WANG AN SHIH

王 安 石

(VOL. II)

WANG AN SHIH

王 安 石

a Chinese Statesman and Educationalist
of the Sung Dynasty

(VOL. II)

BY

H. R. WILLIAMSON, M.A., D.Lit.

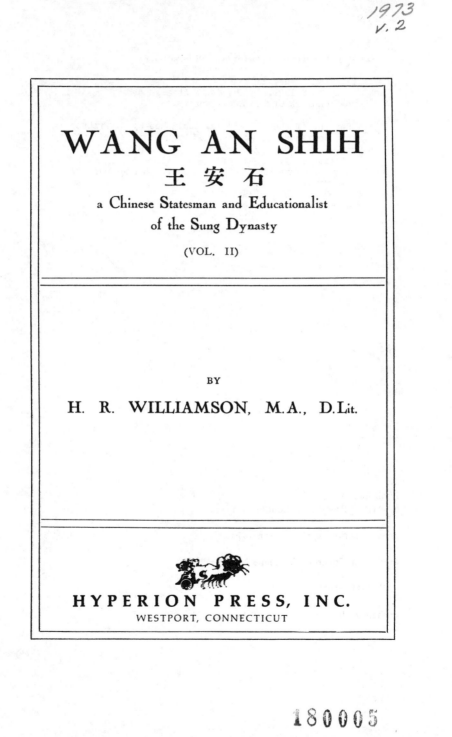

HYPERION PRESS, INC.
WESTPORT, CONNECTICUT

Library of Congress Cataloging in Publication Data

Williamson, Henry Raymond.
    Wang An Shih ... a Chinese statesman and
educationalist of the Sung Dynasty.

    Reprint of the 1935-37 ed. published by A. Probsthain,
which was issued as v. 21-22 of Probsthain's oriental
series.
    Bibliography: v. 2, p:
    1. Wang, An-shih, 1021-1086. 2.   China—Politics
and government.
DS751.W35 1973   951'.02'0924 [B]   73-901
ISBN 0-88355-095-4

Published in 1937
by Arthur Probsthain, London, England

First Hyperion reprint edition 1973

Library of Congress Catalogue Number 73-901

ISBN 0-88355-097-0

Printed in the United States of America

TABLE OF CONTENTS
(VOL. II)

PAGE

CHINESE BIBLIOGRAPHY

Complete Works of Wang An Shih (王 臨 川 全 集).

Poetical Works of Wang An Shih (王 荆 文 公 詩).

New Interpretation of the Government System of the Chou Dynasty, by Wang An Shih (周 官 新 義).

Dynastic History of the Sung Dynasty, Sections on Biography, particularly as affecting the Emperor Shen Tsung, Wang An Shih and his brothers Wang An Li and Wang An Kuo, Economics, Military System, Government System, Educational System, and Astronomy (二 十 四 史 宋 史).

The Canonical History of Shang Lu, Sung Dynasty period (續 資 治 通 鑑 綱 目).

The Imperial History of the Sung Dynasty (御 抽 通 鑑 韓 覽).

The Ancient T'ang Dynasty History, Biographical Section (舊 唐 書 列 傳).

Index to the Imperial Encyclopædia (四 庫 全 書 提 要).

Encyclopædia of Literature (文 獻 通 考).

Biographical Dictionary (中 囘 人 名 大 辭 典).

Complete Works of Chu Hsi, Books 49, 62, and 64 (朱 子 全 書).

Biographies of Famous Officials, by Chu Hsi (名 臣 言 行 錄).

Biography of Wang An Shih, by Liang Ch'i Ch'ao, in Vol. I of his Complete Works (飲 冰 室 叢 集 卷 一).

Critical Biography of Wang An Shih, by Ts'ai Shang Hsiang (王 荆 公 年 譜 考 畧).

Lives of Famous Chinese, published by Association Press of China.

Biographical Table of Wang An Shih, by Chan Ta Ho. (詹 大 和 著 王 荆 文 公 年 譜).

Complete Works of Lu Hsiang Shan, Book 19 (陸 象 山 文 集).

Chinese Classics in various editions.

CHAPTER I

SUBSEQUENT HISTORY OF THE REFORM POLICY

(1086–1093 : DEATH OF HSUAN JEN)

IN this chapter we shall endeavour to give the reader a general idea of the course of events from the death of Wang An Shih in the fourth month of 1086, to the death of the Empress-Dowager Hsuan Jen in the ninth month of 1093.

This period as a whole is characterized by the maintenance of Ssu Ma Kuang's policy with regard to the reforms of Wang An Shih, and by the elimination of the latter's party from influential positions at the capital. But it is also the period in which the party opposed to Wang An Shih split up into three distinct factions. So that affairs at Court were determined to a large extent by partisan politics throughout this period. It will be necessary only to indicate the main trend of events.

First it should be noted that Ssu Ma Kuang survived the death of his great political antagonist by five months only, as he passed away in the ninth month of 1086, at the age of 68. Since his recall from Lo Yang, he had been the most influential man at Court, and in a period of little over a year had succeeded in erasing almost every trace of Wang An Shih's regime. The History records that he was given a magnificent funeral, and that the Emperor and Empress-Dowager attended in person at the obsequies. All business at the capital was suspended, and a mandate issued that he was to be given special honour by the holding of memorial services in all parts of the country.[1]

He had been failing in health for some time, so by way of securing for him the necessary assistance in government affairs Lü Kung Chu had been appointed President of the Legislative Assembly in the fourth month of 1086. Wen Yen Po was also recalled to act as Advisor to the Grand Council on important

---

[1] " T'ung Chien," Yuan Yu, 1st year, 9th month.

I

matters. Han Wei had assumed the Presidency of the "Men Hsia Sheng" in the fifth month, and Ch'eng I had been given a special commission with a view to revising the educational system of the country.

Before his death Ssu Ma Kuang had suggested that the system of recommending men for the government services, which had been almost entirely suspended during the regime of Wang An Shih, should be revived. But such recommendations were to have special reference to a man's ability for the various departments of State. He suggested that men should be recommended in one or other of ten different categories.[1]

In the sixth month Teng Chien, Li Ting, and Lü Hui Ch'ing suffered degradation and transfer. Similar treatment was meted out to Chang Tsao in the ninth month. These were all prominent supporters of the Wang An Shih regime.

Lü Ta Fang and Liu Chih were introduced to the Grand Council in the eleventh month, the latter in the capacity of "Yu Ch'eng" (右 丞) of the Administrative Assembly. Prior to this, in the ninth month Su Shih had been appointed to the Literary Council (翰 林 學 士).

In the first month of the following year, 1087, the New Interpretations of the Classics which had been prepared under the supervision of Wang An Shih, and his Dictionary (字 說) were banned by the government. This meant of course that they would no longer be acceptable to the examiners in charge of the official examinations.[2]

In the fourth month Li Ch'ing Ch'en was transferred to Ho Yang Fu for his opposition to the changes made in Wang An Shih's policy. Liu Chih (劉 摯) was promoted a step; Wang Ts'un joined the Grand Council, and An T'ao (安 燾) became President of the Board of War in the sixth month.

Han Wei (韓 維) was transferred to Teng Chow (鄧 州) on account of some slander or other, and Ch'eng I (程 頤) was degraded in the eighth month, after a squabble with Su Shih. The faction spirit comes into prominence at this time,

[1] "T'ung Chien," Yuan Yu, 1st year, 7th month.
[2] "T'ung Chien," Yuan Yu, 2nd year, 1st month.

three distinct parties being discernible. There was first the Lo (洛) party, headed by Ch'eng I, with Chu Kuang T'ing (朱 光 庭) and Chia I (賈 易) as his influential associates. The second was the Shu (蜀) or Ssu Ch'uan party, with Su Shih as leader, and Lü T'ao as his right-hand man. The third was the "Shuo" or Northern party (朔) whose chief representatives were Liu Chih (劉 摯), Liang T'ao (梁 燾), Wang Yen Sou (王 巖 叟), and Liu An Shih (劉 安 世).

The remarks of the historian [1] on this matter are of interest. He writes : " By this time all the officials who had helped Wang An Shih in the reign of Shen Tsung had been scattered. But the spirit of resentment had entered into the very marrow of their bones, and they were stealthily watching for an opportunity to return to power. And yet the ministers of the Court began to form factions, and to indulge in mutual recriminations. Only such great souls as Lü Ta Fang (呂 大 防), Fan Tsu Yü (范 祖 禹), and Ssu Ma Kuang (司 馬 光) formed no faction."

The emperor was greatly concerned at the spread of this faction spirit, and sought the advice of Hu Tsung Yü (胡 宗 愈) as to how it might be controlled. The latter advised him to seek for men who were not of any recognized faction to serve the State. If he made that his ruling principle, the country would be saved from what promised to be a most grievous calamity.[1]

But from this time up to the death of the Empress-Dowager in the ninth month of 1093, the Histories record little but transfers, degradations, dismissals, and banishments, all based on party prejudices, jealousies, and strife.

Chia I (賈 易) was the first to succumb, being transferred to Hua Huai Chow (懷 州) in the latter part of 1087.

In the first month of 1088 the Kuang Hui Ts'ang Granary System was revived.

Lü Kung Chu became Chief Adviser of State affairs in the fourth month of this year, but died in the second month of 1089.

---

[1] "T'ung Chien," Yuan Yu, 2nd year, 8th month.

The old examination system was restored in the fourth month of that year, the Law course and curriculum of Wang An Shih's regime being abolished.[1]

Ts'ai Ch'ueh was banished to Hsin Chow (新 州) in the fifth month. Liu An Shih took the initiative in this, and was supported by Fan Tsu Yü and Wen Yen Po, the latter wishing to banish him to the still more remote and wilder spot of Ling Ch'iao (嶺 嶠). Fan Ch'un Jen (范 純 仁) and Wang Ts'un (王 存) opposed the move, the former saying, " Thorns have been allowed to grow on this road for the last seventy years (i.e. no banishments of this sort have occurred during this time). If we take the initiative in reopening it, I fear similar punishment will await us later on."

For their stand on this case both of these men suffered degradation and transfer in the sixth month.[2]

Wen Yen Po resigned from all connection with the government in the second month of 1090, at the advanced age of 85.

In the eighth month of the same year Liang T'ao, Liu An Shih, and Chu Kuang T'ing were all degraded and transferred for their opposition to the appointment of Teng Jun Fu to the Literary Council. The latter was supposed to be a partisan of Ts'ai Ch'ueh, who in turn was regarded as the leader of the Wang An Shih party. There is a note in the history at this point indicating that the influence of Wang An Shih still persisted, and was strong enough to cause considerable apprehension in the minds of those at Court.[3]

Su Che was promoted to the Grand Council in the second month of 1091, being dubbed a second Wang An Shih by one of his critics. On the other hand, his brother Su Shih, having been indicted by Lü Ta Fang and others, was degraded and transferred in the sixth month to Yang Chow. Lü Ta Fang was also instrumental in getting Liu Chih away from Court in the eleventh month. Ch'eng I received his *coup-de-grâce* in the third month of 1092, at the instigation of Su Che, and

---

[1] " T'ung Chien," Yuan Yu, 4th year, 4th month.
[2] " T'ung Chien," Yuan Yu, 4th year, 6th month.
[3] " T'ung Chien," Yuan Yu, 5th year, 8th month.

two months later Wang Yen Sou, under suspicion of his being a partisan of Liu Chih, was also transferred.

In the sixth month of 1092 the following formed the Grand Council, viz. : Su Sung, Su Che, Fan Pai Lu, Liang T'ao, Cheng Yung, Han Chung Yen, and Liu Feng Shih.[1]

Su Shih was recalled to a post in the Board of War in the ninth month, but did not stay long. Su Sung, Fan Pai Lu, and Liang T'ao were all transferred early in 1093. Fan Ch'un Jen was recalled to the Grand Council in the seventh month of 1093.

The Empress-Dowager Hsuan Jen died in the ninth month of that year.[2] Her death marks a definite period in the history of the reform policy, as with the assumption of the reins of government by Che Tsung, a reversion to Wang An Shih's policy occurred. This forms the subject of the next chapter.

[1] "T'ung Chien," Yuan Yu, 7th year, 6th month.
[2] "T'ung Chien," Yuan Yu, 8th year, 9th month.

CHAPTER II

SUBSEQUENT HISTORY OF THE REFORM POLICY

(ATTEMPTED REVIVAL OF THE NEW MEASURES UNDER CHE TSUNG : 1094–1100)

WE have already noted the death of Hsuan Jen, the Empress-Dowager, in the ninth month of 1093. She had been the leading figure in affairs of State for nearly nine years. The chief events of her regency as given by the History are the recall of the old guard of loyal officials to Court, the abrogation of the (so-called) oppressive Measures instituted by the Reform Party, the presentation of territory to the Hsi Hsia (西 夏) in the north-west, and the restoration of peace to the empire. It is noted that the ruler of the Liao Tartars had warned his officers that as the Chinese had restored the regime of Jen Tsung (仁 宗) in the person and rule of Hsuan Jen, that they must cease to make trouble on the borders.[1]

On the death of the Dowager, Che Tsung became independent, and assumed the reins of government. The Historian [2] notes that there was great trepidation at this time amongst the Court functionaries, as they were in doubt as to what attitude he would adopt towards the Reform policy. They were not left in doubt for long, for immediately after his assumption of power Che Tsung recalled Liu Yuan (劉 瑗) and nine others of Wang An Shih's party.

Fan Tsu Yü (范 祖 禹) thereupon sent in a memorial of warning, pleading that the rule of Hsuan Jen had been beneficial to the country. He warned the young Emperor that certain officials would now make it their chief aim to get redress from the Court for the banishment of all those who had been connected with Shen Tsung's regime. He urged upon the Emperor that

---

[1] " T'ung Chien," Yuan Yu (元 祐), 8th year, 9th month.

[2] " T'ung Chien," Yuan Yu (元 祐), 8th year, 10th month.

he should investigate the facts, and seek to adjudicate fairly the rights and wrongs of the case. He asserted that those who had been dismissed had in reality wronged Shen Tsung, and that if they were now recalled they would also do the present Emperor serious injury, and probably ruin the country.

Su Shih added his signature to this memorial, which he termed " a very timely document ".

As, however, the Emperor made no acknowledgment of this memorial, nor indeed of a second from the same source, in which Fan Tsu Yü affirmed that not a single good appointment had been made since Che Tsung had assumed the reins of government, Fan approached the Emperor personally with the following statement :—

" During the early days of Shen Tsung's reign, Wang An Shih and Lü Hui Ch'ing expounded and promulgated a number of new laws, completely altering the character of the previous administration. They introduced a large number of unworthy men into office, much to the detriment of good government, while the famous and experienced officials, the loyal and patriotic ministers, were either ignored or compelled to leave the Court.

" They also initiated war measures which only incited the resentment of the border tribes. The whole empire was grievously distressed, and the people were scattered throughout the country.

" When Shen Tsung eventually came to his senses he dismissed the two leading reformers from Court. But their followers, who had been given appointments in various parts of the country, remained, and their influence persisted. Such were Ts'ai Ch'ueh, who had raised several important questions : Wang Shao, who proposed the idea of recovering the Hsi Ho territory ; Chang Ch'un, who had reopened the troublesome question of the reduction of the Hunan tribes ; Shen Ch'i (沈　起), who had incited the Annamese to revolt ; and Shen Kuo, who had instigated trouble on the western frontier (Ssu Ch'uan). These had involved the army and people in enormous losses, some 200,000 lives having been sacrificed.

" Then there was Wu Chü Hou (吳 居 厚), who had initiated new Smelting Regulations ; Wang Tzu Ching (王 子 京), who had introduced new Tea Laws for Fuchien ; Ch'ien Chou Fu (鶱 周 輔), who had promulgated new Salt Regulations in Chiang Hsi ; Li Chi (李 稷) and Lu Shih Min (陸 師 閔), who had organized the Tea Monopoly in Ssu Ch'uan ; and Liu Ting (劉 定), who had pushed the Militia Act (保 甲) in Hopei.

" These things had incited the people to resentment, and plots for rebellion were well under way.

" But the situation was saved when your grandmother and yourself came into power, to the delight and relief of the people.

" However, the officials of the Wang An Shih regime who suffered dismissal and degradation are now awaiting just such an opportunity as the changes which you are contemplating afford. They will get the impression, mistakenly of course, that you were opposed to the abrogation of the new laws. If they are appointed to the Court services now, they are bound to make certain suggestions of an injurious character which, if you adopt, will bring the empire into a hopeless state of confusion and distress." [1]

This, however, in no wise affected the emperor's purpose, for he restored Chang Ch'un and Lü Hui Ch'ing to office in the twelfth month, and transferred Liu An Shih (劉 安 世) to Ch'eng Te Chun (成 德 軍) for his opposition to this move.[2]

In the second month of 1095 still more of Wang An Shih's party were recalled to high office. Li Ch'ing Ch'en (李 清 臣) and Teng Jun Fu were appointed to the Grand Council, while Lü Ta Fang (who had been a member of the Grand Council for eight years during the regency of the Empress-Dowager) and Su Che (蘇 轍) were both allowed to resign.[3]

[1] " T'ung Chien," Yuan Yu (元 祐), 8th year, 10th month.
[2] " T'ung Chien," Yuan Yu (元 祐), 8th year, 12th month.
[3] " T'ung Chien," Shao Sheng (紹 聖), 1st year, 2nd month.

The resignation of Su Che followed on a warm discussion between him and Li Ch'ing Ch'en on the reform policy, the latter having advocated a complete restoration of Wang An Shih's measures. In his reply Su Che acknowledged that there were certain features of Shen Tsung's regime which were worthy of perpetuation. He contended, however, that the changes introduced during the regime of the regency had been demanded by the needs of the times, and maintained that all the good features of Shen Tsung's administration had been preserved. He thought that if Che Tsung now recalled to Court those who had been left unemployed for so long, who were merely nourishing private enmities, and on whose lips the name of Shen Tsung was ever present,[1] a serious calamity would befall the State.

In his memorial he had used the expression " the measures promulgated during Shen Tsung's reign were mostly in line with those advocated by the ministers of Han Wu Ti's day" (漢 武 帝). This enraged Che Tsung, who replied, "How can you possibly compare Shen Tsung with Han Wu Ti?" This led Su Che to retire and await the emperor's decision as to his future.[2]

Fan Ch'un Jen did his best to demonstrate to the Emperor that Su Che's comment on Han Wu Ti was not intended to be derogatory to Shen Tsung, but this had no effect on Su Che's determination to resign. He eventually was appointed to Ju Chow (汝 州) as prefect.

The nature of the change in the Court attitude to the reform policy may be gauged by the fact that at the official examinations, the candidates who in their essays lauded the regime of Wang An Shih were now given good places in the lists, while those who discussed the regime of the Empress-Dowager and

[1] The reference, of course, is to the policy of Wang An Shih.

[2] " T'ung Chien," Shao Sheng (紹 聖), 1st year, 2nd month. Chu Hsi narrates an incident as follows : " Che Tsung would persist in using an old table, which was so unsightly that the Dowager Hsuan Jen ordered him to change it for a new one. Che Tsung replied : ' This was my father's table.' Then the Dowager was greatly disturbed, as it indicated the emperor's desire to follow in his father's footsteps." From *Complete Works of Chu Hsi*, vol. 62, p. 4.

Ssu Ma Kuang in favourable terms were generally placed at the bottom.

Tseng Pu, another old colleague of Wang An Shih, was recalled to the Literary Council at this time.[1] He had opposed Ssu Ma Kuang's proposal to revive the Commissioned Services Act (差 役 法) and had spurned his appeal for help in the same by remarking, "I drew up the regulations for the Public Services Act (免 役 法), how can I conscientiously support its rescindment, and the revival of this absolutely contradictory measure ?" In the interim he had been in positions in Taiyuanfu and Chiang Ning.

Chang Shang Ying (張 商 英), another prominent opponent of the regime of the Empress Dowager, was appointed to the Censorate in the fourth month.[2] He had submitted a memorial lauding the reign of Shen Tsung as being the greatest of all time, and incidentally maligning Ssu Ma Kuang, Lü Kung Chu, Liu Chih, and Lü Ta Fang.

Su Shih (蘇 軾) was now permitted to resign and was appointed to Ling Chow.

A most important decision was now made in regard to the title of the reign to be adopted. It was the custom throughout the Sung Dynasty for different periods of an emperor's reign to be designated by some title which would indicate the main characteristics of the period. Tseng Pu suggested that Che Tsung should style this particular period " Shao Sheng " (紹 聖), i.e. " Continuation of the Glorious Work of Shen Tsung ". Teng Jun Fu supported this proposal, suggesting that just as Wu Wang had enhanced the reputation of Wen Wang, and as Ch'eng Wang (成 王) had carried on the glorious achievements of Wu Wang, so Che Tsung would be able to continue the great work of his father Shen Tsung.

---

[1] " T'ung Chien," Shao Sheng (紹 聖), 1st year, 2nd month. Text reads " appointed as ' Ch'eng Chih ' (承 旨) ", which probably meant Secretary to the Council.

[2] " T'ung Chien," Shao Sheng (紹 聖), 1st year, 4th month. His appointment was as " Yu Cheng Yen " (右 正 言).

" So," records the historian, " everyone knew without doubt what were the inclinations of the Emperor." [1]

Chang Ch'un was now appointed Grand Councillor. He immediately nailed his colours to the mast, asserting that Ssu Ma Kuang should be branded a traitor to his country, in that he had not maintained the laws and regulations of Shen Tsung's reign.

This brought a reprimand from Ch'en Huan (陳 瓘), who affirmed that the most urgent need before the country at the present juncture was the elimination of the faction spirit.

Fan Ch'un Jen resigned as a gesture of disapproval with this appointment of Chang Ch'un.[1]

Ts'ai Ching (蔡 京) was appointed to the Ministry of Finance,[2] and Lin Hsi (林 布) given a high position in the Chung Shu Sheng (中 書 省).[3] The former, under the regime of Ssu Ma Kuang, had put the Commissioned Services Act into operation in his area within a period of five days, but now he completely changed front, and urged Chang Ch'un to revive the Public Services Act of Wang An Shih, and proposed that it should be done without discussion.

His suggestion was adopted, but the revived Measure was styled the " Ch'ai Ku Liang Fa " (差 顧 兩 法), which from its name indicates that it was a sort of compromise between the Conscription-of-Labour Laws of Ssu Ma Kuang and the Hiring-of-Labour Laws of Wang An Shih.[4]

Another very important action was taken at this time. Ts'ai Pien (蔡 卞), the brother of Ts'ai Ching and son-in-law of Wang An Shih, was commissioned to rewrite the History of Shen Tsung's reign. During the regency of Hsuan Jen, Fan Tsu Yü had been appointed to write the history of that period. This had been compiled and issued under the title of " Shen Tsung Shih Lu " (神 宗 實 錄). Ts'ai Pien had

---

[1] " T'ung Chien," Shao Sheng (紹 聖), 1st year, 4th month.
[2] Appointment was to " Hu Pu Shang Shu " (戶 部 尚 書).
[3] Appointed as " Chung Shu She Jen " (中 書 舍 人).
[4] " T'ung Chien," Shao Sheng, 1st year, 4th month.

submitted a memorial criticizing the character of this record, affirming that it contained many false and misleading statements, and appealing that a new edition might be prepared.

The Emperor consented to this, and Ts'ai Pien undertook the task. The character of this new work was evidently as prejudiced in favour of Wang An Shih as the older work had been against him, i.e. if the remark of the historian is to be accepted as true. For he writes, "Ts'ai Pien collected his materials for the compilation of this work from Wang An Shih's diary. He embellished the record so as to conceal the real nature of his traitorous conduct, and by manipulating the facts altered the colour of the previous record completely." [1]

It should be noted here that while the previous record sought to emphasize the faults of Wang An Shih, it endeavoured to show Shen Tsung in a good light.

In the fourth month (intercalary) the Agricultural Loans Measure was revived, but again under a new name, and was probably of somewhat different form from the older Measure. It was revived under the name of the "Ch'ang P'ing Granary Laws" and superintendents were specially appointed in each circuit for the promotion and administration of the Measure. [2]

Steps were also taken to restore the system of examinations which had been the vogue under Wang An Shih. In the fifth month candidates were ordered to specialize in the meaning of the Classics. In the sixth month the ban on Wang An Shih's dictionary was lifted. [3] Men like An T'ao (安 燾), Huang Li (黃 履), and Ts'eng Pu (曾 布) were all restored to office or promoted.

In the seventh month the posthumous rank and honours of Ssu Ma Kuang, Lü Kung Chu, and others of their party were taken away from them, and a proclamation issued throughout the land that Lü Ta Fang, Liu Chih, Su Che, Liang T'ao, and

---

[1] " T'ung Chien," Shao Sheng, 1st year, 4th month.
[2] " T'ung Chien," Shao Sheng, 1st year, 4th month intercalary.
[3] " T'ung Chien," Shao Sheng, 1st year, 6th month.

other officials of the Hsuan Jen regime had been guilty of
traitorous conduct.   This action was taken as a substitute for
the much sterner proposal of Chang Ch'un that Wen Yen Po
and thirty others of the anti-Wang-An-Shih party should be
sent into banishment.[1]

The " Kuang Hui Ts'ang " regulations of the Hsuan Jen
regime were rescinded in the eighth month : the " Trade Tax
Measure " was revived, and Lü Hui Ch'ing was appointed
Governor of Ta Ming Fu (太 名 府).[2]

In the twelfth month of 1094 Ts'ai Pien presented his new
edition of the History of Shen Tsung's reign, and was promoted
to the Literary Council as a reward for his labours.   Those
who had been responsible for the previous edition, viz. Fan Tsu
Yü, Chao Yen Jo (趙 彥 若), and Huang T'ing Chien
(黃 庭 堅) were transferred (practically equal to banishment)
to distant outposts like Yung Chow (永 州), Li Chow (澧 州),
and Ch'ien Chow (黔 州).[3]

The Militia Act was revived in the second month of 1095,[4]
Hsü Chiang (許 將) and Ts'ai Pien were admitted to the
Grand Council,[5] and Ts'ai Ch'üeh, who had recently died,
had the title of " Grand Tutor " (太 師) conferred upon him,
also the posthumous designation of " Loyal and Loving "
(忠 懷).[5]

Cliques now began to appear in the government party,
Chang Ch'un and Ts'ai Ching evidently not being quite of
one mind.   One Ch'ang An Min (常 安 民) was accused of
trying to form a party under Ts'ai Ching's name, which
was opposed to the government, and of being a partisan of the
Su (蘇) faction.   Chang Shang Ying and An T'ao, who took
his side, were cashiered along with him.[6]   Fan Ch'un Jen also

[1] " T'ung Chien," Shao Sheng, 1st year, 7th month.
[2] " T'ung Chien," Shao Sheng, 1st year, 8th month.   Evidently he had
received no court appointment prior to this, although it was the Emperor's
intention to give him one.
[3] " T'ung Chien," Shao Sheng, 1st year, 12th month.
[4] " T'ung Chien," Shao Sheng, 2nd year, 2nd month.
[5] " T'ung Chien," Shao Sheng, 2nd year, 10th month.
[6] " T'ung Chien," Shao Sheng, 2nd year, 11th month.

suffered degradation and transfer to Sui Chow (隨 州) for his attempt to secure a repeal of the sentence of banishment which had been passed upon Lü Ta Fang and his associates.[1]

Fan Tsu Yü and Liu An Shih were banished definitely in the seventh month of 1096, the former to Ho Chow (賀 州) and the latter to Ying Chow (英 州).[2]

In the first month of 1097 Li Ch'ing Ch'en was cashiered,[3] and in the second month Ssu Ma Kuang, Lü Kung Chu, and Wang Yen Sou were all further degraded in rank and deprived of honours, regardless of their being dead or alive.[4] Partisans like Han Wei, Sun Ku (孫 固), Fan Pai Lu (范 百 祿), and Hu Tsung Yü (胡 宗 愈), all were deprived of their offices or posthumous emoluments.

The same month the still more severe step of banishing certain influential opponents of Wang An Shih's regime was taken. Lü Ta Fang, Liu Chih, Su Che, Liang T'ao, and Fan Ch'un Jen were all banished to Ling Nan (嶺 南), Lü Ta Fang dying on the road. Others who had not been so prominent in their opposition, but who were under suspicion of allying themselves with the opposition party, some thirty in all, were cashiered. Even Wen Yen Po, who had been granted the title of Grand Tutor (太 師), had this reduced to that of Junior Tutor of the Heir to the Throne (太 子 少 保).[4]

In the third month it is recorded that Chang Ch'un wished to execute all those who had been banished, but this drastic step was prevented by Che Tsung, who said he had not yet executed any minister, and did not want to do so. As an alternative to this it was agreed that the writings of these men, including the memorial of Ssu Ma Kuang, which had got scattered, should be collected and kept as a record of their crimes. The suggestion was actually made that the blocks of Ssu Ma Kuang's great History should be burned, but happily

---

[1] " T'ung Chien," Shao Sheng, 2nd year, 11th month. There is no note of Lü Ta Fang's banishment prior to this.

[2] " T'ung Chien," Shao Sheng, 3rd year, 7th month.

[3] " T'ung Chien," Shao Sheng, 4th year, 1st month.

[4] " T'ung Chien," Shao Sheng, 4th year, 2nd month.

this was not carried out [1] ("because it included a preface by Shen Yung," says the historian).

The death of Wen Yen Po is recorded in the fifth month of 1097, at the ripe age of 92. To the credit of the ministers of those days be it said that they restored to him his title of "Grand Tutor" and granted him the posthumous designation of "Loyal and Famous" (忠 烈).[2]

Ch'eng I (程 頤) was banished to Fu Chow (涪 州), Ssu Ch'uan, in the eleventh month, refusing a grant of a hundred taels from the Treasury.[3]

The Trade and Barter Measure was revived in the eleventh month,[3] but as no details are given it is impossible to say whether any essential changes were made from the original Measure or not.

The deaths of Liang T'ao and Liu Chih in banishment are reported under this month.

With the opening of the year 1098 the title of Che Tsung's reign was altered to "Yuan Fu" (元 符)[4] or "Great Seal". This was due to the discovery of a jade seal, made during excavations and repairs to a residence in the village of Liu Yin Ts'un (劉 銀 村) in the county of Chien Yang Hsien (咸 陽 縣). The seal bore the inscription, "We have received the 'decree' from Heaven. Our dynasty is already long-lived. May we prosper for ever."

This seal was sent to the Court, where Ts'ai Ching and his colleagues examined it, and pronounced it a royal seal of the Ch'in (秦) dynasty. It was then given the designation of "Heaven's gift of the Transmitted Kingdom". A Court function of universal congratulation was held, and the reign title changed to that of the "Great Seal". The discovery of this seal was evidently considered peculiarly felicitous to those who were in charge of affairs and indicated that the policy of restoring Wang An Shih's laws and regulations had received

---

[1] "T'ung Chien," Shao Sheng, 4th year, 3rd month.
[2] "T'ung Chien," Shao Sheng, 4th year, 5th month.
[3] "T'ung Chien," Shao Sheng, 4th year, 11th month.
[4] "T'ung Chien," Yuan Fu (元 符), 1st year, 1st month.

the approval of Heaven, and promised a long continuance of the present dynasty.

A step still more severe than any which had preceded it was now taken, the sins of the fathers being visited upon the children. In the third month the son of Wen Yen Po, called Chi Fu (及 甫), was imprisoned in the T'ung Wen Kuan (同 文 舘), and the descendants of Liu Chih and Liang T'ao, who had both died in banishment, were ordered to be manacled and banished to Ling Nan. This drastic action was taken because it was thought that Wen Yen Po had been an accomplice of Ssu Ma Kuang, and that Liu Chih and Liang T'ao had been plotting against the throne.[1]

Ts'ai Ching was now made Head of the Literary Council, and An Tu (安 都) made Grand Councillor.[1]

Chang Ch'un and Ts'ai Pien then tried a further stratagem with the object of defaming their political opponents, by appealing that the late Empress-Dowager Hsuan Jen should be deprived of her royal rank and title, and that a mandate be issued from the throne reducing her to the status of a commoner. In this, however, they were foiled by Che Tsung, who burned their first memorial, and trampled underfoot a second of the same character.[1]

A further rift in the ranks of the government party occurred in the fourth month. Tseng Pu had aroused the suspicion of Chang Ch'un, who sent Lin Hsi (林 希) to spy on his activities in the Board of War. Tseng Pu, however, gained the confidence of this spy, so Chang Ch'un secured his dismissal from office.[2]

Further punishment was inflicted upon the members of the anti-Wang-An-Shih party in the seventh month, Fan Tsu Yü and Liu An Shih being banished to Hua Chow (化 州) and Mei Chow (梅 州) respectively. Shortly afterwards Fan died, anticipating the arrival of his executioner by a very short period, i.e. if the History is to be regarded as reliable on this point.[3]

---

[1] " T'ung Chien," Yuan Fu, 1st year, 3rd month.
[2] " T'ung Chien," Yuan Fu, 1st year, 4th month.
[3] " T'ung Chien," Yuan Fu, 1st year, 7th month.

A kind of Inquisition [1] was established in the ninth month of 1099 to secure information of all who were plotting against the existing regime. This was the suggestion of Chang Ch'un, An Ch'un (安 惇), Ts'ai Ching, and Ts'ai Pien. People now began to speak with bated breath of the two Ch'uns and the two Ts'ais. No less than 830 people were punished as a result of the activities of this Inspectorate.

Che Tsung died without heir in the first month of 1100, and was succeeded by his younger brother Tuan Wang (端 王). It is broadly hinted by the Historical Commentator that Chang Ch'un had murdered Che Tsung.[2]

[1] "T'ung Chien," Yuan Fu, 2nd year, 9th month, intercalary. The Inspectorate was styled "K'an Hsiang Su Li Chü" (看 詳 訴 理 局), which was set up with the idea of overturning the acts of grace which had been promulgated during the time of Yuan Yu in the interests of the anti-Wang-An-Shih faction.

[2] "T'ung Chien," Yuan Fu (元 符), 3rd year, 1st month.

CHAPTER III

SUBSEQUENT HISTORY OF THE REFORM POLICY

SECOND ATTEMPT AT REVIVAL OF THE NEW MEASURES, UNDER HUI TSUNG AND TS'AI CHING. (PERIOD 1100–1126)

TUAN WANG was the eleventh son of Shen Tsung,[1] and assumed the throne under the regal title of Hui Tsung (徽 宗). The first acts of the new emperor, or actions taken under his name, were all of a contrary character to those taken by his predecessor, and it looked for a time as though the pendulum would swing again, and the policy of Wang An Shih be once more overturned. Ts'ai Pien [2] and An Ch'un were cashiered, Hsing Shu (邢 恕) [3] and Chang Ch'un were banished,[4] and Ts'ai Ching degraded.[5]

Ssu Ma Kuang, Wen Yen Po, and others of their following, thirty-three in all, were restored to their old rank, title, and emoluments,[3] Ch'eng I was restored to office,[5] and Han Chung Yen and Tseng Pu were made Grand Councillors.[5]

These moves evidently were made with the idea of securing some kind of neutral policy in the government, which would neither be slavishly devoted to Wang An Shih's ideas nor rabidly opposed to them. However, the balance of power seemed rather to lie with those who were against Wang An Shih than for him, with the possible exception that Tseng Pu was retained in office. He had been out at elbows with Chang Ch'un, but was an old colleague of Wang An Shih, and had recently also had a fair share in reviving some of his measures.

But outwardly at least it was an attempt to establish neutrality.

---

[1] " T'ung Chien," Yuan Fu (元 符), 3rd year, 1st month.

[2] " T'ung Chien," Yuan Fu (元 符), 3rd year, 5th month.

[3] " T'ung Chien," Yuan Fu (元 符), 3rd year, 6th month.

[4] " T'ung Chien," Yuan Fu (元 符), 3rd year, 7th and 10th months.

[5] " T'ung Chien," Yuan Fu (元 符), 3rd year, 10th month.

In the 11th month of 1100 the reign title adopted was that of "Chien Chung" (建 中) or "Neutrality Established".[1]

This attempt did not wholly succeed apparently, for in the 11th month of the following year, i.e. 1101, Ts'ai Ching was restored to favour, and immediately secured the change of the reign title to that of "Ts'ung Ning" (崇 寧), the significance of which was to exalt that part of Shen Tsung's reign during which Wang An Shih was in supreme power.[2]

So once again the attempt was made to restore the policy of Wang An Shih, but with what measure of sincerity we shall see later.

In 1102 Ssu Ma Kuang and his associates, forty-four in all, were again deprived of their official status,[3] and over fifty of the officials who had displayed partiality for the anti-Wang-An-Shih faction and ideas during the regency of Hsuan Jen and also during the latter years of Che Tsung's reign (styled "Yuan Fu") were proscribed, i.e. their names were put on record in the Government offices as those who were not to be given any public appointments in the future.[3]

Tseng Pu, who evidently was in Ts'ai Ching's way, was transferred to Jun Chow (潤 州), and Ts'ai Ching and Hsü Chiang (許 將) became Grand Councillors. This was in the 5th month of 1102.[4]

In the 8th month of 1102 a semblance of the Public Services Act, styled the "I Fa" (役 法), was revived.[5]

---

[1] "T'ung Chien," Yuan Fu (元 符), 3rd year, 11th month. The idea was to designate by the reign title an attitude of neutrality in the matter of government policy, the policy of Yuan Yu (元 祐) and Shao Sheng (紹 聖) periods both being regarded as extreme, one way or the other. This, however, lasted for barely twelve months. See next note.

[2] The reign title was now changed again definitely in favour of Wang An Shih's policy, the characters "Ts'ung Ning" meaning reverence for the policy of Hsi Ning's days, i.e. the policy of Wang An Shih.

[3] "T'ung Chien," Ts'ung Ning (崇 寧), 1st year, 5th month.

[4] "T'ung Chien," Ts'ung Ning (崇 寧), 1st year, 7th month.

[5] Called "Shao Sheng I Fa" (紹 聖 役 法). See "T'ung Chien," Ts'ung Ning, 1st year, 8th month.

In the 9th month a stone tablet, inscribed with the names of 120 traitors, headed by Ssu Ma Kuang, Wen Yen Po, Lü Kung Chu, and Lü Ta Fang, was set up outside the Tuan Li Gate (端 禮 門) of the capital. Then a list was drawn up of the chief officials who had served during the reign of Shen Tsung, and also during the reign of Che Tsung. These were carefully divided first into two large classes, termed loyal and disloyal respectively. These again were subdivided into three classes according to their grades of loyalty and disloyalty, and each rewarded or punished according to their merit or blame. In the main divisions it was discovered that forty-one were classed as loyal and over five hundred as disloyal.

Many of the latter were banished.[1]

In 1103 the Tea Monopoly was revived, and also the Salt voucher regulations reinstated.[2]

In the 4th month the pictures of Ssu Ma Kuang, Lü Kung Chu, and others of kindred political colouring were removed from the Ching Ling Kung (景 靈 公) and the name of Ch'eng I (程 頤) was erased from the roll in the Mi Ko (秘 閣).[3]

All the sub-districts (prefectures) were ordered to set up a replica of the traitors' tablet in each county. The superscription of the tablet was to be " An Shih Kung An Min " (安 石 工 安 民) or " Wang An Shih's Work for the Salvation of the People ". The History records an appeal made by some one to omit the words " for the salvation of the people ", or to put the title at the foot of the tablet where it would not be so prominent. It also narrates the refusal of a certain stonemason to cut the stone because of the respect which the people had for Ssu Ma Kuang.[4]

A large arsenal was established in the capital in the 9th month of 1103.[4]

In the 4th month of 1104 all officials were commanded to make

[1] " T'ung Chien," Ts'ung Ning (崇 寧), 1st year, 9th month.
[2] " T'ung Chien," Ts'ung Ning (崇 寧), 2nd year, 2nd month.
[3] " T'ung Chien," Ts'ung Ning (崇 寧), 2nd year, 4th month.
[4] " T'ung Chien," Ts'ung Ning (崇 寧), 2nd year, 9th month.

a report on the progress that was being made in their respective districts with the revival of the New Measures.[1]

Ts'ai Ching was invested with the title of Duke of the State of Chia (嘉 國 公), in the 5th month.

In the 6th month the pictures of all the famous ministers of Shen Tsung's reign were ordered to be hung in the Hsien Mu Ko (顯 謨 閣). The Commentator on the History says that these would only include such as Wang An Shih, Lü Hui Ch'ing, Chang Ch'un, Ts'ai Ch'ueh, etc. Men like Ssu Ma Kuang, Su Shih, Su Che, Ou Yang Hsiu, Han Ch'i, Fu Pi, Chou Tun I, the two Ch'engs, Chang Tsai, would not be thus honoured.[2]

But quite special honour was to be accorded Wang An Shih, for his spirit tablet was ordered to be placed in the Confucian temple, ranking in order next to that of Mencius. He was also to have a share in the sacrifices to Confucius.

The Commentator says that the name of Hui Tsung was loathed for generations because of this particular act.

The names of the " Traitors " were now assembled again, to the number of 309, cut in stone, and erected in the Ming T'ang (朝 堂).[3]

In the 7th month the Land Tax Survey Measure (方 田 法) of Wang An Shih's regime was revived.[4]

During the next year, 1105, friction developed between Ts'ai Ching and his brother Ts'ai Pien, resulting in the latter being transferred to Honanfu. The comment in the History is to the effect that Ts'ai Pien's one object was to revive the whole of Wang An Shih's Measures.[5] Subsequent acts of Ts'ai Ching would seem to indicate that Ts'ai Pien was the more sincere and thorough of the two in this purpose, for soon after he had left the Court, that is during the 5th month of this year, the ban on brothers and sons of the " Traitors " was lifted,

[1] " T'ung Chien," Ts'ung Ning (崇 寧) 3rd year, 4th month.
[2] " T'ung Chien," Ts'ung Ning (崇 寧), 3rd year, 6th month, Kuang I com.
[3] " T'ung Chien," Ts'ung Ning (崇 寧), 3rd year, 6th month.
[4] " T'ung Chien," Ts'ung Ning (崇 寧), 3rd year, 7th month.
[5] " T'ung Chien," Ts'ung Ning (崇 寧), 4th year, 1st month.

and the banished ministers and descendants of the " Yuan Yu
Party " (元 祐 黨), i.e. those who had helped Hsuan Jen
during her regency to abolish Wang An Shih's Measures, were
recalled from their banishment, on condition that they did not
come to the capital.[1]

This would seem to indicate that Ts'ai Ching was playing for
his own hand, seeking to extend his own influence, and form
his own party. For he had adopted the idea of restoring the
Wang An Shih regime, not because he was sincerely anxious to
do that for its own sake, but because it afforded one means of
attaining his personal ambition.

He had, however, to contend with a very superstitious
emperor, and this was to determine their relations for quite a
considerable period. In the 1st month of the next year (1106)
a comet was visible for the whole day in the west.[2] The Emperor
decided that the proper response to make to this Heavenly
warning was to smash up the " Traitors' " tablet. This was
done at dead of night without consulting Ts'ai Ching. When
the latter was informed of what had been done he was furious.
But worse was to follow. Before long the planet Venus was
visible in the daytime. The Emperor decreed that this, too, was
in the nature of a Heavenly warning, calling for some changes in
government policy, so this time he decided that the ban must be
lifted on all " Traitors ", and that the recently revived " Land
Tax Survey Regulations " should be suspended. He also
initiated further policy of a generous character towards the
opponents of Wang An Shih, recalling all those who had been
banished on that account.[2]

Ts'ai Ching was degraded in the 2nd month of 1106, but
was again restored to office in the 1st month of 1107,[3] on giving
some sort of guarantee that he had no ulterior motive in seeking
to revive the regime of Wang An Shih. His son Ts'ai Yu

---

[1] " T'ung Chien," Ts'ung Ning (崇 寧), 4th year, 5th month.

[2] " T'ung Chien," Ts'ung Ning (崇 寧), 5th year, 1st month.

[3] ' T'ung Chien," Ta Kuan (大 觀), 1st year, 1st month, probably because
of an eclipse which had been prophesied but did not occur on the 1st of the 12th
month of the preceding year.

(蔡 攸) was also given important office, and as a token of the policy now to be adopted, several of the old opponents of the Reform policy were once again banished.

However, another Heavenly warning in the shape of a comet appeared in the early part of 1110, and this was made the pretext for relieving Ts'ai Ching of his appointment once more, and Chang Shang Ying (張 商 英), an old associate of Wang An Shih's party, was appointed to the Grand Council.[2] He had but a short term of office, however, for in the 8th month of 1111 he was transferred to a provincial appointment.[3]

After this the " Land Tax Survey Regulations ", the revival or abrogation of which seems by this time to have signified the attitude of the Government in power towards Wang An Shih, was once more rescinded,[4] only to be revived again in 1112, when Ts'ai Ching was restored to favour again. He was given a residence in the capital, and called to Imperial audiences once in three days.[5]

During 1113 Wang An Shih was honoured with the post-humous designation of Shu Wang (舒 王), a title higher than that of Duke, with which he had been previously invested, making him practically equivalent to a member of the Imperial family.[6] His son Fang was granted the title of Earl of Lin Ch'uan (臨 川 伯). This was done on the occasion of the opening of the new Confucian temple in K'ai Feng Fu, styled the Pi Yung Tien (辟 雍 殿), and, of course, the act served to emphasize the honour that was to be paid to Wang An Shih in connection with the Confucian sacrifices.

Taoist ideas and practices were gaining ground rapidly about this time, through the encouragement of the Emperor,

---

[1] In the 11th month of 1109 he had been called upon to resign his government appointment, but allowed to live in the capital. In the 5th month of 1110 he was sent to take up his residence in Hang Chow.

[2] " T'ung Chien," Ta Kuan (大 觀), 4th year, 6th month.

[3] " T'ung Chien," Cheng Ho (政 和), 1st year, 8th month.

[4] " T'ung Chien," Ta Kuan (大 觀), 4th year, 7th month.

[5] " T'ung Chien," Cheng Ho (政 和), 2nd year, 2nd and 5th months.

[6] " T'ung Chien," Cheng Ho (政 和), 3rd year, 1st month.

and the " Chin " (金) or Golden Tartars were rapidly rising to
power. The Hsi Hsia (西 夏) inflicted several severe defeats
upon the Chinese in the years 1115–16. Ts'ai Ching, however,
was extending his influence throughout this period. In the 9th
month of 1119 he was accorded equal honour with that given
by Shen Tsung to Wang An Shih, being invested with the
title " K'ai Fu I T'ung San Ssu " (開 府 儀 同 三 司).[1]

In 1120, however, he once more was permitted to resign
from the Grand Council, and the following year the " Land
Tax Survey Regulations " were yet again rescinded, together
with certain educational regulations known as the " San She
Fa " (三 舍 法) which formed part of the Reform Policy.

The period 1121–4 is marked by the increasing power
of the Golden Tartars and their aggressive attitude towards
China. The Chinese suffered several serious defeats at the hands
of the Liao or " Iron " Tartars, and to their increasing chagrin
witnessed the alliance of the Hsia (夏) and the Golden Tartars
(金) against themselves in the year 1124, 1st month.[2]

In the 12th month of that year Ts'ai Ching was restored to
supreme power, and marked his return by reviving the old
Government system of Shen Tsung's reign. The three Government organs, known as the " San Sheng " (三 省), had no one
man occupying the chief position in them, and that only.
Some one holding another concurrent post was appointed for
that purpose. This was to prevent any individual from wielding
undue authority.

Under the date of the 9th month, 1125,[3] the Histories note the
incident of a madman shouting at the Palace Gates that he had
been specially commissioned by the spirit of Shen Tsung to
prophesy that a great change was about to take place in Government affairs. The appearance of a fox in the palace is also
recorded, and the fact that it sat on the throne. This was
evidently taken to indicate that some drastic changes should be

---

[1] " T'ung Chien," Hsuan Ho (宣 和), 1st year, 9th month.
[2] " T'ung Chien," Hsuan Ho (宣 和), 6th year, 1st month.
[3] " T'ung Chien," Hsuan Ho (宣 和), 7th year, 9th month.

made, and as the Golden Tartars had killed the Chinese
ambassador for refusing to prostrate himself before their ruler
and had captured the whole of the Yen (燕) area and surrounded
T'aiyuanfu (太 原 府), the Emperor suggested the removal
of the capital from its present site to Nanking. This, however,
was opposed by Wu Min. The Heir-Apparent was installed in
his father's place as Emperor, Hui Tsung being given the title
of " Chiao Chu Tao Chun T'ai Shang Huang Ti " (敎 主
道 君 太 上 皇 帝).[1] All this was contrary to the will of the
heir-apparent, notes the historian.

Now the execution of Ts'ai Ching and five others was
demanded as retribution for bringing the empire to this sorry
plight. The sentence does not seem to have been carried out,
however.

In the 1st month of 1126[2] the Golden Tartars crossed the
Yellow River. Hui Tsung fled, and Li Kang (李 剛) was
commissioned to defend the capital. Terms of peace were
arranged of a character most humiliating to China. For in
addition to being called upon to pay enormous sums of money
and to surrender large tracts of territory, they had to agree to style
the ruler of the Tartars as " Uncle " implying the inferiority
of the Chinese, and to send their acting emperor as a hostage
to the enemy camp. In the 2nd month the Tartar army withdrew
from the city, and Li Kang went to Nanking to escort Hui
Tsung back to the old capital.

The opportunity was now taken to lay the blame for all this at
the door of Wang An Shih and all who had followed his policy.
His Dictionary was once more officially banned. We gather
from the Histories [3] that students had got quite accustomed to
using this dictionary and to the study of Wang An Shih's
interpretations. Yang Shih (楊 時) thereupon appealed to
the throne that he should no longer be honoured with a place

[1] The Emperor was addicted to Taoism, so the title given him really made him
head of that sect.
[2] " T'ung Chien," Ching K'ang (靖 康), 1st year, 1st month.
[3] " T'ung Chien," Ching K'ang (靖 康), 1st year.

in the Confucian ritual. This was approved by the Emperor, who also lifted the ban on the opponents of Wang An Shih's regime and banished Ts'ai Ching to Chan Chow in the 7th month of 1126. He died on the way.[1]

Some semblance of a fight was put up by the Sungs against the Tartars, but aided by the Hsia, who besieged Hsi An Fu (西 安 府) in the 9th month, they once more crossed the Yellow River, surrounded Lo Yang (洛 陽), and compelled the Sungs to sue for peace.

One Kuo Ching gathered the Militia, and determined to defend the capital. He was, however, defeated, and in the 4th month of 1127 the whole of north China passed under the sway of Chin. Hui Tsung and his heir, with some three thousand members of the Imperial line, were all taken captive.[2]

In the 5th month of 1127 the Sungs moved to the south, where Chang Pang Ch'ang first set himself up as emperor. Later, however, he resigned in favour of K'ang Wang (康 王), son of Hui Tsung, who with the wife of Che Tsung, styled "Meng Shih" (孟 氏), now to be honoured as Empress, set up the Court of the Southern Sung Dynasty in Hangchow (杭 州).

[1] "T'ung Chien," Ching K'ang (靖 康), 1st year, 7th month.
[2] "T'ung Chien," Chien Yen (建 炎), 1st year, 4th month.

CHAPTER IV

THE LIFE OF WANG AN SHIH

(ACCORDING TO THE DYNASTIC HISTORY OF SUNG)

WANG AN SHIH (王 安 石), also known as Wang Chieh Fu (王 介 甫), was a native of Lin Ch'uan[1] (臨 川) in the prefecture of Fu Chow (撫 州). His father was Wang I (王 益), who held a post as Accountant in the Military Judiciary at the capital [2] (都 官 員 外 郎).

In his early years Wang An Shih was a keen student, and remembered everything he read. His essays were composed with lightning-like rapidity, and apparently with little thought. But when completed they aroused the admiration of everyone who read them, both for their content and style.

While he was still a young man, some of his written work was submitted to Ou Yang Hsiu by his friend Tseng Kung (曾 鞏). The former was so impressed that he began to spread his name abroad, with the result that at the examination for the doctor's degree (進 士) he was placed in the highest class.[3]

After this he was appointed as secretary to the military commandant of the Huai-Nan circuit (淮 南).[4]

According to the government regulations in force at the time, officials were entitled, on the completion of their first term of probation, to submit a thesis to the educational authorities, so as to qualify for the examination for the higher ranks of the civil service [5] (館 職). Wang An Shih, however, refused to

---

[1] Province of Chiang Hsi, the modern Lin Ch'uan Hsien (臨 川 縣).

[2] 都 官 員 外 郎 is Accountant in one of the twenty-four departments of the Shang Shu Sheng connected with criminal administration.

[3] This I take it to be the implication of the context. The writer would convey the impression that Wang An Shih gained this degree, and his particularly lofty place in the list, by the influence of his patron.

[4] The details of Wang An Shih's various official appointments will be discussed in the main body of the work, so are not commented upon in detail here.

[5] This seems to have been the current procedure.

avail himself of this privilege, thus forming a notable exception
to the general rule.[1]

He was next appointed to Chin Hsien (鄞 縣) as magistrate.
During his term of office there he repaired the grain-mounds
and restored the embankments. He drained marshlands and
flooded areas, which was greatly to the advantage of agriculture.
He also instituted a system whereby loans of grain were made
to the people, thus ensuring a constant supply of fresh grain
in the granaries. This was considered a very beneficial arrangement by the local populace.

His next appointment was at Shu Chow (舒 州), where he
took up the position of Military Attaché.

Wen Yen Po, who was a member of the Grand Council,[2]
then appealed to the Emperor that Wang An Shih should be
promoted to the official hierarchy without the observance of
the usual procedure.[3] He affirmed that Wang An Shih was of
a modest and retiring disposition,[4] and suggested that if the
Emperor would do as he recommended it would serve as a
warning [5] to those who so shamelessly pressed their claims
for advancement.

[1] The text reads 王 安 石 獨 否, the character 獨 occupying a
strongly adversative position. " He was the sole exception to the general rule "
is what is implied.
[2] Wen Yen Po was promoted Grand Councillor in the 1st month of 1048
and was dismissed from that office in the 10th month of 1051. His recommendation
of Wang An Shih at this time was probably towards the close of his period
in this appointment.
[3] This would seem to mean that Wang An Shih might be excused the taking
of the " kuan chih " examination (see above) and possibly exempted from under-
going the one year's probation at the capital which usually followed on success
at this examination. It might also mean the disregarding of the length of service
in government employ which was another factor in the usual procedure of
promotion.
[4] 恬 退 The characters are used together of a man living a quiet and
retired life, as opposed to taking part in public life. See Giles' Dictionary under
character No. 11,220.
[5] The character 激 usually means to stimulate, but that cannot be the
meaning here. There is one use of the character in connection with 刷 (to wash
away, as with a hosepipe), which gives a clue to the meaning in this passage.
See Giles' Dictionary under character No. 886, 楊 清 激 濁 (to elevate the
pure and wipe out the impure).

Wang An Shih was then commanded to take the higher examination, but he refused.

Ou Yang Hsiu then recommended him for a position in the Censorate, but he excused himself on the ground of his grandmother's advanced age. Realizing that his home circumstances [1] demanded a post with better financial prospects, Ou Yang Hsiu once more interposed on his behalf, and secured for him a position in the Board of Husbandry (羣 牧 判 官).

Then, at his own request, he was transferred to Ch'ang Chow (常 州) as sub-prefect. But this appointment was changed to that of Chief Justice of the Chiang Tung circuit (提 點 江 東 刑 獄). Later, again, he was called to the capital, and appointed to the Ministry of Finance (度 支 判 官). This was in 1058. [2]

His government proposals were of an ambitious and unusual character. He brought remarkable powers of debate to the support of his theories. He was extremely self-confident, [3] and obsessed of the idea that he was to make a great contribution towards the reform of everything connected with the government and social order of his day. This led him to submit his memorial of a myriad characters [4] to the throne (synopsized as below) :—

" The finances of the State were getting progressively more straitened, and the public life more and more corrupt and decadent. These things he attributed to the prevailing ignorance of the real method of government, and to a deviation from the example of the ancient rulers.

---

[1] This allusion to Wang's circumstances gives a clue to the reason for his repeated refusals to proceed to the capital to take up any appointment there. He was better off in a provincial appointment than he would have been if he had proceeded to the capital and had been compelled to undergo probation without pay in one of the Bureaus there, with correspondingly heavy expenses.

[2] The dates in this record are very scanty and vague. See Biographical Tables for further details.

[3] 果 扵 自 用, lit. " determined in furthering his own notions ".

[4] 萬 言 書, but actually only 8,565 words, near enough, however, to justify the appellation. A full translation of this important memorial is given in Chapter VII of Vol. I.

" He affirmed, however, that it was only requisite to follow the *ideas* of the ancient rulers (and not slavishly imitate all the *details* of their laws and regulations). If a policy of that type could be initiated, he affirmed that the reforms and changes he sought to introduce would not unduly alarm the people nor create a public disturbance. On the contrary, he was of the opinion that it would certainly bring the government administration into conformity with the ancient models.

" His main thesis was that the total resources of the empire should be so organized as to produce increased revenue for the State, and that all the available revenue should be devoted to the meeting of the State's financial needs.[1] He said that in ancient times the rulers were never distressed by lack of funds, their one and only concern being lest they should not attain to the right method of administering the finances of the country.

" He next proceeded to state his opinion that there were far too few capable men in the service of the government, and that there was in the country generally a dearth of usable men (from whom could be drawn the numbers required to make up the deficiency).

" He urged the Emperor not to presume on a continuation of the good fortune which had hitherto characterized the progress of the dynasty, or to assume that he would not have serious cause for anxiety one day in regard to his responsibilities for the government and the protection of the Empire.

" He therefore warned the Emperor of the danger which lurked in the pursuance of a policy of *laissez-faire*,[2] and appealed that he would command his high officers to devise immediately some measures which would gradually bring about the much desired improvements, so that the needs of the times might be met.

" But he also asserted that the proposals he himself would make were not such as time-serving and conventionally-minded

[1] 因 天 下 之 力 以 生 天 下 之 財 取 天 下 之 財 以 供 天 下 之 費.

[2] 苟 且 因 循 " negligent and conventional ".

officials would advance, and that they were generally spoken of by critics as either impracticable or commonplace." [1]

When, later on, Wang An Shih became a member of the Grand Council [2] he based most of his proposals for reform on this particular memorial.

A short time after the presentation of this memorial he was appointed to the Chi Hsien Yuan (集賢院). Hitherto he had repeatedly refused to consider appointments of this character,[3] and the big officials had begun to think that his mind was not set on political advancement. This created a great desire amongst those at Court to see such a man. So whenever a good post was offered him, their one concern was lest he should not accept it.

The next year (1062) he was appointed Keeper of the Emperor's Diary (同修起居注). He at first refused to accept this, though it was repeatedly offered to him day after day. Eventually a special messenger was sent to offer him the commission in person, but still he refused to receive it. He turned away from the messenger, but the latter followed hard after him begging him to take it. At last Wang An Shih retired to the privy, whereupon the messenger laid the commission on his desk and made for home. However, Wang An Shih sent the document back. Eight or nine times he refused this position before he was finally prevailed upon to accept it.

Later on he was appointed to the Edicts Office (知制誥) and also made Chief Inspector of Justice of the capital (糾察在京刑獄). From this time on he ceased to refuse Court appointments.

A certain youth, who was the owner of a fighting quail,

[1] 迂濶 is roundabout. 熟爛 usually means thoroughly cooked, a metaphor for "well-known", "commonplace". Note that the synopsis of the memorial ends here.

[2] The text reads 當國, which implies that Wang An Shih was then a member of the Grand Council. It was during his office as Vice-Grand Councillor that many of his important reforms were instituted.

[3] 館閣之命, appointments to the various Government Bureaus at the capital.

was requested by a friend to make him a present of it. This request he felt bound to refuse, whereupon his friend, presuming on his familiarity, snatched the bird from him and ran away. The owner gave chase to the thief, and in the scuffle which ensued killed him.

The judge of K'ai Feng Fu passed sentence of death. Wang An Shih opposed this decision, arguing from the law that the taking of property, public or private, which belonged to another was robbery. In this case the owner (of the bird) was obviously unwilling to hand it to his friend, but it had been taken without the owner's consent, and so in the first instance it was clearly a case of robbery.

He then proceeded to argue that the chasing of the thief by the owner was obviously with intent to apprehend him in the interests of the law, and that, although the culprit should have been killed in the process, it ought not to be regarded as a crime at all.[1]

So Wang An Shih accused the judge of having made an illegal decision. This, however, the court officials concerned refused to admit, so the matter was referred to the High Court of Justice. This Court upheld the decision of the local judge and demanded that Wang An Shih should be punished by being requested to present an apology at the Civil Office (閤 門). This he refused to do, affirming his innocence.

The Censorate then appealed that action should be taken against him, but the Emperor ignored the matter.

Later, a mandate was issued by the throne to the effect that after an edict had been issued by the Emperor, the Edicts Inspection Board (舍 人 院)[2] were not to appeal for any alterations or erasions to be made in the text. This suggested action Wang An Shih strenuously opposed. He affirmed that if it were

---

[1] 當 勿 論, probably meaning that no charge whatever ought to have been made.

[2] i.e. editors or copyists of the Imperial edicts, forming a kind of Censorate of mandates. Distinct from the ordinary Censorate or 御 史 臺, or 諫 官, the former being privileged to criticize policy or impeach officials, and the latter deemed specially responsible for admonishing the Emperor.

THE LIFE OF WANG AN SHIH 33

carried out the office of the Edicts Inspection Board would be rendered nugatory. He also asserted that it would tend to make the power of the high officials absolute, and that even though these might be free from private prejudices and be above action based on purely personal considerations, such procedure as was proposed was constitutionally wrong. Should it become the recognized procedure, there would be weaker officials who would not dare to pay sole regard to the interests of the Emperor,[1] while the more powerful ones would presume on their knowledge of the Emperor's mind to issue orders in their own name. The Censorate official would not dare to oppose such influential men, and so this was a matter which excited his serious apprehension (as there would be no opportunity for the defects of these attitudes to be remedied).

It was inevitable that such statements as this should be regarded by the most influential officials as an offence, and so their animosity against Wang An Shih was greatly increased.

On the death of his mother he returned home, and remained in retirement until the death of the Emperor Ying Tsung (英宗), during whose reign, although called to Court several times, he took up no office.

Wang An Shih was a native of the State of Ch'u (楚) and a scholar. His name, however, was unknown at Court. So he secured the help and patronage of the influential families of Han (韓) and Lü (呂) to get better known. He became very intimate with Han Chiang and his younger brother Han Wei, also with Lü Kung Chu (呂公著), through whose patronage and advertisement he first became famous.[2]

[1] If it became the law that edicts once issued could not be changed, there would be weaker officials who would not dare to issue stringent orders.

[2] Liang Ch'i Ch'ao's comment on this is that Wang An Shih was recommended together with Han Wei by Wen Yen Po, and together with Lü Kung Chu by Ou Yang Hsiu, so that as far as Han Wei and Lü Kung Chu recommending him is concerned, such action seems on the face of it unreasonable. But Han Wei certainly spoke for Wang An Shih later on, as the ensuing record shows. However, the imputation of the writer that Wang An Shih cultivated the acquaintance of influential families for his own purposes seems quite alien to his disposition and the facts.

While Shen Tsung was still a prince in status,[1] Han Wei (韓 維) acted as his secretary and adviser. When anything he suggested met with his master's approval he was accustomed to say : " This is the idea of my friend, Wang An Shih." Later on, when Han Wei was appointed as steward to the Heir-Apparent, he recommended Wang An Shih to take his place. This made Shen Tsung very anxious to make his acquaintance, so as soon as he came to the throne he commissioned Wang An Shih as Governor of Chiang Ning Fu (江 寧 府). After some months he called him to the capital to take up the post of Literary Councillor (翰 林 學 士) and also made him sub-expositor of the Han Lin College (侍 講).

In the first year of Hsi Ning (熙 寧),[2] in the 4th month, he was first called to take part in Imperial audiences. The Emperor asked him what he thought was the most important matter to which those in charge of the government should give their attention. He replied : " The selection of the right method is of first importance." The Emperor then inquired : " What do you think of T'ang T'ai Tsung ? " (were his methods satisfactory ?). Wang An Shih replied : " Why discuss T'ai Tsung ; you ought to take Yao and Shun (堯 舜) as your models. Their method of government was direct and simple. They dealt with essential matters in a practical manner, and their ideas are not difficult to carry out. But, alas, later students fail to realize this, and imagine that their method of government cannot be revived."

The Emperor continued : " You would impose an extremely hard task upon me. I feel myself to be so insignificant, and fear that I have neither the character nor the ability to do as you suggest. Perhaps, however, with the help of your counsel I might attain to such heights."

On another occasion the Emperor detained Wang An Shih

---

[1] The characters 藩 邸 mean " the court or capital of a feudatory prince ". See Giles' Dictionary under character No. 3397.

[2] The designation of this particular period of Shen Tsung's reign. In the times of the Sung dynasty these designations were frequently changed, usually because of some outstanding event of public importance taking place at the time.

for private conversation after the other officials had dispersed. When they had seated themselves, the Emperor said: "It was only after T'ang T'ai Tsung (唐 太 宗) had secured the help of Wei Cheng (魏 徵) and after Liu Pei (劉 備) had secured the assistance of Chu Ko Liang (諸 葛 亮) that they accomplished anything worthy of note. But, of course, these two were extremely rare characters."

Wang An Shih replied: " If you are really to become another Yao and Shun, you will certainly need the help of a Kao (皋), a K'uei (夔), a Chi (稷), or a Hsieh (契). If you are to do what Kao Tsung (高 宗) did, you will assuredly need the help of a Fu Yüeh (傅 說). As a matter of fact, Wei Cheng and Chu Ko Liang are not greatly esteemed by those who know what real government should be. They are not worth mentioning in this connection.

" When one considers the vastness of the empire and its enormous population; when, again, we take into account the fact that we have enjoyed a century of peace, and that those who have been devoting themselves to literary pursuits have not been few, it is surprising that we should still have to deplore the lack of suitable men to help in the government services. I am afraid that as you are not quite clear as to the method of government that should be adopted, and as you have not yet made up your mind to put into effect sincerely (the needed reforms), even though you should secure a Kao, a K'uei, a Chi, or a Hsieh, to act as your ministers, they would be so hindered by meaner men that their proposals would never be carried out."

The Emperor replied: " But every generation has its mean men. Were there not the four infamous ministers even in the days of Yao and Shun ? " [1]

" True," retorted Wang An Shih, " but the rulers recognized them as such, and inflicted due punishment. By that very fact they became so famous. If they had given a free rein to such nefarious men, can you imagine that such notabilities as Kao,

---

[1] (共 工, 驩 兜, 三 苗, 鯀.)

K'uei, Chi, and Hsieh would have been content to compromise
their principles by serving them for the whole of their lives ? "

In the district of Teng Chow (鄧 州) a case arose of a woman
attacking her husband with a knife in the night, on account of
his unbearable conduct. She had inflicted serious injuries, and
the general opinion at the Court was that the death penalty
ought to be imposed. Wang An Shih, however, differed from
everybody else, contending that according to the law a sentence
of two grades below that decreed for injury with intent to kill
was just. The Emperor concurred in Wang An Shih's opinion,
and a mandate was issued to that effect.

Wang An Shih was appointed vice-Grand Councillor in
1069 (參 知 政 事). The Emperor remarked : " No one seems
really to know you. The general impression is that you are
acquainted only with bookish ideas,[1] and have no knowledge
of practical politics." He replied : " But a knowledge of the
methods of government as found in the Classics is exactly what
is required for practical politics. Modern scholars are very
commonplace folk, and it has become the fashion to think that
a knowledge of classical methods is useless for practical affairs
of State."

The Emperor inquired : " What contribution would you
deem of first importance ? " Wang An Shih replied : " To
change current practices, and set up (new) laws and ordinances,
is the greatest need of the times."

This statement gained the approval of the Emperor, who
thereupon issued his decree that the Financial Reorganization
Bureau (制 置 三 司 條 例 司) should be set up. Ch'en
Sheng Chih (陳 升 之) (who had concurrent control of the
Board of War) was put in joint charge with Wang An Shih.
The latter also ordered his partisan Lü Hui Ch'ing (呂 惠 卿)
to assist.

In this way the various new Measures, viz. the Neng T'ien
Shui Li (農 田 水 利) or " Land Reclamation and River
Control ", the Ch'ing Miao (青 苗) or " Agricultural Loans ",

---

[1] i.e. Wang An Shih was supposed to possess only literary and not administrative qualifications.

the Chün Shu (均 輸) or "Equitable Transport", the Pao
Chia (保 甲) or "Militia Act", the Mien I (免 役) or "Public
Services Act", the Shih I (市 易) or "Trade and Barter
Regulations", the Pao Ma (保 馬) or "Militia Mounts
Measure", the Fang T'ien (方 田) or "Land Tax Survey",
were promulgated one after the other, and were generally
spoken of as the New Laws.

More than forty special superintendents were commissioned
to supervise the execution of these new laws, and sent out into
different parts of the country with that object in view.

The Agricultural Loans Measure involved the diversion of
the funds available for the purchase of grain in connection with
Government Emergency Granaries [1] to a special fund which
was to be used for disbursement amongst the people on interest
at 24 per cent per annum. The loans were to be distributed in
the spring and repaid in the autumn.

The Equitable Transport Measure involved the alteration
in character of the Transport Service (發 運) into the
Equitable Distribution Service (均 輸). Reorganization of the
system of handling tribute grain and other goods was the aim.
Funds and goods were allocated to enable the officials in charge
to buy the requisite supplies for government needs in the
cheapest market, and in the most conveniently placed centres.
Those in charge were to be kept informed of the probable
requirements of the Imperial Treasury and Granary, so that
they could secure such supplies beforehand and have them in
readiness against every emergency.

The Militia Act aimed at registering the country people
(for regular periods of military training). One able-bodied
male out of every two in a family was liable to be called up.
Ten families formed a corps. Each man received a bow or
cross-bow and was instructed in military drill.

The Public Services Act consisted of a money levy based
on the property classification of the various families. The

---

[1] The actual measure seems to have included the existing stocks of grain as
part, if not the whole of, the capital fund. See Chapter XIII in Vol. I.

38 WANG AN SHIH

proceeds of the levy were to be devoted to the procuring of
hired labour for the public services. The levy extended to
families with only one male, or even to those families in which
there was no male member at all, and to all classes which hitherto
had been exempt from liability for public work. In these
particular cases the levy was styled "Public Services Aid
Money" (助 役 錢).

The Trade and Barter Measure permitted a person to contract
loans of either money or goods with the officials, who accepted
land, buildings, or other property by way of security. Interest
was charged at the rate of 24 per cent per annum, but if the loan
was not repaid by the specified time an extra 2 per cent per
month was demanded as a fine.

The Militia Mounts Measure was as follows :—

All militia (保 丁) within the five districts [1] adjacent to
the capital who were willing to keep a horse were allowed one
to each family. The animals were either taken from the National
Stud or were purchased by the keeper of the animal with money
granted for that purpose by the government. There was to
be an annual examination of the animals' condition, and dead
or sick animals had to be replaced.

The Land Tax Survey comprised the measuring out of the
land into plots of 1,000 "pu" square.[2] Each year, in the 9th
month, the officials were to measure the plots, and determine
the classification of each according to its relative productivity.
Five classes of land were recognized, and taxation assessed on
this basis in an equitable manner.

In addition another Measure was instituted, styled (免 行
錢) "Mien Hang Ch'ien" or "Direct Trade Tax Measure".
This was a tax levied directly by the Government on all sales
of goods brought into the capital, the total amount to be
received from this source being estimated on the profits which
the "hangs" (行) or big trade houses (which had managed

[1] i.e. 永 興 and 秦 鳳, 河 北, 京 東, 京 西, 京 畿.
[2] One square was equal in area to 41 ch'ing, 66 mu, 160 pu. One ch'ing is
equal to 15.13 acres, so the total area would be about 630 acres. See Giles'
Dictionary under character No. 2195.

this business hitherto) had made, and also including the levy for which these trade houses had been responsible themselves (apart from the taxes which they had levied in the name of the government).[1]

There resulted from all these proposals nation-wide discussion of land and water schemes, the reclamation of fallow land, and the restoration of neglected grainplots and dykes. The people vied with one another in making all available land suitable for cultivation.

An order was also issued ordering the people to bid, by sealed tender, for market stands and sites, which led to an increase in the prices of these. Increases also took place in the quantities of tea and salt (which the people were compelled by law to use). In Hopei (河 北) a Government Purchase Bureau was set up in connection with the Granary system, the object of which was to accumulate large stocks of grain on the waterways in readiness for transport.

In these ways the various taxes and levies were increased and the people everywhere became discontented.[2]

Lü Hui, the chief censor, impeached Wang An Shih on ten counts, and was cashiered in consequence. Wang An Shih then recommended Lü Kung Chu for the vacancy thus caused.

Han Ch'i (韓 琦) then submitted an indictment of Wang An Shih's policy. As the Emperor was inclined to agree with Han Ch'i's point of view, Wang An Shih asked to be relieved of his post. The Emperor ordered Ssu Ma Kuang (司 馬 光) to write the official reply. In this he included the words: " The officials are in a turbulent mood, and the people seriously discontented." When Wang An Shih heard of this he was greatly annoyed and sent in a rejoinder fiercely justifying himself. The Emperor humbly apologized,[3] Lü Hui Ch'ing being

---

[1] According to the Wen Hsien T'ung K'ao, vol. 20, p. 13, the salaries of Government officials concerned were also to be covered by the proceeds of this tax.

[2] The character of the various New Laws and their effect is fully discussed in the main body of the present work. So criticism of this statement is reserved for detailed discussion later on.

[3] (帝 爲 罷 辭 謝.)

commissioned to convey the apology to Wang An Shih.
Han Chiang (韓 絳) also appealed to the Emperor to recall
Wang An Shih.

When the latter entered the Court to offer his thanks for the
Emperor's consideration, he took the opportunity to complain
of the way in which all officials, both at Court and outside, both
high and low, even the officials of the Censorate, were forming
cliques against him. He said that if the Emperor was desirous
of overcoming the Conventionalists he must put the weight
of his authority against theirs. For if their authority was greater
than his, it would naturally turn the scale in their favour and the
whole empire would become conventional. But if the Emperor's
authority was seen to be greater than theirs, then naturally the
whole empire would follow his lead. He said : " When the
weight and the thing to be weighed are laid in the balance and
found to be of exactly equal weight, even though it was a matter
of 30,000 ounces, the scale would be turned one way or the other
by the addition or removal of a single ounce or dram. There
are at present certain evil-minded folk who are determined to
hinder Your Majesty in your great purpose, and to nullify
every attempt that we make to revive the ancient methods of
government. The times are critical. It is a time in which we
shall see whether the authority of the Emperor or that of the
Conventionalists is to win the day. If you add the least little
bit of weight to their authority they will become supreme. This
accounts for all the turmoil that exists."

The Emperor saw the force of this. So Wang An Shih
resumed his post, and Han Ch'i's idea was forestalled.

Wang An Shih and Ssu Ma Kuang had been the best of
friends for some time. The latter with the idea of discharging
a friendly duty sent the former three letters entreating him (to
change his policy). This only excited Wang An Shih's displeasure. The Emperor offered Ssu Ma Kuang the vice-
Presidency of the Board of War, which, however, he refused.
Wang An Shih having resumed his post, the idea of giving
Ssu Ma Kuang this appointment was abandoned.

Lü Kung Chu, although he had been recommended by Wang

An Shih for official appointment, appealed for the repeal of the New Laws, and was, in consequence, transferred to Ying Chow (潁 州). Liu Shu (劉 述), Liu Ch'i (劉 琦), Ch'ien K'ai (錢 顗), Sun Ch'ang Ling (孫 昌 齡), Wang Tzu Shao (王 子 韶), Ch'eng Hao (程 顥), Chang Chien (張 戩), Ch'en K'uei (陳 薆), Ch'en Chien (陳 薦), Hsieh Ching Wen (謝 景 溫), Yang Hui (楊 繪), and Liu Chih (劉 摯), who were all officials of the public Censorate, and officials of the Imperial Board of Censors such as Fan Ch'un Jen (范 純 仁), Li Ch'ang (李 常), Sun Chueh (孫 覺), and Hu Tsung Yü (胡 宗 愈), all resigned their posts because their criticisms of the New Laws met with no response from the Emperor.

Li Ting (李 定) from some judicial appointment at Hsiu Chow (秀 州) was suddenly promoted to the Censorate. Three vice-Grand Councillors, viz. Sung Min Ch'iu (宋 敏 求), Li Ta Lin (李 大 臨), and Su Sung (蘇 頌), returned the order which announced this appointment, placing it in a sealed envelope. The censors Lin Tan (林 旦), Hsieh Ch'ang Ch'ao (薛 昌 朝), and Fan Yü (范 育), all impeached Li Ting as being unfilial. Every one of these was relieved of his position. Fan Chen (范 鎮) submitted three memorials criticizing the Agricultural Loans Measure, and as he was degraded on account of this, he resigned all his offices.

Lü Hui Ch'ing having resigned to fulfil his mourning obligations, Wang An Shih was at a loss to find some one to whom he could entrust his duties. But he secured Tseng Pu (曾 布) for his trusted colleague, regarding him as second only to Lü Hui Ch'ing. In the 12th month of 1070 Wang An Shih was appointed Grand Councillor (同 中 書 門 下 平 章 事).

In the spring of the following year a typhoon occurred in the Ching Tung and Hopei Circuits, and the people were greatly alarmed. The Emperor issued a mandate ordering the Chung Shu Sheng (中 書 省) to adopt a policy of inactivity in order to appease the wrath of Heaven as evinced by this natural phenomenon. He proposed that all the hired labourers from these two Circuits (which were engaged on public works) should be sent back to their homes, and that local officials who had not furnished the government with specific information about the typhoon conditions should be reprimanded.

But Wang An Shih did not publish this order.

In the K'ai Feng district there were numerous cases of people inflicting self-injury, such as the cutting off of their fingers or the breaking of their wrists, in order to avoid being enrolled in the Militia under the Militia Act. Han Wei (韓維), the governor, brought these matters to the notice of the Emperor, who inquired of Wang An Shih as to the truth or otherwise of this report. Wang An Shih replied : " One cannot be quite sure. But even if the reports are true we need not be surprised, for even the high officials and educated people are greatly concerned and disturbed because of the New Laws. So it is more than probable that amongst the 200,000 people of K'ai Feng there are some who are so stupid as to permit others to disturb them. But are we, because of this, to be afraid of carrying out anything at all in the way of reform ? "

The Emperor replied : " But when the people unite their voices (on any matter of public import) we shall only overcome the difficulty by complying with their request.[1] This is a matter about which one cannot but feel apprehensive."

A crowd of people from the Tung Ming district pressed round Wang An Shih one day as he was riding, and complained about the oppressive character of the Aid Money Measure (助役錢). Wang An Shih, in reporting this mattter to the Emperor, said : " The magistrate of the district is Chia Fan (賈蕃), who is son-in-law of Fan Chung Yen (范仲淹). The latter is partial to the Conventionalists, and so has incited the people to take this action." He went on to say : " In governing the people, it is of first importance to ascertain the real facts, and to find out whether any particular policy is or is not to the true advantage of the state. In no case should we show the people a too lenient front. If we let them have their way,

---

[1] Probably based on the principle enunciated in Mencius, viz. 天視自我民視天聽自我民聽, which is translated by Legge as follows : " Heaven sees according as my people see : Heaven hears according as my people hear." Mencius, Book V, pt. 1, ch. v, v. 8.

they will presume to approach the palace precincts, create a
great commotion, and besiege the throne with their clamorous
appeals. They will rely upon their numbers to get their way.
But that would not be conducive of good government."

Wang An Shih's arguments were mostly of this arrogant
and unreasonable order.

The Emperor wished to instal Han Wei (韓 維) as Chung
Ch'eng (中 丞) (an important official of the Censorate).
However, Wang An Shih being resentful of the way in which he
had criticized him and his policy, hinted to the Emperor that he
was inclined to side with the Conventionalists, and that he was
opposed to the Emperor's policy. This led Han Wei to refuse
the proffered appointment, and then only did Wang An Shih
desist from his opposition.

Ou Yang Hsiu then appealed that he might be allowed to
resign all his public responsibilities. Feng Ching (馮 京),
however, appealed that he should still be retained in office.
Whereupon Wang An Shih said : " Ou Yang Hsiu is a protégé
of Han Ch'i, whom he regards as indispensable to the State.
To appoint such a man to a provincial district will be the ruin
of it. To give him a Court appointment will have disastrous
consequences. What is the use of keeping such a man ? " [1]

Fu Pi (富 弼) had been relieved of his rank of Imperial
Commissioner (使 相) on account of his opposition to the
Agricultural Loans Measure. Wang An Shih remarked that such
a penalty was altogether too light to be effective in repressing
such disloyal activities. He even went so far as to compare Fu
Pi with such notorieties as Kung (共) and Kun (鯀).

Yu Ying (尤 瑛), of the Board of Astronomy, then appealed
that Wang An Shih should be dismissed, as the heavens had
been long overcast, and the stars were pursuing an irregular
course. [2] As a result of this Yu Ying was branded as a criminal
and sent to Ying Chow (英 州).

---

[1] Liang Ch'i Ch'ao affirms that this is a fabrication. See later chapter where
the matter is discussed in detail.
[2] Anything unusual in the natural order was interpreted as an omen of something wrong in the government.

T'ang Chung (唐 坰), whom Wang An Shih had promoted to the Censorate, vehemently denounced his patron in the Imperial presence. But as a reward for his pains he was degraded and banished to a distant outpost,[1] where he died.

Wen Yen Po (文 彦 博) in a memorial criticized the Trade and Barter Measure (市 易 法) on the ground that it involved the government in business competition with the people, and contended that this had caused the collapse of Hua Shan (華 山). Wang An Shih replied: " It is quite conceivable that the earthquake at Hua Shan has been sent by heaven as a warning to mean folk. But the Trade and Barter Measure was devised to relieve the poor people of long-standing distress and with a view to repressing the monopolists. What profit is there in it for the government ? "

Wang An Shih kept back this memorial, and got Wen Yen Po transferred as Garrison Commissioner of Wei (魏).

So by this time Lü Kung Chu and Han Wei, who had been instrumental in establishing Wang An Shih's reputation; Ou Yang Hsiu and Wen Yen Po, who had recommended him for office; Fu Pi and Han Ch'i, who had employed him in their own entourage; and Ssu Ma Kuang and Fan Chen, who had been his personal friends, were all degraded or cashiered by him with the utmost severity.

The president of the Board of Rites proposed that the tablet of T'ai Tsu (太 祖), the first Emperor of the Sung dynasty, should be transferred to the central position (facing east) in the Imperial Ancestral temple. Wang An Shih, on the contrary, proposed that the tablet of Hsi Tsu (僖 禧), the great-great-grandfather of T'ai Tsu, should be transferred to this position from its place in the reserved chamber. Although general opinion was against Wang An Shih, the majority failed to override his arguments.[2]

[1] Evidently to a very subordinate office.
[2] The normal practice in regard to the Imperial Ancestral temple was for it to contain seven tablets, five of the Emperor's immediate ancestors and two relatively more remote. The primordial position was usually occupied by the tablet of the most remote who was regarded as the founder of the Imperial line. This tablet occupied a position of sole honour on the west, or as the text reads

On the evening of the fifteenth of the first month (1074) Wang An Shih, who had been escorting the Imperial chariot on horseback, made as though he would ride through the Hsuan Te gate (宣 德 門). The guard at the gate checked him, and began to beat his horse back. Wang An Shih took umbrage at this and put in a plea for the punishment of the offender. Ts'ai Ch'üeh (蔡 確), the censor, urged that the guard was but doing his duty out of respect for the Emperor. Wang An Shih, he affirmed, ought to have dismounted at that point, and that it was right that he had been checked. However, the Emperor ordained that the guard should be beaten and his superior officer reprimanded. This, however, failed to satisfy Wang An Shih.

Wang Shao (王 韶), having reported the successful termination of the Hsi Ho (熙 河) campaign, the Emperor,

東 向 之 位 facing east. The tablets of the other six were ranged three on each side, north and south respectively.

But there was no certainty as to who should occupy this position during the Sung dynasty, and so the primordial place had been left vacant.

When Ying Tsung died in 1067 the question of these tablets and their position became very acute, as in addition to the tablets of T'ai Tsu, T'ai Tsung, Chen Tsung, and Jen Tsung, his immediate predecessors, there had been included also the tablets of Hsi Tsu, the great-great-grandfather of Shen Tsung, and Shun Tsu, his great-grandfather. That made seven in all, but no more than six places were possible, unless one tablet was moved into the primordial position.

There were some who thought that this position ought eventually to be reserved for T'ai Tsu, as being the one who had done most to establish the royal line, but on the other hand there were those who thought that the primordial position should be given to Hsi Tsu.

On the accession of Shen Tsung the question was solved by removing the tablet of Hsi Tsu to the reserved chamber (祧 廟) and moving up the tablets of the others one place, still keeping the primordial position vacant.

However, in the year 1072 the question was revived, and Wang An Shih supported the appeal of the Civil Office that the tablet of Hsi Tsu should be restored to the Imperial temple and that it should occupy the primordial position. This was done on the ground that the ancestry of the Sung line prior to Hsi Tsu could not be ascertained, and so it was argued that his tablet should be kept in the primordial place in the Imperial Ancestral temple, just as the Shang Dynasty honoured the tablet of Hsieh (契) and the Chow dynasty the tablet of Chi (禝).

Wang An Shih had opposed the removal of the tablet of Hsi Tsu to the reserved chamber, so now as Prime Minister he supported its restoration, and placing it in the highest position (taken from the Dynastic History of Sung, Li Chih (禮 志), vol. 106).

in his gratification at the news, and being peculiarly grateful to Wang An Shih for suggesting the campaign, presented him with his bejewelled girdle.

During the spring of 1074 there had been prolonged drought, the face of the country being covered with swarms of famine refugees. The Emperor displayed great grief, and at a Court audience expressed his opinion that all oppressive or unjust measures should be repealed. Wang An Shih replied : " Floods and drought are part of the regular course of nature, and could not be avoided even by such great rulers as Yao (堯) and T'ang (湯). Your Majesty need exercise no undue anxiety on that score. All that is necessary is that certain adjustments should be made in affairs as a response to this natural calamity."

The Emperor replied : " But this is no minor affair. My fear arises from the fact that we have not made such adjustments as you suggest. I fear that we have been taking far too much money from the people by the operation of the Direct Trade Tax Measure (免 行 錢).[1] They naturally are resentful at this, and utter rebellious speeches. Everyone, from the more intimate officers to members of the royal family, speaks of the oppressive character of this particular measure. The Empress and the Dowager are for ever bewailing it. They fear lest the capital should be thrown into confusion, and that the people generally might become disaffected by the drought."

Wang An Shih replied : " I do not know who the intimate officers may be to whom you have referred. But if the Empress and Dowager have talked about it, it must have been due to the instigation of Hsiang Ching (向 經) and Ts'ao I (曹 佾)."

Feng Ching interpolated the remark that he too had heard of complaints as to the oppressive character of this measure, whereupon Wang An Shih retorted : " All high officials, who are disgruntled for any reason, flock to Feng Ching, and this may account for the fact that he alone has heard about it."

Cheng Hsieh (鄭 俠), the superintendent of the An Shang

---

[1] A direct tax on all trade in the capital. (See Chapter XVI in Vol. I.)

Gate (安 上 門), then submitted a memorial, together with drawings, illustrating the pitiable condition of the famine refugees as he had observed them, showing the young supporting their aged, and parents leading their children, etc. He affirmed that the drought was due to Wang An Shih, and that rain would surely fall if he were dismissed.

The memorialist was punished for this act of temerity and banished to Ling Nan (嶺 南).

The Grand Dowager Tz'u Sheng (慈 聖), the grandmother of Shen Tsung, and the Dowager proper Hsuan Jen (宣 仁), mother of Shen Tsung, weeping copiously, complained to the Emperor that Wang An Shih had thrown the whole empire into confusion. Then even the Emperor began to have his doubts (about Wang An Shih) [1] and transferred him to the governorship of Chiang Ning Fu (江 寧 府) with the rank of Grand Councillor of the Kuan Wen Tien (觀 文 殿 大 學 士).

Lü Hui Ch'ing (呂 惠 卿), who on the conclusion of his mourning period had been irregularly promoted no less than nine grades, from the post of Vice-President of the Board of Rites to the Presidency of the Board of Civil Appointments (吏 部 尙 書), had been inveigled by Wang An Shih into an entire agreement with his policy. So the latter now recommended him for the position of vice-Grand Councillor, and proposed that Han Chiang should succeed himself as Grand Councillor. These two maintained Wang An Shih's policy in its entirety, not deviating from it in the slightest degree.[2] On account of this Han Chiang was given the nickname of the " Propagating Abbot " (傳 法 沙 門) and Lü Hui Ch'ing was termed " Divine Protector of the New Laws " (護 法 善 神).

But, as a matter of fact, Lü Hui Ch'ing was scheming to get the reins of government into his own hands, and so was anxious

---

[1] There is no evidence of the Emperor's doubting Wang An Shih at this or any other period.

[2] Some alterations were made, such as the " Self-Assessment Measure " initiated by Lü Hui Ch'ing during Wang An Shih's absence, and also the banishment of Cheng Hsieh, which was foreign to Wang An Shih's policy of treating his political opponents.

to prevent Wang An Shih from returning to power. He took advantage of certain elements in the Cheng Hsieh case to injure his brother, Wang An Kuo (王 安 國), and revived the case of Li Shih Ning (李 士 寧) with intent to bring about the complete downfall of Wang An Shih.

Han Chiang, hearing of this plot, secretly informed the Emperor of it, and appealed that Wang An Shih might be recalled. So in the 2nd month of the next year (1075) he once more assumed the position of Grand Councillor Supreme. After he had received the Emperor's mandate of recall he travelled to the capital in double quick time.

After his Interpretation of the Three Classics had been presented, his rank was promoted to that of Shang Shu Tso P'u She (尚 書 左 僕 射) and Men Hsia Shih Lang (門 下 侍 郎).[1] His son, Fang (雱), was offered a post in the Lung T'u Ko (龍 圖 閣) or Imperial Library. Fang excused himself from the acceptance of this position, and Lü Hui Ch'ing suggested that he should not be pressed to change his mind. This led to the breach between Wang An Shih and Lü Hui Ch'ing becoming more obvious. The latter was indicted by Ts'ai Ch'eng Hsi, so he retired home to await the Emperor's decision on the matter. Fang then instigated Teng Chien (鄧 綰), the Chief Censor, to make still further charges against Lü Hui Ch'ing, accusing him of infamous profiteering in connection with the case of Chang Jo Chi (張 若 濟), the official at Hua Ting Hsien (華 亭 縣). Chang Jo Chi was incriminated and Lü Hui Ch'ing transferred to Ch'en (陳).

A comet appeared in the east during the 10th month of the same year. The Emperor called for general criticism, soliciting opinions as to what features of the current administration were not to the advantage of the people.

---

[1] These two offices made him supreme in each of the three Government Assemblies. He was already head of the Chief Legislative Assembly (中 書 省), now he held the chief positions in the Chief Administrative Assembly (尚 書 省) and also as before the head position in the Chief Record Office (門 下 省).

Wang An Shih and his faction then compiled the following statement :—

"In the fifth year of Chin Wu Ti (晉 武 帝) one comet appeared in ' Chen ' (軫) and another in his tenth year. He ruled in all for twenty-eight years, a period which was at variance with the predictions of the astrologers.[1] The way of heaven is remote and difficult to foretell. It is true the ancient rulers engaged official diviners, but what they actually relied upon (in making their prognostications) were the observable facts, particularly the way in which public affairs were conducted. The phenomena of the astronomical world are innumerable, and it is inevitable by forcing interpretation of them so as to seem to have connection with mundane affairs that certain coincidences of a lucky character should occur.

"It will be admitted that it is inconceivable that such men as Chow Kung (周 公) and Shao Kung (召 公) should deceive Ch'eng Wang (成 王). The latter mentioned that Chung Tsung (中 宗) had occupied the throne for a particularly lengthy period. He was told that this was due to his being dignified, respectful, cautious, and obedient. So that he himself had

---

[1] The appearance of comets was regarded as an augury of ill omen. The particular position in the heavens in which these were first discernible was also regarded as signifying its particular reference to mundane affairs. There is confusion between this account in the Pen Chuan and that given in the Dynastic History of Chin Wu Ti's reign. In the latter the comet which appeared in the " Chen " (軫) constellation is given as appearing in the 10th year of his reign, while in the Sung History it is given as appearing in the 5th year. There were comets, however, in both the 5th and the 10th years of his reign. Following the Dynastic History of Chin Wu Ti as being more likely to be correct, we note that the comet which appeared in the 5th year was regarded as foretelling the death of some member of the royal family, so in the 10th year the death of the Empress is recorded as being related to the appearance of this comet. War in the Ch'u region was evidently supposed to be the concomitant of the appearance of the comet in the 10th year. But in one or other of these cases there was supposed to be indicated the demise of the Emperor at a date earlier than that on which his reign terminated. It is to this fallacious prognostication on the part of the astrologers that Wang An Shih refers in this passage.

I have been unable to relate the year "I Ssu (乙 巳) to the reign of Chin Wu Ti. Perhaps this is an error in copying ".

(Taken from the Dynastic History of Chin Wu Ti, " T'ien Wen Chih " (天 文 志), vol. 13, p. 16.

determined the decree of heaven by not daring to indulge in reckless ease in connection with the government of the people. [1] From this it can be seen that the length of reigns in the Hsia and Shang dynasties was related solely to the moral character of the emperor concerned.

" P'i Tsao (裨 竈) foretold the outbreak of a fire, and his prophecy was fulfilled. (When he gave a second warning of a similar occurrence) the people wished to offer special sacrifices to ward off the threatened calamity, and to show their respect for P'i Tsao's reputation as a prophet. Kuo Ch'iao (國 僑) [2] refused to heed this request, so P'i Tsao said : ' Do you pay no attention to my words ? Another big fire will occur in Cheng (鄭).' Kuo Ch'iao still refused to pay any attention and no fire occurred.

" If men of such repute as P'i Tsao can make false predictions, what reliance can be placed upon the statements of our modern astrologers ? The traditional books on divination have been banned for generations (which shows that our rulers have placed no reliance on such matters) and it is also impossible to know how many mistakes have been made in copying them out.

" Your Majesty is of the highest personal character. You are not only superior in that respect to Chung Tsung, but you have carried out in their entirety the exhortations of the Dukes Chow and Shao. What need have you of the advice of stupid and blind ' astrologers ' ? We hear that the Grand Dowager and the Empress Dowager are greatly concerned about the appearance of this comet, but I hope they will receive comfort from the advice we now present."

To this the Emperor replied : " The people are really seriously distressed by the operation of the new laws."

Wang An Shih rejoined : " The people are resentful of natural phenomena such as excessive heat, cold, or rain. There

---

[1] Cf. Legge, Book of History, part v, bk. xv, par. 4, and, in fact, the whole of the section, which is entitled " Against Luxurious Ease " (無 逸).

[2] i.e. Tzu Ch'an of Cheng (鄭 子 產), of some repute as a reformer, mentioned by Wang An Shih as one who had carried out measures similar to his own.

is no need for you to be anxious about their resentment in regard to this particular matter."

The Emperor retorted : " But it would be better if they had no cause for resentment at all, even on account of natural phenomena." [1]

This remark annoyed Wang An Shih, who kept to his rooms on the pretext of being ill. The Emperor tried to console him and exhorted him to resume his duties.

Wang An Shih's associates then took counsel together and advised him, saying : " Unless you comply with the Emperor's wishes our political enemies will take advantage of your absence to rush in with their theories. If the Emperor uses them, our own authority and influence will decrease and our faults will be brought to light." Wang An Shih thereupon agreed to return, whereupon the Emperor, overjoyed to welcome his favourite again, followed his wishes absolutely.

At this time the expedition against Annam was mooted. A spy had procured a copy of the proclamation issued by the Annamite chief, asserting that he was leading forth his forces to deliver the Chinese people from the poverty and distress which the Agricultural Loans Measure and the Public Services Act had imposed upon them. This enraged Wang An Shih, who forthwith drew up with his own hand a manifesto denouncing the Annamite king.

The Hua T'ing Hsien case had been in abeyance for some time. So Fang, the son of Wang An Shih, took counsel with two of his father's partisans, viz. Lü Chia Wen (呂 嘉 問) and Lien Heng Fu (練 亨 甫), with a view to taking further action with regard to Teng Chiens' exposure of Lü Hui Ch'ing's crime. By adding evidence from other documents they succeeded in getting (Chang Jo Chi), his accomplice, imprisoned in the Imperial gaol.

This was done without Wang An Shih being consulted.

[1] The idea in the Emperor's mind seems to be that he wished the people to be free from calamities of the natural order which may be regarded as beyond men's power, and therefore that all the more should rulers seek to avoid giving them ground for complaint in matters which are in the power of the government to arrange.

A subordinate informed Lü Hui Ch'ing, who was then in Ch'en (陳). He thereupon charged Wang An Shih with having rejected all he had ever been taught, accusing him of being too zealous an admirer of the worst type of faction promoter.[1] He accused him, too, of disobeying the Emperor's orders, and of issuing mandates in his own name. He asserted that he had done despite to the throne, and had forced the Emperor to act contrary to his own wishes. He affirmed that his innumerable crimes, which had been perpetrated with such determination the last few years, proved him to be more guilty than the disappointed place-seekers of ancient time, who were so notorious for their disobedience and rebellion. He also made public certain letters of Wang An Shih, in which the following phrase occurred: " Keep this from the knowledge of the Emperor."

When the latter made this known to Wang An Shih, he was at a loss to account for the business, as he had no idea who was responsible for its initiation. However, on inquiry from his son Fang, he learned the whole story. His father reprimanded him so sternly that Fang lost his temper, and as a result a carbuncle broke out on his back, from which he died.

Wang An Shih also vehemently denounced Teng Chien for his share in the proceedings, and for his presumption[2] in recommending his son Fang and his son-in-law Ts'ai Pien (蔡 卞) for promotion. This resulted in Teng Chien incurring punishment together with Lien Heng Fu.

[1] Su Ch'in (蘇 秦) was the leader of the anti-Ch'in war party at the period of the latter State's rise to power. He advocated an alliance of the six states to the east of Ch'in, viz. Han, Chao, Wei, Yen, Lu, and Ch'i in a north and south line, and so this was called the " Yueh Tsung " (約 縱) or Perpendicular Alliance. Chang I (張 儀), on the other hand, sought to ally the states on an east–west line, in favour of Ch'in, by more peaceful Measures. Their party was termed the " Lien Heng " or Horizontal Alliance (連 橫). These terms later came to be used of any sort of divisive or faction-making policy, the person advocating it being termed a " Tsung Heng Chia " (縱 橫 家).

[2] Teng Chien was a comparatively small official. For him to recommend the relations of Wang An Shih, the Grand Councillor, was presumption.

It should be noted that Teng Chien had secured his position in the Censorate through his subservience to Wang An Shih, and that in the controversy which had arisen between his leader and Lü Hui Ch'ing he had vigorously assisted Wang An Shih. When the Emperor showed his displeasure with Wang An Shih, Teng Chien, fearing lest he himself should lose his influence, appealed that Wang An Shih might be retained in office, and used the most extravagant language in his praise.

Lien Heng Fu was a dangerous and small-minded fellow who had been advanced in the government service through his servile flattery of Fang. But now both he and Teng Chien were rejected by Wang An Shih.

Since the latter had resumed his office of Grand Councillor he had made frequent requests for retirement on the ground of ill-health. After the death of his son, Fang, his grief proved unbearable, and he urgently requested that he might be relieved of all administrative responsibilities. The Emperor's dissatisfaction was greatly increased,[1] and he was relieved of his office and transferred to Chiang Ning Fu (江 寧 府) with the standing of civil and military commissioner for Chen Nan (鎮 南), while retaining his rank of Grand Councillor.

During the following year (1077) his appointment was changed to that of Warden of the Chi Hsi Kuan (集 禧 觀), and the title of Duke of Shu (舒 國 公) was conferred upon him. He tried several times to resign his Commissioner's seal, but in the third year of Yuan Feng (元 豐), i.e. 1080, he was appointed to be Tso P'u She (左 僕 射), also Grand Councillor of the Kuan Wen Tien (觀 文 殿 大 學 士). Later again his title was changed to Duke of Ching (荊 國 公) and the words " T'e Chin " (持 進) or " Specially Promoted " were added.

After the accession of Che Tsung (哲 宗) in the year 1085–6, he was given the additional honorary appointment of

---

[1] The text reads as though the Emperor was dissatisfied with Wang An Shih's conduct. But may not his dissatisfaction have been with Wang An Shih's determination to resign, and not with any flaw in his conduct, or the character of his policy ? Otherwise how are we to account for the honours with which he loaded him ?

Superintendent of Public Works (司空), but soon after this he died in 1086, at the age of 65.[1]

On his death he was granted the posthumous title of Grand Tutor (太 傅).

During the period of Che Tsung's reign known as " Shao Sheng " (紹 聖) he was given the further posthumous designation of " Wen " (文) or " Accomplished ", and his spirit tablet was erected alongside that of the Emperor Shen Tsung in the Court temple.

In the third year of Ts'ung Ning, i.e. 1104, during the reign of Hui Tsung (徽 宗), his tablet was placed in the Confucian temple, and he shared in the sacrifices which were offered to the national sage along with Yen Hui (顏 回) and Mencius (孟 子). He was later rendered still greater homage by the conferring of the title of " Shu Wang " (舒 王).

In the reign of Ch'in Tsung (欽 宗), 1126-7, Yang Shih (楊 時) successfully appealed that the homage paid to Wang An Shih in the Confucian temple should be proscribed by Imperial decree. In the time of Kao Tsung (高 宗), successor of Ch'in Tsung (1127-1163), on the suggestion of Chao Ting (趙 鼎) and Lü Ts'ung Wen (呂 聰 問), not only was the sacrifice to Wang An Shih in the Confucian temple prohibited, he was also deprived of the title of " Wang " (王) or " Prince ".

After Wang An Shih's new interpretation of the Odes, History, and Chou Li had been completed and presented to the throne, they were distributed to the different educational authorities, and received by general consent the designation of " Hsin I " or " New Interpretation " (新 義).

During his later years, while resident at Chin Ling (金 陵), he wrote his " Tzu Shuo " (字 說) or Dictionary. This contained many forced and fanciful interpretations, of a type much akin to those adopted by the Buddhists and Taoists. But for a time educationalists were forced to teach and adopt these interpretations. The superintendent of examinations demanded their sole use in his selection of candidates for the various government

---

[1] Biographical tables all agree in making him 66 at death (Chinese reckoning which usually adds one year to foreign reckoning).

appointments, free interpretation of the candidates being banned. In this way the traditional commentaries of the early Confucianists were absolutely discarded.

Wang An Shih despised the Annals (春秋), forbidding its use by the educational authorities. But what was still more hateful, he termed it a mere collection of Court records, both scrappy and confused.[1]

Prior to his attainment of high office, Wang An Shih's reputation resounded throughout the capital. He was said to be of an abstemious disposition, living a very parsimonious life, rarely washing his clothes or even his face. He was, however, regarded as a man of worth by many of his contemporaries.

But Su Hsün (蘇洵)[2] was the one man bold enough to term him an unnatural fellow, such as rarely failed to achieve a reputation for infamy. He also wrote a pamphlet (辯姦論) which was really an attack upon Wang An Shih. In this he asserted that he was a combination of Wang Yen (王衍) and Lu Ch'i (盧杞).

Wang An Shih was a strong-willed and envious man, brooking no opposition in his government policy, regardless of whether it was feasible or not. He held tenaciously to his own point of view, which once fixed, he never changed. When he introduced his ideas for reform of the administration, his colleagues and associates in the government all considered his proposals impracticable. So he then produced a special interpretation of the Classics which made them appear to coincide with his pet theories. When discussion was raised, he poured forth a torrent of words, so that the majority were unable to convince him of the error of his ways. He went to the length of asserting that calamities in the natural world need excite no alarm; that the example set by the Emperor's ancestors was not adequate as a model; and that the opinions and criticisms of other men were not worthy of consideration. He

[1] 斷爛朝報. The question of Wang An Shih's attitude to this particular classic, about which the Confucianists were so sensitive, is discussed in the main body of the work. See Chap. VIII.
[2] i.e. 蘇老泉, the father of Su Shih and Su Che.

dismissed the older ministers of experience from the Court and employed in their place the members of his own faction, mostly youthful and clever, but shallow-minded men.

After a period in high office he was led to resign owing to an occurrence of drought. But after an interval of over a year he returned to office again. This time, however, he was only in the capital for about a year, when he was dismissed. During the ensuing period of about eight years, i.e. for the remainder of Shen Tsung's reign, he was not called again to take part in the government.

Wang An Shih's son, Fang, styled also Yuan Tse (元 澤), was a quick-tempered, treacherous, and mean fellow, entirely lacking in self-restraint. He was, however, extremely clever, who, before he was capped (20 years of age), had published works to his name of several tens of thousands of characters. At 13 years of age he received information from a soldier of Ch'in (秦) concerning the territory near the T'ao river (洮 河). With a sigh he said : " By rendering the requisite help we may get possession of this territory. If we allow the Hsi Hsia to take it, it will strengthen our foes and increase the trouble on the border."

Later on, when Wang Shao had begun operations in the Hsi Ho area, he received the strong backing of Wang An Shih, which was given because Fang had made the above suggestions to his father.

Fang gained his Doctor's degree (進 士) and was appointed to a military post at Ching Te (旌 德). He was very proud and overbearing in his manner, lording it over his fellows. He thought it inconsistent with his dignity to serve in small appointments.

He wrote over thirty pamphlets earnestly discussing the affairs of State, an exposition of Lao Tzu's doctrines, and several lengthy commentaries on Buddhist works.

When Wang An Shih was Grand Councillor-in-Chief, he mostly employed young men as his colleagues. Fang also wished to hold office under his father, and is reported to have made the following remark to him, viz. : " It is true that the son of a minister may not hold any administrative position, but he is entitled to an expository post." In order that the Emperor might get to hear of him and possibly give him some post, Wang An Shih adopted the device of printing Fang's political pamphlets and his commentary on the Tao Te Ching (道 德 經). These were put on sale and in this way his name and work were reported to the Emperor. Teng Chien and Tseng Pu also recommended him. So after an interview with the Emperor, he was given the post of Chamberlain to the heir-apparent and also appointed to the concurrent post of expositor of the Ts'ung Cheng Tien (崇 政 殿).

The Emperor often held private conversations with him, and he received a commission to write a commentary on the Odes and Book of History. He was later appointed to the T'ien Chang Ko (天 章 閣) as advisor and also as instructor in the royal family.

When his commentaries were completed he was offered a new post in the Lung T'u Ko (龍 圖 閣), which, however, he refused on account of ill-health.

The reforms of Wang An Shih were really undertaken at the instigation of Fang, for the latter was always praising Shang Yang (商 鞅) as a man of strong character. It is to him that the statement is attributed that "unless certain powerful opponents of the new laws were executed, it would be impossible to carry them out effectively". For on a certain occasion, when Wang An Shih and Ch'eng Hao were engaged in conversation, Fang swaggered in with hair all dishevelled and a woman's hat dangling in his hand. He rudely demanded the subject of their conversation. Wang An Shih replied : " Certain features of the new laws are meeting with the objection of the people, so we were just talking the matter over." In a loud voice Fang interposed the remark : " The heads of Fu Pi and Han Ch'i should be hung in the market-place, then and then only can your new laws be carried out." "Not so," replied his father uneasily, " you are quite mistaken, my son."

Fang died at the age of 33, and was given the posthumous title of " Tso Chien I Tai Fu " (左 諫 議 大 夫).

Chu Hsi (朱 熹),[1] in his discussions on Wang An Shih, says : " He presumed on his superiority over his contemporaries in literary skill and moral character, and assumed personal responsibility for the moral and political reform of the empire. After he had made the acquaintance of the emperor Shen Tsung, he was promoted minister of State.   At that time everyone thought that he would make some great contribution to the welfare of the country.   So great was their expectancy that they even began to think they might witness a revival of the splendour and prosperity of the Golden Age of Yao, Shun, Yü, T'ang, and Wen-Wu.

However, Wang An Shih devoted himself to financial and military matters, as being, in his opinion, of prime importance. He introduced and employed evil men in the government service, rejecting the assistance of the loyal and upright.   By the pursuance of a reckless and rigorous policy he caused the people clamorously to deplore the loss of all joy in life.

Later on a crowd of infamous men continued his tyrannical policy, the poisonous influence of which extended gradually to the furthest limits of the empire, until in the times of Ts'ung Ning and Hsuan Ho (1102–1126) confusion and grievous disaster resulted.

This represents the general opinion.

Shen Tsung was desirous of appointing a new minister of State and asked Han Ch'i as to whether he thought Wang An Shih was suitable for such a position.   Han Ch'i replied : " Wang An Shih has gifts and ability more than adequate for the post of literary Councillor, but I do not consider him the right man for a ministerial post."   Shen Tsung, however, ignored this advice and proceeded to appoint Wang An Shih minister of State, a step which was equally unfortunate, both for the Sung Dynasty and Wang An Shih himself.

---

[1] Chu Hsi has several sections on Wang An Shih in his works, which are quoted in the Chapter on Wang An Shih's reform policy.   See Chapter X.

Chapter V

THE SUNG HISTORIES

IF the character and work of Wang An Shih are to be justly estimated, it is essential that some inquiry should be made into the character of the records upon which the traditional opinion of him is based.

The account of Wang An Shih's life and work (as given in the preceding chapter) is taken from the Dynastic History of Sung. This was compiled at the end of the Mongol Dynasty, A.D. 1341, by T'o K'o T'o (托 克 托) or T'o T'o as he is sometimes called. The general opinion of the character of this History may be gleaned from the following quotations.

In the Index to the " Ssu K'u Ch'uan Shu " (四 庫 全 書 提 要) we read :—

" The main object of the compilers of the History of Sung was to expound the teachings of the various schools of ethico-philosophical thought. Other matters were given scanty attention. Consequently the errors and defects are innumerable." [1]

T'an Ts'ui (檀 萃), of the times of Ch'ien Lung, A.D. 1736-1796, writes :—

" The Sung Histories are extremely confused and of doubtful worth. They are full of unjust criticisms. For they bear the impress of the faction spirit of the period, which permeated the minds of the writers of the records from which the Mongols took their materials, to such an extent that the facts were deliberately warped and embellished, the faults of their own faction concealed, and guilt unjustly imputed to their opponents." [1]

Chao I (趙 翼), also of the time of Ch'ien Lung, in his work

---

[1] Liang Ch'i Ch'ao, p. 9.

entitled Hai Yü Ch'ung K'ao (陔 餘 叢 考), gives numerous
examples of the errors, omissions, mutual contradictions, and
deliberate misrepresentations with which the Sung Histories
abound, both in the general and biographical sections.[1]

In the Index to the Ssu K'u Ch'uan Shu reference is made
to attempts that were made to rectify the character of the Sung
Histories, so as to give posterity a more reliable account on
which to base their judgment.   One such attempt was made
by Ko Wei Ch'i (柯 維 騏) of the time of Chia Ching
(嘉 靖), A.D. 1522–1567, who styled his book the " Sung Shih
Hsin Pien " (宋 史 新 編) or New Edition of the Sung
Histories.   The other was from the pen of Shen Shih Po
(沈 世 泊), who styled his work the " Sung Shih Chiu Cheng
Pien " (宋 史 就 正 編) or " Corrected History of Sung ".[1]

Liang Ch'i Ch'ao and Ts'ai Shang Hsiang, who gave much
time and thought to the subject of Wang An Shih's life and
work, concur in the opinion that the Sung Histories are woefully
unreliable as a guide to his real character and achievements.
They point out that although the Mongol compilers of the
History had no prejudices against Wang An Shih, they took
no pains to ascertain the real facts, and merely adopted as the
basis for their record the traditional material which was ready
to hand.

The nature of this material will be discussed below.   First
we will translate a section from Ts'ai Shang Hsiang's preface
to his Life of Wang An Shih, as follows [2] :—

" Wang An Shih has been dead for seven hundred years.
Those who first sought to vilify his memory based their
detractions upon private sources of information.   Once private
sources of information had been adopted for the compilation
of the Canonical History, many extraneous matters naturally
crept in, so that it has become practically impossible for any
later investigator to correct the record completely."

---

[1] Liang Ch'i Ch'ao, p. 10.
[2] Ts'ai Shang Hsiang. Introduction to his " Investigation into the Biography
of Wang Ching Kung " (王 荊 公 年 譜 考 略 序). The latter is in
Works, vol. xviii, p. 8.

He then quotes from a very interesting letter, written by Wang An Shih to an official resident at Shao Chow (韶 州), styled Chang Tien Ch'eng (張 殿 丞), as follows :—

" From the time of the Three Dynasties, each state kept its own historical records. The historiographers of those days were mostly drawn from the same families generation after generation. There were frequent instances of such men sacrificing their lives in the course of their duty, preferring to suffer in this way than to act in any manner which conflicted with the high ideals of such an office. That accounts for the trustworthy character of their records.

" Later on, however, the various state historiographers ceased to function (as the Empire had been united), and none but those of the highest positions and greatest influence, no matter how valorous, noble, or useful their lives may have been, if they had not received recognition by the Court, found a place in the national histories.

" What is still more deplorable is that the historiographers of recent times have all been drawn from official families. Now such men as these, in the public discussion of affairs at Court (when every one has the opportunity to express his own point of view, and agree or disagree with what is said), dare to term the loyal as treacherous, and deliberately misrepresent facts, without fear of punishment or shame, being concerned merely to glut their own individual preferences and prejudices.

" If they act thus in the open forum, what can be expected of them when they take up their pens and indite in secret their judgments of historical personages ? They can set out the facts in such a way, and so embellish them, as to leave the reader in doubt as to whether a really praiseworthy man is entitled to fame or not, or even whether he ought not to be vilified. Those who are already dead have no means of redress, and those who remain alive have no means of arriving at the real truth of what is so cleverly narrated. So that the writers are able to prosecute their nefarious task without fear of consequences. In such circumstances can it be expected that they will not practise deceit ? "

This letter was written in reply to a note of appreciation of the work of Wang An Shih's father, during his term of office at Shao Chow. Chang Tien Ch'eng was living there at the time he wrote this message of appreciation, and expressed his regret that such distinguished work as his father had done there should not be put on record. Wang An Shih, in thanking the writer for his message, asserts that he is quite satisfied to have such an appreciation from an unbiassed critic, and that to him it is a matter of no significance whatever whether his father finds a place in the Histories or not.

These considerations led him to expatiate on the character of historians in general, and of those of his day in particular.

Ts'ai Shang Hsiang says that the main idea of this letter of Wang An Shih is truly prophetic of the treatment which later historians were to mete out to him, and continues :—

" It was the ancient practice for the historical records of one dynasty to be compiled by the historiographers of their successors, who in so doing of necessity depended for their materials upon such sources as were available. The Mongols compiled the history of the Sung Dynasty, but availed themselves solely of private sources of information in so doing. During the reign of Shen Tsung, when the reforms of Wang An Shih were first mooted, the Court simply 'buzzed' with discussion. But discussion centred in the New Laws, and so there was a definite and ascertainable reason for the differences of opinion which emerged.

" When, however, we come to the times of Yuan Yu (元 祐), i.e. the first half of Che Tsung's reign, not only did the officials then in control completely abrogate the whole of the new Measures, but a calamitous spirit of faction and feud spread everywhere. And what was particularly deplorable was that when Fan Tsu Yü (范 祖 禹) and Lü Ta Fang (呂 大 防) were drawing up the first record of Shen Tsung's reign, there also appeared the work of Shao Pei Wen (邵 伯 溫) entitled the 'Wen Chien Lu' (聞 見 錄); the works of Ssu Ma Kuang entitled the 'Wen Kung So Yü' (温 公 瑣 語); and the ' Su Shui Chi Wen ' (涑 水 紀 聞), together with the Tung Hsien Pi Lu ' (東 軒 筆 錄) of Wei Tao Fu (魏 道 輔). All these works were of a private character, drawn up with the idea of satisfying the private enmities and pre-dilections of the writers (and yet their opinions got incorporated in the Histories).

"These works were followed by the Vermilion History (朱 墨 史) of Fan Ch'ung (范 沖) and the ' Ch'ang Pien ' of Li Jen Fu (李 仁 甫 長 編), both of which were of the type deplored by Wang An Shih (in his letter above) as being such as the dead could not appeal against, and of which the living could not ascertain the real facts. Such works, as we have seen, were a serious cause of concern to Wang An Shih. How strange then that these writers should make all the distress of the country revert to Wang An Shih alone, even asserting that the loss of the northern part of the empire in the Sung times was due to him. Surely that is an exaggerated view of the case.

"From the time the Sung Dynasty migrated to the south up to the initiation of the Mongol Dynasty, a period of some two hundred years, there arose a succession of reckless critics and calumniators, too numerous to mention. From the Mongol to the mid-Ming times there were such as Chow Te Kung (周 德 恭), who affirmed that Shen Tsung personified the infamous rulers of all history, and such as Yang Yung Hsiu (楊 用 修), who asserted that Wang An Shih was a com-bination of the notoriously wicked ministers of all time.

"But prior to these was published the work reputed to be by Su Shih (蘇 軾), entitled the ' Wen Kuo Hsing Chuang ' (溫 國 行 狀), comprising more than 9,400 words, at least half of which is taken up with adverse criticism of Wang An Shih. But this work ostensibly was an account of the life and career of Ssu Ma Kuang, so that it is impossible to believe that such an unreasonable work is from the pen of a man like Su Shih.

"Later on in the Ming times there were writers like T'ang Ying Te (唐 應 德), who published his ' Shih Tsuan Tso

64 WANG AN SHIH

Pien' (史 纂 左 編), in which is included a biography of Wang An Shih comprising 26,500 words. Yet in all this there is not a single good thing recorded of him. Can such productions be discussed in the category of historical writings?"

It is easy to see from the above account by Ts'ai Shang Hsiang that he considers the traditional opinion of Wang An Shih, which is embodied in the Dynastic History of Sung as compiled by the Mongols, to be based on a great deal of evidence emanating from the political enemies of Wang An Shih, and that it may therefore be discounted as being both partial and prejudiced. That his opinion is not baseless will appear from the following account of the compilation of the history of the reign of Shen Tsung.

First it is of importance to note that three attempts were made to compile the history of Shen Tsungs regime, and that each of these was directly related to Wang' An Shih's political policy.

Shen Tsung died in 1085. He was succeeded by his son Che Tsung, who was then only 10 years old. Consequently his grandmother Hsuan Jen, who had been opposed to Wang An Shih's policy, was appointed Regent. She recalled Ssu Ma Kuang, Wang An Shih's greatest political antagonist, to Court, and in the short space of a few months the New Measures were all abrogated. It was at this period, viz. the first year of Che Tsung's reign (1086), that the first official attempt was made to record the history of Shen Tsung's reign.

The work of compilation was entrusted to Fan Tsu Yü (范 祖 禹), Huang T'ing Chien (黃 庭 堅), Lu Tien (陸 佃), and others. It is evident that Lu Tien was not of one mind with his colleagues as to the character of this record. This appears from an account of a discussion which is reported to have taken place between him and Huang T'ing Chien on the subject, during which the latter is reported to have said, " According to your view of the matter we ought to produce ' Flattery' History " (佞 史). To this Lu Tien retorted, " And if we have sole regard to your point of view, the resultant

will be (謗 書) a 'Blasphemous' record." Ts'ai Shang
Hsiang affirms that the compilers of this record drew their
materials in the main from the " Su Shui Chi Wen " (涼 水
紀 聞) of Ssu Ma Kuang.[1] As he was the main opponent of
Wang An Shih's policy, it was inevitable that he should have
recorded views of Wang An Shih and his work which were
of a very unfavourable character. From the character of the
administration which Ssu Ma Kuang initiated, and which was
in full swing when this history was in process of compilation,
it is reasonable to surmise that Lu Tien's opinion of the record
was fairly correct.

The date of this first compilation is given as the 2nd month
of 1086.[2]

When Che Tsung became independent in 1094, the political
pendulum swung to the other extreme, and members of the
Reform party were restored to power. One of the first things
they did was to call for a revised history of Shen Tsung's reign.
Several memorials were submitted by the various government
departments, complaining that the previous record was
extremely faulty and pernicious, the whole object of it being
to throw the blame on Wang An Shih for everything that was
considered injurious in the previous reign. The Emperor
thereupon ordered an investigation to be made into the sources
of the previous record, and according to Chang Ch'un (章 惇),
An T'ao (安 燾), and others, it was discovered that much of
the material found in it was founded on mere rumour and
hearsay, and that even where written sources had been used,
they were not reliable.[3]

So in the 4th month of 1094 Ts'ai Pien (蔡 卞), the son-
in-law of Wang An Shih, was appointed Editor-in-chief of the
Imperial History Redaction,[3] and in the 10th month of the
same year announced the completion of the work. It seems
to be admitted by the authorities that Ts'ai Pien adopted the

---

[1] Ts'ai Shang Hsiang, vol. xxv, " Jih Lu," p. 2.
[2] Ts'ai Shang Hsiang, vol. xxv, " Jih Lu " (日 錄), p. 1.
[3] " T'ung Chien " under " Shao Sheng ", 1st year, 4th month. Also Liang
Ch'i Ch'ao, pp. 10 and 11.

diary of Wang An Shih as the main source for the compilation of the new work. He took the old record, and after comparing the accounts therein recorded with the statements found in Wang An Shih's diary, made numerous corrections and deletions with a vermilion pen, and so this particular history is known as the " Chu Mei Pen " (朱 墨 本) or " Vermilion Ink Record ".[1] By way of distinguishing it from the first record the latter has been styled the " Mei Pen " or " Black Ink Record ".

As the first attempt was based on Ssu Ma Kuang's diary and was therefore inevitably prejudiced against Wang An Shih, it is only fair to assume that as the second was based on the diary of Wang An Shih it was equally prejudiced in his favour. It should, however, be pointed out that Ts'ai Shang Hsiang and Liang Ch'i Ch'ao, while hesitating to affirm that the " Vermilion Ink Record " was absolutely just to the facts, think it was justifiable as an attempt to correct the extremely antagonistic character of the previous work.[2] The fault for initiating this type of writing lies with the producers of the " Black Ink Record ", who had thus broken with the ancient precedents of Chinese historiographers by allowing factious interests to colour the nature of their historical writings.[3]

It should also be observed that after the revised History had been presented to the throne and accepted as the canonical version of Shen Tsung's reign, the compilers of the first record were punished by degradation to distant outposts, Fan Tsu Yü, Chao Yen Jo (趙 彥 若), Huang T'ing Chien, Lü Ta Fang (呂 大 防), and even Lu Tien suffering in this way.[4]

During the reign of Che Tsung's successor, Hui Tsung (徽 宗), one Liu Cheng Fu (劉 正 夫) reopened the question by asserting that both the previous records suffered from the party prejudices of their compilers, and that a third edition should be prepared which would be strictly impartial,

---

[1] Ts'ai Shang Hsiang, vol. xxv, p. 3.
[2] Ts'ai Shang Hsiang, vol. xxv, p. 5.
[3] Ts'ai Shang Hsiang, vol. xxv, p. 2.
[4] " T'ung Chien " under Shao Sheng (紹 聖), 1st year, 12th month.

so that posterity might be furnished with a trustworthy account of the Shen Tsung–Wang An Shih regime.[1]

Hsü Chi (徐 勣) supported this plea with the remark that both the previous records were faulty in that they represented the prejudices of political partisans. He affirmed that Fan Tsu Yü and his colleagues had depended solely on the diary of Ssu Ma Kuang, and that Ts'ai Pien and Ts'ai Ching (brothers) had relied solely upon the diary of Wang An Shih. It was inevitable that the results in each case should be unsatisfactory, and so he urged the Emperor to order a third compilation which would be strictly neutral and fair.[1]

The mandate for this was forthwith issued by the Emperor,[2] but it was not carried out during Hui Tsung's reign. Meanwhile the Court was transferred to the south in 1126, and the matter considerably delayed. Eventually the third edition was compiled and issued in 1134 in the reign of Kao Tsung (高 宗). This is the work which would be taken by the Mongol compilers of the Sung History as their chief source of information, and it is therefore important that its character should be investigated.

First of all it should be noted that the chief editor was Fan Ch'ung (范 沖), the son of Fan Tsu Yü, who was the chief compiler of the " Black Ink Record ". As he was under the influence of the faction spirit and as in addition he was nursing feelings of vengeance on those who had done despite to his father's work and memory, he added still more slanderous statements about Wang An Shih than had been included in the " Black Ink Record " and eliminated from the " Vermilion Ink Record " numerous proofs of his good character and administration. It is recorded that he actually burnt Wang An Shih's diary and the " Vermilion Ink Record " as well, leaving no traces of either work.[3]

As the party of Wang An Shih, or rather those who had

[1] Ts'ai Shang Hsiang, vol. xxv, p. 6.
[2] According to Ts'ai Shang Hsiang this mandate was issued in the period " Chien Yen ", i.e. (建 炎) early, so it would be 1127-8. It was, however, not completed until 1134 as stated.
[3] Liang Ch'i Ch'ao, p. 12.

assumed his name and policy for reasons not altogether dis-
interested, had entirely ceased to count in political circles at
this time, there was no one to come forth and expose the revengeful character of this third record, and so later works on the
period were not only of similar complexion to this, but even
still more unfair to Wang An Shih's character and achievements.

Of such a character were the " Jih Lu Pien " (日 錄 辨) of
Yang Chung Li (楊 中 立) ; the " Ch'ang Pien " (長 編)
of Li Jen Fu (李 仁 甫) ; and worst of all the " Erh Ch'en
I Mei " (二 陳 遺 墨), the authors of which works were not
content to take the materials of the third Record (henceforth
styled the " Vermilion Ink History ") as their basis, but added
a considerable amount of extra material from many other private
works.[1] These works, in addition to those which have been
specially referred to above, all emanated from the pens of those
who were antagonistic to Wang An Shih and his policy.

One other matter of considerable importance remains to be
noted in this connection. At the end of Wang An Shih's
biography, as found in the Sung Histories, there is included a
paragraph summarizing the opinions of Chu Hsi on his character
and work.[2] This is possibly a precis of Chu Hsi's somewhat
numerous expressions of opinion on Wang An Shih which are
found in his " Complete Works ".[3] Doubtless T'o K'o T'o
would have these writings before him, as well as other works
from the Chu Hsi school,[4] when he compiled the Sung
Histories.

It is well known that the opinions of Chu Hsi were almost
sacrosanct for centuries, being regarded as the standard of
Confucian orthodoxy, generally speaking, right through to
the late years of the Manchu Dynasty. It is for this reason that
those writers who took up the cudgels in Wang An Shih's

---

[1] Ts'ai Shang Hsiang, vol. xxv, p. 2.
[2] See Translation in Chap. IV.
[3] " Chu Tzu Ch'uan Shu " (朱 子 全 書), vol. lix, pp. 17–29, etc.
[4] Such as for instance the " T'ung Chien Kang Mu " (通 鑑 綱 目),
which is one cf the main sources of historical information for this work, and " The
Lives of Famous Officials " (名 臣 言 行 錄).

behalf, and were led to write in a different strain from Chu Hsi, have been given little prominence, and accounts for the fact that the views of Chu Hsi, which in the main are antagonistic to Wang An Shih's policy, have remained the popular tradition.

Chu Hsi was a later disciple of the " Lo " school of ethico-political thought. The founder of this was Chow Lien Hsi (1017–1073). He was followed by the two Ch'engs, Ch'eng Hao (1032–1085) and Ch'eng I (1033–1107). The succession was maintained by Yang Chung Li, or Yang Kuei Shan (楊 龜 山) as he is also called (1053–1135). His writings were extremely opposed to Wang An Shih. He is the author of the " Jih Lu Pien " noted above, and the one who so strenuously argued that the downfall of the northern Sung Dynasty was due to him and his policy. Although Chu Hsi comes later in time (1130–1200), he is a direct descendant of this school,[1] and his views of Wang An Shih and his work bear the impress of his connection with it.

At the close of the northern Sung Dynasty (1126) and after the removal of the capital to the south, the descendants of those who had opposed Wang An Shih's policy remained in possession of the field. So that the views of those antagonistic to his regime persisted as the official tradition, and naturally enough were adopted by the Mongol compilers of the Sung Histories.

Liang Ch'i Ch'ao writes, " The reason for the erroneous impression of Wang An Shih and his policy which has persisted for so long is to be found in the prejudices and exaggerations of the descendants of the officials of the ' Yuan Yu ' regime (1086–1094). After the transfer of the Court to the south, the views of the ethico-political school (represented by the Ch'engs and Chu Hsi) predominated in the popular estimation. This led to the baseless opinions of this school becoming the permanent tradition ".[2]

This then reveals the real significance of the statement in the " Ssu K'u Ch'uan Shu T'i Yao " that " the chief concern of the Mongol editors of the Sung Histories was to record the

---

[1] See *Chu Hsi and His Masters*, Dr. J. P. Bruce, p. 58.
[2] Liang Ch'i Ch'ao, p. 13.

matters connected with ethics and philosophy, other things being given scanty attention ".

But the " scanty attention " they gave to " other things " has led to serious injustice being done to the memory of Wang An Shih, for it has contributed greatly to the general misunderstanding of the man and his work which has characterized the thinking of the scholarly class of China for over eight hundred years.

CHAPTER VI

THE TIMES OF WANG AN SHIH

THE Sung Dynasty (A.D. 960–1278) is famous for its cultural greatness. It represents a period in which literature, philosophy, and the fine arts, particularly painting and the production of porcelain, flourished. When, however, we come to consider such questions as national prestige, and military and economic stability, we find that the Dynasty is characterized by great weakness.

Historically we speak of the Northern Sung, represented by the first half of the Dynastic period (960–1126), and the Southern Sung (1127–1278). During the latter half of the first period the Northern Tartars gradually encroached upon the territory of the Sungs, culminating in 1126 in the great onslaught, which compelled the Sungs to evacuate their capital of K'ai Feng Fu and migrate to the south of the Yang Tzu river. Here, after a period of wandering on the part of the representatives of the Imperial line, the Sung rulers finally established a new capital at Hang Chow in 1139.

So it came about that the China of those days was divided into two great areas, the territory controlled by the Sungs being confined to the southern half of the country, while their enemies, the " Chin " or " Golden " Tartars, remained in possession of the northern half for the next hundred years, after which the Mongols gained the whole empire. (See Map No. 2.)

Wang An Shih was born in 1021 and died in 1086, so he belongs to the mid-period of the Northern Sung Dynasty. In order, however, to relate him properly to his times, it is necessary to review the history of the Sung Dynasty preceding his day, for it was during that period that the main problems arose with which he and his policy were concerned. The manner in which he tried to find a solution for these problems is the story of his own political career, which

71

is outlined in the first volume of this work. The policy which he inaugurated during his term of high office aroused such controversy, and influenced political life so greatly, that events for the next fifty years or so gyrated about him and his work. So that the subsequent history for that period at least must also be reviewed, if we are to judge the character of Wang An Shih's political achievements.

Briefly stated, the period may be said to be characterized by the aggression of the Tartars in the north : by the military weakness of the Sungs : by the impoverishment of the national finances and inequitable taxation of the people : by the pursuance of a *laissez-faire* policy in matters of government administration, and by considerable dissension and party strife in the world of officialdom.

Wang An Shih's policy aimed at increasing the military and economic resources of the empire, with a view to stemming the northern invasion, while at the same time seeking to relieve the economic distress of the poor. But his proposals were of so radical a character, and he pressed them with such determination, that he soon found himself deserted by the old guard of conventionally minded officials, and was perforce compelled to take matters very largely into his own hands. However, he possessed the complete confidence of the Emperor Shen Tsung, and so was able to make practical experiment of his military and economic theories, and to override the opposition of his political foes. That, however, was possible only as long as Shen Tsung remained upon the throne. After his death, with the advent of Hsuan Jen to the regency and the restoration of Ssu Ma Kuang to power, Wang An Shih witnessed the over-throw of all his policy. For the ensuing period of half a century controversy waxed fierce around his name and political measures.

At times his own adherents were in the ascendancy and at others his political foes became supreme. For one long period of thirty years, immediately preceding the downfall of the Northern Sung Dynasty, during which Ts'ai Ching (蔡 京) was the most prominent political figure, Wang An Shih's policy was used largely as a cloak to hide the selfish purposes of those in power. With the migration of the Sungs to the south in 1126–7, influential opinion became more or less stabilized against Wang An Shih and his political theories.

That in outline is the history of his policy. We must now give some account of the preceding history, and endeavour to account for the military weakness of the Sungs and the aggressive tactics of their northern foes.

This military weakness had its roots in the very beginning of the Dynasty. During the times of the Posterior Chow, the emperor Shih Tsung (世 宗), A.D. 954–960, and his successor Kung Ti (恭 帝) put up a brave resistance to the inroads of the invading Ch'itans (契 丹). The armies of Kung Ti were under the command of Chao K'uang Yin (趙 匡 胤), but his troops, while engaged against the enemy, mutinied at Ch'en Ch'iao (陳 橋) about six miles to the north of K'ai Feng Fu in 960.[1] In the course of this mutiny, so the histories relate, Chao K'uang Yin was compelled to assume the Imperial robes by his subordinates, and became the first ruler of the Sung Dynasty with the title of T'ai Tsu (太 祖).

As he took the oath of allegiance he is reported to have said, " You, my subordinates, have made me emperor out of your own desire for wealth and position. Is it likely that you will obey my commands ? "[2] This statement reveals the source of his constant apprehension that he might be deprived of his regal power in the same manner as he had dispossessed his predecessor Kung Ti, and accounts for one of the outstanding features of his policy. For some two centuries prior to his accession the authority of the throne had been constantly challenged by the rise to power of military leaders. T'ai Tsu endeavoured to prevent the recurrence of such trouble by steadily weakening the authority and power of his military associates, and centralizing control of all military matters in his own person.

But, as Liang Ch'i Ch'ao points out,[3] in concentrating on

---

[1] Outlines of Chinese History, by Li Ung Ping, p. 171.
[2] Liang Ch'i Ch'ao, p. 15.
[3] Liang Ch'i Ch'ao, p. 16.

this internal problem, he failed to do justice to the external menace. For although he succeeded in bringing into submission and allegiance a number of independent princes and rebellious generals in Honan, Ssu Ch'uan, An Hui, and Chiang Su, he failed to take sufficiently aggressive measures against the " Liao " (遼) or " Iron " Tartars in the Yu Chow (幽 州) region (where the modern Peiping is situated). The reason he neglected to do so was his fear that if the campaign were undertaken, it might lead to the secession of several of his more powerful generals. As a direct result of his failure to take energetic action in this direction, the " Iron " Tartars became very presumptuous and aggressive.

T'ai Tsu's successor, T'ai Tsung, succeeded in recovering a tract of territory in the north-west, comprising parts of modern Shansi, known as Pei-Han (北 漢). Further to the north-west the Hsi Hsia (西 夏), of Tangut descent, rebelled in 981. T'ai Tsung very unwisely sent a former leader of theirs, Li Chi P'eng (李 繼 捧), against the rebels. Naturally enough he soon joined forces with his old associates, and aided by an alliance with the Ch'itans, they gradually increased so greatly in numbers and prestige as to form in themselves a powerful foe of the Sung Dynasty.[1] T'ai Tsung, in no wise deterred by this new menace, gathered all his available forces, and led them against the Ch'itans in the Yu Chow area. In the end, however, the Imperial army suffered a complete defeat. They lost more than half of their number, T'ai Tsung himself was wounded, and was compelled to flee for his life to K'ai Feng Fu. As a result of this defeat the martial spirit of the Sungs weakened greatly. A second campaign ordered by the emperor resulted equally disastrously, as Korea and two districts in modern Hopei, viz. Cho (涿) and I (易), were surrendered to the Tartars.[2]

During the reign of Chen Tsung (眞 宗), 997–1022, some preliminary successes were registered by the Sungs against the foe, but later they were repeatedly and ignominiously

[1] Liang Ch'i Ch'ao, p. 17.
[2] Outlines of Chinese History, p. 177.

defeated. In 1004, the enemy captured the modern Ho Chien (河 間) in south Hopei province, and reached T'an Chow (檀 州) near the Yellow River, about forty miles north-east of K'ai Feng Fu. It was then suggested that the capital should be transferred south of the Yang Tzu river, or to distant Ssu Ch'uan. One K'ou Lai Kung (寇 萊 公), however, stiffened the emperor's resolution to oppose this, and they remained in the old capital. But a very humiliating treaty of peace with the Liaos was made, whereby the Sungs were obliged to pay to their enemies an annual sum of one hundred thousand ounces of silver and two hundred thousand rolls of silk.[1]

After the accession of Jen Tsung (1022–1063) further trouble arose with the Hsi Hsia in the north-west. Their chieftain, named Yuan Hao (元 昊), assumed the title of emperor of Hsia, and defeated the Sungs in two great battles at San Ch'uan and Yang Mu Lung. The Liaos took advantage of these reverses to make further encroachments, and captured ten cities with little or no resistance. They exacted also one hundred thousand ounces of silver and one hundred thousand rolls of silk by way of extra tribute, and what was still more humiliating the Hsi Hsia then demanded a subsidy of similar amount.[2]

In 1066 the victorious Ch'itans adopted the dynastic title of Liao (遼), and their ruler, Yeh-lu-hung-chi (耶 律 洪 基), made himself the eighth emperor of the dynasty by raising his ancestors of seven generations to imperial rank.

So that in 1067, when Shen Tsung assumed the reins of government and Wang An Shih was appointed to high office, the Sungs were practically acknowledging the suzerainty of the Liaos in the north and the Tanguts in the north-west. The burden and disgrace of this past policy of weakness and disaster lay heavily upon the hearts of all loyal officers. The military weakness and economic distress attendant upon these reverses, and the huge annual exactions of their enemies, had become problems vital to the permanence and welfare of the whole nation.

[1] Outlines of Chinese History, p. 178.
[2] Outlines of Chinese History, p. 180.

That was the first factor in the situation with which Wang An Shih had to deal.

A second factor, contributing to the military weakness of the nation at this time, is to be found in the existing method of recruiting, distributing, and treatment of the regular army.

The practice of employing paid forces and organizing them into a standing army dates from the T'ang Dynasty, and was continued by the Sungs.[1] But in the times of the latter dynasty the troops for the most part consisted of the riffraff of the countryside, supplemented in times of famine or flood by the unfortunate victims of these natural calamities. All troops for garrison duty on the borders were commissioned from the capital, where the great majority of the forces were stationed. This was part of the scheme initiated by the first Sung emperor to ensure as far as possible that military authority centred in the capital.

There were also operative regulations for the periodical transfer of forces from one post to another, or from the capital to the borders and vice versa. The officers, who received their commissions directly from the emperor, were frequently changed. The effect of this policy was to make of the army an incohesive force, although it was intended to prevent officers and men from becoming so familiar with each other as to plan for rebellion, or the declaration of independence.

While the idea behind this policy was good, and receives its meed of praise from Chinese historians, it resulted in a weakening of the military power of the empire, as it prevented the rise of a real spirit of *esprit de corps* in the army.

There was also a lamentable lack of discipline among the regulars. Several hundred thousand of the troops were congregated in the capital and precincts, in receipt of regular pay, but allowed to laze about, rarely if ever engaging in military drill or manœuvres, or gaining any instruction in the proper use of their weapons.

Further, the impression gradually gained ground that the

---

[1] Liang Ch'i Ch'ao, pp. 18 and 19.

soldiers were a class by themselves, different from ordinary citizens, and unfitted either for peace or war. The generality of the people began to look upon soldiering as a disgrace, and regarded the troops with something approaching contempt. This, too, tended to deprive the troops of a real martial spirit.

This state of things made of the troops a poor and ineffective fighting force, rendering them quite incapable of coping with their more warlike and aggressive neighbours of the north and north-west. It represented also one of the important matters calling for the earnest attention of any enterprising and loyal servant of the Empire.

In the first volume of this work the attempts made by the emperor Shen Tsung and Wang An Shih to deal with the aggression of the enemy and the problems arising from the weakness of the regular army are fully outlined, and need not be recounted here.

It will be readily perceived, however, that the economical situation in the country was adversely affected by all that has been related above.

The number of troops on the pay-roll of the country was in itself a constant drain on the exchequer. At the opening of the Sung Dynasty the number enrolled in the regular army was about 200,000, and as other expenses were low in proportion, there was usually a balance in hand each year. But by the year 976 the number had increased to 378,000. In 995 this had advanced again to 666,000, while in 1017 during the reign of Chen Tsung the number was 912,000. In 1041, with Jen Tsung on the throne, no less than 1,259,000 were enrolled, a number which was generally maintained through the reign of Ying Tsung (英 宗) and up to the beginning of Shen Tsung's rule.[1]

Such increases in the numbers of troops in receipt of pay, combined with the heavy expenditure on the frequent transfers from post to post, contributed greatly to a serious depletion of resources in the National Treasury.

The number of officials was also ever on the increase, and

Liang Ch'i Ch'ao, p. 20.

the salary list mounted in proportion. The great State
Ceremony was held once in three years, at which it was the
custom to make special gifts to the officials. The average
amount expended on these was approximately five million
" strings ". But in the year 1004 it had increased to seven
million. There were also special occasions of ceremony or
sacrifice at which similar gifts were conferred. The " Tung
Feng " (東 封) [1] ceremony involved an expenditure of eight
million, the " Ssu Fen " (祀 汾) [2] and " Pao Ts'e " (上 賓
册) [3] a sum of 1,200,000 " strings ". Then at the royal
ancestral sacrifice the outlay was gradually increased until it
reached the colossal total of 12,000,000 " strings ".[4]

Before the time of K'ai Pao (開 寶) in 968 there were no

---

[1] This relates to the royal sacrifice at T'ai Shan (泰 山), situated to the
east of K'ai Feng Fu, hence called " Eastern Ordinance ". This sacrifice was
also known as " Feng Ch'an " (封 禪), the former character of which means
" a mound of earth on the mountain " at which the worship of Heaven was
conducted, and the latter character " a levelling of the ground on some lower
peak ", at which the worship of Earth took place. This sacrifice usually took
place at the invitation of the local people, in honour of the Emperor's virtue and
good reign. At this, as on other occasions of great ceremony, the officials and
people received some special favours from the ruler.

[2] The " Ssu Fen " was a sacrificial ceremony taking place in the modern
Shansi, in the neighbourhood of Fenchowfu. The modern city is located on the
north bank of the Fen river, and is usually called Feng Yang (汾 陽). As
this sacrificial ceremony is related to have taken place at Fen Yin (汾 陰), the
location must have been on the south of the Fen river, possibly just opposite
the modern city. It would appear as though the ceremony here had particular
relationship to the God of Earth, styled Huang Ti Ch'i (皇 帝 祇). The
writer has noticed all through the district stones in the fields bearing the inscription
" Hou T'u Chih Wei " (后 土 之 位), which shows how prevalent the
worship of the God of Earth was in that neighbourhood.

[3] The adding of honorific titles to the Emperor's name usually took place at
the request of important officials, and was regarded as an occasion of mutual
congratulation and conferring of gifts. This is what is meant by " shang pao
ts'e " (上 賓 册).

[4] The " ming t'ang " (明 堂) was the great Royal Hall of Ceremonies.
Here not only did the great Royal family sacrifices take place, but also the
Imperial sacrifices to Shang Ti (上 帝). Here, too, were held audiences with
visiting princes, and gifts conferred to old servants of the dynasty, as well as to
those of special merit.

figures of a reliable character from which one might gauge
the state of the national budget. But in the year 995 the annual
income was 22,245,000 " strings " and a balance in hand was
reported at the end of the year. Between 1017 and 1022, the
annual income had leaped to 150,850,100 " strings " and the
total expenditure was 126,775,200. From 1056 onwards there
was a recurring annual deficit of about twenty million " strings ".
In 1065, during the reign of Ying Tsung, and just preceding
the advent of Wang An Shih to power, the income was
116,138,400 while the expenditure was 131,864,300.[1]

Such was the state of the government finances. The economic
condition of the people generally was no better. The officials
on the whole seem to have been lacking in initiative and took no
steps towards the improving of the people's livelihood. Taxes
were not light. Much waste ground was allowed to lie fallow
which might have been reclaimed. The farmers were compelled
to contract loans at unthinkable rates of interest. During the
reign of T'ai Tsung (太 宗) an edict was issued prohibiting
the charging of over 100 per cent on loans.[2]   Forty and fifty
per cent was thought nothing unusual.   The land was worked
so incessantly by the poorer farmers that it gradually deteriorated,
and failed to give even a normal yield.   " The fields of the rich
were beautiful and flourishing, inasmuch as they did not im-
poverish their lands by continuous tillage, and were able to
make improvements. But the poor farmer overcrowded his
fields and exhausted the natural productivity of the soil, thereby
reducing his ability to support his family." [3]

During the reign of Jen Tsung a new plan of assessing the
land tax was adopted by dividing the land into squares of fixed
area, with the idea of making taxation more equitable.[4]

The general conditions obtaining about this period may be
gauged from the following documents, one by Wang Ch'uan
Shan (王 船 山) being a quotation from his essay, " A Dis-

[1] Liang Ch'i Ch'ao, pp. 20 and 21.
[2] Economic History of China, by Mabel Ping-Hua Lee, Ph.D., p. 74.
[3] Economic History of China, by Mabel Ping-Hua Lee, Ph.D., pp. 78 and 79.
[4] Economic History of China, by Mabel Ping-Hua Lee, Ph.D., p. 279.

cussion of the Sung Dynasty," and the other a memorial presented by Wang An Shih on the topic of " A Century of Peace ".

Wang Ch'uan Shan writes [1] :—

" The emperor Jen Tsung reigned for forty-one years, and by pursuing a policy of *laissez-faire* managed to keep the country free from war. But this peace was purchased at such a cost that insurmountable difficulties were imposed upon his successors. Each year he paid 500,000 ' strings ' to the Ch'itans, asking with shamed face that they would regard it as the gift of one friendly nation to another. . . . He also paid heavy tribute to the Hsi Hsia to keep them from making incursions into Chinese territory. But the emperor showed no particular concern about these matters.

" While these crafty and powerful foes were awaiting their opportunity on the north and north-west, the officials of the empire no more thought of opposing them than they did of opposing Heaven and Earth, while those at Court waxed eloquent over trifling matters of ceremony. It was this that weakened the dynasty.

" How extremely fortunate it was that there were no fierce beasts of prey like Ye-Lu-Te-Kuang of Liao and Li Chi Ch'ien (李繼遷) of Hsia roaming abroad at this hour, and so the Sung rulers were able to avoid disaster temporarily by means of bribery. But if they had not adopted this particular method of keeping the peace, it would only have been necessary for a Liao general like Liu Liu Fu (劉六符) to give a shout, and the soul of Sung would have perished from fright.

" Jen Tsung might have done better if he had possessed the help of a really capable minister. There were of course some men of outstanding ability like Fan Chung Yen, who were cognisant of the real character of the situation, and were anxious enough to redeem it. He was however not the equal of Wang An Shih. Others, like Fu Pi, Han Ch'i, Wen Yen Po, and Ou Yang Hsiu have become justly famous for their character,

---

[1] Sung Lun Chuan Liu (宋論卷六), quoted Liang Ch'i Ch'ao, p. 21.

learning, and literary ability. But they could do little more than patch up Court quarrels and rectify certain of the emperor's personal defects. They failed absolutely to get at the root of the trouble, and so made no adequate response to the exigencies of a really desperate situation.

"Apart from these outstanding men, the majority of the Court functionaries were just a batch of honest old worthies, pretending that all was well within the empire, and acting as though trouble or calamity was impossible. The expression of Chia I (賈 誼) is apposite, viz., 'They were like a man who having put a lighted torch under a bundle of firewood, then goes to sleep on the top, who, as long as the fire does not reach him, keeps on saying, "All's well."' [1]

"Wang An Shih's memorial [2] was submitted to Shen Tsung in the year 1068. It consists of twelve hundred words, more than half of which are taken up, in true diplomatic fashion, with a rehearsal of the virtues of the preceding emperors of Sung, and with a particular and detailed account of the virtues of Jen Tsung, of whose regime Wang An Shih had personal knowledge. He singled out for special mention the emperor's reverence for Heaven and his consideration for men. He refers to his aversion to war; his determination to save a man from suffering the extreme penalty of the law if at all possible; his endeavour to reward all men justly for their deeds; his readiness to listen to the advice of his ministers; his rigid censorship of all officials aiming at the elimination of tyrannical practices; and his concern that the people should increase both in numbers and happiness."

Then, however, he interposes a very big " but " and indicates the features of Jen Tsung's reign which call for criticism and reform, as follows :—

"For many generations now our dynasty has suffered too much from the pursuance of a policy of *laissez-faire*, and from a lack of attention to the ancient methods of government.

---

[1] Liang Ch'i Ch'ao, p. 22.
[2] Prose Works, vol. x, pp. 5–7.

When attention has been given to such matters it has led to a consideration of methods of a decidedly inferior character. There has been a dearth of advice on the part of officials and others as to the best methods of reforming such a state of affairs. Jen Tsung associated chiefly with eunuchs and women within the palace, and whenever he emerged to consider public business, there were brought before his notice only such matters of trifling significance as subordinate officers might suggest. Never did the emperor discuss with his great scholars and officials the old royal road of empire, after the manner of the ancient kings. Everything has just been allowed to take its course without any effort being made to direct or control affairs. So that for a long time facts and appearances have remained undistinguished.

"I am not asserting that no honour has been paid to good men, but I do say that unfortunately mean men have been allowed to enter in. Neither do I wish to convey the impression that occasionally the right policy has not been adopted, but again unfortunately, it is true that wrong and pernicious counsel has been allowed to prevail.

"As examples I would suggest that it is quite wrong to select government officials on the basis of their skill in rhyming-couplets, or on memory or recitation tests of the Classical literature, instead of establishing schools for the proper training of officials. It is wrong also to promote men in the government services merely because of the length of time they have been in that service, or the positions they have previously occupied, instead of adopting an efficient method of inspection. Military officers have been selected on quite haphazard methods, and they have been changed so frequently that any proper estimation of their work has been rendered impossible.

"I would refer also to the fact that a multitude of aspirants for office has arisen, who by attaching themselves to this or that great man of affairs, have contrived to the boycotting or banishment of any person of independent mind and with a programme of his own. This policy has led to fearful slackness on the part of superiors and subordinates alike, so that they have become content with the mere appearance of activity. Should perchance a man of real ability get appointed, he was constrained to act mostly just like a servant or menial.

" The people have become thoroughly unhappy and resentful at the incessant toil which is imposed upon them by the officials, and they see no hope of deliverance. No officials have been appointed to look into the questions of land and water, which are so vital to the people's livelihood. Soldiers are kept in the army until they are old or decrepit, neither are they given proper training. No efficiently trained officers have been appointed to lead them, nor are they allowed a sufficient period in any one post to enable them to get a proper grip of their task. The regular army consists of a crowd of riffraff, and is concentrated at the capital, so that in this respect there has been no improvement on the policy of indifference and slackness which characterized the five dynasties.

" Members of the royal family have been given positions regardless of their ability or training, and no attempt has been made to conform to the older regulations in such matters.

" And as for the economic problem, no scheme at all has been devised to cope with it. Although the emperor has called for economy in the way of living all round, the people are still poor. What then avails it that concern is displayed or restraint exercised ? The nation still remains weak.

" Fortunately the northern barbarians have not been at their strongest during these years, and no great calamity like the great flood of Yao's time or the famine of the time of T'ang has occurred. The fact that we have experienced a century of tranquillity is due rather to the favour of Heaven than to the credit of men."

From these and other sources we gather that Jen Tsung must have been of a very easy-going disposition, and on the whole indifferent to the real condition of the empire. We gather further that his predecessor Chen Tsung must have been very extravagant and incapable. It would appear, too, that in the main the big officials were either too concerned for their own ease and affluence or too much beset by circumstantial difficulties to be able to make any seriously constructive contribution towards the remedying of the existing weakness and poverty. But evidently Shen Tsung was of stronger character than his predecessors, and Wang An Shih of different calibre from previous ministers, so they set themselves resolutely to the task of fundamental reconstruction and reform.

Wang An Shih is commonly criticized for devoting himself primarily to financial and military measures. But the state of things being as outlined above, how could he do otherwise? The policy of economy which others had urged [1] was of course logical and necessary. But Wang An Shih went the further step of attempting to increase the productive capacity of the country. His measures were devised with that in view, or the strengthening of the military resources of the nation. Disregarding for the moment the question as to how far he succeeded or failed, one must admit that his objectives were directly related to the need of the times.

It has been urged that with a monarch so intelligent and purposeful as Shen Tsung on the throne, and with a minister of such calibre and character as Wang An Shih at his right hand, that their joint efforts should have resulted in a permanent peace and enhanced prosperity. That a certain measure of success did attend their efforts in these directions any fair critic of his life and work will probably concede. That greater success was not achieved is due to the difficulties of the time on the one hand and to the comparatively short period in which he was in office on the other.

It is with one of the greatest difficulties, characteristic of the age, that we are now to deal, viz. the rise of the faction spirit.

There are hints of the existence of this spirit in both the documents quoted above. Wang Ch'uan Shan refers to the officials at Court waxing eloquent over trifling matters of ceremony, and to the patching up of Court quarrels. Wang An Shih mentions the multitude of aspirants for office who attached themselves to this or that great person, and the boycotting of

---

[1] e.g. Ssu Ma Kuang.

any official who showed an independent spirit and unusual turn of mind.

Liang Ch'i Ch'ao [1] goes into the matter at some length, showing not only that the faction spirit existed before the times of Wang An Shih, but also indicating the main reasons for its rise, viz. (1) that literary ability was prized too much and military prowess despised ; (2) that power was concentrated in an excessive degree at the capital . . . financial and military power being in the hands of two or three high ministers of State ; (3) that the selection of men for these posts was limited to the personnel of two or three Bureaus or Censorates, also located at the capital. The result was that all who wished for official position gravitated there, for this was the only avenue to power and fame. Naturally enough this excited a good deal of rivalry in scholarly and official circles. As a matter of fact, if we wish to describe in a sentence the history of the Sung times, it may be termed, " A history of struggle for political power."

The mean and selfish struggled for personal aggrandizement, and worthier men for the achievement of their ideals. It was inevitable that personal feelings should run strong in such conditions, and that there should be a good deal of mutual slander and recrimination which tended to the forming of factions.

The rise of these factions may be traced in part also to the apathy of the majority of the Sung emperors, who with a few exceptions devoted themselves to a life of ease and pleasure, and were prone to entrust the affairs of State to any official who would flatter them. This feature is particularly prominent in the cases of Che Tsung and Hui Tsung, but a certain readiness to listen to the advice of this or that favourite statesman characterizes them all. When the individual statesman in favour happened to be a thoroughly good and able man, affairs of State were moderately well conducted, but when the power fell into the hands of unscrupulous charlatans, who played for

---

[1] Liang Ch'i Ch'ao, pp. 25–39.

their own hand most of the time, the government was thrown into the utmost confusion.

Liang Ch'i Ch'ao traces the growth of the faction spirit of Wang An Shih's day to the quarrels of Fan Chung Yen (范 仲 淹) and Lü I Chien (呂 夷 簡) in the times of Jen Tsung and Ying Tsung. Strife waxed particularly fierce over the question of the succession after the death of Jen Tsung, who died without heir. Fan Chung Yen having been dismissed from Court for the stand he took on this question, the great officials began to take sides with one or other of the two leaders, each terming the other a " faction ". Later Lü I Chien was dismissed and Fan Chung Yen recalled and installed as Chief Minister. This incident led the poet Shih Chieh (石 介) to write :—

" The promotion of any worthy man,
　　Is like plucking up a weed. (Many roots come up with it.)
　　While the dismissal of a traitor,
　　Is like the skinning of a chicken's foot. (The whole skin
　　　comes off.) "

After Fan had been restored to office, he began to eliminate a number of plausible men and supernumeraries. This, coupled with the fact that Fan was in too great a hurry to reform matters, caused a good deal of displeasure and hostile criticism. Later, again, he began to oppose the practice of sons falling into their father's official shoes, and to increase the severity of the tests for office. The plausible and evil-minded naturally found these moves to their detriment. So they began to slander and vilify Fan, and much criticism of his " faction-forming tactics " began to penetrate to the emperor's ears. The result of all this opposition was that men like Tu Yen (杜 衍), Han Ch'i (韓 琦), and Fu Pi (富 弼) were all dismissed together with Fan Chung Yen. The leader of the opposition, Wang Kung Ch'en (王 拱 辰), thereupon boastfully remarked, " I have bagged them all in one net."

The verdict of history as far as the traditional opinion is concerned, is in favour of Lü I Chien and against Fan Chung Yen. Liang Ch'i Ch'ao is of contrary opinion, but acknowledges that associated with Lü I Chien were many who later showed themselves to be quite capable and upright men. He considers that the explanation for their siding with a man like Lü I Chien is to be found, not so much in the justice of his cause, as in the fact that the times were characterized by a spirit of partisanship based on personal considerations.

This spirit was greatly intensified by a discussion which ensued when Ying Tsung, the nephew of Jen Tsung, succeeded his uncle in 1063. His father An I (安 懿 王) was already dead, and discussion centred on the point as to whether he should be designated " Uncle " of the emperor, thus maintaining unbroken the old Imperial line, or whether he should be designated " Father " of the emperor, thus creating a new line. Wang Kuei (王 珪) and Fan Chung Yen took the former view, while men of note, like Ou Yang Hsiu and Fu Pi, took the other. Eventually a compromise was reached by styling him " ch'in " (親) or " close relative ", leaving the question at issue unsolved. But so intense was the spirit of both sides on this " nice " point, that the chief Censor, Lü Hui, demanded the execution of Han Ch'i and Ou Yang Hsiu.

Although the leaders of both sides are deemed by posterity to be worthy and honourable men, nevertheless during the " squabble " no epithet was mean enough or no slander vile enough to serve the factious purposes of one or the other.

We see, therefore, that when Wang An Shih came forward with his proposals for political reform, the atmosphere was already well charged with the faction spirit. The period of his greatest influence is characterized by still further intensification of it. For during that time Fu Pi, Han Ch'i, Ssu Ma Kuang, even Ou Yang Hsiu and Wen Yen Po, and innumerable others either resigned or were degraded and transferred on account of their opposition to his policy. A good deal of the opposition was doubtless sincere, and actuated by considerations of policy only. But it is also true that much of it was born of personal and factious considerations.

Ssu Ma Kuang eventually took the lead of the Conservative party against Wang An Shih and the Radicals. But during the reign of Shen Tsung the Radicals remained in supreme power, their opponents either living in retirement for the time or serving in provincial and comparatively insignificant positions.

But a complete change of scene occurred on the death of Shen Tsung, when his mother Hsuan Jen assumed the regency during the minority of Che Tsung, then only ten years old. She recalled Ssu Ma Kuang to supreme power in 1086, and in the short space of a single year the whole of Wang An Shih's policy was overthrown. After the death of Ssu Ma Kuang, men of his party, like Lü Ta Fang (呂 大 防) and Fan Ch'un Jen, carried on the government. This party became known as the "Yuan Yu Tang" (元 祐 黨) because they functioned under the auspices of Hsuan Jen, the designation of whose regency consisted of the two characters Yuan Yu (元 祐).

The scene changed again on the death of the regent empress in 1094, when Che Tsung himself assumed the reins of government, for he immediately dismissed the members of the "Yuan Yu" party, and reinstated Tseng Pu (曾 布), Chang Ch'un (章 惇), and others of Wang An Shih's following, who attempted to restore the whole of their leader's measures.

An interlude of uncertainty was created in the period 1099–1101, owing to certain differences arising in the ranks of Wang An Shih's party, but in 1101, with Hui Tsung on the throne, the pendulum once more swung definitely in his favour. That, however, took place under the leadership of Ts'ai Ching (蔡 京), during whose period of influence political principles were ruled out, the whole reign being characterized by unscrupulous personalities and party considerations. The members of the Yuan Yu party were ruthlessly proscribed and persecuted. The attitude of the emperor to political matters was determined solely by superstitious fancies. But Ts'ai Ching, although he suffered from the vicissitudes of political fortune, remained for a long period the most influential man of his time. Ultimately, however, he became responsible for the greatest obloquy that has become attached to Wang An Shih's name. Being utterly selfish and unscrupulous, he made the revival of a semblance of Wang An Shih's policy [1] a mere pretext for the furthering of his own interests.

The details of this period of factious strife are described in another portion of this work, and need not be repeated here. It is, however, necessary to point out that the Conservatives, hitherto led by Ssu Ma Kuang, split up into three separate factions, known respectively as the Lo Yang school, the Ssu Ch'uan school, and the Northern school. The first had Ch'eng I as leader, the second was dominated by Su Shih, and the third by Liu Chih. This split only further intensified the faction spirit of the later Sung times, and in the end led to still further defamation of Wang An Shih and his followers.

So pungent did the criticism become that the downfall of Northern Sung was laid at the door of Wang An Shih. But that question is fully discussed in the chapter on his Reform policy.[2]

What has been said above is sufficient to show that this spirit of faction and feud played a large part in the fortunes of the Sung Dynasty as a whole and of Wang An Shih and his policy in particular. It has also determined to a considerable extent the verdict of history hitherto upon his character and work.

For it should be observed that the Northern Dynasty closed with the spirit of opposition to Wang An Shih in the ascendant : that those who had advocated his policy either sincerely or insincerely were then in utter disfavour or banishment, and that the tendency has been for the opinions then current to persist until comparatively recent times.

[1] Cf. Article on Political Parties of the Northern Sung Dynasty, by Dr. J. C. Ferguson, *Journal of N. China Branch of R.A.S.*, vol. lviii.

[2] Dr. Ferguson gives the following causes for the downfall of the Sung Dynasty and its migration to the south, viz. :—

(1) Fierce assaults along the whole northern frontier by militant tribes and the urgent necessity of supporting large armies for the defence of empire.

(2) Conscription of a large proportion of the young men of the country to serve in the army.

(3) Large increase in the taxes directly levied upon the people.

(4) Extravagance of the Emperors, culminating in the person of the last Emperor, Hui Tsung.

(5) The prevalence of superstitious beliefs.

(6) The lack of a sufficient number of trained men.

CHAPTER VII

THE GOVERNMENT SYSTEM OF THE SUNG DYNASTY IN THE TIME OF WANG AN SHIH

THE main organs of government administration during the Sung Dynasty, excluding the Grand Council which is discussed below, were divided into four. Three of these, viz., the Chung Shu Sheng (中 書 省), the Shang Shu Sheng (尙 書 省), and the Men Hsia Sheng (門 下 省), were responsible for civil affairs. The fourth, styled the Shu Mi Yuan (樞 密 院), was the chief military executive. The Civil Administration as a whole was termed the " San Sheng " (三 省).

The Chung Shu Sheng was the chief legislative organ of the government, being responsible for the making and changing of laws and for the censoring and promulgation of Imperial mandates. The following is a list of the principal officials of this organ, viz. :—

1. Chung Shu Ling (中 書 令), vacant in Sung times.
2. Shih Lang (侍 郎), acting head of this organ, and also acting head of the Shang Shu Sheng, occupying the place of the Yu P'u She (右 僕 射) in the latter department.
3. Yu San Ch'i Ch'ang Shih (右 散 騎 常 侍).
4. She Jen (舍 人), of whom there were four, who acted as censors of edicts from the throne.
5. Yu Chien I Tai Fu (右 諫 議 大 夫), vice-censor of the Emperor.
6. Ch'i Chü She Jen (起 居 舍 人), recorders to the throne.
7. Yu Ssu Chien (右 司 諫).
8. Yu Cheng Yen (右 正 言).

The Shang Shu Sheng was the chief executive organ of the government, divided into departments or ministries, such as Revenue and Finance, Rites and Ceremonies, Civil appointments, Works, Justice, etc.

The principal officials of this Assembly were as follows :—

1.   Shang Shu Ling (尙書令), vacant in Sung times.
2.   Tso P'u She (左僕射), who acted as head of the Men Hsia Sheng (see below).
3.   Yu P'u She (右僕射), acting head of this organ, and also of the Chung Shu Sheng, as above.
4.   Tso Ch'eng (左丞).
5.   Yu Ch'eng (右丞).
6.   Tso Ssu (左司).
7.   Yu Ssu (右司).
8.   Lang Chung (郎中).
9.   Yuan Wai Lang (員外郎).

The Men Hsia Sheng seems to have been the Government Record Office, with particular responsibility for supervising all affairs connected with the Imperial Household. In addition to preserving all government documents, and exercising supervision over numerous smaller bureaus at the capital, this particular organ was responsible for all Court functions, sacrifices, equipages, jewels, etc.

The chief officials were as follows :—

1.   Shih Chung (侍中), vacant in the times of the Sung Dynasty.
2.   Shih Lang (侍郎), acting Head of this Department, and concurrently acting as Tso P'u She of the Shang Shu Sheng (see above).
3.   Tso San Ch'i Ch'ang Shih (左散騎常侍).
4.   Kei Shih Chung (給侍中), of whom there were four.
5.   Tso Chien I Tai Fu, Censor of the Emperor (左諫議大夫).
6.   Ch'i Chü Lang (起居郎).
7.   Tso Ssu Chien (左司諫).
8.   Yu Cheng Yen (右正言).

It has been noted in the previous chapter that the emperors of the Sung Dynasty were scrupulously careful to avoid the possibility of too much power being gained by military leaders. The arrangements made for the civil administration were also

originally devised with that in view. No one person was to
be appointed actual head of any of these three organs of government, and even the acting heads were not to be allowed to hold
that office solely. The latter arrangement might seem at first
sight to tend to increase rather than decrease a minister's
influence. But as he must hold position in at least two
assemblies at the same time, this would bring his actions under
the censorship of two organs, and it was thought that this
would tend to prevent his attaining to sole power in any one
of them. However, as we know, the system failed of its objective
in the case of Wang An Shih and others. (See below.) One
man was acting head of the Chung Shu Sheng and the Shang
Shu Sheng at the same time, and another, who was acting
head of the Men Hsia Sheng, also held important office in the
Shang Shu Sheng. These two men were also members of the
Grand or State Council, which for convenience we will style
the " Nei Ko " (內 閣). Men who held these positions, in
addition to being styled Chung Shu Shih Lang (中 書 侍 郎),
Men Hsia Shih Lang (門 下 侍 郎), were also given the title
of Grand Councillor (同 平 章 事). So we find that Wang
An Shih, on his promotion to the Grand Council, was styled
" T'ung P'ing Chang Shih " (同 平 章 事), which is still
further defined by Chan Ta Ho as " T'ung Chung Shu Men
Hsia P'ing Chang Shih " (同 中 書 門 下 平 章 事),
which would seem to have made him head of all three civil
assemblies. However, in the " T'ung Chien " it is stated that
Han Chiang (韓 絳) was also given similar appointment at
the same time, so they must have divided the responsibility
between them.

We must now inquire into the composition and status of
the Grand Council. This was composed of Grand Councillors,
styled " T'ung P'ing Chang Shih " (同 平 章 事) as above,
and also of a number of vice-Grand Councillors, termed " Ts'an
Chih Cheng Shih " (參 知 政 事), who also held concurrent
appointments in one or other of the government organs noted
above. For instance, when Wang An Shih was appointed
vice-Grand Councillor he was also given the position of " Yu

Chien I Tai Fu " (右 諫 議 大 夫) in the Chung Shu Sheng. In addition, the head of the Shu Mi Yuan, or chief military organ, who was styled " Shu Mi Yuan Shih " (樞 密 院 使), had the standing of a vice-Grand Councillor, and was admitted equally with them to the meetings of the Grand Council.

The membership of the Grand Council varied, as far as numbers were concerned, at different times. The following list, covering most of Shen Tsung's reign, will indicate this in a general way, viz. :—

1069. Wang An Shih, Fu Pi, Tseng Kung Liang, Ch'en Sheng Chih, and T'ang Chieh.

1070. Wang An Shih, Tseng Kung Liang, Ch'en Sheng Chih, Han Chiang, and Feng Ching.

1071. Wang An Shih, Han Chiang, Feng Ching, Wu Ts'ung, and Wang Kuei.

1072. Wang An Shih in sole power as Grand Councillor, with Feng, Wu, Wang, Ts'ai T'ing, and Ch'en Sheng Chih.

1073. Wang An Shih in sole power as Grand Councillor, with Feng, Wu, Wang, Ts'ai T'ing, and Ch'en Sheng Chih.

1074. Wang An Shih until 2nd month, when Han Chiang took his place, helped by Lü Hui Ching.

1075. Wang An Shih returned in 10th month. Han Chiang as colleague until the 8th month. Wu Ts'ung, Wang Kuei, Yuan Chiang, and Tseng Hsiao K'uan.

1076. Wang An Shih in sole power until the 10th month, when he resigned and Wang Kuei and Wu Ts'ung were appointed in his place, helped by Feng Ching.

1077. Wang Kuei and Wu Ts'ung, with Feng Ching and Yuan Chiang as vice-Grand Councillors.

1078. As for 1077, with the addition of Sun Ku, Lü Kung Chu, and Hsueh Hsiang.

1079. As for 1078, with the exception that Ts'ai Ch'ueh displaces Yuan Chiang.

1080. As for 1079, with the addition of Chang Ch'un.

1081. Wang Kuei alone as Grand Councillor, with Sun Ku,

Lü Kung Chu, Hsueh Hsiang, Ts'ai Ch'ueh, Han Chen, and Chang Tsao, as vice-Grand Councillors.

1082. Wang Kuei and Ts'ai Ch'ueh, and vice-Grand Councillors as for 1081, with Chang Ch'un, P'u Tsung Meng, and Wang An Li in addition.

1083. Wang Kuei and Ts'ai Ch'ueh as Grand Councillors, with vice-Grand Councillors as for 1082, with the exception that An Shou and Li Ch'ing Ch'en took the places of Sun Ku and P'u Tsung Meng.

1084. Wang Kuei and Ts'ai Ch'ueh, with vice-Grand Councillors as above, Wang An Li resigning in the 7th month.

1085. Wang Kuei, Ts'ai Ch'ueh, and Han Chen as Grand Councillors, with others as for 1084. Ssu Ma Kuang was recalled in the 5th month.

1086. Ssu Ma Kuang, Han Chen, Lü Kung Chu, Wen Yen Po, Ts'ai Ch'ueh.

It will be seen from the above that although the system in vogue during the earlier half of the Sung Dynasty was devised with the object of preventing too much power getting into the hands of one man, we know that in the reign of Shen Tsung, owing to the special conditions which obtained then, that one man was in sole power as Grand Councillor for quite a considerable period, either Wang An Shih himself, or Han Chiang, and later Wang Kuei. This indicates the keenness of Shen Tsung to press the reform policy of Wang An Shih, and also shows that in so doing it was necessary to centralize authority to the maximum degree.

The Grand Council was, of course, the highest and most influential of all government bodies, and acted, with the Emperor, as Chief Executive of the Government. In the cases mentioned above, where only one man was left in the Council, he was Chief and Sole Minister of State, and as such practically all-powerful.

There were, however, other recognized organs of government, which while possessing neither legislative nor executive power, were nevertheless very influential. Such as for instance the Censorate. There were evidently three types, at least, of

Censors. There was first the Imperial Censorate, consisting of at most two men, viz., the Tso Chien I Tai Fu (左 諫 議 大 夫) of the Chief Executive Assembly and the Yu Chien I Tai Fu (右 諫 議 大 夫) of the Chief Legislative Assembly. These were also styled " Chien Kuan " (諫 官). Then there was the Censorate of Mandates and government orders, records, etc., composed of the " She Jen " (舍 人), and possibly other officials of the three chief organs of government. In addition to these there was the public Censorate, called the " Yü Shih T'ai " (御 史 臺), which had the right to impeach all officials.

Apart from this highly organized system of Censors, it was also possible for recognized officials to present memorials to the throne, in which not only could affairs be discussed, but also the conduct of affairs by this or that individual could be criticized.

So that it was open to every person of importance to express himself freely on any matter of public import, and for the Emperor if he so desired to be kept informed of the real state of the country and the character of the administration.

Civil officials received their appointments from a department of the Shang Shu Sheng, called the Li Pu (吏 部) or Appointments Board. Such matters as the inspection of an official's record and recommendation for promotion or otherwise were supervised by a sub-department of this Board, known as the Shen Kuan Yuan (審 官 院). Normally military appointments were made by the Shu Mi Yuan (樞 密 院) or " Board of War ", but in Wang An Shih's term of high office these came also under the control of the Shen Kuan Yuan, which was divided into two sections for the purpose, one controlling civil and the other military appointments.

Appointments to the government service depended on examination and recommendation, the higher ranks of the service being recruited from those who had either passed the higher examination for admission to the hierarchy (館 職) or who by virtue of special ability were recommended by highly placed officials for such special privilege.

There were numerous bureaus established at the capital, apart from those which have been mentioned above, mostly of a literary character, styled "Kuan" (館), "Yuan" (院), "Tien" (殿), "Ko" (閣), and the like, into which those who had attained to the ranks of the hierarchy were admitted, and occupied themselves with literary and expository work until they were selected for still more responsible positions in the actual administration of affairs.

One of the most important of these was styled the Mi Ko (祕 閣) or the Mi Shu Sheng (祕 書 省), which was divided into three departments, called respectively :—

1.　Chi Hsien Yuan (集 賢 院).
2.　Shih Kuan (史 館).
3.　Chao Wen Kuan (昭 文 館).

The first may be styled the Classical Library, in which apart from the writings of an exclusively classical character, those dealing with ethics and philosophy were stored, copied, or expounded.

The second was the Historical Library in which all works of a historical character were kept.

The third had charge of all other literature, the works of famous authors, biographies, etc.

The supervision of these Libraries or Literary Bureaus was undertaken by the Grand Councillors, the first in order of rank taking charge of the Chao Wen Kuan, the second in order of rank supervising the Shih Kuan, and the third, if there was such, taking over the Chi Hsien Yuan. When there were only two Grand Councillors, the first in order of rank had charge of the Chao Wen Kuan and the Shih Kuan, and the second charge of the Chi Hsien Yuan.

Other Bureaus were more definitely in the nature of Secretariats, like the Han Lin Yuan (翰 林 院) and the Chih Chih Kao (知 制 誥), which together were known as the Liang Chih (兩 制). The former was sometimes termed the "Nei Chih" (內 制) or "Internal Secretariat", while the latter was called the "Wai Chih" (外 制) or "External Secretariat".

The first of these was concerned with the drawing up of all documents connected directly with the Court and the higher ranks of officials at the capital. They drew up all the orders of the Emperor, Empress, and princes, together with pardons, treaties, correspondence with foreign rulers, etc. They were consulted as a group on important matters of State, and expository duties were often required to be undertaken by individual members.

The " External Secretariat " was concerned with documents of a public character, like the composition of edicts, orders to the provincial officials, and local authorities. Correspondence relating to official appointments and transfers passed through their hands.

The country was divided for administration purposes into Circuits, or " Lu " (路), of which there were twenty-five in Wang An Shih's time. The chief circuit officials were the Chieh Tu Shih (節 度 使), who was superintendent of military affairs, the Chuan Yün Shih (轉 運 使), or Transport Officer, who had charge of financial affairs, revenue, taxation, transport of grain and other goods connected with revenue and the like, and the T'i Tien Hsing Yü (提 點 刑 獄) or Chief Justice, who was directly responsible for the supervision of all litigation and punishments.

Under these again were the various prefectural, sub-prefectural and district officials, both of a civil and military character.

CHAPTER VIII

THE CHARACTER OF WANG AN SHIH

IT is only natural that varying opinions should have been expressed concerning the character of a man around whose person and work the political storms of sixty years gyrated. The policy which Wang An Shih inaugurated became ostensibly the chief *casus belli* between the political factions which arose during the forty years succeeding his death, and was responsible, in name at least, for the rise and fall of the most famous statesmen of that period. Political partisanship tends to create personal prejudices, particularly against prominent protagonists of an opposing policy. Bearing these considerations in mind, we are not surprised to find that the traditional opinions of Wang An Shih's character are so widely divergent. By one authority [1] (*sic !*) he is described as a "towsel-headed and unsavoury rascal" and by another as "a famous man of his day, who regarded wealth and worldly honours as a fleeting cloud, untainted by avarice and lust".[2] Thanks to the painstaking labours of Ts'ai Shang Hsiang, who has closely investigated the subject, material is available to enable us to express some sort of judgment on these opposed points of view, and to help us to formulate a more correct opinion of the character of this remarkable man.

The Dynastic History of Sung, biased against him as it is, credits Wang An Shih with diligent devotion to his studies in his youth.[3] The fact that he gained his "chin shih" degree at the early age of 21 is sufficient evidence that his time was well spent in the pursuit of learning in those days. His poem

---

[1] In the "Pien Chien Lun" (辨 姦 論), said to be by Sü Hsun. But see next chapter.

[2] By Huang Lu Chih (黃 魯 直), a contemporary, famous poet and calligraphist.

[3] See Chapter IV, Life of Wang An Shih, according to the Histories.

98

entitled " Reminiscences " reveals his possession of a high moral ideal in youth, for he then set himself to imitate the example of the most famous ministers of history.[1] During the period of his residence at the capital, when he was sitting for his " chin shih " degree, he found himself strongly attracted by the virtuous example of his friend Li T'ung Shu, and acknowledges that he received fresh stimulus from him to live a worthy life.[2]

He gained the respect of the famous Han Wei Kung during his first term of office at Yang Chow. Even the Wen Chien Lu, another of those works which are strongly prejudiced against him, credits Wang An Shih with a reputation for hard study while he was there.[3] His love of home and natural longing for the renewal of family associations is shown in the poem quoted above. His own determination to succeed is shown by his deploring the lack of progress and failure to fulfil the promise of youth in the case of his acquaintance Fang Chung Yung, during his first visit home in 1044.[4] The friends of his younger days he admits were very few. But those which he had were men of the highest character, such as Tseng Tzu Ku, Sun Cheng Chih, and Wang Feng Yuan. Others with whom he conducted regular correspondence included such men as Sun Shen Lao, Wang Shen Fu, Liu Yuan Fu, Han Ch'ih Kuo, Ch'ang Ì Fu, Ts'ui Po I, Ting Yuan Chen, and Hsi Shen Fu, all of whom were of most estimable repute.

In a letter written to Sun Sheng Chih he affirms his loyalty to principle, and admiration of those who devote themselves strenuously and assiduously to mental and moral self-cultivation.[5] And writing to Wang Feng Yuan he expresses his determination to emulate the example of his friend, who had elected to suffer poverty and hardship rather than sacrifice his principles or compromise his conscience.[6]

[1] See Vol. I, p. 12.
[2] See Vol. I, p. 9.
[3] See Vol. I, p. 16.
[4] See Vol. I, p. 15.
[5] Works, vol. xvii, p. 29.
[6] Works, vol. xviii, p. 19, end of letter No. 1.

No wonder then that in 1044 Tseng Tzu Ku ventured to recommend him to Ou Yang Hsiu as a sincere and self-respecting young man, of such rare character and ability that the State could not afford to lose his services. A little later Ch'en Hsiang also recommended him for appointment, lauding his reputation for high character and learning, and speaking most highly of his literary and administrative ability.[1] In 1051 Wen Yen Po in recommending Wang An Shih termed him "modest and retiring, and unwilling to push himself forward".[1] This was after he had served for several years at Chin Hsien, where he had gained a fine reputation for devotion to duty and ability to deal with problems besetting the economic life of the people. The Dynastic History credits him with having earned the gratification of the people there.

His refusal to take the "kuan chih" examination about this time seems to have been based solely on the needs of his family, which reflects creditably upon his filial disposition.[2]

In 1055 Wang An Shih first made the personal acquaintance of Ou Yang Hsiu, who for some time had been very desirous of meeting with him. The following year he recommended him to the throne, along with Lü Kung Chu and two others, testifying to the ability and high character of his nominee, emphasizing in particular his unswerving loyalty to principle. As just prior to this Wang An Shih had persistently refused to accept special favours from the Emperor in regard to the "kuan chih" examination, and had also declined an offer of admission to the official hierarchy by Imperial privilege, and as the idea was getting abroad that he had ulterior motives in so doing, Ou Yang Hsiu particularly refers to the fact that he had conscientious reasons for refusing to avail himself of these exemptions.[1]

In a letter written to his friend Li Tzu Shen about this time he expresses his desire to make " right " his universal standard of action.[3]

[1] Liang Ch'i Ch'ao, p. 46.
[2] See Vol. I, p. 25.
[3] See Works, vol. xviii, p. 7.

Ou Yang Hsiu continued to exert his influence on Wang An Shih's behalf for several years after this. Throughout the next ten years, in appointments at the capital, at Ch'ang Chow, and Chiang Tung, his reputation remained unsullied. In 1058 he submitted his famous Memorial of a Myriad Characters, which shows not only that he possessed a keen sense of responsibility for the state of the country, but that he had the courage to criticize the conventional attitude of the great officials of the day.[1]

His duties in the Ministry of Finance, and as librarian of the Chi Hsien Yuan, were all fulfilled with credit. The History notes that everybody at the capital was pleased when he notified his acceptance of the latter appointment in 1061.[2] Promotion followed rapidly during the next two years. During this period his moral courage showed itself in the " fighting quail " case, and his fight for the rights of the Censorate.[3]

In 1063 he resigned all his offices to keep the prescribed period of mourning for his mother, who had died in the 8th month, and he remained at home throughout the four years of Ying Tsung's reign 1064–7.

So far Wang An Shih had been growing steadily in the public estimation. He was now a man of forty-six, and had given little or no ground for adverse criticism of his personal character. The fact that when Shen Tsung ascended the throne he appointed Wang An Shih as governor of Chiang Ning in 1067, and soon after called him to the capital to take up the post of Literary Councillor, and that the latter appointment was made after Han Wei, Lü Kung Chu,[4] and Tseng Kung Liang had recommended him in the highest terms to the Emperor, is sufficient evidence that up to this point in his career he had maintained his reputation unimpaired.

It is only after his appointment to high office at the capital that criticism becomes rife. In the main, however, the criticism of contemporaries was confined to his policy. The exceptions

[1] See Vol. I, Chap. VII.
[2] See Vol. I, p. 93.
[3] See Vol. I, p. 95.
[4] It is doubtful whether Lü Kung Chu ever recommended Wang An Shih.

are attacks on his character by Lü Hui, T'ang Chung, and a reputed but unsubstantiated calumny by Su Hsün. These attacks, because they form notable exceptions to the general attitude of his contemporaries, and because they were taken as the basis for slanderous statements later on, must be discussed in some detail.

Soon after Wang An Shih's promotion to vice-Grand Councillor the Chief Censor, Lü Hui, in the 6th month of 1069, impeached him on ten counts,[1] introducing his indictment by a general attack on his personal character.

In this Lü Hui terms him a plausible hypocrite and dangerous plotter of the type of Shao Cheng Mao (少 正 卯),[2] whom Confucius executed, and Lu Ch'i (盧 杞)[3] of the times of T'ang Te Tsung. He affirmed that these two notorieties were men whose real character was not easily discerned, and so it was not strange that Wang An Shih had not yet appeared in his true colours. While he seemed to be without guile, he was in reality deceitful and proud, insolent and overbearing, and a very dangerous enemy of the State.

In support of his main thesis Lü Hui outlined his charges in detail, affirming that he was prepared to testify to their truth with his life. The charges are given below, with a precis of Liang Ch'i Ch'ao's comments [4] on each, viz. :—

1.   " Wang An Shih proudly refused to make apology for a wrong decision in connection with the case of the fighting quail,[5] although called upon to do so.

---

[1] " T'ung Chien," Hsi Ning, 2nd year, 6th month.

[2] Shao Cheng Mao was an infamous official of the State of Lu, who was executed by Confucius during his term of office as Minister of Crime. It is reported that Confucius said of him : " He has five evil characteristics, each of which is worse than robbery. He has a vicious mind, his will is set on doing evil, he is a clever liar, versed in wickedness, and a rank hypocrite." (Quoted from the Chia Yü 家 語.)

[3] Lu Ch'i was a minister of the times of T'ang Te Tsung. He was a very eloquent man, of simple appearance, but treacherous in disposition. He was very autocratic and self-opinionated. He inaugurated a system of taxation, based on the number of rooms and the area of land possessed. He created general turbulence at Court and rebellion on the borders. (From the Tz'u Yuan.)

[4] Liang Ch'i Ch'ao, pp. 253–5.

[5] See Vol. I, p. 95.

" He made various pretexts for refusing to accept the calls of the Emperor Ying Tsung to take office under him, but promptly accepted your (i.e. Shen Tsung's) call to the governorship of Chiang Ning Fu, just because it happened to suit his personal convenience. This attitude towards Ying Tsung shows his insolence."

Comment.—It is difficult to say whether Wang An Shih's judgment of this case was right or wrong. Anyway he erred on the side of mercy. His refusal to apologize is an indication of his sincerity, and not of his pride, for he felt he was in the right, and therefore had nothing for which he could apologize.

It is true that he did not serve in any official capacity under Ying Tsung, refusing on three separate occasions to do so.[1] He did, however, appeal for some minor post near his home.[1] There is no doubt that he was suffering from ill-health and embarrassed by family difficulties during Ying Tsung's reign. There is no other evidence of his despising Ying Tsung, although it is quite feasible to suggest that he did not think there was much chance to push his political ideas under him. When Shen Tsung came to the throne, not only had Wang's home circumstances improved, but he felt the new Emperor more likely to give favourable opportunity to him for the expression of and experiment with his political theories.

2. " Wang An Shih refused to take small appointments, but avidly accepted the governorship of Chiang Ning Fu and a place on the Literary Council (Han Lin Yuan). In these matters he was ruled by considerations of personal advantage only, paying no regard to moral principles."

Comment.—But he occupied minor posts under Jen Tsung, so it cannot fairly be said that he showed unwillingness to do so. What personal advantage there was in his so doing would seem to be related to his home circumstances, his attitude being entirely based on consideration for them. The fact that he accepted higher posts and Court appointment under Shen Tsung was because home circumstances allowed of it for one

[1] Works, vol. ix, p. 18, especially No. 2.

thing, and because he felt Shen Tsung was a kindred spirit
for another.

3. " Wang An Shih, in his capacity as teacher to the
Emperor, appealed that he might sit in the Imperial presence,
thus not only demonstrating his ignorance of correct distinctions, but also his tendency to self-glorification."

Comment.—It was the custom in the Han and T'ang dynasties
for ministers to sit in the Imperial presence. At the beginning
of the Sung Dynasty, one Fan Chih (范 質), feeling himself to
be under suspicion because of his connection with the preceding dynasty of the Posterior Chow, refused to sit, and that
changed the ancient custom, ministers of later time always
standing at Court audiences. Wang An Shih sought to revive
the more ancient custom, urging that the practice of ministers
sitting together with the Emperor, demonstrated that the
functions of both were of equal importance as regards the
conduct of State affairs. In this he was supported by many
influential scholars of the time. Ch'eng I (程 頤) in 1086
appealed that he might sit in the Imperial presence in his
capacity as tutor to the Emperor.

4. " Since Wang An Shih has assumed office as vice-
Grand Councillor he has repeatedly remained behind after
Imperial audiences for private conversation with the Emperor.
He has taken advantage of such opportunities to bring pressure
to bear upon the Emperor to affix his seal to certain documents,
thus preventing action of an opposing character from his
associates. If such matters turned out well he would take credit
to himself, if ill, he would lay the blame upon the Emperor."

Comment.—One might appositely inquire as to what amount
of credit he got for anything. And as to blame reverting to
Shen Tsung, the indications are all of a contrary character.
Later on it became the practice of critics to endeavour to shield
Shen Tsung at the expense of Wang An Shih.

5. " In making decisions on important cases-at-law like
that of the Teng Chow Fu assault incident,[1] he was actuated

---

[1] See Chap. IV, p. 36.

by purely personal motives. He thus made a travesty of public justice."

Comment.—The judgment as delivered by Wang An Shih in this case was first suggested by Hsü Shun (許 遵), the official of the district. In the case itself there were no persons intimately connected with Wang An Shih, so it is difficult to see what purely personal reason he could have had for adjudicating the case as he did.

6. "Wang An Shih pressed the claims of his brother An Kuo for official appointment, and exacted vengeance of the examiner who failed to give him high place at the examination. During the six months since he came into high office, he had presumed on his influence to an altogether unwarranted degree. None dared to oppose his will, but those who sought his favour rushed to his door in crowds. His tendency to form private factions was already a great menace to public life."

Comment.—One might set against this the very obvious reticence on the part of Wang to push the claims of his relatives. Wang An Kuo was recommended by such men as Han Chiang, Wu Hsiao Tsung (吳 孝 宗), and Shao Kang (邵 亢), which showed that he had sufficient ability for whatever posts were conferred upon him. His biographical sketch in the Dynastic History [1] indicates that he failed at his first attempt to gain the Doctor's degree, but that later he was recommended for it, not however by Wang An Shih.

7. "Wang An Shih has made appointments entirely on his own authority, transferring court officers who were not of his own party to outside positions. For these he professed to have the Emperor's authority, but actually issued the orders in his own name. He has thus exceeded the bounds of his legitimate authority, and broken long-established precedent. By his arrogance and assumption in this matter he has transgressed the principles of good government."

Comment.—According to the Historical records many matters of importance were being held up in the Civil Office for days, so Wang An Shih in his desire for efficiency and

[1] See Chap. XV.

punctuality, was compelled to take strong action. But he had the authority of the Emperor for so doing.

8. " Wang An Shih is overbearing in his relations with his associates, and brooks no opposition. He was so furious with T'ang Chieh (唐 介) for his opposition that a disgraceful scene was enacted in the Imperial presence. Later on T'ang Chieh succumbed to his chagrin, dying of a carbuncle which broke out on his back as a result of this incident. Wang An Shih had no consideration for anybody but himself and for no other opinion than his own."

Comment.—T'ang Chieh was an obdurate opponent of Wang An Shih, and was over sixty when he died. His death was probably due entirely to natural causes, although it is quite possible that his chagrin at not getting his way hastened his end.

9. " When the proposal was made that your Majesty's brother Ch'i Wang (岐 王) should be removed from the Court, Wang An Shih opposed you when you demanded that the man who suggested this infamous proposal, Chang Pi Kuang (張 弼 光), should be punished. He has thus lent his support to a policy of separating the members of the royal family."

Comment.—The Histories of the time frequently refer to the trouble caused by the presence of the Emperor's brothers at Court. This particular brother, Ch'i Wang, had frequently asked to be granted the fiefship of a principality. In the final edict on the subject issued in the first year of Che Tsung, the following occurs :—" The former Emperor (Shen Tsung) allowed his brothers to remain at Court out of grace, and not because it was considered to be the right thing." The Emperor's mother was also opposed to their residence at Court. Wang An Shih supported Chang Pi Kuang because he thought the latter was actuated by the best of motives in making his proposal.

10. " Wang An Shih has gradually seized contol of all finances of the State and in collaboration with his partisans in the Board of War, is scheming to get all military and financial

authority into his own hands. He has appointed three of his own faction to high office, and commissioned eight of them to travel through the country on the pretext of devising measures of financial economy, but really with a view to throwing the whole country into turmoil. The injurious character of his policy is already apparent, and so far no one can see any advantage accruing from it."

Comment.—It is quite clear that centralization of financial control was essential to the success of Wang An Shih's policy. The partisans referred to included such men as Ch'eng Hao (程 顥), Liu I (劉 彝), Hsieh Ch'ing Ts'ai (謝 卿 材), and Hou Shu Hsien (侯 叔 獻), all of whom were men of the highest character.

The above are the ten points of Lü Hui's indictment. He wound up with a warning to the Emperor not to be inveigled by Wang An Shih's persuasive eloquence into extending to him his intimacy and confidence. He affirmed that as evil-minded men got their way the loyal would gradually desert him, and disorder inevitably result. He asserted that he had discovered Wang An Shih to be possessed of no forethought, but to be solely interested in proposing changes and in doing things differently from others. He warned the Emperor that his rhetorical and literary powers were merely a cloak for his evil purpose.

The reason for Lü Hui's attack is found in his own Biographical Sketch in the Dynastic History, where it is clearly stated that he submitted this indictment because of Wang An Shih's support of Chang Pi Kuang's appeal for the removal of Ch'i Wang from the Court, to which he himself was obstinately opposed. The narrative includes the following : " Lü Hui, vexed beyond measure at failing to secure Chang Pi Kuang's punishment, sent in a memorial of impeachment of Wang An Shih."

It should be noted that this indictment received no acknowledgment from the Emperor, and that Lü Hui was transferred to Teng Chow (鄧 州) as governor, in response to his own request that he be relieved of his office of Chief-Censor.

It will be remembered, too, that Wang An Shih threatened to resign on account of this indictment, but was persuaded to stay on. Later, when Wang An Shih became somewhat doubtful of the Emperor's attitude to him, the latter recalled to his mind the way in which he had refused to credit the charges made by Lū Hui, even though the latter had compared him to such villains as Shao Cheng Mao and Lu Ch'i.

The second notable attack on the character of Wang An Shih occurred in the 8th month of 1072,[1] when T'ang Chung, after he had submitted twenty memorials on current affairs, all of which had been ignored, attacked the reformer and his associates in the Imperial presence. His main points were that Wang An Shih had acted in an autocratic and arbitrary manner, that he despised his political opponents as worthless folk, and made conformity to his own ideas the criterion of personal worth. He wound up his attack by likening Wang An Shih to Lu Ch'i and Li Lin Fu (李 林 甫)[2] (the latter also being a notoriety of the T'ang Dynasty).

This attack, like that of Lü Hui, can be traced to personal chagrin. For T'ang Chung (唐 坰) had not received the promotion which he had expected from Wang An Shih, and in addition had suffered the ignominy of having twenty memorials ignored. So that both these attempts to defame Wang An Shih's character, the only ones of note that can be substantiated as having been made by actual contemporaries, were the outcome of personal spleen, and one looks in vain in the records of current events for any solid justification of their more serious charges.

Other attacks of a defamatory character, averred to be by Wang An Shih's contemporaries, have found a place in the Traditional Histories. Such as for instance what was said to be the opinion of Su Hsün, the father of Su Shih and Su Che, which is found in the Dynastic History of Sung, in the

---

[1] "T'ung Chien," Hsi Ning, 5th year, 8th month.
[2] Li Lin Fu, a member of the royal family of T'ang, very influential at Court during the reign of Hsuan Tsung (A.D. 713–755). Seemingly mild, he was a very specious and cunning man, who held strong views on political matters.

biographical notice of Wang An Shih. This reads as follows :—

" Wang An Shih was regarded as a man of worth by many of his contemporaries. Su Hsün, of Ssu Ch'uan, however, was an exception, terming him an unnatural fellow, of such a type as rarely failed to become notorious for villainy. He also wrote a pamphlet, entitled the ' Pien Chien Lun ' (辨 姦 論) or ' Recognition of Infamous Ministers ' which was intended to refer to Wang An Shih. In this he asserted that he was a Wang Yen (王 衍) and a Lu Ch'i (盧 杞) combined." [1]

The words which are supposed to refer to Wang An Shih in the pamphlet referred to read as follows [2] :—

" Here is a man who is for ever quoting the works of Confucius and Lao Tzu, who pretends to be treading in the footprints of Pai I (伯 夷) and Shu Ch'i (叔 齊), who is calling to his standard those scholars who are out for fame, but who so far have failed to get their way. These have conspired together to fabricate reports that this man is of such a calibre that Yen Yuan or Meng-Tzu are about to appear again in his person. But in reality he is a cunning and dangerous enemy of the state, of extraordinary ways, a Wang Yen [3] and a Lu Ch'i combined. The ruin he will effect is beyond the powers of speech. It is elemental to human nature not to forget to wash one's face or launder one's clothes, but this fellow is of different mould. He dresses like a banished criminal, eats food only fit for dogs and pigs. With towseled head and unwashed mien he descants of Poetry and History. Can such be termed natural ? But when in everything a man

[1] See Chap. IV.

[2] Ts'ai Shang Hsiang, vol. x, p. 1.

[3] Wang Yen, a native of Chin Yang (晉 陽), who attained to the rank of Minister of Education (司 徒) in the times of the Western Chin Dynasty (西 晉), A.D. 265–313. He was a man of great repute, both for high intelligence and administrative ability. But he was specially renowned for his versatile mind and ready wit, being, so it is reported, particularly skilled in changing his ground when " cornered " in debate (口 中 雌 黃). He is also said to have had a predilection for the teachings of Buddhism and Taoism (Tz'u Yuan, Biographical Dictionary).

does he shows an unnatural disposition, rarely indeed does such
a one fail to turn out to be a notorious villain.   He is a Shu
Tiao (竪 刁), an I Ya (易 牙), or a K'ai Fang (開 方).[1]
As these were men of repute in their day, they were enabled
to prosecute their deep-laid schemes of villainy, so that even
though there might be a purposeful monarch on the throne,
and ministers in power who were desirous above all things
to secure men of character for the government services, they
might be so deceived as to recommend and employ them.
There is no doubt at all about such a man bringing calamity
upon the state, which will be more ruinous than that wrought
by these three notorieties."

Chang Fang P'ing is reported to have confirmed the authorship of this tract as emanating from the pen of Su Hsün, in his
obituary notice on the death of the latter,[2] and the further
evidence is adduced that Su Shih, in writing a letter of thanks
to Chang Fang P'ing, also admitted his father's authorship for
this scurrilous attack.[3]

Ts'ai Shang Hsiang has gone into this matter in great detail,
and produces incontrovertible evidence to prove that each
of these three documents is a fabrication.[4]   It would un-
necessarily burden the narrative to introduce his proofs at this
point.   The reader who is sufficiently interested may turn to
the next chapter for these.[5]   But it is important to note that
Su Shih cultivated the friendship of Wang An Shih during the
latter's later life,[6] and also composed the document conferring
the honorific title of Grand Tutor upon him after his death.
This document was composed in the early days of Che Tsung's
reign, when Hsuan Jen was acting as regent, and Ssu Ma Kuang

[1] Three clever officials of Ch'i Hsuan Wang (683–641 B.C.) and of his
successors Hsiao and Chao (641–611 B.C.). I Ya was the notorious cook of Huan
Kung, of whom it is related that he offered his own child and cooked him for
his master. K'ai Fang, Shu Tiao, and I Ya formed a conspiracy later on and set
up Chao Kung, after killing the son of Hsiao Kung.
[2] Ts'ai Shang Hsiang, vol x, p. 7.
[3] Ts'ai Shang Hsiang, vol. x, pp. 9 and 10.
[4] Ts'a i Shang Hsiang, vol. x, pp. 10 and 11.
[5] Chap. IX.
[6] Ts'ai Shang Hsiang, vol. xxiii, pp. 2 to 5.

was in supreme power in the Grand Council. We quote the following apposite sentences from this document, viz. :—

" Heaven endowed him with a character of such lofty determination that he was enabled to influence the whole country . . . His loyalty and devotion to duty have never been equalled . . . The manner in which he retired from office demonstrates his freedom from every taint of vainglory . . . I (the Emperor) cannot endure the thought that I shall never see or hear him again." [1]

" It is unthinkable," writes Liang Ch'i Ch'ao, " that if Su Hsün had written such slanderous statements about Wang An Shih as are reported above, that his son should have written about him in such lofty strain. For to write in such glowing terms about one whom his father had vilified in a public manner would have been a glaring instance of unfiliality." [2]

Ssu Ma Kuang is also reported to have written equally vituperous stuff in his private diary and in the " Su Shui Chi Wen ", which make out Wang An Shih to be utterly debased.[3] But statements of that kind are inconsistent with Ssu Ma Kuang's general attitude to Wang An Shih personally. He was of course his greatest political antagonist, and on his restoration to power after the death of Shen Tsung, overturned the whole of his policy in the year 1085. It is also true that though they had been friends for a time, after Wang An Shih's promotion to high office they had drawn apart on questions of government policy.

In 1069, during a discussion on the character of Wang An Shih, Ssu Ma Kuang had described him as a man of good character, but self-willed.[4] He also said that the reason why he was so generally reviled was because of his connection with Lü Hui Ch'ing.

After the death of Wang An Shih, Ssu Ma Kuang, in writing to Lü Kung Chu, says :—

" For literary genius and personal character, Wang An Shih

[1] For complete translation see Vol. I, pp. 386–7.
[2] Liang Ch'i Ch'ao, p. 240.
[3] Liang Ch'i Ch'ao, p. 241.
[4] " T'ung Chien," Hsi Ning, 2nd year, 9th month (賢 而 愎).

had many exceptional points of excellence. He was, however, of an unpractical mind, and was too fond of pursuing wrong ideas. This led him to treat with scant courtesy the loyal and upright, and afforded an opening for the specious and cunning to attach themselves to his party, with the result that everything connected with the government has been brought to a sorry pass. But just as we have amended his errors and corrected his defects, he has most unfortunately passed away. Un-principled folk will inevitably take the opportunity to slander him on a hundred counts, but my own opinion is that the Court ought to honour him with the highest marks of respect, so as to show contempt for such shallow-mindedness. . . ." [1]

Ssu Ma Kuang may have thought Wang An Shih self-willed and of an unpractical and obstinate mentality, but certainly he could not have descended to such depths as to attribute to his arch-antagonist in politics such a mean and despicable character as the works ascribed to his authorship suggest.

Ts'ai Shang Hsiang asserts that these slanderous statements attributed to Su Hsün and Ssu Ma Kuang are fabrications by later writers like Yang Shih (楊 時), Shao Pai Wen (邵 伯 溫), Fan Ch'ung (范 沖), and Wei Tao Fu (魏 道 夫), who deliberately represented them as emanating from notable contemporaries of Wang An Shih, in the hope that they would gain credence thereby.[2] All these writers belong to the time of the Southern Sung when deliberate efforts were made by the party opposed to Wang An Shih and his following, to defame his personal character.

" It is deplorable," says Liang Ch'i Ch'ao, " that these utterly false representations of contemporary opinion about the character of Wang An Shih should have been incorporated in the Dynastic Histories, and thus have tended to create in the minds of later generations erroneous notions about him." [3]

It has already been remarked that the Mongol editors of the Sung histories were indifferent to the real facts regarding

[1] Liang Ch'i Ch'ao, p. 238.
[2] Ts'ai Shang Hsiang, vol. xxiii, p. 5.
[3] Liang Ch'i Ch'ao, p. 241.

the character of men and events which they sought to place on record.[1]   Had they not been so, they would certainly have found place for opinions of quite another stamp about Wang An Shih's character, which were expressed by notable contemporaries, and which are available to investigators to-day. They would, for instance, have included in his biographical notice the statement of Huang Shan Ku (黃 山 谷), who, in composing an inscription to accompany a picture of Wang An Shih, wrote :—

"Wang An Shih regarded riches and honours as a fleeting cloud.   He was not addicted to the accumulation of wealth, and remained aloof from every form of vice.   He was a real gentleman." [2]

Chu Hsi has put on record his opinions of Wang An Shih and his policy, and as his opinions are particularly important, they are worthy of discussion in some detail.   In answer to the inquiry of one of his disciples, as to what he thought of Wang An Shih as a man, he is reported to have said, " Lu Hsiang Shan (陸 象 山) has already written upon this subject, and there is no need to discuss the matter further." [3]

Lu Hsiang Shan, or, as he is more generally styled, Lu Chiu Yuan (陸 九 淵), was a contemporary of Chu Hsi, who for a time was closely associated with him.   They gradually drew apart on questions of interpretation, Chu Hsi emphasizing the philosophical aspect of everything, while Lu Chiu Yuan was keener on stressing ethical implications.   It would appear, however, that Chu Hsi accepted Lu's opinion of Wang An Shih's character as being fair and adequate.   Let us see now what that opinion was.

The source of our information is found in an inscription which Lu Chiu Yuan was commissioned to write for a memorial shrine, which a public spirited official of Lin Ch'uan (Wang's ancestral home) named Ch'ien (錢) had erected in his honour.[4]

[1] See Chap. V.
[2] Liang Ch'i Ch'ao, p. 237.
[3] Complete Works of Chu Hsi, vol. lix, p. 17.
[4] Complete Works of Hsiang Shan, vol. xix, pp. 7 to 12.

From this inscription it appears that during the period 1119–1126 the old residence had fallen into complete ruin, so his fellow townsmen proceeded to erect a monument on the site to Wang An Shih's memory. This was repaired again in the period 1131–1163 (probably in 1147–8). After a further period of forty years, the magistrate Ch'ien, who had devoted himself to the extension of educational facilities in the district, was grieved to find this memorial to Wang An Shih in dilapidated and neglected condition. So he gave orders for its restoration and enlargement. The work was completed in 1188, the monument being adequately safeguarded against vandalism, and regulations drawn up for periodical ceremonies of remembrance to be held at the shrine. In the first month of 1188 the inscription composed by Lu Chiu Yuan was carved in stone and dedicated as part of the memorial.

The full text of this inscription is extant in Lu's Works, from which the following pertinent extracts are taken, viz. :— [1]

" Wang An Shih, working in collaboration with the Emperor Shen Tsung, sincerely endeavoured to revive the illustrious age of Yao and Shun. The confidence which Shen Tsung reposed in his minister was of such a character that, in the words of Tseng Lu Kung, ' Wang An Shih should have been willing to sacrifice life itself in order to justify it.' It is evident from succeeding history that Wang An Shih lived up to his own advice to the emperor, viz., ' that both ruler and minister should work to the limits of their capacity and strength in the fulfilment of their duty to the people, regardless of consequences or reward.'

It is, however, most unfortunate that Wang An Shih failed to fulfil the great purpose of his life, his knowledge being inadequate to the carrying out of his noble intention.

During the reign of the Emperor Jen Tsung, Wang An Shih was called to Court to report on his work in Chiang Tung. He then submitted his memorial of ten thousand words (the Wan Yen Shu 萬 言 書), which was a just and candid

[1] Complete Works of Hsiang Shan, vol. xix, pp. 7 to 12.

exposition of current affairs. In this he analysed in detail the defective character of the government. It was a most timely and apposite document.

This memorial was the basis for Wang An Shih's various proposals for reform, and to the practical execution of which he devoted his energies during the first half of Shen Tsung's reign. The main thesis of this memorial was that current methods of government were not in line with the ancient pattern. It was this consummate passion of his (for the restoration of the ancient regime) which contributed in large measure to his failure to carry out the great purpose of his life. For the imitation of Yao and Shun need not necessarily imply that their various measures should be revived in every detail.

However, those critics who described him as a fawning courtier, or an opportunist, or as one who had relinquished his former principles, or as one who violated his principles by plausible but erroneous arguments, with the object of gaining prestige and influence, cannot be said to know Wang An Shih.

When men find themselves at loggerheads with one another, they invariably indulge in slanderous vilification. Men like Chang An Tao (張 安 道), Lü Hsien K'o (呂 獻 可), and Su Ming Yun (蘇 明 允),[1] who attacked his character prior to his assuming high office, were of this type. Wang An Shih had his defects, but they were not of the kind which these attributed to him.

For he was a man of heroic mould and will, entirely free from love of luxury, vice, wealth, or even fame. He stood aloof from those who pursued a merely conventional policy in such matters. He was an outstanding example of moral purity and determination. And as for his ideal, his purpose was to sweep the country clean of merely conventional practices, and to eliminate every trace of the *laissez-faire* policy of those officials who either refused to recognize, or failed to see, the necessity for administrative reforms. He sought to follow

[1] These are different designations for Chang Fang P'ing, Lü Hui, and Su Hsün.

Confucius and Mencius in matters of principle, and to equal the achievements of I Yin and Chow Kung in affairs of government.   He himself was free from all desire for fame, and yet at one time his reputation was so great that some of the most famous men of his day were ready to act as his subordinates. Can this be said to have been accidental ?

He was fortunate in having gained the ear and confidence of Shen Tsung, one of the great sovereigns of history, who, after having sat at his feet, called him to be high minister of state. In this, Shen Tsung shows himself a worthy successor of Ch'eng T'ang (成 湯) in his appointment of I Yin (伊 尹) and of Kao Tsung (高 宗) in his appointment of Fu Yueh (傅 說).   Whenever Wang An Shih suspected the slightest wavering of Shen Tsung's confidence, he resigned on the pretext of ill-health, and only when the Emperor had given him satisfactory proofs of regret and complete confidence, would he return to his post.

When the new laws were being drawn up and promulgated, discussion became rife and the whole Court resounded with turbulent criticism.   Before they had been long in actual operation, opposition was roused from every quarter.   Wang An Shih then sought to buttress up his position by reinterpreting the Chow Li (周 禮), giving lucid and detailed interpretations from this (as being in line with his proposals), and was so confident that his ideas were right that he pressed them with increased determination and resolution.

This led to strenuous opposition on the part of the high officials of the time, and one by one they left the Court. Meaner men seized their opportunity.   They cleverly availed themselves of the opening which his determination presented for flattery, with the result that the loyal and honest deserted him, and the crafty got their way.   Wang An Shih failed to perceive the peril of all this, and this must be accounted a defect.

One would hesitate to say that each of the measures propounded by Wang An Shih was absolutely perfect or that he adopted the right way of reforming the abuses of his times. His opponents were not sufficiently conscientious and he was excessively determined. So that both sides failed to make the contribution for which the times called.

But this consideration may be urged in his favour. Those who attacked his policy in the main excessively slandered him, but failed to produce adequate reasons for their detractions. Very few indeed took up what may be termed a moderate attitude, the vast majority adopting an extreme position. So they not only failed to gain the support of the Emperor for their views, but failed also to convince Wang An Shih of the error of his ways. On the contrary, their opposition, being of the type it was, only served to increase his determination to carry out his ideas. So his opponents must share the blame for whatever guilt attaches to the promoters of the reforms.

The great officials of the earlier part of Che Tsung's reign, in their rescindment of his measures, were not free from prejudices of a partisan character. The worth of the jewel lies in the fact that its flaws as well as its fine points are both clearly revealed. That the ancient records are reliable is due to the fact that affairs were honestly recorded, regardless of their being right or wrong, good or bad. As the records are free from partiality, they serve for the encouragement or warning of succeeding generations.

But when facts are concealed, or unduly emphasized, when facts are only partially recorded or spurious additions are made to them, with the idea of making the records conform to one's personal likes and dislikes, violence is done to one's conception of real scholarship. For mean folk are thereby afforded an excellent pretext for exacting vengeance on their opponents.

Wang An Shih roused the ire of his political opponents by terming them mere conventionalists, or mean fellows. When his opponents were restored to power they altered everything which he had introduced. Chagrin played its part in this, and no one can deny that they went beyond what the circumstances called for. Later again in the times of Shao Sheng (1094-8), when the pendulum swung again in Wang An Shih's favour, the actions taken against his political opponents were due to the extreme and unwarranted attitude of their predecessors, so

the blame for this is not all to be laid at Wang An Shih's door.
From that time on to the period Ts'ung Ning (1102-7) the
political pendulum swung to and fro. The spirit of faction
and feud wrought dire results. But chief blame attaches to
the historiographers of the times of Yuan Yu (元祐), i.e.
1086-1094, for the way in which they recorded the events of
Hsi Ning's time, i.e. 1068-1078. For this incited unworthy
men to adopt the revival of Wang An Shih's policy as a pretext
for exacting vengeance on their political opponents. Both
sides suffered from this.

Modern scholars, who fill the schools with their prejudiced
opinions about Wang An Shih, cannot be termed good students
of history (i.e. they are unable to distinguish between right and
wrong in the attitudes of their predecessors).

The neglect in which Wang An Shih and the work which
he accomplished have been allowed to lie, is due to this prevalence
of unfavourable criticism and fear of taking his side. All the
more commendable, therefore, is this act of the magistrate
Chien in undertaking the restoration of this memorial shrine.
The shrines of goblins and sprites are nowadays maintained in
the best repair, but if Mr. Ch'ien had not taken the matter in
hand, the shrine of Wang An Shih, the hero of his day, who
resisted the evil tendencies of his time with a character of
outstanding worth, and with ability such as is unequalled by
the spirits of hills and streams, would have remained in a
grievously dilapidated condition.

I take it that you, Wang An Shih, although you refused
to heed the opinions of your contemporaries, will not be
altogether displeased with what I have written about you in
this tablet." (Inscription ends here.)

Generally speaking, Chu Hsi was opposed to the policy of
Wang An Shih. Opinions on his life and work which are
attributed to him, and which the Mongol editors have included
in the Dynastic History of Sung, present him in no very
favourable light. But, as a matter of fact, from the many
references to Wang An Shih and his reforms which are found
in the writings of Chu Hsi, one gathers that he finds it very

difficult to be consistent in the matter. But apart altogether from questions of policy, on which Chu Hsi must be regarded as critical and usually antagonistic, his endorsement of Lu Chiu Yuan's opinion of Wang An Shih's character is decidedly welcome and important. The inscription for Wang An Shih's memorial shrine was written by Lu Chiu Yuan late in life, and must be considered as an expression of his cool and deliberate judgment.

We have, however, something direct from the pen of Chu Hsi which credits him with noble character and high ideals, a eulogy which is somewhat tempered, it must be admitted, by his criticism that Wang An Shih was haughty and self-confident. But when the person under criticism is of opposite political colour, such epithets lose a good deal of their seeming significance. We will reproduce the passage from his works, as follows :—

" Wang An Shih was a man of high and resolute principle, but lacked magnanimity of temperament. He had the noblest of ideals, but had only commonplace intelligence. His theories and proposals, being limited to his own observation and judgment, were of quite ordinary or even second-rate quality, yet he regarded them as being so exceptional as to make him of sagely capacity. This, to him, seemed to obviate the necessity of scientific investigation into things with a view to extending his knowledge, or of denying himself so as to return to propriety. He thus remained oblivious of the inadequacy of his own ideas, or the necessity of complementing his own limited capacity. Hence he committed the primary mistake of adopting a headlong and self-opinionated attitude to matters of the gravest import to the State, and became extremely obstinate and self-centred later on. It was this which accounted for the failure of his policy." [1]

Opportunity will be taken later on to discuss Chu Hsi's attitude to Wang An Shih's policy, and the reasons for its failure. What we are primarily concerned with at the moment

[1] Complete Works of Chu Hsi, vol. lix, p. 22.

is his opinion of his character. His view of Wang An Shih's intelligence and mental complexes is naturally influenced by his opinion of Wang An Shih's policy, and is not necessarily to be considered a fair criticism of his character. But when he owns, as he does, that Wang An Shih was a man of pure and resolute principle, and possessed of the highest ideals, we are on solid ground, and may conclude that Chu Hsi had the deepest respect for Wang An Shih as a man.

One of the great criticisms levelled against Wang An Shih is that he employed unworthy men. This matter bears upon the question we are discussing. For if he deliberately chose to employ such, it would reflect seriously upon his character. If such were found amongst those whom he selected to serve him, although he did not deliberately do so because they were evil-minded, he would stand convicted at least of faulty judgment of men.

In a memorial which he submitted on the employment of officials, Wang An Shih wrote :—

" Since your Majesty came to the throne, you have been led (because of the scarcity of capable men for the government services) to appoint a number of officers who are of inferior ability and doubtful character. If such men as these are given scope for their activities, public life will perforce be corrupted. The remedy for this state of things lies in your seeking for loyal and upright men to act as your more intimate officers." [1]

From this we gather that Shen Tsung, probably in his haste to get things done, had engaged men unsuitable for government posts, and that Wang An Shih himself was well aware of the peril of pursuing such a policy.

In our investigation into this aspect of our subject, it will be necessary to give some account of the men who were prominently associated with Wang An Shih during his political career. The Traditional Histories are unreliable as a guide on this question, as it is their practice to dub all who co-operated with him in the promulgation of his reforms as " wicked, treacherous, traitorous, specious " and the like.

[1] Works, vol. x, p. 4.

We will therefore follow Liang Ch'i Ch'ao [1] in his investigation into the characters of a number of the more important officials who received their appointments from Wang An Shih, or who were associated with him in his public work.

Ch'eng Hao, Liu I, Hsieh Ch'ing Ts'ai, and Hou Shu Hsien, four of the eight who were commissioned by Wang An Shih to make the preliminary economic survey, all have their characters sufficiently well established in the Histories and further comment is unnecessary. They were all good men. Of the remainder, three, viz. Wang Ju I (王 汝 翼), Tseng Hang (曾 伉), and Wang Kuang Lien (王 廣 廉), have left no records and it is impossible to estimate their characters. Of the eighth, viz. Lu Ping (盧 秉), it was reported that he administered the Salt Laws in an oppressive manner in association with Hsieh Hsiang (薛 向).

As a consequence of this charge Lu Ping appealed that he should be allowed to resign and offered to return his surplus receipts to the government, a most rare occurrence. This shows him to be a man of good character. As he had conducted border affairs with conspicuous ability, both Shen Tsung and Wang An Shih were anxious to retain his services, and to offer him some important post. However, he asked to be allowed to return home to care for his father, and he was permitted to do so.

Ch'en Sheng Chih (陳 升 之), who was associated with Wang An Shih for some time in the Financial Reorganization Bureau, had been Grand Councillor for five years prior to receiving this appointment, and had also acted as Chief Censor for a number of years, during which he introduced over a hundred matters of public import. He had great ability, but is designated by the historians as " a wicked and servile flatterer, selfishly devoted to his own interests ". An impartial investigation into his career fails to substantiate this verdict.

Wang Kuei (王 珪) was in high office for eighteen years, and was a loyal supporter of Wang An Shih's policy. The Histories give him a good character up to the time of his engagement with Wang An Shih, but have nothing good to say of him afterwards. He was a man of moderate abilities, and of somewhat colourless character.

Lü Kung Chu (呂 公 著) was one of Wang An Shih's important associates for a time, but later attached himself to Ssu Ma Kuang and helped him to abolish the New Laws. The Historians praise him for this *volte face* and make him out to be a very fine man in consequence. They endeavour to deny to Wang An Shih the credit for his selection and promotion of such a good official, by suggesting that he used him only in order to bring pressure upon his brother, Lü Kung Pi (呂 公 弼), who, as governor of K'ai Feng Fu, was giving Wang An Shih some trouble by his opposition. On the evidence of the Histories we may assume that he was a man of good character, and as he was employed by Ssu Ma Kuang there can be no doubt of his ability. His " repentance " with regard to the reform policy is said to be due to over-emphasis on accumulation of revenue by the adminstrators of the New Laws, which made them injurious to the livelihood of the people.

Han Chiang (韓 絳) was another of Wang An Shih's more intimate associates, who became Grand Councillor, and succeeded him when he retired. Han Ch'i (韓 琦) highly recommended him to Shen Tsung, so that Wang An Shih was not his sole patron. In his earlier years he had gained a reputation for administering justice with strict impartiality, and for having done much to relieve the distresses of the people. In his capacity of censor he exposed many defects and evils in the Court and official circles, which was by no means an easy thing to do. He subdued a revolt at Ch'ing Chow (青 州), and as governor of Ch'eng Tu (成 都) and K'ai Feng Fu he frequently espoused the cause of the people against the wealthy and influential classes.

Jen Tsung said of him, " You alone amongst my ministers are not content to let things slide." His favourite " quip " was, " The secret of the nation's wealth lies in the ground." He was the first to suggest that the Commissioned Services Act (差 役 法) should be revised. On several occasions he

recommended Ssu Ma Kuang for appointment, so was free
from any party spirit. All the above are quotations from the
Canonical Histories, and refer to his career before association
with Wang An Shih. After that they have nothing good to
say of him.

Yuan Chiang (元 絳) was also appointed Grand Councillor
on Wang An Shih's recommendation. He was a great favourite
of Shen Tsung, and his achievements and character are such
that even the most prejudiced historian could not ignore them.
But at the end of his Biographical sketch they add, " Yuan
Chiang really thought quite differently about questions of
government from Wang An Shih, but was small minded
enough to toady to him. It was as a partisan of Wang An
Shih that he attained to the position of Grand Councillor, and
so there is little of a pure and consistent character to record
of him."

Lü Hui Ch'ing (呂 惠 卿) was one of two (the other being
Tseng Pu (曾 布)) who did most in a personal capacity to
assist Wang An Shih with his reform policy. Ou Yang Hsiu
first introduced him to the notice of Wang An Shih, describing
him as a learned, able, and upright gentleman. Later on Lü
Hui Ch'ing and Wang An Shih had their differences, and
some suspicion arose between them, which however seems to
have been more on Lü's side than on Wang's. For the latter
in his correspondence makes it clear that what differences had
arisen between them were not of any personal character, at
least so far as Wang An Shih was concerned. He exposed
certain private letters of Wang An Shih, an action which is
reported to have aroused the Emperor's suspicion of his
favourite. When Wang An Shih resigned the first time from
the position of Grand Councillor, Lü Hui Ch'ing succeeded
him and introduced two measures of his own,[1] styled the Self
Assessment Measure (手 實 法) and the Sale of Temple
Property Measure (鬻 祠 法), both of which Wang An Shih
rescinded on his return to power. Lü Hui Ch'ing in this
interim period also banished Cheng Hsieh, which displeased

[1] Liang Ch'i Ch'ao, p. 294.

Wang An Shih, who all through was opposed to meting out too severe a punishment to his political opponents.

Liang Ch'i Ch'ao thinks that Lü Hui Ch'ing was not of too good a character, though he was far from being as evil as the historians make him out to be.

Tseng Pu (曾 布) was the younger brother of Tseng Kung, and his contribution to the furtherance of the reform policy was exceedingly important. He cleared up many difficulties about the working of the New Laws, and helped to unravel knotty points raised by Court functionaries about them. Some of his expositions are to be found in the " Wen Hsien T'ung K'ao " and they show him to be possessed of considerable literary and dialectical gifts. With the exception of his objection to Lu Chia Wen's method of carrying out the Trade and Barter Measure, he gave his support to the reform policy throughout. For his opposition to that particular measure or method of administering it, which he affirmed was putting the Government into the same category as the wealthy usurers, he was transferred to Jao Chow by Lü Hui Ch'ing.

When Ssu Ma Kuang became Prime Minster he requested Tseng Pu to make certain adjustments in the Public Services Act. He replied, " The latter, as far as the detailed regulations are concerned, is my own work. If I were to consent to make these alterations, as you suggest, I should be violating my sense of duty."

Later on he opposed Ts'ai Ching (蔡 京) and along with his family suffered at his hand.

For the stand he took on these two occasions he is termed " disloyal " by the historians. But it looks strangely like " loyalty " to the impartial observer.

Chang Ch'un (章 惇) received his first high appointment from Wang An Shih, this being to establish the Financial Reorganization Bureau. Later he was engaged upon military expeditions in the Hupei and Hunan areas. In 1080 he was appointed vice-Grand Councillor, after Wang An Shih had retired from public life. Before long he was degraded on account of his father's crime, and appointed to Ts'ai Chow.

Later again, he strenuously opposed Ssu Ma Kuang's revival of the Commissioned Services Act. His speeches were so strong that they were termed " rebellious " by the Court officials, and he was dismissed.

When Che Tsung took over the reins of government he was recalled and became Prime Minister. He reinstated all of Wang An Shih's measures. This aroused violent discussion at Court. He then attempted to deprive the Empress Regent, Hsuan Jen, of her royal titles, and made certain suggestions about Che Tsung's successor which met with general disapproval. He was degraded step by step until he was banished to Mu Chow (睦 州) where he died.[1]

His remarks about the succession were probably to the point, as Hui Tsung, who eventually succeeded Che Tsung, was hopelessly licentious and superstitious, and contributed in no small degree to the downfall of the Sung Dynasty. But he was blameworthy in his banishment of the ministers of the previous regime, and in his appeal for the deposition of Hsuan Jen. He might be termed " revengeful " but neither " wicked " nor " traitorous ".

Wang Shao (王 韶), Hsiung Pen (熊 本), Kuo K'uei (郭 逵), and Chao Hsieh (趙 卨) were all military men, who carried out the expeditions entrusted to them with ability and success.

Hsieh Hsiang (薛 向) was recommended to Jen Tsung by Wang An Shih in the year 1060. In 1068 he was appointed Transport Officer for the Chiang-Huai Circuit (江 淮 發 運 使), and soon after given a temporary appointment as Superintendent of the Financial Reorganization Bureau. He was much trusted and his achievements were of a brilliant character. His services in the Department of Husbandry and in connection with the transport system led to many improvements. During the Hsi Ho expedition he organized the transport system efficiently and without blemish. Even the historians praise him highly but conceal the fact that he was recommended by Wang An Shih. He was a man of outstanding ability and character.

[1] Liang Ch'i Ch'ao, p. 297.

Teng Chien (鄧綰) seems to have been of a different stamp. He had a fawning disposition which was loathsome to Wang An Shih, who frequently bemoaned the fact that he had patronized and helped him.

Ts'ai Ch'ueh (蔡確) held no important post under Wang An Shih.

Ts'ai Pien (蔡卞) was the younger brother of Ts'ai Ching, who did most to bring calumny upon the name of Wang An Shih. He was associated with his brother for a while, and achieved considerable notoriety by so doing. But eventually they parted company through a difference of opinion, which is to Ts'ai Pien's credit.

Ts'ai Ching (蔡京) was not employed by Wang An Shih in any position of note, but he availed himself of Wang An Shih's policy later on to further his own interests. In the opinion of Liang Ch'i Ch'ao he was a thoroughly unworthy character.[1]

After a survey of forty-eight individuals who were associated with Wang An Shih, and who may be said to owe their positions to him, Liang Ch'i Ch'ao finds that by far the greater proportion of them are deserving of classification as both worthy and capable. About one-fifth are of mediocre type. Only two, viz. Teng Chien and Wang Tzu Shao, he considers thoroughly bad. (The latter was eventually degraded by Wang An Shih.)

So to this limited extent only is it true that Wang An Shih used men who were not of the right character and ability. He himself after his retirement acknowledged that he had failed to discriminate in some cases,[2] and that dangerous men of evil ways had appeared amongst his intimate acquaintances.[3] But considering all the circumstances it is remarkable that the unworthy turned out to be so few. Both he and the Emperor were keen to introduce their reforms as quickly as possible, as they considered the need of the country to be desperate.

[1] This is confirmed by Chu Hsi, Complete Works, vol. lix, p. 8.
[2] Works, vol. x, p. 18 (智不足以知人). Also Works, vol. xviii, p. 12.
[3] Works, vol. xvii, p. 7 (險詖常出於交游之厚).

In one of his essays Wang An Shih writes, " The calamity of the floods of Shun's time created a crisis of such urgency that it was not possible to delay action until the right man could be secured.   Amongst the men around the throne only Kun (鯀) possessed the practical ability to deal with the emergency. So although he turned out to be disobedient to orders, and did his utmost to injure his associates, it was impracticable to dispense with his services."

Here we have in epitome an ancient example of Wang An Shih's difficulty in the matter of using men.   Owing to their divergent political views the high minded and capable of the older guard of officials had all deserted the Court, so he was compelled to find new associates outside their ranks.   That factor, coupled with an eagerness to do things quickly, no doubt accounts for the few who failed to justify his trust.

We have seen that he was aware of the peril of using the wrong men, and that he was ready enough to acknowledge his own mistakes in the matter.   What more can we expect ?   The failures were comparatively few in particularly difficult circumstances, so the criticism levelled against his character in this connection loses much of its force.   The statement that his policy failed largely through the use of unworthy men is a different proposition which will be discussed in the chapter on the Reform Policy.   Such criticism refers mainly to the large body of local administrators of the measures with whose appointment Wang An Shih had nothing to do, but whose character was of vital importance to the fate of his policy.

The next question which calls for discussion is the way in which Wang An Shih treated those who differed from him, whom we may style his political enemies.   This will afford some help towards the estimation of his character.

In this respect Wang An Shih stands out most nobly, for in general he extended the utmost generosity and even leniency to his political opponents.   As the government of those days was conducted, it was impossible to keep a man in high office who was deliberately blocking government policy. It was therefore necessary that those who radically differed from him should be removed to posts in which their opposition would be comparatively innocuous. His procedure in practically every case was that those who held divergent views from him on essential points of policy were given provincial appointments consonant in the main with their dignity and deserts.

There was only one instance of the banishment of an official during his regime, viz. that of Cheng Hsieh, and this really occurred in the interval of Wang An Shih's resignation, while Lü Hui Ch'ing was in power. To this action Wang An Shih, as we have seen, raised strong objection. The worst that can be used against him in this case is that Cheng Hsieh was imprisoned during his term of office.

In the case of Lü Hui, who was the first to vilify the personal character of Wang An Shih, and who had more than hinted that he ought to be executed, as he had urged the decapitation of Ou Yang Hsiu before him, was given quite a good appointment at Teng Chow.[1]

Fan Ch'un Jen (范 純 仁) was transferred to Ch'eng Tu after a severe indictment of Wang An Shih's policy. After his arrival in Ssu Ch'uan he forbade the local officials under his charge to carry out the New Laws. This act was equivalent to treason, nevertheless he was merely transferred to Ho Chow as prefect.[2]

Su Shih (蘇 軾) was transferred from the Ministry of Finance to be Chief Justice of Honan.[2] Chang Fang P'ing (張 方 平) was transferred to Ying T'ien Fu [3] (應 天 府). Ssu Ma Kuang having refused the portfolio of Minister of War,[4] made several attempts to resign from his position at the capital before he was allowed to take up a provincial appointment at Yung Hsing Chun (永 興 軍). Later, at

[1] "T'ung Chien," Hsi Ning, 2nd year, 6th month.
[2] "T'ung Chien," Hsi Ning, 2nd year, 8th month.
[3] "T'ung Chien," Hsi Ning, 3rd year, 1st month.
[4] "T'ung Chien," Hsi Ning, 3rd year, 2nd month, also 10 month, and 4th year, 4th month.

his own request, he was granted a sinecure at Lo Yang (洛陽), where he was enabled to proceed with his monumental labours on the History of China.

Sun Chueh (孫 覺) was transferred from his position as Chief Justice at the capital to Kuang Te Chun (廣 德 軍).[1] Lü Kung Chu of the Censorate was transferred to Ying Chow (英 州) as prefect.[2]   Chao Pien, having resigned from the Grand Council, was appointed as governor of Hang Chow (杭 州).[2]   Lin Tan (林 旦), Hsieh Ch'ang Chao (薛 昌 朝), and Fan Yü (范 育), all of the Censorate, suffered in no way at all, although they had presented a strong indictment of Wang An Shih.   Ch'eng Hao (程 顥), Chang Chien (張 戩), Li Ch'ang (李 常), and Wang Tzu Shao (王 子 韶), also of the Censorate, who had submitted severe criticisms of the New Laws, were all transferred to positions in the provinces.[2]   Lü Kung Pi (呂 公 弼), president of the Board of War, was transferred to the governorship of T'ai Yuan Fu (太 原 府).[3]   Fan Chen (范 鎮), Grand Councillor, was allowed to resign all his offices, but was granted the rank of vice-President of the Board of the Interior.[4]   Han Wei (韓 維), governor of K'ai Feng Fu, opposed the Agricultural Loans Measure, and requested a post in the provinces.   He was pressed to remain at his post, but as he persisted in his desire to resign, he was eventually appointed to Hsiang Chow (襄 州).[5]

It will be remembered that Wang Fang (王 雱), son of Wang An Shih, is reported to have demanded the head of Fu Pi (富 弼) in order that the New Laws might be given a free course. We are asked to infer from this that Fu Pi was a great obstacle in the way of Wang An Shih. We will give the historian credit for the remark that Wang An Shih demurred to the suggestion that Fu Pi should be thus summarily

[1] " T'ung Chien," Hsi Ning, 3rd year, 3rd month.
[2] " T'ung Chien," Hsi Ning, 3rd year, 4th month.
[3] " T'ung Chien," Hsi Ning, 3rd year, 7th month.
[4] " T'ung Chien," Hsi Ning, 3rd year, 10th month.
[5] " T'ung Chien," Hsi Ning, 4th year, 5th month.

disposed of. But we need not surmise about his opinion of Fu Pi, who in 1069 was transferred to Po Chow (亳 州) after he had asked to be allowed to resign.[1] For we have a letter written by Wang An Shih to the aged statesman, permitting him to resign his office of Tso P'u She (左 僕 射) or Left Imperial Advisor. The letter reads as follows [2] :—

" The assistance you rendered to Jen Tsung was invaluable. Your virtue and honour have been maintained unimpaired and unsullied throughout your career. Your loyalty and ability have been an adornment to the State. You ought not to resign your post. I hope, however, that at some future date we shall be able to avail ourselves of your help."

It is particularly important that we should discuss Wang An Shih's later attitude towards his old friends and patrons, such as Han Ch'i, Ou Yang Hsiu, and Wen Yen Po. For these had been largely instrumental, in his earlier days, in securing for him that recognition and opportunity which later on had led to his promotion to high office. After the promulgation of his new measures, however, each of these raised serious objections to his policy. Their differences on political questions, however, do not concern us here, so much as the matter of Wang An Shih's personal relationships with them, and particularly his treatment of them after political differences had arisen.

The traditional histories tend to convey the impression that Wang An Shih meted out scurrilous treatment to these old friends, and suggest that he is guilty of base ingratitude towards them. As the discussion of this subject vitally affects one's judgment of his character, it is introduced at this point.

To begin with Han Ch'i (韓 琦). Along with Fu Pi, he was considered a grievous obstacle in the way of the reform party,[3] so much so that (if we are to believe the accounts in the Histories) Wang's son Fang urged that both should be executed in order that the New Laws should have a free course.

[1] " T'ung Chien," Hsi Ning, 2nd year, 10th month.
[2] Works, vol. xii, p. 4.
[3] See Chap. V.

As in the case of Fu Pi (noted above), we will give the historian credit for recording Wang An Shih's objection to this proposal.

Han Ch'i resigned from the Grand Council in the 9th month of 1067, his resignation synchronizing with Wang An Shih's promotion to the Literary Council. In proffering his resignation Han Ch'i made the remark that Wang An Shih was unsuitable for high office. It should also be noted that Wang An Shih's promotion to the Literary Council is reported to have been at the instigation of Tseng Kung Liang, whose motive for doing so is attributed to his desire to lessen Han Ch'i's influence. In the 2nd month of 1070 Han Ch'i appealed for the abrogation of the Agricultural Loans Measure,[1] and, if the historical account is to be accepted as it stands, his appeal so affected the Emperor that he felt inclined to give it serious consideration. This brought from Wang An Shih a strong reply which evidently failed to convince the Emperor, who still wavered in his attitude to Han Ch'i's memorial. Wang An Shih thereupon kept to his home on the pretext of illness, and appealed for resignation. Then Ssu Ma Kuang added fuel to the fire by quoting, in the Emperor's reply to Wang An Shih's appeal, a sentence to the effect that the officials were in a ferment and the people distressed by the new measures. In the end the matter was settled by an apology from the Emperor, and then Wang An Shih resumed his post. But the same month Han Ch'i resigned from his office as Pacification Commissioner for Ho-pei, on the grounds that his memorial had not been given the attention it deserved. His resignation was accepted, but he kept his former concurrent post of Governor of Ta Ming Fu. Here the historian records that Wang An Shih was anxious to curb Han Ch'i's influence, and so he concurred in this arrangement. Then in the 6th month of 1071, when Ou Yang Hsiu sent in his resignation, Wang An Shih is reported to have said that Ou Yang Hsiu was a partisan of Han Ch'i, whom he regarded as a " pillar of state ", and so he should be allowed to resign. In 1073 Han Ch'i became prefect of Hsiang Chow, a position for which he

---

[1] " T'ung Chien," Hsi Ning, 3rd year, 2nd month.

had appealed in the 7th month of 1068, and had probably held
for a short time. In the 2nd month of 1074, when the Liao
sent their embassy appealing for a new boundary line to be
drawn in the north, Han Ch'i sent in his memorial, criticizing
Wang An Shih's policy in general, and in particular emphasizing
seven features in this which had roused the suspicions of the
northern foe, and urging that these should be abandoned, so
as to disabuse the enemy's mind of any warlike intentions on
China's part. This, on the face of it, seems rather an absurd
attitude for a man like Han Ch'i to have taken up, seeing that
the Ch'itans were the obvious aggressors, and Wang An Shih's
measures were taken with the idea of warding off subsequent
attacks.

It will be clear from the above sketch of the relationships
of the two men during the period of Wang An Shih's influence
that, politically speaking, they were in opposite camps, and that
the circumstances of the time were such as to put a great strain
on the personal relations of them both. But one gathers from
Wang An Shih's correspondence that as far as his personal
feelings towards Han Ch'i are concerned, he maintained his
respect and friendliness for his old patron.

After Han Ch'i had appealed for a provincial appointment,
probably in 1073, Wang An Shih wrote the official reply permitting him to resign from high office. From this letter the
following is taken,[1] viz. :—

"In your capacity as Grand Councillor and Grand Tutor
you have shown yourself to be a great leader in State affairs,
and a staunch upholder of the constitution. You have discharged the onerous duties of your various posts in an
exceptionally able manner. We hope you will make a speedy
recovery from your illness. But as you have repeatedly appealed
that you may be allowed to retire on this ground, and in consideration of the fact that you are deserving of special favour as
a revered statesman of the House of Sung, we feel obliged to
accede to your request, and you are hereby permitted to take
your ease."

[1] Works, vol. xii, p. 3.

There is also included in Wang An Shih's works a letter written later, probably towards the close of his life. (Han Ch'i died in 1075 at the age of 68.) From the tone of this letter one gathers that it was in the nature of a congratulatory epistle on the occasion of Han Ch'i's retirement from some important post, when numerous honours had been conferred upon him. The following is a synopsis [1]: —

"You have exercised your exceptional gifts in the highest offices of the land. You have long been famous for your sincere and pure character. You have earned the highest respect of your contemporaries. In your conduct of your various civil and military appointments, and in your control of the central executive, you have merited praise and incurred blame on a thousand counts. But you have maintained your singleness of purpose throughout. Neither peace nor danger has wrought any change in your fixed will. Your resignation is a matter of vital consequence to the future of the empire. You have also acted conscientiously in retiring from or returning to your official duties. In each case you have been guided by principle. . . .

"Personally I feel greatly indebted to you for many favours. I do not forget that you recommended me for promotion. I feel that it is incumbent upon me to do some great thing for you in return. I regret that I have had to cut myself adrift from you (in political life) lest I should incur the suspicion of being actuated by personal considerations. But I shall never forget your former kindness."

These letters afford sufficient evidence that, as far as Wang An Shih is concerned, there was no waning in his respect for, and no sign of ingratitude towards, his old friend and patron, despite very serious and in one case, at least, unreasonable opposition on Han Ch'i's part to his policy.

His attitude to Ou Yang Hsiu would seem to be equally estimable, although the traditional histories would make it appear to be quite otherwise. For according to them, Ou Yang

---

[1] Works, vol. xix, p. 1.

Hsiu, having reached the age of sixty, and on the ground that he was being continually slandered, requested that he might be allowed to resign all his offices. He was, however, appointed to Ch'ing Chow Fu.[1] From there he submitted a request that he might be permitted to stop the distribution of the Agricultural Loans. (As a matter of fact he had already stopped distributing the money before he sent in the request.[2]) Permission from the Court was withheld. " However," says the history, " the Emperor wished to recall him to Court and give him an appointment at the capital. To this Wang An Shih demurred, so he was transferred to Ts'ai Chow (蔡 州)."

In the 6th month of 1071, Ou Yang Hsiu asked that he might be allowed to retire altogether, on the grounds of old age and failing health.

The historical account continues, " Whereupon Wang An Shih said, ' Ou Yang Hsiu is a partisan of Han Ch'i, and regards the latter as a pillar of State. A man such as he is a menace to public order. If you should appoint him to a county he will ruin it, and if you give him a Court appointment he will work havoc there. What is the use of retaining him ? ' So Ou Yang Hsiu was allowed to resign with the title of Junior Tutor of the Heir-Apparent." [3]

Now if that is all true the criticism of " base ingratitude " on Wang An Shih's part is fully justified. It is necessary that we should quote the result of Ts'ai Shang Hsiang's investigation into this matter, as follows [4] :—

" It was in the summer of 1070, when Wang An Shih was vice-Grand Councillor, that Ou Yang Hsiu ceased the distribution of the Agricultural Loans in Ch'ing Chow Fu. In the 12th month of the same year Wang An Shih was promoted to be Grand Councillor. In the spring of 1071 the following letter of congratulation was sent to him by Ou Yang Hsiu, viz.: ' You are famed as a Confucian scholar, and the

---

[1] " T'ung Chien," Hsi Ning, 4th year, 6th month.
[2] Ts'ai Shang Hsiang, vol. xvi, p. 4.
[3] " T'ung Chien," Hsi Ning, 4th year, 6th month.
[4] Ts'ai Shang Hsiang, vol. iv, p. 1.

hopes of the whole Court are centred in you. You have privileged access to the Imperial presence, and have the intimate confidence of the Emperor.' "

On the assumption that Ou Yang Hsiu was seriously grieved with Wang An Shih's attitude to him at this time, such a statement would partake of the nature of flattery. But from one so straight and sincere as Ou Yang Hsiu such an action is inconceivable.

It is also of importance to note that it was after Lü Hui had attacked Ou Yang Hsiu on the P'u I (濮 議) case in 1066,[1] and after he had been slandered by P'eng Ssu Yung (彭 思 永) and Chiang Ch'i Chih (蔣 之 奇) in 1067, that he began to request provincial appointments, in which he remained from that time on. During the first four years of Shen Tsung's reign he held no Court appointment, being in office at Po Chow, Ch'ing Chow, and Ts'ai Chow successively. During that period he was repeatedly requesting to be allowed to resign altogether on the grounds of ill-health.

The statement attributed to Wang An Shih and quoted in the traditional histories about Ou Yang Hsiu ruining a county and working havoc at Court can be traced to Yang Chung Li's diary of Shen Tsung's reign, the prejudiced character of which it is easy to prove. Unfortunately, later writers regarded this as evidence of Wang An Shih's guilt, without even glancing at the writings of the people concerned.[2]

Ou Yang Hsiu died in 1072, soon after his retirement,[3] and Wang An Shih wrote a panegyric to his memory, lauding his fame as a writer and a man, pointing out the great difficulties which had attended his political career, and testifying to the mutual friendship and intimacy which had subsisted between them in life, and his longing for him after death.[4]

Wang An Shih had no reason to envy Ou Yang Hsiu. He had the ear of the Emperor and a free course for the experiment

[1] "T'ung Chien," Ying Tsung, 4th year, 3rd month.
[2] Liang Ch'i Ch'ao, p. 265.
[3] "T'ung Chien," Hsi Ning, 5th year, 8th month.
[4] Works, vol. xxi, p. 5.

he wished to make with his political ideas. It is incredible that he should have taken up the attitude which critics affirm he adopted towards his friend and patron in later life, and which all the evidence contradicts.

Wen Yen Po (文 彥 博), another of Wang An Shih's old friends and patrons, asked to resign in the 4th month of 1073, and was appointed to Ho Yang (河 陽) [1] with the concurrent post of Adviser to the Board of Works of the Ho Tung circuit. There is no evidence of a character more reliable than that quoted above in connection with Han Ch'i and Ou Yang Hsiu, of any ungrateful treatment of him by Wang An Shih.

We may therefore conclude that on the particular point of Wang An Shih's treatment of his old friends and patrons his character emerges unsullied. Political differences existed between them, but as far as he could, Wang An Shih kept in the friendliest of personal and official relations with them.

It may next be asked why Wang An Shih could not work in co-operation with the more famous and able officials of his time, and why it was necessary to allow them to retire from the capital and take up provincial appointments. Why did he not modify his ideas somewhat so as to gain their sympathetic interest and co-operation, instead of being so determined to push his own ideas even at the cost of losing their assistance ? Does not that show a defect in his character, and amply justify the sobriquet of " Obstinate Minister " which posterity has been pleased to confer upon him ?

What was it that prevented Wang An Shih from co-operating with the older officials of repute ? What led younger men like Ssu Ma Kuang and the two Sus, for instance, to withdraw from the government ? Was the fault entirely with Wang An Shih and his reputed " self-will " or " obstinacy " ?

The answer is probably to be found in the fact that the old guard, such as Fu Pi, Wen Yen Po, Ou Yang Hsiu, and Han Ch'i, had become to a large extent innured to the traditional policy of making as few changes as possible. They were all

---

[1] " T'ung Chien," Hsi Ning, 6th year, 4th month.

getting on in years, and were too old to bother with schemes that involved the introduction of wide-sweeping changes, and the abandonment of many of their cherished ideas. Even men like Ssu Ma Kuang and the younger Sus cannot be absolved from the charge of being unreasonably addicted to a policy of Conservatism and even of *laissez-faire*. Wang An Shih's opinion of the great majority of the old guard and of large numbers of important personages of about his own age was that they were altogether too keen on maintaining the *status quo* and so unreasonably averse to serious changes in any form that it was infeasible for them to serve his purposes in any adequate way.

At the outset of his high official career it is evident that many of these famous officials thought him a man who had excellent ideas, and who might be expected to do great things for the country. Many of the " old guard " did co-operate with him for a time, but gradually withdrew. But it did not take long to show the great majority that Wang An Shih's theories were altogether too radical for their taste, and so they felt compelled to " spue them out of their mouths ".

By the year 1070 the opposition had become so fierce that Wang An Shih began to feel that the case was hopeless and that he had better resign.[1] The Emperor did his utmost to reassure him, but the following letter written by Wang An Shih in response to this " consoling " message shows the nature and extent of his difficulties at that particular time. It reads as follows :—

"Heaven has conferred upon Your Majesty such extra-ordinary wisdom that it ought to be possible to revive the glorious government of Yao and Shun. Without estimating my own strength or ability, and without so much as a thought as to whether I was the man for the times or not, I have, in my assurance that your noble will and purpose could be carried out (entered upon my task) and incurred in my own unworthy person the wrath and opposition of the whole empire.

[1] " T'ung Chien," Hsi Ning, 3rd year, 2nd month.

"Already a year has passed since I took up my very responsible position in the government. During that time I have been able to do nothing to advance the welfare of the country. For all within and without the Court have conspired together to hinder me with their obstructive policy, and by their strenuous efforts to render you suspicious of my motives and aims.

"It is their 'conventionalism' which has brought things to this pass. On your part I fear you cannot but have your doubts, and as for myself I begin to feel I cannot overcome their opposition." [1]

It is then, on Wang An Shih's own showing, to the conventionalism of the majority of his contemporaries that we must look for the reason why he found it impossible to co-operate with them. By the term "conventional" he meant something more than "conservative", although they were certainly that. He meant that they were content to let things slide, and swim with the stream of popular opinion, rather than follow the dictates of their own consciences and the guidance of their own principles. For he had reason to think that many of them were so "conventional" as to be actually inconsistent.

Instances of this might be quoted. Before Wang An Shih began his reform movement, Su Che (蘇 轍) had advocated the loaning of money to the people on interest under the auspices of the government,[2] but he opposed the Agricultural Loans Measure, which was the same thing in principle.

During the reign of Ying Tsung, Ssu Ma Kuang had advocated that apart from the land tax, the farming class should not be expected to contribute anything further in the way of taxation, and that certain sections of the Public Services, like the office of Official Agent (衙 前), should be paid for by the government,[2] and yet he was obdurate in his opposition to the Public Services Act, which incorporated these very ideas.

[1] Works, vol. x, p. 17.
[2] Liang Ch'i Ch'ao, p. 270.

Su Shih (蘇 軾) had formerly advocated the necessity of capturing Ling Wu (靈 武), i.e. the Hsi Ho territory, as it would otherwise be impossible to maintain control of the western border lands, and if that could not be ensured, it would be impossible to check the growing power and menace of the Ch'itans.[1] But he opposed the Hsi Ho expedition which had that as its objective.

Su Shih had also made a strong appeal that the numbers enrolled in the Archers' Corps of Hopei should be greatly increased, and requested that rewards should be offered to encourage the people to join in the movement. But this was very much akin to the Militia Act of Wang An Shih, which he rigorously opposed.[1]

Instances might be quoted also of officials who opposed Wang An Shih's policy during the period of his supremacy, but who themselves advocated similar measures either in whole or in part later on. These are outlined in another part of this Work,[2] and need not be repeated here. But we will remind the reader of just one instance, viz. that of Su Shih, who at one time had said that the hiring system in connection with the public services was absolutely impracticable, but later on affirmed it to be indispensable.[1]

It is such "inconsistencies" as these which marked the attitude of some of his important official contemporaries that seem to justify Wang An Shih in his dubbing them "conventional".

Two other matters should be mentioned as contributing to Wang An Shih's difficulties in this connection, as they account to some extent for his inability to co-operate with his more famous contemporaries.

One is the fact that many of his measures were directed against the wealthy and deprived them of some of their long-standing privileges and luxuries. The big officials were mainly of this class, and their opposition and withdrawal from Wang

[1] Liang Ch'i Ch'ao, p. 270.
[2] Chap. X.

An Shih's company is to that extent natural, and need occasion no surprise.

The other is the remarkable confidence which the Emperor Shen Tsung placed in Wang An Shih, and which led eventually to his wielding sole power in the Empire for several years. This exceptional favour shown by the Emperor to one of his ministers naturally excited the envy and jealousy of other highly placed officials, and added considerably to Wang An Shih's personal difficulties. It must, too, have contributed to his isolation from the majority of the more able and influential men of his time.

Added to all these considerations was the fact that many who opposed him were seeking a cheap notoriety by so doing. Such were Ch'en Shun Yü (陳 舜 俞) of Shan Yin (山 陰), Lo Ching (樂 京) of Ch'ang Ko (長 葛), and Liu Meng (劉 蒙) of Hu Yang (湖 陽), who deliberately refused to carry out the New Laws in their districts, knowing that they would have the sympathy and backing of many prominent men by so doing. It was such attitudes as these which led to Wang An Shih's institution of the " Special Inspectorate " of officials, which excited such resentment and animosity.[1]

When all the above considerations are taken into account one is inclined to marvel, not so much that Wang An Shih failed to win the co-operation of all these famous men of the time, but rather that he was able to hold on so long, and carry so many of his ideas through. He certainly must have been possessed of remarkable strength of character, and an indomitable will. We are not suggesting that in this matter the fault was entirely on the side of his opponents, but sufficient evidence has we trust been adduced to show that the fault was not only on his side either.

The opposition was tremendously formidable and in many instances insincere and pernicious, so that we should not be surprised that Wang An Shih showed the more obstinate side of his strong nature. But as regards his treatment of these

---

[1] " T'ung Chien," Hsi Ning, 4th year, 3rd month.

opponents we have already said that his conduct left little to
be desired.   P'an Po (潘 博) of Nan Hai (南 海) says,
" Wang An Shih used the method of a true follower of
Confucius and not the lawyer's way."   Liang Ch'i Ch'ao [1]
thinks that he treated his political opponents with greater
generosity than they deserved, and that if he had been a little
more harsh with them his policy might have been more successfully prosecuted.   Certainly his treatment of his opponents is
in happy contrast with that meted out by both enemies and
friends in succeeding years.   Under the regime of Ssu Ma Kuang,
Teng Chien and Li Ting were banished, and a little later Ts'ai
Ch'ueh suffered a similar fate.   Under the independent rule of
Che Tsung, with Chang Ch'un in power, and later under Hui
Tsung with Ts'ai Ching in supremacy, banishments, proscriptions, deprivation of rank and honours were the order
of the day.

So that from the standpoint of the subject under discussion,
the fact that Wang An Shih failed to co-operate with the most
famous and able men of his time, would seem to be no serious
reflection upon his character, for in his treatment of his political
foes he erred if anything on the side of leniency.

One other question affecting the discussion of his personal
character is that connected with his remarkable influence over
the Emperor Shen Tsung.   The suggestion of his critics that
he was a mere opportunist, ready to sacrifice his principles to
gain power and position, and that he was one who had forgotten
or rejected all he had learnt of the principles of Confucius, in a
word that he had gained his lofty position by " fawning
flattery ", must now be considered.

Lu Chiu Yuan (陸 九 淵), who composed the inscription
in Wang An Shih's spirit temple, says that those who think
such things cannot be said to know him.[2]

The imputation that in his youth he cultivated the
acquaintance of certain great families with a view to getting

[1] Liang Ch'i Ch'ao, p. 268.
[2] Liang Ch'i Ch'ao, p. 3.

his name known has been discussed already, the sting of such criticism being removed by the general opinion of those who recommended him that he was of a retiring disposition, and by his own confession that he had made few friends.

The offices he held under the reign of Jen Tsung were certainly not gained by flattery. For a glance at his Myriad Character Memorial shows that there was little of a flattering nature in that. It was rather a wholesome condemnation of the government.[1]

The suggestion that he refused to take the " Kuan Chih " examination so frequently because he hoped thereby to purchase a cheap notoriety has also been discussed, and we trust proved to be groundless.

The reasons he gave for his repeated refusals to accept the position of Keeper of the Emperor's Diary under Jen Tsung were that he feared his promotion to that office would excite envy and ill-feeling amongst those who were his senior in rank and position, and that it was necessary for him to return home to care for his mother.

There is nothing in all this to suggest that he had forgotten or relinquished his Confucian principles, or that he had flattered or fawned upon his superiors with a view to his own advancement.

The fact that he refused to take office under Ying Tsung has already been noted, with the reasons therefor, which can all be interpreted as being in line with Confucian ideals of filial piety and " awaiting the time ".

His advance to power under Shen Tsung was certainly very rapid. After his call to Court from the governorship of Chiang Ning Fu he was given the rank of Literary Councillor. While occupying that position he was granted the unusual favour of being admitted to Court audiences, and was frequently detained by the Emperor for private interviews. It seems as though it was in the course of these private conversations that Shen Tsung and Wang An Shih found their affinity. It was

---

[1] See Vol. I, Chap. VII.

then that Wang An Shih encouraged his Emperor to revive
the glorious era of Yao and Shun, and that he encouraged him
to think he had the capacity to do so. It was then, too, that he
reminded him that he would need to be very strong minded
and persevering if he was to make his purpose effective, and also
that he would need the help of such ministers as Kao, K'uei,
Chi, and Hsieh.

Now here perhaps, if anywhere, lurks a suggestion of flattery
and intrigue, of which his critics are only too ready to avail
themselves. It might be interpreted as flattery that Wang An
Shih encouraged his Emperor to think he had the capacity of
becoming a second Yao or Shun, and of intrigue in that he
suggested the need of some specially equipped minister such
as graced the Court in those halcyon days of long ago. For
it is open to the inference that Wang An Shih was recommending
himself as being such a minister.

Even if all this were true, would it be so very wrong for a
minister to make such suggestions, if he were at heart convinced
that he had the capacity to introduce fundamental and wide-
sweeping reforms, and that the principles of those old monarchs
were such as he felt suitable and adaptable to current needs?
We have found, as the narrative of his life and work has been
unfolded page by page and chapter by chapter, that both Shen
Tsung and Wang An Shih were sincere and serious, profoundly
so, in their attempt to inaugurate an era of benevolent, righteous,
and powerful rule.

It certainly appears as though Wang An Shih was convinced
that in Shen Tsung he had discovered a ruler who was sufficiently
interested in the condition of his country and people as to be
determined to give a trial to those political ideals which possessed
his own mind. It seems equally true that Shen Tsung felt that
in Wang An Shih he had found a minister who could help him
to carry out the great purpose of his life, namely, to wipe out
the disgrace which the cession of territory in former reigns
to the Ch'itans had brought upon the House of Sung, and to
atone for the impoverishment which the payment of enormous
sums by way of tribute to the enemy had occasioned his people.

On which topic the following quotation from Wang Ch'uan Shan (王 船 山) is apposite [1] :—

"Shen Tsung had thoughts to which he dare not give public utterance. His great officers were unable to enter into his plans or understand his purpose. So they failed to provide him with the advice and sympathy for which he was looking. Soon after he had assumed the throne he remarked to Wen Yen Po, ' A full Treasury is essential to the needs of our army and for our border policy.' This was before he had called Wang An Shih to Court and shows that his purpose was already fixed . . . He was unable to overlook the peril of the situation, and exercised his mind constantly with plans for its retrieval, but he was not free to speak openly of such matters to those most intimate with him at Court. For if he had made his purpose public he feared the enemy might be instigated to still more aggressive action. So he uttered such words as he could speak to Wen Yen Po and the others in such a way that they might gradually apprehend their significance. They certainly ought to have done so, and they ought to have shouldered their share of the Emperor's anxieties, and made suggestions and plans for the deliverance and stability of their country."

"No wonder," says Liang Ch'i Ch'ao,[2] "when Shen Tsung found that Wang An Shih was a man of kindred aim and purpose with himself, who had ideas as to how the financial resources of the country might be increased, and its military prestige enhanced, who was further of a heroic and persevering disposition, that he gave him his confidence, and that they became so intimate as monarch and minister that Shen Tsung himself spake of them as one man."

It is then not to " flattery and the vain desire for power " that we must look for the cause of Wang An Shih's rapid advancement to favour, but rather to this mutual affinity of nature and purpose that subsisted between him and his monarch.

Without the whole-hearted " backing " of the Emperor, it is certain that Wang An Shih would have failed to carry through

[1] Liang Ch'i Ch'ao, p. 101.
[2] Liang Ch'i Ch'ao, p. 102.

any of his measures.   The opposition was so strong, and in many cases so unreasonable, that he had at times to give the Emperor opportunity for reaffirming his confidence in him and his policy.   That accounts for his threats to resign at different stages in his high political career.   But the Emperor's trust was such that Wang An Shih was able to bring the national finances under their joint supervision and control, and also to bring military appointments under the civil authority.

The following quotation from Wang An Shih's own writings, after he had read the " Tz'u K'o Chuan " (刺 客 傳) or " Record of Famous Assassins ", is apropos :—

" These men, villains though they were, understood the necessity of awaiting the right time for the carrying out of their nefarious schemes.   How much more ought men who profess virtuous principles, to await the proper time for taking up office that they may have the opportunity for putting the same into effect." [1]

We conclude that Wang An Shih's rise to power under Shen Tsung and the confidence which the latter extended to him, was due entirely to the fact that the minister had found a ruler who could promote his ideas for the rehabilitation and prosperity of the State, and so the minister came forward in recognition of the fact that the " proper time " had arrived for him to do so.   Not to " flattery of his monarch ", nor to the " sacrifice of his principles ", but rather to the conviction that time and circumstance had combined in such a way as to constitute a heaven-sent call to devote himself to the public cause, must we look for the explanation of Wang An Shih's remarkable influence over Shen Tsung.

Wang An Shih was a man of high ideals, loving and considerate to his parents and family, loyal to his monarch, and grateful to his friends.   He was generous to his political foes, and did his utmost to maintain friendly relations with some who had proved traitorous to his cause.   He was a very strong-minded man, convinced that he had the right ideas for

[1] Works, vol. xvii, p. 31.

his day. This made him impatient with all who thought
differently from himself, and led to his losing the help and
co-operation of many of the famous men of the time. But
that was not altogether his own fault, as his opponents were
not always as reasonable and conscientious as they might
have been.

There is no evidence that he accumulated great wealth. He
was a man of frugal habits and simple ways. He donated his
residence for a temple and his lands for the support of a
monastery. He more than once referred to the possession of
his official emoluments during retirement as a burden upon
his conscience.[1]

He possessed a high sense of duty and discharged the
obligations of his position with the utmost energy and fidelity.
He believed in hard work. In an obituary notice in memory
of a friend Wu Fan (吳 蕃) he writes, " To develop one's
natural talent to the utmost is to discover the lot appointed
to us by heaven." [2] He himself was an outstanding illustration
of this. He laboured hard to equip himself for public office,
and having gained it, he laboured to the utmost of his capacity,
physical, mental, and spiritual, to justify the Emperor's
confidence, and to promote the welfare of the nation.

He was courageous in the expression of his opinions, and
persevered with his task against all opposition. Take for
illustration another obituary notice from his pen, namely that
to his friend Hsü P'ing (許 平), as follows :—

" He stood aside from conventional notions. He dared to
take his own course. Mockings, revilings, difficulties, all alike
failed to turn him from his path. He sought, not for the praise
of his contemporaries, but for the approval of posterity." [3]

Wang An Shih might have been writing that for himself.
One of his friends has said of him that " he regarded fame
as a fleeting cloud ". Certainly what praise he got from his
contemporaries was of the " fleeting " variety, and posterity

---

[1] Works, vol. x, p. 19 (地 閑 祿 厚 非 分 所 宜).
[2] Works, vol. xxiv, p. 17.
[3] Works, vol. xxiii, p. 29.

in the main has left him either utterly neglected or maliciously reviled.

It is the hope of the writer that what has been attempted in this present work, and particularly in this chapter, will help to restore to him his just place in the estimation of men, and will, in line with the similar efforts of his few friends in every generation, have done a little to remove from the minds of the present students " of things Chinese " any misconception which the traditional accounts of Wang An Shih may have tended to convey.

CHAPTER IX

NOTES ON THE "PIEN CHIEN LUN" (辯 姦 論) AND ASSOCIATED DOCUMENTS

(SYNOPSIZED FROM TS'AI SHANG HSIANG, vol. x, pp. 1–13)

THE " Pien Chien Lun " according to the " Sung Wen Chien " (宋 文 鑑) reads as follows :—

" Events pursue a fixed course, and the principles governing them function in a definite manner. But it is only the man of unshakable principle who can perceive the ultimate issue from the minutest omens. All men know that a red moon signifies wind, and that damp stones indicate the coming of rain. But the course of human affairs, and the connection between the principles of things and their manifestation, are often vague and difficult to discern. But amongst the phenomena about which it is so difficult to prophesy, the most difficult are those connected with the course of nature, and the results of the interaction of the two great natural principles (陰 陽). In this connection even the worthy and talented (賢 者) are not all equally well informed. The cause for their ignorance is to be found in the fact that their own preferences and prejudices disturb their minds, and the seeking of their personal advantage detracts from the influence of their example.

" Of old, Yang Shu Tzu, after an interview with Wang Yen (王 衍), said, ' This is the man who is certain to deceive the whole nation.'   Kuo Fen Yang (郭 汾 陽), after an interview with Lu Ch'i (盧 杞), said, ' If this man gets his way, our descendants will be exterminated.'   Beginning our discussion from this point, the facts (governing the course of affairs connected with these men) are discernible.

" In my opinion, Wang Yen had the appearance and a manner of speaking which could deceive the people and lead to his gaining (unjustly) some considerable fame. But as he was not

envious or desirous of getting on, and was of a complaisant
and easy-going disposition, I would say that if there had not
been such a person as the Emperor Hui of Chin (晉 惠 帝),
or even if a moderately good and intelligent emperor had taken
his place, that even a hundred or a thousand Wang Yens would
not have sufficed to throw the empire into confusion. The
wickedness of Lu Ch'i was without doubt capable of deceiving
the whole nation. But he was not a man of learning, and had
no attractive gifts. His manner and appearance were not such
as would excite comment, and his eloquence was not of that
order which deceives a whole nation. If it had not been for
the depravity and ignorance of Te Tsung, he would never have
been used in high office.

"So that in these two cases, we may say that the insight
regarding the careers of these two which Yang Shu Tzu
(羊 叔 子) and Kuo Fen Yang displayed, still allowed of the
possibility of things not turning out as they had predicted.

"But this man (of whom now I wish to speak) is for ever
quoting the words of Confucius and Lao Tzu, and professes
to be following in the footsteps of Pai I (伯 夷) and Shu
Ch'i (叔 齊). He is calling to his standard those scholars
who are out for fame, but who so far have failed to get their
way. They have conspired together to fabricate reports that
this man is of such a calibre that Yen Yuan or Meng Ko are
going to appear again in his person. But in reality he is a
cunning and dangerous enemy of the state, of extraordinary
ways, a Wang Yen and a Lu Ch'i combined. The ruin he will
effect is beyond the powers of speech. It is elementary in human
nature not to forget to wash one's face or launder one's clothes,
but this fellow is of different mould. He dresses like a banished
criminal, eats food which is only fit for dogs and pigs. With
towseled head and unwashed mien he descants of poetry and
history. Can such be termed 'natural'? When in everything a man does he shows an unnatural disposition, rarely
indeed does such a one fail to turn out to be a notorious villain.
He is a Shu Tiao (豎 刁), an I Ya (易 牙), and a K'ai
Fang (開 方). Such men as they, being of repute in their day,

were enabled to prosecute deep-laid schemes of villainy. So that even were a purposeful monarch on the throne, and ministers in power who were desirous above all things to secure men of character for the government services, it is possible for them to be so deceived as to recommend and employ them. There is no doubt at all that such a man will bring calamity upon the state, which will be even greater than that which was wrought by these three notorieties.

"Sun Tzu said, 'A skilful general attains to no great fame.' If this man fails to get employed in the government serivce, then my words will be regarded as extreme, and the man himself will regret his lack of opportunity. Who then could perceive that the ruin he could cause would be of this character? But if he does get employed in this way, the empire will certainly be ruined by him, and I shall get the reputation of a prophet, which will be regrettable."

Ts'ai Shang Hsiang criticizes this document as a whole as unworthy of a man of the literary and moral reputation of Su Hsün. He considers it quite impossible for him to have attributed to himself the qualities of penetration and foresight such as the document implies. Further, it is impossible to say to whom he refers as the worthy and talented man (賢 者). Prior to Su Hsün's death, Wang An Shih, although of some repute as an able official, had not attained to any position of influence, so that it could not have been of any public consequence what his preferences and prejudices were. Moreover, could a man who is termed "worthy" have such prejudices? Again, Lu Ch'i is affirmed to have been unable (but for the depravity and ignorance of Te Tsung) to have deceived the nation by his eloquence. But the historians affirm that he was of exceptional eloquence and that it was eminently feasible for him to deceive everyone. It should have been quite sufficient, also, for Su Hsün to compare Wang An Shih with Lu Ch'i, as he obstructed the worthy and loyal of his day, was hated by the whole nation, and termed a traitorous minister. In fact he is known as one of the greatest villains of the T'ang Dynasty. Why then should he add the name of Wang Yen to make the comparison complete ?   I Ya slaughtered his own child, Shu Tiao submitted to voluntary castration, K'ai Fang rejected his own father.   These are truly most unnatural things to have done, and later they were led by their Emperor's unbridled licentiousness to work havoc in the empire.   If Su Hsün specially wrote the Pien Chien Lun to prophesy the future of Wang An Shih, and deliberately selected these historical instances and personages as examples, I don't think much of his prophetic gifts!   Equally absurd is the reference to Wang An Shih's personal habits.   Was he a beggar or a wastrel that he should be so neglectful of his personal cleanliness ?

And to whom are we to apply the epithets " lovers of fame ", " disgruntled place-seekers ", and the like ?   Wang An Shih himself was regarded as a man of the highest character and ability by many of the most famous men of his time, like Ou Yang Hsiu, Tseng Tzu Ku, and Wen Yen Po.   His friends, though few, were all of the noblest character and best reputation. The only person to whom this might in any sense be applied maybe was Lü Hui Ch'ing, but it was not until 1058 that Ou Yang Hsiu introduced him to Wang An Shih, and then he spoke of him as a worthy and able man.   Further, Lü Hui Ch'ing did not become Wang's associate in government until 1069, three years after Su Hsün's death.

Chow Kung Chin (周 公 謹) says that according to the opinion of Ch'en Chih Chai (陳 直 齋) the Pien Chien Lun appears to have been written against Wang An Shih, but it may also conceivably refer to the two Ch'engs (二 程). Against this, however, Chu Hsi, in his desire to maintain the fair name of the Ch'engs, argued that the Pien Chien Lun was not originally written with any one person particularly in mind, but that later, when it was seen that Wang An Shih had made a failure of his government policy, writers began to apply the statements contained in it to him.

Ts'ai Shang Hsiang considers both these explanations unreasonable, as it was not until some considerable time after the death of Su Hsün that the Ch'eng school attained to any eminence, and it was not until the period Yuan Yu (1086–1091) that the various politico-philosophical schools engaged in open polemics. There would therefore be no reason for Su Hsün's making this document refer to the Ch'engs. Moreover, in the two other documents connected with this discussion, namely, the memorial inscription (墓 表) attributed to Chang Fang P'ing (張 方 平), and the letter of thanks for the same which is ascribed to Su Shih, the statement is definitely made that the Pien Chien Lun was written with Wang An Shih in mind. Moreover, the suggestion of Chu Hsi that later writers began to apply the statements in the document to Wang An Shih, after his policy had failed, is quite beside the mark, for an investigation of the record of the period of his political influence affords no case of parallelism with the personalities referred to in it. But all these guesses and suppositions were made because of their ignorance of the fact that this document is not by Su Hsün at all.

Ma Kuei Yü (馬 貴 與) in his work the Ching Chi K'ao (經 籍 考) says that " the edition of Su Hsün's works styled the Chia Yu Chi (嘉 祐 集) comprised fifteen volumes. But the editions now current are not styled by that name, and comprise twenty volumes. There have been added to the original such treatises as the Hung Fan (洪 範), Shih Fa (諡 法), etc., and two volumes of extra matter have been added at the end. These I consider represent additions by later hands. Recently I have procured a copy of his works reprinted by Chang T'ang (張 鐘), the Governor of T'aiyuanfu, of the Ming Dynasty (Chia Ching), which was based on the work preserved by the Wang family of Li Nan (灃 南). The name of this and the number of volumes are the same as the edition referred to in the Ching Chi K'ao, and yet in it there is no trace of the Pien Chien Lun." This strengthens the impression that the work cannot be by Su Hsün. In fact there is strong evidence, corroborated by Li Mu T'ang (李 穆 堂), that the work is a fabrication by a member of the Shao family (邵 伯 溫), i.e. Shao Pei Wen.

The following are the chief points raised by Li Mu T'ang, viz. " The Pien Chien Lun was first found in the Wen Chien

Lu (聞 見 錄) of the Shao family. This was published in
1132. Fifteen years later, Shen Fei (沈 斐) published two
addenda to Su Hsün's works, in which were included Chang
Fang P'ing's memorial document (墓 表) which specially
refers to the Pien Chien Lun, and also the letter of thanks from
Su Shih which was written specially on the subject of that
document.

My own opinion is that each of these three documents is a
fabrication, for as one compares the statements in these with
the actual events of the times, many discrepancies are revealed.
The account of it which is found in the Wen Chien Lu is word
for word the same as that found in the memorial notice, and yet
there is no acknowledgment of the fact of its being a quotation.
The reference in both these documents to Wang An Shih having
a large and influential band of associates cannot be true, as in
the days prior to Su Hsün's death, Wang An Shih had attained
to no influential position in connection with the government
such as would have made it feasible for him to have a large
following, and yet the documents referred to state that such was
the case as early as 1056–8 (Chia Yu Ch'u 嘉 祐 初). The
further reference to the document appointing Wang An Shih
to the Grand Council, with its supposed laudation of Wang
An Shih as a sage, must have emanated from the Emperor Shen
Tsung. The actual appointment took place at the earliest in
1069 when Wang An Shih was appointed vice-Grand
Councillor, but Su Hsün died in 1066. Again, in the memorial
notice Chang Fang P'ing styles Su Hsün 'hsien sheng'
(先 生), but Chang was older than Su Hsün, and of superior
status, officially, so to style him in that particular way was
quite contrary to the custom prevalent in the times of the
Northern Sung. It was, moreover, quite unlike Chang Fang
P'ing to be so subservient.

I suspect that the funeral notice and the Pien Chien Lun are
both fabrications of the Shao family. For on the death of Su
Hsün, Ou Yang Hsiu composed the funeral notice, and Tseng
Tzu Ku wrote out the epitaph. Tseng Tzu Ku states expressly
that Ou Yang Hsiu's document was placed within the tomb,

and that his own epitaph was carved upon the tombstone. So it would be very unusual to call for a ' mu piao ' (funeral notice) as well.

Note further that in the ' mu piao ' there occurs the phrase ' Shu wu jen ' (蜀 無 人), whereas in the letter of thanks from Su Shih the very similar phrase ' Ch'in wu jen ' occurs. This strongly points to the conclusion that both these documents are from one pen, i.e. from Shao."

What is absolutely incontrovertible is that in the life record of Wang An Shih there is no suggestion of evil purposes or self-seeking. On the contrary, he was quite obviously keenly devoted to the welfare of his country, and determined to save it from its weakness and peril. All this is in flat contradiction to the statements of the Pien Chien Lun. He may not have had the best method of going about his work, but in aim he was absolutely sincere. The epithet " Chien " (姦) " wicked " or " treacherous " is quite inapplicable to him.

Before going further it will be well to give the substance of the " mu piao " of Chang Fang P'ing and also Su Shih's letter, which are referred to above. The important section of the first document reads as follows :—

" In the early years of Chia Yu (1056–8) the reputation of Wang An Shih began to spread, and his partisans were extremely influential. The commission appointing him to the Grand Council stated that there had been few like him since the dawn of history, and that reports had been spread about which made him practically equivalent to a sage. Ou Yang Hsiu also spoke highly of him, and exhorted Su Hsün to cultivate his acquaintance. Wang An Shih was also desirous to make friends with Su Hsün. But the latter said, ' I perceive that this man is of such an unnatural disposition that he is practically certain to bring disaster upon the state.'

" After the death of Wang An Shih's mother, all the great officials, with the sole exception of Su Hsün, went in person to present their condolences. He stayed at home, and wrote out the Pien Chien Lun. Contemporaries when they saw this document, demurred, and regretted its extreme character. But three years after the death of Su Hsün, when Wang An Shih became influential in matters of government, they began to regard the statements in this document as true. . . ."

On this Ts'ai Shang Hsiang comments as follows :—

" Ou Yang Hsiu and Tseng Tzu Ku had each composed funeral notices for Su Hsün, which was a sufficient guarantee that his name would persist, but to add the ' mu piao ' (墓 表) of Chang Fang P'ing and the letter of thanks from Su Shih, which concern themseves chiefly with the Pien Chien Lun, is not only derogatory to Su Hsün, but also to the composers of the two documents referred to. The former was acknow-ledged as a writer of considerable fame, and to attribute this badly written and confused composition to him is certainly not to his credit. What is stranger still is that he should have included the supposed words of the Imperial commission appointing Wang An Shih to the Grand Council, an event which happened four years after the death of Su Hsün, and when, moreover, Chang Fang P'ing was also at Court. So it is incredible that he should have committed such a blatant anachronism as that.

" For six or seven hundred years no one pointed out this error, but Li Mu T'ang having once exposed it, it was also found that in the Ming Ch'en Yen Hsing Lu (名 臣 言 行 錄) of Chu Hsi, in recording the biography of Su Hsün, that the editors had left out the twenty-four characters referring to the Com-mission appointing Wang to the Grand Council, but had included the rest of the ' mu piao ' references to him. It would seem therefore as though they realized the erroneous character of this reference, but although they had omitted it with the one object of concealing its false character, they just simply added to the evidence for exposing the same."

The letter of thanks which Su Shih is credited with, is as follows :—

" I respectfully acknowledge the second copy of the funeral notice, with its special emphasis on the Pien Chien Lun. As I read this document, I could not restrain my tears, and words fail me. My father died comparatively young, and it was only

in his later years that he attained to any fame. Although his
contemporaries acknowledged him as teacher, yet in the main
they failed to fully comprehend his public utterances and
writings. It is all the less likely that they should understand
the ideas which he had not put formally into speech or writing.
You are the only one who completely understood him and
believed in him. Although that may be regarded as an unfortunate circumstance, yet ' being known by few was considered estimable by Lao Tzu '. When the Pien Chien Lun
was first published, both my brother and myself both regretted
its extreme character, so no wonder others were of the same
opinion. Probably you thought the same when you first
saw it. But since you first took up the matter at court, and it
got inserted in the histories, although it may still be possible
that some may not know of it, later generations will have it as
an imperishable record. Unless you had included it in your
funeral notice, it might still be possible that some would not
believe in the statements made, but after all whether they
believe or not is a matter of small consequence. But if the
nation was to be allowed to remain in ignorance of the deceitful
character of this man's despicable work it would call forth regrets
from later generations that ' Ch'in had no man ' (to expose
such). This shows why it was necessary for the ' mu piao '
to be written, and accounts for my tears. Allow me to renew
my thanks. . . ."

Ts'ai's comment on this is as follows :—

" It is only right that a son should give thanks for the efforts
of any worthy man to make plain the really virtuous character
of a father, to whose character and achievements full justice had
not been done. If Wang An Shih had done despite to the
teaching of his father or deliberately attempted to defame his
literary work, then it might be reasonable to believe that tears
would be wrung from the son when some kind friend exposed
the outrage and revealed his father's virtue. If, again, Wang
An Shih had been hated by Su Shih for some other reason, it
might also be credible. But to give such importance to a
document like the Pien Chien Lun, is hardly the conduct that

one would expect of the filial son of a noble father. If this is really Su Shih's composition then I don't think much of Su Shih.

" The Pien Chien Lun is a private work, the origin of which is a debatable point. For Su Shih to say that it had been discussed at Court and inserted into the histories is a baseless assertion. Four years after the death of Su Hsun, Wang An Shih came into power, and the whole court resounded with criticism of the new laws, but it is inconceivable that they should be concerned about such a document as the Pien Chien Lun. How could Su Shih say that unless Chang Fang P'ing had composed the 'mu piao' later generations would regret that 'there was no man in Ch'in'? Moreover, Su Hsun, Chang Fang P'ing, and Su Shih are all famous essayists and men of good repute. But such documents as the Pien Chien Lun, the 'mu piao', and the letter of thanks are of such a worthless character, that if they are to be attributed to these men, then their literary and moral reputation may be considered to have been lost."

Ts'ai goes into still further detail to show that the Pien Chien Lun is a fabrication, and indicates several sources from from which extracts have been taken and combined to make the resulting composite document. These are the " Chieh Yin Pi Chi" (芥 隱 筆 記) of Kung I Chcng (龔 頤 正), the " Po Chai Pien " (泊 宅 編) of Fang Yun (方 勺), the Wen Chien Lu (聞 見 錄) of Shao (the fish-bait incident), the " Pi Shu Lu Hua " (避 暑 錄 話) of Yeh Meng Te (葉 夢 得), the indictment of Wang An Shih by Lü Hui (呂 誨), and a tract by Su Hsun on Kuan Chung (管 仲 論).

These are outlined in Ts'ai Shang Hsiang, vol. x, pp. 1–13, to which the reader desirous of following up the matter in further detail is referred.

CHAPTER X

WANG AN SHIH'S REFORM POLICY

IN the chapter on Wang An Shih's character, we reached the conclusion that the slanderous statements which have found their place in the traditional records cannot be substantiated, and that all the evidence is in favour of his having been a man of pure life and sincere purpose. His literary ability is generally acknowledged to be of a very high order. As an official in the provinces and in minor posts at the capital, he earned a great reputation for devotion to duty, and for administrative ability of exceptional character. But after his assumption of high office under Shen Tsung the policy he inaugurated in collaboration with him, but with which his own name will be for ever associated, met with severe criticism and opposition, and for various reasons all the more famous and influential officials at the Court were compelled to resign their appointments at the capital. But in spite of that fact, until the time of Shen Tsung's death in 1085, Wang An Shih's policy was maintained with little or no change for a period of sixteen or seventeen years.

It is our purpose in this chapter to estimate the character of his political policy. We shall endeavour to evaluate it in essence and results, try to account for the opposition which was aroused and which continued with such persistence, attempt to explain the reason for its abrogation, and assess the popular judgment upon it as represented by Chu Hsi [1] and others.

In a discussion of this character the nature of the times in which Wang An Shih lived must be taken into account. Dr. Ferguson [2] terms him a product of the age in which he lived. As a whole chapter has been devoted to this subject, it will be sufficient here merely to summarize the main

---

[1] Chu Hsi, Complete Works, Discussion on Wang An Shih, vol. lix.

[2] *Journal of North China Branch of Royal Asiatic Society*, Article on Wang An Shih by Dr. J. C. Ferguson, vol. xxxv.

characteristics of the period, in so far as they may be regarded as having contributed to the shaping of his policy.

Briefly, then, the features of his time are as follows, viz. : Foreign aggression in the north and north-west, accompanied by the military weakness and economic stringency of the Sungs. A strong tendency to conservatism and the pursuance of a policy of *laissez-faire* on the part of the great majority of the official clan. A dearth of capable and honest administrators, and the lack of an efficient system whereby this defect could be remedied. A low scale of salaries for those engaged in the various government services conducing to the prevalence of peculation and graft in official circles. A tendency amongst the Court officers to form factions. The existence of a powerful capitalistic class upon whom the poorer farmers and traders were dependent for the maintenance of their livelihood, and from whose manipulations of finance the government treasury was losing large sums of possible revenue. These are some of the more prominent characteristics of the age in which Wang An Shih lived.

It is also of first importance to consider the character and purpose of the Emperor Shen Tsung, for they have vital connection with Wang An Shih's policy.

The Dynastic History of Sung, which, as has frequently been pointed out, reflects in the main the opinions of Wang An Shih's political enemies, gives the following résumé of Shen Tsung's character, viz. :—

" He sought for public criticism, investigated the conditions under which the people lived, was merciful to the poor and aged, and generous to the distressed." [1]

The nature of the Dynastic Histories being such as has been described above, and containing as they do many signs of dissatisfaction with Shen Tsung for associating himself so closely with Wang An Shih and his policy, it is only natural to infer from the above description, as Liang Ch'i Ch'ao does, that Shen Tsung must have been a really great ruler, one of the

---

[1] Dynastic History of Sung. Shen Tsung Chi Tsan (神 宗 紀 贊).

greatest since the Ch'in and Han Dynasties.[1] Otherwise the traditional histories could not ascribe to him such characteristics, nor is it likely that he would have been granted the title of " Shen " (神) or " August " as his historical designation.

His purpose was revealed soon after he had ascended the throne, for then it is related that he remarked to Wen Yen Po, " In view of the situation on the frontiers a full treasury is essential for military exigencies." [2] His ancestor in the imperial line, Sung T'ai Tsu (宋 太 祖), had hoped to inflict a crushing defeat upon the northern barbarians, and with that object in view had created a special bank, styled the " Ching Fu Tien " (景 福 殿), in which he had planned to assemble a sum equal to two million bales of raw silk for military expenses. Shen Tsung soon after his accession changed the name of this bank, and composed the following poem in honour of the occasion :—

> " The five dynasties in succession decayed,
> While the northern hordes exceedingly prospered,
> I Tsu (藝 祖) established the Imperial line,
> And formed his plans for revenge.
> This special bank he forthwith set up,
> With intent to collect a great army,
> Can I, his successor, ever forget,
> His great and noble purpose."

Later on, Shen Tsung ordered the establishment of thirty-two special banks, in which he intended to accumulate large sums from the revenue surplus. On this occasion he wrote the following lines in commemoration, viz. :—

> " Far into the night I wrack my brain,
> Proud of the sacred task,
> Committed unto me,
> Anxious too,
> For I am doubtful of our prowess in arms.
> When, oh when, will victory be ours ? "

---

[1] Liang Ch'i Ch'ao, p. 100.
[2] Liang Ch'i Ch'ao, p. 102.

Wang Ch'uan Shan says, " Shen Tsung had thoughts to which he dare not give public utterance. The great officers round the throne failed to appreciate his real intent, and so failed to give him the counsel for which he was seeking."

It is evident from this that Shen Tsung's plans were beyond the understanding of his immediate advisers, or at least, beyond their will or capacity to execute. " No wonder," says Liang Ch'i Ch'ao, " when Shen Tsung made the acquaintance of Wang An Shih, and discovered the type of man he was, that he regarded him as his own right hand." [1]

Wang An Shih had the very ideas which he deemed necessary for the carrying out of his great purpose of redeeming the national shame of many generations, and possessed moreover the right character for putting them into effect. It was but natural, in such circumstances, that the ruler should elect such a man to be his high minister of State, and extend to him his unreserved confidence and wholehearted trust.

Shen Tsung then had as his great purpose the strengthening of the military resources of the empire with a view to thwarting the aggressive tactics of his neighbours in the north and north-west, and even of reclaiming territory which once had been under the sway of the empire in the glorious days of the T'ang Dynasty. It was essential as a corollary to this that the finances of the national treasury should also be greatly increased.

Wang An Shih entered with full sympathy into the plans of the Emperor, and as his high minister of State it was but natural that he should give prime attention to financial and military matters. Chu Hsi makes this a point of severe criticism.[2] In so doing he evidently had in mind the traditional conception of the duties of a high minister of State, in accordance with which such an officer should seek to influence the Emperor by the exposition of moral principles and the rectification of his conduct so that he would, as a matter of course, institute laws which would be both just and beneficent, and make his

---

[1] Liang Ch'i Ch'ao, p. 102.
[2] Liang Ch'i Ch'ao, p. 248. See also " T'ung Chien ", Yuan Yu, 1st year, 4th month.

country prosperous. In line with this traditional conception
it would be beneath the dignity of a high minister of State
to meddle in such mundane matters as finance and military
expeditions.

It is reported that Wang An Shih, shortly after his appointment to high office, suggested to Shen Tsung the possibility
of his becoming another Yao and Shun. It was not then foreign
to Wang An Shih's ideas that he should use moral suasion or
emphasize ethical principles in his relationship with the
Emperor, and in the formulation of his policy. His various
memorials to the throne are sufficient evidence of that. But
at the same time, he perceived that the state of the country
demanded practical reforms. So while not neglecting the
importance of ethical considerations, he devoted himself to
the creation of a number of political measures tending towards
the material prosperity of the empire. "In each and every
case," says Liang Ch'i Ch'ao, "his idea was to enhance the
prosperity of the state and to improve the people's economic
condition." [1]

Ssu Ma Kuang criticized Wang An Shih as being of
"unpractical mind", and as "being unacquainted with
practical affairs". But the most cursory glance at the character
of the various reform measures which he promoted is sufficient
to disprove such assertions. He may not have given sufficient
consideration to the fact that there were not enough high-
minded men in the government service to ensure the success
of his different projects, or he may have overlooked the fact
that as his measures in the main were directed against the
wealthy and influential classes, they would raise such opposition
that his measures must eventually fail to produce those
permanent results which he expected. Or again he may not
have given sufficient thought to the fact that some of his
measures would interfere with the customary and easy-going
ways of the common people, and that this would make many
of his regulations irksome to them. If that is what Ssu Ma

---

[1] Liang Ch'i Ch'ao, p. 105.

Kuang meant by his " being unpractical " or " unacquainted
with practical affairs " he may perhaps be considered justified
in making the statement. But if he meant that Wang An Shih
was ignorant of the need of his country, and lacked the ideas
for meeting that need in practical fashion, his criticism is quite
beside the mark. Chu Hsi remarks that " the times called for
reform and that Wang An Shih had the right ideas for his
day ".[1]

It is characteristic of Wang An Shih that he combined moral
enthusiasm with a " penchant " for practical politics, as we
trust will appear in the course of the discussion. He may not
have secured the perfect method of dealing with his country's
ills, but he certainly set to work in sincere and practical fashion
to find a remedy for them.

Possibly Ssu Ma Kuang meant that Wang's policy was
" idealistic " and therefore " impracticable ". Critics often
refer to Wang An Shih's theories as " unusual ", " utopian ",
and the like. Liang Ch'i Ch'ao says that his measures were
closely akin to those advocated by State socialists, and such as
modern governments find extremely difficult to carry out.[2]
Certainly when one considers the vast extent of the Chinese
empire, the lack of communications, the ignorance of the
people on matters political, and other features characteristic
of the empire nearly a thousand years ago, this experiment
of Wang An Shih may be classed as " idealistic " in character.
But it is not on that ground to be regarded as " impracticable ".
For, as we shall see, in spite of all the difficulties that have been
enumerated, a certain measure of success attended his efforts.
Further, if only his political opponents had maintained those
features which the trial period of Shen Tsung's reign had shown
to be both " practicable " and " advantageous ", eliminating
only those points which experience had shown to be either
" impracticable " or " deleterious ", it is quite probable that a
permanent contribution of great value would have been made

[1] Chu Hsi, Complete Works, vol. lix, p. 24.
[2] Liang Ch'i Ch'ao, p. 109.

towards the solution of the economic problems of the Chinese people.

Holcombe asserts that " basically, the ills of China are of an economic character ".[1]   It is true that in Wang An Shih's day, the chief question facing the mind of any serious statesman was the economic condition of the country.   We have shown that the national budget was showing a serious deficit every year,[2] that the government officials were poorly paid,[3] and that the aggressive tactics of border foes called for ever increasing expenditure on the military forces of the empire. In such circumstances it was inevitable that a man of Wang An Shih's character should devote prime attention to financial and military matters.   Chu Hsi makes this to be his great crime, but when all the factors of his times are taken into consideration, the fact that he did so is greatly to his credit.

Let us now examine his method of dealing with the basic problem, namely, that of finance.   His great object was to provide the government with increased revenue.   According to Ssu Ma Kuang the only way to do this was to increase the taxation of the people.   Against this Wang An Shih proposed his theory that the revenue could be increased without adding to the burdens of the people.   Although this seemed to Ssu Ma Kuang " impracticable " and " unheard of ",[4] Wang An Shih proceeded to demonstrate its eminent " practicability ".

The obvious thing to suggest in a time of national financial stringency is " economy ".   This naturally appealed to Wang An Shih and his political opponents alike as one way out of their difficulties.   But while men like Ssu Ma Kuang were content with the suggestion, and with pointing out the difficulty of making any substantial reductions immediately, Wang An Shih got to work, and actually effected considerable reductions in a very short space of time.   For this Shen Tsung must take a share of the credit, for the reduction on the national budget

---

[1] *The Chinese Revolution*, by A. N. Holcombe.
[2] See Chap. VI, Vol. II, of this work.
[3] See Vol. I, p. 65.
[4] Vol. I, p. 106.

was effected largely, if not altogether, on the various items under the heading of Court expenditure.[1]

Another method which suggested itself, and which to some extent Wang An Shih adopted, was to increase the revenue by enlarging the borders of the Imperial territory, thereby adding to the population of the empire, and naturally increasing the revenues by extending the poll-tax to larger numbers. Concurrently it was hoped that the area of arable land would be greatly extended by schemes of colonization of the border territories in the north-west. Tribes of the south and west which had so far maintained their economic independence he sought to bring under the authority of the Imperial Court, and impose regular taxation upon them. These objects were all included in his military policy.

Economy, however, could only be regarded as a minor expedient, and there were obvious limits to the possibilities of extending the national territory. Wang An Shih had something more fundamental and permanent to suggest for increasing the revenues. He felt that the resources of the country could be increased. Ssu Ma Kuang had said that this was impossible, that the available resources had already been fully exploited, and divided between the people and the government in due proportion. So that as he saw it, any addition to the government's portion would mean a deprivation of the people's share, which would be inimical to their livelihood.[2]

Wang An Shih, however, proceeded to demonstrate that the government could increase its revenues without injury to the livelihood of the people; in fact his method was to increase the productive capacity of the people, so as to improve their livelihood on the one hand and add to the government revenues on the other.

Nowadays we should talk of developing the mineral resources of the country, improved methods of production, and the like. China is well known to be very rich in coal and iron, with lesser

[1] Vol. I, p. 126.
[2] Vol. I, p. 65.

reserves of copper, lead, zinc, tin, and silver. In a comparatively
short space of time she has become the leading producer of the
world for antimony and tungsten.[1] But in the days of Wang
An Shih there was very little demand for these metals, except
for the production of coins, weapons, utensils, ornaments, etc.
The time was too early to consider any vast industrial development which could have called for the use of these metals.

Commerce and agriculture were the two great national
assets of the time, and it was to these that Wang An Shih gave
prime attention. The small trader represented the great bulk
of the merchant population. Wang An Shih by the promulgation of the " Trade and Barter Measure " sought to free these
from disabilities such as the accumulation of stocks represented
by buying these up in the name of the government. In this
way he hoped to encourage increased production, and effect
a better trade situation. In addition, by the loan system which
was a part of this measure, he sought to help them to continue
production in times of difficulty. For by this system they
were offered loan facilities at much lower rates of interest than
they would have to pay normally to the money-lenders.

Further, he encouraged trade with the border tribes by his
scheme of colonization in the north-west, and by the lifting
of the embargo on the export of copper. These were all
measures designed to increase the financial resources of the
empire.

For the farmers, whose livelihood and economic prosperity
was still more vital to his programme, he devised many schemes.
His Agricultural Loans Measure was intended not only to
relieve the farming class of the intolerable burden of interest
which the callous money-lenders exacted of them in difficult
times, but also to ensure that the work of agriculture should
be regularly conducted without such hindrances as lack of
capital involved. His irrigation projects, and measures for
river control, were designed to ensure an adequate water

---

[1] See *Annals of the American Academy of Political and Social Science*, Nov.,
1930. Article on the " Economic Significance of the Mineral Wealth of China ",
by John W. Frey.

supply on the one hand, and to prevent flooding on the other. In this way also large tracts of land would be reclaimed and brought under the plough. The farming class was helped in other ways too. His Public Services Act exempted the lower classes (of whom the farmers formed the great bulk) from the exactions of the old Labour Conscription Acts. They were thus able to devote themselves more thoroughly and regularly to their work on the fields.

These, too, were methods of increasing the nation's resources.

In other directions, a saving of expenditure was brought about, thus increasing the revenue at the disposal of the government. His "Equitable Transport Measure" was designed to save the heavy expenditure on conveying the tribute grain from the distant parts of the empire, and he prevented great losses on the actual transport of grain by employing merchant boats in competition with the Government Transport Services. Reference has been made to the economy he made on Court expenditure. His Militia Act aimed at the reduction of the regular army with correspondingly less expenditure on the same, while at the same time providing for the training of far greater numbers of militia to take their place.

Then his various taxation measures were all devised with a view to increasing revenue. The great object of his "Equitable Land Tax Measure" was that all land from which taxation could legitimately be derived should be made subject to taxation, while at the same time ensuring that taxation should be fairly apportioned according to the relative productivity of the land. His Public Services Act aimed at a more equitable assessment of the people, bringing many classes under the Act who had hitherto been exempt, and ensuring that those who could pay did pay proportionately to their finanical assets, while those who were too poor to contribute to the national exchequer were relieved of their responsibility for so doing.

From this brief sketch of his economic policy it will be seen that in aim, at least, the measures devised leave nothing to be desired. Each was definitely constructive, in that either economy or increased productivity was the objective in each case. The only classes who were called upon to pay increased levies were the wealthy, whom he conceived as having been too leniently dealt with hitherto, whereas the measures were uniformly devised for the relief of the poorer classes. So interpreted they were equitable, and even beneficent, as well as efficient measures of finance, and Wang An Shih may be considered to have justified his contention that there were ways of increasing the revenue without increasing the taxation. His economic policy, as far as its aim is concerned, we may then pronounce sound and good.

But that is not sufficient. We must examine the measures in their actual operation and investigate their effect before pronouncing final judgment upon them. If Chu Hsi is correct, these very measures were deemed cruel and oppressive, so much so that the people clamoured to be saved from them, as they had deprived them of all joy in life.

It is necessary, therefore, that this statement should be fully examined as to its truth or falsity, and with that in view it will be desirable to look at each of the Measures in detail, first investigating the nature and implications of the measures, and then endeavouring to estimate the value of each in actual results as far as such are ascertainable, allowing room in our judgment for the opinions of important critics of a contemporary and later age.

We will begin with the Public Services Act (免 役 法). This was devised with the idea of abolishing the old system of Labour Conscription for State services which had hitherto been operative, and supplanting it by a system of paid labour for all types of public work. The funds for this were to be gained from taxation according to property qualification, the poorer classes being entirely exempt from taxation on this account. It partakes of the nature of the Income Tax Measure so common in Western countries at the present day As such it must have been welcome to the poorer classes at least, for not only were they exempted from taxation in connection with it, but all the services which they might be called upon to render

for the officials were to be paid for. Under the older Labour
Conscription Act the poorer classes would have been called
upon at the whim of the local official for such services as road-
making, dyke construction, porterage and transport, escorting,
the work of servants, doorkeepers, scavengers, and the like.
The demands of the public services did not always coincide with
the needs of agriculture, and doubtless much interference with
farming pursuits resulted, in addition to the fact that no pay
could be expected. The poorer classes, then, ought to have had
no reason for complaining that this measure operated in any
oppressive way.

The middle and higher classes under the old Conscription
Act had been liable for services of a clerical, commercial,
financial, and administrative character. They had either undertaken these themselves, or had hired others to do the work for
them. But it was their responsibility, and not only did they
receive no certain remuneration for this work, but they were
often involved in heavy financial losses. Under the Public
Services Act these classes provided a definite sum of money
for the maintenance of these services, and they themselves were
eligible to receive the remuneration for such work which was
now provided for by the Act of Wang An Shih.

It is conceivable that even these classes were better off under
this Act than under the old one. In fact Ssu Ma Kuang said
that the richer classes were better off under this Act than they
had been under the old, and that was a reason why in his opinion
it should be abrogated.[1] Tseng Pu affirmed that all classes
were better off, if the hitherto exempted classes were excepted.

In all probability the real " grouse " about this measure came
from this hitherto privileged section of the populace. It will
be remembered that under the old Conscription Act, officials,
priests, and families with one male member, or none, had been
exempted from all liability for the public services. Under the
new Act of Wang An Shih, all these were brought within the
meaning of the Act, provided that their property qualification

---

[1] See Vol. I, p. 236.

demanded it. These were, as one critic pointed out, the class who could make themselves heard. Especially in the case of the officials was this true. Wang An Shih was also warned that once this proposal became law, the local officials would be deprived of their most powerful instrument of intimidation and graft. It is only natural to expect that the officials, who had hitherto been exempt from paying this tax themselves and who were being deprived of their most lucrative medium of " graft ", should find the new Act inconvenient, and raise their voices in protest.

As regards the priests, these were usually attached to temples and monasteries, which possessed " glebe-lands " and received considerable income from gifts of devotees and local residents. Their quota would doubtless come from these sources, and little hardship would be experienced by them. The families with only one male member or with no male at all would only be taxed if their financial standing rendered them liable. So looking at this Measure all round, it is difficult to see where it could be termed oppressive or injurious.

Against the testimony of Ssu Ma Kuang, that the Measure operated to the detriment of the poorer classes, we can place the witness of Su Shih and Su Che, who after ten years of actual experiment, protested strongly against the abrogation of the new Measure. The evidence of these two is all the stronger from the fact that both had formerly been powerful advocates of Labour Conscription. Now the former was prepared to say that " even a sage could not improve upon the hiring system ".[1]

The only points they could urge against it were that money was being collected in excess of the actual needs of the public services in the various districts, and that city residents were being asked for more than their legitimate share. It was urged that half the rates charged should have sufficed. In this, as in other Measures where collections from the people were to be made by local officials, it is probable that malpractice occurred,

[1] Vol. I, p. 238.

and that if the Measure was operated in any way detrimentally to the livelihood of the people, it would be due to the character of the local officials rather than to the intrinsic character of the Measure itself.

The other great criticism levelled against this Measure was that paid agents of the government, like police and those in charge of public funds, etc., would of necessity prove unreliable. But there was plenty of testimony on the other side. Moreover, one of the provisions of the Act was that guarantors should be found for all who were holding responsible positions.

Ssu Ma Kuang also made much of the point that under the New Measure certain classes were taxed which had formerly been exempt. He must have been referring to city residents of the fourth and fifth classes. It does not follow, however, that the Measure was oppressive on that account. It should also be noted that when Ssu Ma Kuang revived the Labour Conscription Measure he retained certain features of Wang An Shih's Act, such as the " Aid Money ", payment of Official Agents, and permitting those classes liable for services who could afford it to hire substitutes.

Taking this Measure as a whole, it would seem to have been generally acceptable and beneficial. The salaries of officials were increased by it, while the numbers of farmers employed on public works were considerably reduced. This freed greater numbers for agriculture. Further, considerable revenue accrued to the government, while at the same time the public services were efficiently maintained. It was financially sound and ethically just. What more can be expected of a political measure ?

It was the abrogation of this particular Measure by Ssu Ma Kuang which caused Wang An Shih most grief. He felt that this Measure at least ought not to have been rescinded.

The Agricultural Loans Measure was designed to help the farmer to tide over the spring season, when his resources were usually getting low. Formerly they contracted loans with the money-lenders at exorbitant rates, or refrained from doing so, in which case their fields were allowed to lie fallow, and they were compelled to face the prospect of no crops and consequent poverty. From the farmer's point of view, this Measure should have been most welcome. It is true they had to pay interest to the government instead of to the money-lender, but the rate was definitely fixed at 24 per cent per annum, which was considerably less than they would have had to pay to others.

Wang An Shih affirmed that the government expected no revenue from the working of these loans, but that it was impossible to work the Measure without this amount of interest, as this was required to meet the salaries of officials engaged and other expenses.

This Measure, however, was fruitful of great criticism and opposition on the part of prominent officials of the time. Han Wei Kung and Ou Yang Hsiu [1] pointed out certain defects in its operation, and the latter refused to distribute the loans in his own district of Ch'ing Chow Fu. The main ground of their opposition seemed to be that the local officials in charge of the Measure were compelling people to take the loans against their will. Compulsion of this sort was prohibited by the government, but one can readily perceive that it was impossible to make such prohibition effective.

There was also allowance for reduction of the interest on the loans in poor years, and for the distribution of free relief in times of absolute dearth. But it was pointed out by critics that the officials would in such cases compel the people to take out further loans instead of granting these privileges, and that led to the piling up of debts which they could not possibly repay.

Wang An Shih, in his memorial on Five Matters,[2] emphasized the dangers inherent in the working of this Measure, chiefly on the ground that the officials would not administer it according to his own ideas. Evidently this was the main cause of opposition. It must not be forgotten that Li Ts'an had administered the Measure successfully in Shensi, and Wang An Shih had certainly carried out the idea in Chin Hsien to the great gratification of the people.

[1] For Ou Yang Hsiu's Memorial see Ts'ai Shang Hsiang, vol. xvi, pp. 3–5.
[2] Works, vol. x, pp. 2 and 3.

Another difficulty pointed out by critics in connection with this measure was doubtless very real, namely that the poor people were only too ready to contract the loans, but not so ready to repay. This had led to the system of demanding guarantors from the local gentry, who naturally resented having to pay up considerable sums for absconding neighbours.

But evidently the greatest cause for objection, which could probably be substantiated, was the compelling of people to take loans against their will, and for this the local officials were again responsible. It was considered creditable for them to disburse large sums, and they were only too keen to get the " kudos " which would accrue from such " success ".

There are, however, many things to be urged in favour of the Measure, and many witnesses can be produced in evidence of its popularity and successful working.

There is the testimony of Wang Kuang Lien, transport officer of Ho Pei, that " all the people are not only pleased but grateful ", and that of Li Ting, who said that the people in the south were all gratified by its promulgation. There is evidence from Wang An Shih's own correspondence that the people welcomed the Measure and that success had attended its operation. He wrote to Tseng Kung Li [1] (曾 公 立) that " it was thought that the people would not ask for the loans, but it was found that they welcomed the opportunity to do so ". To quote again his memorial on Five Matters, he writes :— " Of old the poor paid interest to the money-lenders, but now they pay to the officials. The latter demand lighter rates of interest, and the people are thereby saved much distress." Again, in a letter written to Shen Tsung after Wang An Shih had retired from office at the capital, he writes, " We prepared the Measure most carefully before promulgating it, and despite much criticism we may be said to have attained to success." [2]

Such criticisms as these, however, may justly be discounted

---

[1] Works, vol. xviii, p. 9.

[2] Works, vol. xv, p. 2. 收 功 於 異 論 之 後 taken from 賜 元 豐 勅 令 格 式 表.

as coming either from members of Wang An Shih's own party
or from the promoters of the Measure.

Fortunately, criticism of a favourable character from other
sources is available. Take the following quotation from Chu
Hsi, found in his work, the " Chin Hua She Ts'ang Chi "
(金 華 社 倉 記)[1] :—

" After an investigation into the opinions of former worthies,
and looking at the matter also from the standpoint of a modern
critic, who has experimented with it, I am bound to admit that
the idea of the Agricultural Loans Measure cannot be termed
' bad '. It was, however, faulty in that money was distributed
instead of grain ; that the distribution centres were confined
to the ' hsien ' and not set up in the villages ; that it was
administered by the government officials solely, and not in
co-operation with the local residents ; and that the aim before
the promoters was to accumulate profits as quickly as possible,
instead of being chiefly concerned with the welfare of the
people.

" This accounts for the fact that Wang An Shih could
administer it successfully in one ' hsien ' (縣) and yet failed
to administer it successfully throughout the empire. The fact
that the measure had good possibilities accounts for the further
fact that my master, Ch'eng Tzu (子 程 子), who at first
severely criticized it, was later on compelled to change his mind,
and came to regret his extreme utterances on the subject."

For the moment we will confine ourselves to the change of
mind on the part of Ch'eng Hao,[2] which is extremely important,
inasmuch as it represents the conversion of one of the most
extreme critics of the Measure in Wang An Shih's time. For
he had then written, " It is impossible to carry into effect a
measure which everyone regards as impracticable." Later on,
on Chu Hsi's evidence, he had come to regret such utterances.
This must have been because he had come to see that the
Measure after all was practicable, and that it had within it the
possibilities of successful and beneficent operation.

[1] Chu Hsi, Complete Works, vol. lxiv, p. 11.
[2] i.e. Ch'eng Tzu (程 子) above.

We shall deal with Chu Hsi's own criticism later on.

When Ssu Ma Kuang came into power he abrogated the Agricultural Loans Measure in the 2nd month of 1086. But in the very next month Fan Ch'un Jen appealed for its restoration, on the ground that the national exchequer was depleted.[1] This would suggest that the Measure was regarded by him as being at least profitable to the government. This was contrary to the intention of Wang An Shih, as we have observed, but indicates that in the end it worked out that way.

But what is more significant is that Ssu Ma Kuang himself, in the 8th month of 1086, affirmed in a memorial that " the great idea of the Agricultural Loans Measure was in the interests of the people, and all that was necessary (to make it successful) was that compulsory practices in connection with its administration should be prohibited ".[1]

Such a change of front on the part of these most prominent opponents of the Measure in Wang An Shih's day, after the lapse of seventeen or eighteen years, must have occurred because the Measure had proved itself to be beneficial.

Let us turn now to the criticism of Chu Hsi. He affirms that the idea of the Measure was good. As a matter of fact he himself initiated a similar Measure during his term of office in Ts'ung An Hsien, in the prefecture of Chien Ning (建 寧 府). This he affirmed was based on the She Ts'ang Fa (社 倉 法) of the Chow (周) and T'ang Dynasties, but that during the long period which had elapsed since the inauguration of the Measure, certain defects had arisen, particularly in regard to the fact that the people in the remote places could not take advantage of any distribution which was made, as the distributing centres were located in the " Hsien " and " Chow " cities only. Further, the laws connected with the Measure were so strict that the local officials were unwilling to go to the trouble of opening the granaries even in famine times. The result was that the grain gradually deteriorated, so that when the officials

---

[1] Liang Ch'i Ch'ao, p. 127.

were compelled through force of circumstances to break the
seals, they found the grain unsuitable for human consumption.

These defects he considered could be remedied by his own
scheme, which he had put into effect in his own district, as
follows :—

In 1168 he had organized a " She Ts'ang " (社 倉) or Loan
Granary, initiating the scheme with a gift of six hundred piculs
from the government. This grain, he as official, together with
two local gentry, had undertaken to distribute by way of
relieving the distress of the people . . . on which they had
secured permission to charge 24 per cent interest, to be repaid
in grain. . . . In times of dearth the rate of interest would be
reduced by half, and in times of absolute famine the grain would
be distributed free.

He affirmed that after fourteen years of operation on these
lines, the original loan of 600 piculs had been returned to the
government, and that in addition they had in stock 3,100 piculs
which had been accumulated out of the interest paid on the
loans.

At this juncture, as there was such a large stock in hand,
he proposed that the procedure should be continued, but that
the interest might be greatly reduced, only 3 per cent being
demanded. He suggested, however, that lay residents should
be put in charge, and that they should be under the inspection
of the officials.

In conclusion, he affirmed that such a procedure was of
permanent benefit, both to the government and the people,
" and recommended that it should be applied universally." [1]

This, on the one hand, is adequate testimony to the
practicability and benefit of such a measure, and on the other
serves to indicate the reasons for such lack of success as attended
the efforts of Wang An Shih in connection with it. Chu Hsi
states that under the provisions of Wang's Measure money
was distributed instead of grain. This would undoubtedly
arouse the cupidity of some people. Also in pointing out that
the distribution centres were too few, and that the people who

[1] Chu Hsi, Complete Works, vol. lxiv, pp. 9–11.

most needed the loans were by their remoteness from the centres unable to take full advantage of the Measure, and also in suggesting that local residents should be asked to co-operate in the administration of the scheme, he has probably indicated the weak points in Wang An Shih's Measure. For in keeping the distribution of the loans in the hands of the officials, it was impossible on the one hand to create as many centres as were essential to the efficient working of the Measure, and it was inevitable on the other that malpractices should arise.

Had all the officials of the " hsiens " been of the same calibre as Wang An Shih or the circuit officials of equal character and ability as Li Ts'an, no doubt the Measure would have worked satisfactorily to all concerned. For it might have been possible after the lapse of several years to reduce the rates of interest, which, after all allowances have been made, were still too high to enable the farmers to derive any great and permanent benefit from the loans. But Wang An Shih thought it essential that officials should be used for the work, and that in accordance with his policy of centralization of authority, it was necessary for the government to control the administration of the Measure. Had he gone the further step, which was taken by Chu Hsi, of enlisting local gentry of repute to supervise the actual working of the Measure, using the officials for inspection purposes only, it would have been unnecessary to charge such a high rate of interest.

However, that is criticism of a *post hoc* character, and we must not lose sight of his difficulties. He was in office for a comparatively short period of nine years, the country was vast, and communications were difficult. It was impossible to alter the character of the officials in that short space of time. He was opposed, in many cases, most unreasonably by the more famous officials of the time, and lost the support and prestige which their co-operation would have given to him. His own statement of the purpose of this Measure must be given due weight, viz., " we have the repression of the rich, and the relief of the poor in mind." [1]   In these respects at least he succeeded,

---

[1] " T'ung Chien," Hsi Ning, 2nd year, 9th month.

and although his success was but relative, the Measure had in it the possibility of real and permanent worth.

When Chu Hsi was criticized for adopting a Measure which was an imitation of this particular Act of Wang An Shih, he replied, " But this was the only good measure Wang An Shih introduced." [1]

As to the implication of the last clause, we naturally reserve judgment, but it serves to show that Chu Hsi thought this measure at least was a good one.

Liang Ch'i Ch'ao's criticism of this Measure is that as it involved the government in direct banking transactions with the people, it was so far faulty. But he gives Wang An Shih full credit for perceiving that something in the nature of a government bank was essential to all industrial and banking enterprise of a private character.[2]

Our own judgment is that in view of the times, and taking the nature of his difficulties into account, Wang An Shih devised a very creditable measure for the relief of the poor and the repression of the rich. If he had been longer in office he would gradually have adapted the measure so as to make it of permanent and universal benefit. The measure operated beneficially to the poor, comparatively speaking that is, but aroused the opposition of the wealthy, who objected to being compelled to accept loans, for which they had no need. That they were so compelled was due to the character of the officials operating the measure, and not to the character of the measure itself.

" The Equitable Transport Measure " (均 輸 法), " Reformed Transport Measure " (漕 運), and the " National Trade and Barter Measure " may conveniently be considered together.

The objects of the first are clearly stated by Wang An Shih himself, viz., " The control of prices and the collection and distribution of the nation's resources will be more fully controlled by the government. Dearth and surplus will be

---

[1] Liang Ch'i Ch'ao, p. 129, quoted from Chu Hsi, " Chu Tzu Yü Lei " (朱 子 語 類).

[2] Liang Ch'i Ch'ao, p. 128.

mutually adjusted. Transport will be more economically managed, and greater efficiency secured. This will tend to eliminate burdensome taxation and the farming class will be proportionately relieved. In these ways it is conceivable that the government revenue will be adequately provided for, and the resources of the people suffer no serious injury." [1]

Evidently this Measure was promulgated primarily with a view to reducing the expenses of collecting and transporting the grain which was contributed by the people as taxes. By giving the Transport Officers a capital sum, and giving them liberty to buy and sell according to varying conditions, and transporting Court supplies from as near as possible to the capital, it was thought that many other advantages such as are outlined above would accrue.

As, however, the Measure also permitted the exchange of other commodities which the Court might require, and as also the operation of the Measure tended to put the control of prices into the hands of the government, the Measure gradually called into existence a form of National Sale and Barter agency for all kinds of goods. The "Equitable Transport Measure" operated for a very short period, being merged into the "National Trade and Barter Measure", of which we must now speak.

This Measure gradually evolved out of attempts to solve certain practical problems, originating with Wang Shao's scheme for colonization of the north-west, and his endeavour to establish improved trade relationships with the alien tribes inhabiting the border territory. The government was to establish trade stations, and finance them, in convenient places along the borders, exchanging, purchasing, or selling goods as they had opportunity. Prices would be fixed by the government. Later on the profits accruing from this business were to be devoted to the colonization of the territory with Chinese citizens, bringing the land under the plough, and offering a wider field for commercial activities. The national revenue would thereby be supplemented.

[1] Works, vol. xvii, pp. 22 and 23.

Later again, the idea of the scheme was extended to the capital, and branches set up in all important centres throughout the empire. As thus extended in scope it aimed chiefly at the relief of the small trader, who hitherto could only dispose of his surplus stocks to the wealthy trade combines who offered whatever prices suited them, whereas under the provisions of the new Act the government would purchase these surplus stocks at more equitable rates. The people were also permitted to make exchanges of goods at will, and even contract loans. This again furthered the tendency for the control of market prices to pass into the hands of the government, and for the State gradually to become the one big trade monopoly.

Criticism of this Measure was mainly of two kinds, one that it was beneath the dignity of the State to engage in the sale and barter of such goods as ice, coal, fruits, etc., and the other that it was detrimental to the people's livelihood. By the " people " must have been meant the " big trade combines ", at whose profit-making proclivities the Measure was largely aimed. Undoubtedly it must have caused great trouble and necessitated a huge body of officials to deal with such matters.

However, Wang An Shih's reply to these criticisms was probably justified. He said, " The Trade and Barter Measure has been drawn up with the utmost care, with a view to removing long-standing difficulties connected with the people's livelihood, and also with the idea of eliminating the baneful influences of the wealthy and monopolist classes. No financial advantage accrues to the government from it."

So that in essence and aim it was another measure designed to relieve the small trader and curb the activities of the wealthy.

The main reason urged for its rescindment in the 12th month of 1085 was that no profit had been gained by the government out of it,[1] so that in this respect at least Wang An Shih's contention was justified.

Liang Ch'i Ch'ao terms this the least satisfactory of Wang An Shih's measures.[2] He credits him with having a good

[1] " T'ung Chien," Yuan Feng, 8th year, 12th month.
[2] Liang Ch'i Ch'ao, p. 135.

and beneficent ideal in devising it, but considers that it was essentially defective in that it combined banking and trade under the auspices of the government. He considers that banking belongs essentially to the sphere of private enterprise, although he admits that some sort of government supervision is necessary. For the first part of this contention he has the support of Mr. Baldwin, the present leader of the British Conservative party, who is reported to have expressed himself recently as follows :—

" The fundamental conception of doctrinaire Socialism is that the State should have a virtual monopoly of spending. From this conception it is a short step to the advocacy of the control of banking by a public corporation. . . . But in the formation of those central banks, which have done so much to reconstruct the shattered, and to launch the new countries of Europe, the cardinal principle has been to complete the divorce of banking from government control." [1]

This divorce of control Mr. Baldwin terms financial orthodoxy, and considers it of solid advantage to the people generally. His objection to government monopoly of banking would seem to be that a government might be tempted to adopt a financial policy dictated by other than purely financial considerations.

Liang Ch'i Ch'ao, while objecting to government monopoly of banking, which he considers was involved in this measure of Wang An Shih, yet gives him credit for perceiving that in this vital matter of national economic policy, some sort of government control of banking was necessary.

His second objection to the measure is that eventually it was bound to defeat the very object for which it was devised. Ostensibly it was inaugurated to fight private banking and trade monopolies, but in effect it tended to make the government the sole trade and banking monopoly. So that private commercial enterprise he considers was bound to suffer rather than prosper from its operation.

[1] *Times Weekly*, 23rd May, 1929. Speech to the City of London.

Another aspect of the Measure was that prices of all commodities should be fixed by the government. Of which the criticism of Lancelot Lawton with regard to Stalin's policy is apposite. He writes, " It was one of Stalin's ideas that all produce was to be taken over by the State at fixed prices. Past experience shows that such prices will always be determined, not by economic principles, but by the financial straits of the government." [1]

This is not the place to enter upon a discussion of the tenets of State Socialism. The criticism of this particular measure from that angle must be left to abler minds. The idea of the writer is that Wang An Shih did not foresee the development of this State and Barter Measure into what was virtually a State monopoly of banking and commerce. From other writings on the subject of State monopolies we gather that in principle Wang An Shih was opposed to all such. His prime object in devising this measure was to relieve the small trader of surplus stocks, and to encourage continued and increased production. He had as secondary object the relief of such from the depredations of the professional money-lenders. Also in attempting to fix the prices of all commodities he was seeking to prevent the trade combines from fleecing the people, and taking advantage of times of dearth and emergency to exact extravagant profits. From a scheme of colonization and the attempt to improve relations with the border tribes, through an experiment to relieve the small trader of serious disabilities, the measure gradually developed far beyond the intention of Wang An Shih, and became contradictory of it. It would seem that this measure, while definitely beneficent in aim, turned out to be economically unsound.

The Improved Transport Measure was designed to prevent peculation on the part of those who were responsible for the transport of the tribute grain, and thus obviate the continuance of serious losses to the government. Wang An Shih introduced the system of private competition with the government transport service. This, even though it seems to have been based on no

---

[1] *Sphere*, 22nd March, 1930. Article on " Russia To-day. Back to Serfdom ".

higher principle than that of " setting a thief to catch a thief ", turned out to be remarkably effective.[1]

The Equitable Land Tax Survey Measure was not originated by Wang An Shih. But he revived it as a just method of assessing the land tax. This Measure was not, as some have supposed, an attempt to make the State the sole owner of land.[2] The people were allowed to buy and sell land, but certain limits were imposed as to the amount which any individual could possess. It was devised to ensure that all the land was surveyed, and periodically classified, so that taxation could be equitably levied in accordance with the productive capacity of the land owned. Under the provisions of this Act, all non-productive land, and land required for public purposes, such as roads, ditches, dykes, and the like, was not to be taxed. Further, as the total amount to be collected from any district under the new Act was not to exceed the amount collected under the working of the older regulations, it allowed for a more equitable distribution of the responsibility for the land tax, those who had the more productive land paying more in proportion than those who were working poorer soil. It was infinitely preferable to the imposition of a flat rate based on superficial area, regardless of the quality of the land possessed.

His river conservancy measures and plans for reclamation of flooded land were all on the right lines. Ts'ai Shang Hsiang quotes an interesting account of the work of Wang Feng Yuan's wife at T'ang Chow in connection with this reclamation project. She personally undertook the reclamation and improvement of her brother's land, devoting the proceeds to charity. This gained for her a great reputation, and because she had other fine characteristics, the people took their problems to her rather than to the official. For her work in this connection she was rewarded by the government with ten rolls of silk and ten bushels of wheat.[3]

---

[1] Dynastic History of Sung, " Shih Huo Chih " (食 貨 志), vol. 128, section 3, p. 10.
[2] *Makers of Cathay*, Allan, p. 103.
[3] Ts'ai Shang Hsiang, vol. vii, p. 4.

This record has peculiar interest, in that this lady was cousin to Wang An Shih's wife, and evidently was keen on setting an example of diligence and loyalty to her less tractable neighbours. It also gives us an insight into the way this policy was executed, the method of rewarding those who carried out the provisions of the measure being particularly interesting.

The problem of river control and land reclamation is always with the government of China. The Yellow River is constantly silting up, and frequently breaks through into the surrounding plain. Large funds and the best engineering brains of the world will be needed to solve this great problem. Wang An Shih, with his " river-plough " scheme, it must be admitted, was dealing with the problem in a very crude way, but still he must be given the credit for attempting to solve it according to his light. To make even this crude attempt was infinitely preferable to " doing nothing ", which seemed to represent the attitude of his political opponents.

It has been suggested above that Wang An Shih was opposed to the system of government monopolies. He certainly wrote strongly against the government tea monopoly,[1] and evidently would have extended his opposition to monopolies of other kinds, like gold, iron, and silver. Salt seems to have been in the hands of large dealers, who purchased salt certificates from the government which entitled them to receive delivery of specified quantities of the commodity at the production centres. This system had been inaugurated in 1048 at the instigation of Fan Hsiang, and had been revived in 1058 after a short reversion to full monopoly rights by the government.[2]

Wang An Shih is criticized by some writers for having instituted a currency depreciation measure, but the evidence for this seems insufficiently attested. The subject is discussed later in this work.

With the whole of Wang An Shih's fiscal policy before us, certain things can definitely be said. He had the interests of

---

[1] Works, vol. xvii, p. 21 (論 茶 法).

[2] *Annals of the American Academy*, Nov., 1930. Article on the " Public Administration of Salt in China " by Esson M. Gale.

the poorer classes at heart. One fails to see any sign of
" oppression " in his policy. " Repression " of the profiteering
proclivities of the capitalists there certainly was. Deprivation
of certain hoary privileges which the official and wealthier
sections of the community had hitherto enjoyed, was a
characteristic of his policy, but that can hardly be termed
" oppression ".

He was out to redistribute the wealth of the country more
equitably. He took from the rich to relieve the poor. He was
determined to increase the national revenues, but he did this
not by grinding the faces of the poor, but by taking more from
those who could well afford to pay. As Dr. Ferguson says,
" While Wang An Shih laid great stress upon the foundations
of prosperity being in the increased wealth of the nation, yet
his intense sympathy with the people, and his anxiety for their
welfare, ennobled all his plans with a high standard of moral
worth." [1]

In aim he was sincere and his measures were devised with
beneficent objects. Those who suffered from his economic
policy were the " privileged " and influential sections of the
populace. These were naturally more " articulate " than
others, and so in the accounts which have come down to us,
the side of the case which they represent is emphasized in such
a way as to give the impression that his measures were
" oppressive ". If the poorer classes suffered at all from his
policy, it was not due to anything inherent in the measures
themselves, but to the way in which they were administered
by the local officials, whose " acquisitive " tendencies, " love
of wealth and fame " were ingrained in their very natures.

If it be urged, as indeed some critics have done, that Wang
An Shih failed to make full allowance for this, and that therefore
he is culpable, the same argument applies to any other minister
who should attempt to introduce any financial measure at all.
If Wang An Shih's reforms failed because the local officials
were corrupt, then even the old system of government must
have been working at least equally badly. It is suggested that

[1] Article on Wang An Shih, by Dr. Ferguson, as above.

Wang An Shih and his party thought that by paying the officials more, their self-respect would be enhanced and they would not be so prone to follow corrupt practices. "But," laments Chu Hsi, "they still continued their dishonest ways." [1]

So that whatever criticism may be applied to Wang An Shih in this connection, applies equally to every other attempt at reform made during that age, whether conservative or liberal in character.

The Militia Act and the Militia Mounts Measure were also part of his economic policy in certain respects, but as they were primarily concerned with the military situation, we have not discussed them under the head of his fiscal programme. But it must be remembered that in seeking to reduce the regular forces and replace them with voluntary or civil levies, without increasing the military expenditure on the normal budget, and at the same time actually increasing the military force at the disposal of the government, the measures had their definite place in his economic policy.

It has already been pointed out that the threatened invasion from the Tartars in the north and the Tanguts in the north-west determined Wang An Shih's military policy to a large degree, and that it was definitely with the idea of coping with that threat that these two measures were devised.[2]

The condition of the regular forces can be gauged from the criticism of such men as Ou Yang Hsiu, Fan Chen, and Su Shih, none of whom can be considered friendly towards Wang An Shih's policy in general. The former termed the standing forces "a mere pretence of an army" and severely criticized their arrogance, indolence, and ineffectiveness.[3] Fan Chen said that the regulars were quite useless as a fighting force, and that the enormous number enrolled acted deleteriously to agriculture, by drafting off those who should have been at work on the fields. He considered some system of people's levies and the revival of the soldier-farmer policy essential.[4] Su Shih said

[1] Chu Hsi, Complete Works, vol. lix, p. 18.
[2] See Vol. I, pp. 177–8.
[3] Liang Ch'i Ch'ao, pp. 156–8. [4] Liang Ch'i Ch'ao, pp. 155–6.

that 50 per cent of the regular forces might be disbanded without doing the State any injury, as through age or physical incapacity. quite that proportion were useless.[1]

So disbandment of large numbers of regulars was one of the chief features of Wang An Shih's military policy. He was aware, however, of the danger of doing this too hastily, and emphasized the necessity of doing it in gradual fashion, urging in fact that large reductions could be effected without taking any drastic action at all, as considerable numbers left the army through various reasons, and all that was necessary was that these should not be replaced. The standing army at the opening of Shen Tsung's reign numbered 1,162,000 men, whereas at the time of Wang An Shih's retirement from the Grand Council there were only 568,688 on the roll.[2] This was practically equivalent to the reduction of the 50 per cent which Su Shih had advocated.

His next step was to ensure that the disbanded regulars should be supplanted by corps raised from the people, who were to be drilled in the intervals between the agricultural seasons, provided with trained officers and weapons, and gradually rendered available, first for police duty locally, and eventually for actual warfare. It will be noted that the Measure gradually extended both in nature and scope, but that the original intention of its promoters was to get the people of the north and north-western districts trained first.

The expenses were to be secured from the Military Treasury, and in the main provided for by the saving on the regular army which the stopping of recruiting made possible.

By the year 1076 no less than 7,182,028 men were enrolled in the Militia.[3]

In the appeal for abrogation which Ssu Ma Kuang made when he was restored to power, the points emphasized were the larger numbers enrolled, that the officials in charge of the measure were not keeping to the original conditions of the

[1] Liang Ch'i Ch'ao, pp. 161–3.
[2] Dynastic History of Sung, vol. 187, sect. 140, 1.
[3] Dynastic History of Sung, vol. 192, sect. 145, VI, iii.

Act as promulgated, and that the people were being treated badly
by those responsible for its administration. He urged further
that agriculture was being interfered with, that the farmer
forces would never become effective as a fighting force, and that
the Measure would result in the increase of robbery and
brigandage.[1]

Wang Yen Sou quarrelled not so much with the Measure
itself, as with the way in which it was being administered. The
greater part of the people's dissatisfaction was caused by the
character and practices of the officials in charge, who had no
desire to benefit the country.[2]

The numbers were of course huge, but the task before them
was tremendous, and considering that the militia were to do
duty as local police as well as be held in reserve for actual
warfare, the numbers cannot be considered excessive. As
regards interference with agriculture, we gather that at the most
fifty days in the year were to be given to drill, which probably
meant five days each month during ten months in the year.
In many cases this was reduced to twenty-seven days and some
even were called up for only eighteen days per annum. Complete exemption was possible in famine times or through other
exceptional circumstances.[2]

The men were of necessity called up in relays, and as
agriculture has its definitely busy seasons, no doubt the two
months which were excepted, would be the sowing and harvest
seasons. For the rest of the year it is usually possible for the
farmer to have his days off every month.

The character of the officials has of course to be taken into
account, and while in intent and actual character the Measure
may have been designed so as not to interfere with agriculture,
it is extremely probable that in the actual carrying out of the
Act such interference did occur. The officials would doubtless
take advantage of the opportunity afforded by this Measure
to use the people for work other than military drill, and no

[1] Dynastic History of Sung, vol. 192, sect. 145, vi, iii.
[2] Dynastic History of Sung, vol. 192, sect. 145, p. 10.

doubt bribery had to be resorted to in some cases to get free from their clutches.

As to the point of efficiency, we have the testimony of Chang Ch'un, who in regretting the abrogation of the Militia Act, said, in 1095, that the militia after training were superior to the regular forces.[1]   And still more powerful testimony is afforded by the word of Ssu Ma Kuang himself who, in attempting to supplant the Act by the older regulations for the Archers, said that in the militia a large body of well-trained men was available for this work.[2]

Unfortunately there was no actual experiment made with the militia as a fighting force, so it is impossible to say from experience how the plan would have worked out from that point of view.   The real spirit of the Measure was never restored after Ssu Ma Kuang's attempts at abrogation, and such offers as were made by men like Ch'in Yuan to lead the militia against the invading Chins were rejected.

But the contention of Ch'en Ju Ch'i that if the Militia Act had not been rescinded the invaders would have met with stout opposition seems justifiable.   With this Liang Ch'i Ch'ao is in agreement.[3]

Chu Hsi says it was Wang An Shih's plan to make this scheme fully effective throughout the empire, but that he did not succeed in doing so.   He speaks approvingly of the idea, and commends one Fan Chung Ta for having carried out the idea splendidly in Yuan Chow.[4]

It was, of course, a very difficult Measure to carry through, as the ordinary civilian population anywhere is naturally opposed to being called upon for regular periods of military training.   In the case of this particular Measure not only was there that obstacle to override, but also the dissatisfaction of numbers of regulars who must have been disbanded, willy-nilly, through the operation of the Act.   Add to that the large amount of opposition from official quarters, based largely on

[1] Vol. I, p. 208.   [2] Vol. I, p. 205.
[3] Liang Ch'i Ch'ao, p. 188.
[4] Chu Hsi, Complete Works, vol. lxiv, p. 19.

factious considerations, and it is remarkable that Wang An Shih made as much progress as he did with this Measure.

Liang Ch'i Ch'ao thinks the Militia Mounts Measure was unsatisfactory in that the people were compelled to replace diseased or dead mounts, and that it was wrong for the government to lay the burden of feeding the animals on the local population.[1] Those are obvious defects, but against these must be put the facts that the people had the use of the animals, and that horses in sufficient quantity were not available in the national stud. Horses were essential for the use of the militia, and so by force of circumstances he was induced to adopt the idea.

The whole plan was, of course, practically equivalent to the conscription of the available male forces of the empire for warfare. But as Wang An Shih had his face turned towards the ancient precedents, he could think only in terms of the ancient practices, and hence he failed to introduce conscription such as Western nations or the Japanese have devised, i.e. regular periods of two or three years with the army for all males. Justification for the attempt he made is to be found in the situation of his time, and evidently his fears and preparations were more than justified, for half a century later the whole of north China passed into the hands of the northern foe. So he should be given credit for realizing that a measure of compulsory military training was necessary and justifiable at that period.

His policy of redistributing the regular forces arose from the loss of morale which large numbers of troops congregated at the capital tended to induce, and also from the expense which the constant transfers of the regulars from the capital to the various border and garrison posts involved. It was also designed to correct the defects caused by constant changes of officers, and the consequent loss of that cohesion which longer periods and greater intimacy might produce. He endeavoured to guard against the danger, which former experiments in this direction had shown to be possible, by keeping all the forces

---

[1] Liang Ch'i Ch'ao, p. 190.

under direct supervision of the Crown. Later modifications tended to loosen this central control, and the institution of dual authority led to ensuing defects and to the decay of the martial spirit which characterizes the dynasty later on. But for these Wang An Shih should not be held responsible.

With regard to the various military campaigns which were conducted during Wang An Shih's regime, the conventional criticism is that these were not only unnecessary, but that they were the means of bringing fresh disasters upon the country. So that as with regard to his fiscal policy generally he is termed a " tax-gatherer ", so with regard to his military policy he is termed a " war-maker ".

It is necessary, therefore, that we should examine this criticism to see whether or not it is justified by the facts, as far as these are ascertainable.

In the section on Military Campaigns it has been shown that these were four in number, two of which were designed to bring hitherto unsubjugated aboriginal tribes into submission, i.e. the Man and the Miao tribes of Hunan and Ssuch'uan respectively. Of the other two, one was designed to recover an important strip of territory, in the north-west of Kansu, which in Wang's time was held by Thibetan tribes, and the other was against Annam in the south-west.

We will deal first with the north-western campaign, as being relatively more important from the standpoint of general military policy.

As has already been pointed out, the real objective in this campaign was to cripple the growing power of the Hsi Hsia or Tanguts, who had become increasingly threatening in their attempts to dominate the territory west of the Yellow River represented by the modern Shensi and Kansu provinces.

The Hsi Hsia, who were of Tangut descent, had received permission to settle in the north-eastern part of Shensi, in the neighbourhood of the modern Ning Hsia, in the T'ang Dynasty during the reign of T'ai Tsung (A.D. 627–650). They were also permitted to retain their tribal form of government under a chieftain chosen from their own number. During the formidable rebellion of Huang Ch'ao (黃 巢) during the reign of Hsi Tsung (A.D. 874–889) the Hsi Hsia helped the Imperial cause, in return for which Topassukung (柘 拔 思 恭), their chieftain, was given the title of Duke of Hsia, and allowed to assume the imperial family name of Li (李).

When the Sungs came into possession of the empire the Duke of Hsia was requested to change his family name from Li to Chao (趙) (i.e. the family name of the Sungs). As the power of the Ch'itans was growing rapidly at this time, and it was uncertain as to whether the Sungs or they would eventually predominate, the Tanguts devised a policy of watchful waiting, paying tribute to whichever of the two happened to appear strongest at the time.

But during the reign of Jen Tsung (1023–1063), under the leadership of Yuan Hao (元 昊), the Hsi Hsia were raised to the rank of a first-class Asiatic state. He raised a standing army of 500,000 men, extended his boundaries greatly to the north and west, and assumed the imperial title of Emperor of Great Hsia (大 夏). He then proceeded to ravage the Sung territory in north Shensi, and also in north-eastern Kansu, so that the Sungs were constantly having to fight to retain such places as Yen Chow and Lu Chow (in north Shensi) and Huan Chow and Ch'ing Chow (in north-eastern Kansu).

So menacing did they become that it was thought cheaper to purchase immunity from attack than to prolong the war, so in 1043, by a treaty of peace, it was provided that the Sung Emperor should give to the Tanguts each year 250,000 ozs. of silver, 250,000 pieces of silk, and 250,000 catties of Chinese tea.[1]

It must also be remembered that the Ch'itans or "Liao" (遼) Tartars had already captured large slices of territory in the north of Shansi and Hopei provinces, and were ever threatening to exact more territory. They, like the Tanguts, were but temporarily appeased by huge tribute gifts.

So that there was the prospect of the Sungs having to share their domain with these two powerful enemies on the north and north-west frontiers when Wang An Shih came into

[1] Outlines of Chinese History, by Li Ung Ping, p. 180.

power. For over a score of years the policy of paying tribute
had prevailed and no one had come forward with any proposals for dealing with the menace in an effective way.

It has been pointed out that it was Shen Tsung's purpose to
cope with this menace, and Wang An Shih entered into his
plans with enthusiasm. He not only initiated his plans for a
great force of militia to be created, but took steps to recover the
territory in the north-west of Kansu known as Ho Huang
(河 湟). It will be seen from this historical sketch of the
previous history of the Hsi Hsia and their relationships with
the 'Ch'itans that something had to be done to limit their
aggressiveness. By weakening the Tanguts, Wang An Shih
thought that it would be easier in the end to deal with the
Ch'itans. To weaken the Tanguts he thought it necessary to
regain the Ho Huang region, then in the hands of Thibetan
tribes, whose loyalty to the Sungs was in doubt. That would
give them a greater measure of security, as it would block the
great north-west gate into China against the foe, and at the
same time make the position of the Tanguts less secure, as they
would then have to face the prospect of attacks from the west
as well as from the south and east.

Viewed in this light the attempt to recover Ho Huang was but
the first step in a far-reaching scheme of military strategy.
For in its ultimate aim it was devised to weaken the Ch'itans
by crippling the power of a possible and powerful ally.

So that there is no question that in this particular campaign
it was not so much a matter as to whether or not Wang An Shih
took the initiative. That had already been taken by the Tanguts
long ago, and moreover even in the early years of Shen Tsung's
reign, before Wang Shao proposed his definitely military policy,
they had continued their aggressive tactics. In the Histories [1]
we read that in the 3rd month of 1069 the Tanguts took Ch'in
Chow (秦 州) with great slaughter, that in the 10th month
of 1069 the city of Sui Te Chow (綏 德 州) had to be fortified

---

[1] " T'ung Chien," Hsi Ning, 2nd year, 3rd month.

against them.[1]   Also that in the 8th month of 1070 the Tanguts raided Yü Lin Fu (榆 林 府) and Ch'ing Chow (慶 州) with their cavalry,[2] and that in the 3rd month of 1071 that had approached the vicinity of Hun Yuan (渾 源) and Fu Ning (撫 寧).[3]   In the document which Wang Shao presented to the throne in the first year of Shen Tsung's reign (1068) advocating the policy of recovering Ho Huang, he mentions the fact that every year the Tanguts had been attacking Ch'ing T'ang (青 唐), thus threatening to advance definitely from that direction.[4]

All the above preceded in point of time the actual undertaking by the Sungs of military measures in the region, of which the first note in the histories is in the 8th month of 1071, when Wang Shao was appointed Pacification Commissioner for the region.[5]

It would seem from all the evidence that Wang An Shih was taking defensive measures against an aggressive and invading enemy in this campaign, with the ultimate object of restoring territory which had formerly belonged to China, and which had been lost by the weak and vacillating policy of previous rulers.

Ssu Ma Kuang on his advent to power in 1085 thought of evacuating the territory already conquered by Wang Shao, and only desisted from his purpose when Sun Lu (孫 路) pointed out the dangers of fresh invasion which such a policy would create.[6]   During the regency of Hsuan Jen after Ssu Ma Kuang's death, a weaker policy must have prevailed, for we read in the account of her public acts as regent that she surrendered territory to the Tanguts.[7]   We know too from the ensuing history that when the Golden Tartars took K'aifengfu,

1 "T'ung Chien," Hsi Ning, 2nd year, 10th month.
2 "T'ung Chien," Hsi Ning, 3rd year, 8th month.
3 "T'ung Chien," Hsi Ning, 4th year, 3rd month.
4 Liang Ch'i Ch'ao, p. 207.
5 "T'ung Chien," Hsi Ning, 4th year, 8th month.
6 Liang Chi Ch'ao, p. 213.
7 "T'ung Chien," Yuan Yu, 8th year, 9th month (舉 邊 砦 之 地 以 賜 西 夏).

the Tanguts had advanced as far as Sianfu in Shensi, so evidently they were acting as allies with the Tartars, as Wang An Shih had foreseen.[1]

With all these considerations in mind, it would seem that such military action as Wang An Shih took in this case was unavoidable, unless he was going to allow his country's enemies to encroach at will upon the national territory.

His policy with regard to the tribes in Hunan and Ssu Ch'uan seems equally justifiable. For these tribes had long been independent, their leaders having the status of Chinese officials, but refusing real allegiance to the Chinese government. They had furthermore been acting in an oppressive manner towards their Chinese neighbours, and had become a great menace to the internal peace of the State.[2] Viewed from the standpoint of an attempt to restore peace and order and to unify the country, military measures seemed unavoidable.

With regard to the expedition against Annam, the traditional opinion again is that the incursion of the Annamite forces in the 11th month of 1075 was due to Wang An Shih's policy of extending the frontiers of the empire by warlike means.

Under the 2nd month of 1073, the History, in relating the appointment of Shen Ch'i to Kuei Chow (桂 州), has the following :—

" On Wang An Shih's promotion to high office, he began to plan to make a name for himself in connection with the extension of the frontiers. There was one Hsiao Chu (蕭 注), magistrate of Yun Chow (邕 州), who was fond of discussing military matters, and in emulation of Wang Shao and others who had gained high rank and position (through their military successes) he submitted a memorial to the following effect :—

" ' Although Annam sends tribute to us, they are really intent on making war against us. If the present opportunity of taking their territory is lost, they will give us great trouble later on. For they have just been defeated by the Chan Ch'eng

---

[1] T'ung Chien.
[2] Liang Ch'i Ch'ao, pp. 215-220.

(占 城) armies and, according to my information, the available fighting forces left to them number no more than 10,000. So it ought to be easy to reduce them.'

" The mandate was then issued that Hsiao Chu should be appointed as Commissioner for Kuei Chow, with power to take action in this matter. However, when Hsiao Chu entered the Court for the Imperial interview, and the Emperor asked him about his plans for subjugating the Annamese, Hsiao Chu discoursed on the difficulties of the undertaking.

" Whereupon Shen Ch'i (沈 起), an official of the Finance Board, said that the Annamese were an insignificant enemy, and there was no reason at all why they should not be subjugated. This led to Shen Ch'i's being appointed in place of Hsiao Chu.

" Shen Ch'i took his orders from Wang An Shih, and gave himself wholeheartedly to the policy of attacking and arousing the Annamese. This was the cause of their defection." [1]

Liang Ch'i Ch'ao's criticism [2] of the above is based on the biographical account of Hsiao Chu which is found in the Sung History. He finds that Hsiao Chu's plan for the subjugating of Annam is mentioned in that, but that there is nothing said about the date on which his memorial on the subject was submitted. It also relates that Hsiao Chu was appointed to Kuei Chow, and contains the account of the interview with the Emperor, during which Hsiao Chu was asked the question as to what plans he had for the subjugation of the Annamese.

His reply is then given as follows : " True, I did talk about this matter before, but as for the last fifteen years the Annamese have been increasing their forces and organizing themselves under instruction, we may not lightly plan for their subjugation."

We know that Hsiao Chu did actually proceed to Kuei Chow and took up office there, as there is an account of his trip of inspection through the country, and the report that he found everything in good shape to his own satisfaction.

---

[1] " T'ung Chien," Hsi Ning, 6th year, 2nd month.
[2] Liang Ch'i Ch'ao, pp. 223–6.

The account of the interview with the Emperor which is recorded in the History must then have preceded his taking up office at Kuei Chow, and as in that interview he refers to his plan for subjugation of the Annamese as having been propounded fifteen years previously, it must have been made some time in the years 1056–7, when Wang An Shih was in the National Stud and had taken no part in affairs of State, and Wang Shao had as yet made no name for himself in military circles.

Further, later on in the History, under the date of 11th month of 1075,[1] it relates that " the Annamese had been intimidated by the presence of twenty divisions of regulars which had been stationed on the borders, and that one, Liu I (劉彝), had been appointed as Commissioner for Kuei Chow in place of Shen Ch'i, who had been punished for his war policy by transfer to Ch'u Chow (處 州). It also relates that Liu I then made preparations for war with the Annamese because he had been informed that it was possible to subjugate them, and that when the Annamese came to trade with them, he induced the people under his command to refuse to transact business with them. When the Annamese complained of this action in a memorial to the Emperor, he refused to transmit this. So the Annamese entered China by three routes, one from Kuang Fu (廣 府), a second from Ch'in Chow (欽 州), and the third from K'un Lun Kuan (崑 崙 關). They invested Ch'in Chow (欽 州) and Lien Chow (廉 州), killing over 8,000 of the local militia. When this news leaked out, Shen Ch'i was punished by banishment to Ch'eng Chow (郢 州) and the name of Liu I was erased from the official register ".

In the Dynastic History of Sung, under the Biographical Account of Wang An Shih, we have still another reason given for this invasion, as follows [2]:—

" A spy had secured a copy of the proclamation issued by Lu Pu, the Annamite chief, asserting that he was leading forth

<hr>

[1] " T'ung Chien," Hsi Ning, 8th year, 11th month.
[2] See Chap. IV.

his army to deliver the Chinese people from the poverty and distress which the Agricultural Loans Measure and the Public Services Act had imposed upon them. This enraged Wang An Shih, who forthwith drew up a manifesto (declaring war upon the Annamese) denouncing the Annamese king."

We have then three reasons given by the traditional Histories for this incursion of the Annamese forces, one the war-making policy of Shen Ch'i at the instigation of Wang An Shih, the breaking off of trade relations with the Annamese at the instigation of Shen Ch'i's successor, Liu I, and the oppressive nature of the New Laws promulgated by Wang An Shih. It appears evident that somehow or other the historians are determined to make Wang An Shih responsible for the invasion. However, in each of the accounts there are indications that the initiative was taken by the Annamese, as far as military action was concerned. And previous history leads one to infer that this was highly probable.

For in the period 1034-7 Te Cheng (德 政); the Annamese king, led over a thousand troops to attack a small tribe headed by one Ch'en Kung Yung (陳 公 永) because the latter wished to offer his allegiance to China. In 1036 he attacked Ssu Ling Chow (思 陵 州), Hsi P'ing Chow (西 平 州), and Shih Hsi Chow (石 西 州), all in the Ying Chow prefecture (邕 州), burning homes and carrying off the people and their cattle. In 1043 he devastated Chan Ch'eng (占 城), carrying off the king. In 1050, when Neng Chih Kao revolted, Te Cheng led out his forces numbering over 20,000 to assist them. In 1059, with Jih Tsun (日 尊) on the Annamese throne, they attacked Ch'in Chow (欽 州). The next year they attacked Ying Chow (邕 州), and a memorial was presented reporting on the intentions of Jih Tsun to proclaim his entire independence of the Chinese government, stating that he had assumed the title of Emperor and that he had adopted the dynastic title of Ta Yueh (大 越) Kingdom, with the imperial designation of Pao Hsiang (寶 象).[1]

---

[1] Liang Ch'i Ch'ao, p. 224.

During the reigns of Chen Tsung, Jen Tsung, and Ying Tsung their incursions continued, so that whatever may have been the immediate cause of the invasion of 1075, it would seem that the Annamese had long been asking for punishment.[1]

The issue of the war confirms one in the opinion that Wang An Shih undertook this campaign because he was forced to do so, and not because he was anxious to extend the borders of the empire by confiscating the territory of the Annamese. For in the end the Annamite king Li Ch'ien Te (李 乾 德) was pardoned and restored to his former status, Annam remaining a tribute State.

As in regard to his fiscal policy we deem the epithet of " tax-gatherer " unjustified, so in regard to his military policy it seems equally unjust to term Wang An Shih a " war-maker ". For in each of the campaigns he undertook he was actuated by no other motive than that which should actuate any patriotic minister, viz. to take such steps as would ensure the territorial integrity of the empire and the suppression of rebellious elements within it. He was more anxious to stem invasion from outside than to invade alien territory, and such advances as he did make were made with the object of restoring lost territory and counteracting further plans for encroachments.

A full chapter has been devoted to Wang An Shih's educational policy,[2] to which little can be added. He was evidently desirous of extending the school system of government education, and did something towards carrying his plans into effect. But his short term in high office prohibited the possibility of applying his ideas to the whole country. So perforce he had to be content with the revision of the examination system, by means of which the government officials were selected. By seeking to make the candidates concentrate on a method of classical study which tended to make them more practically minded, and so more useful in actual administration, he was making a very valuable contribution to the educational problems of his time.

[1] T'ung Chien.
[2] See Essays in this volume.

The nature of the questions which he himself set at the official examination shows that he intended the candidates to think and not merely to rely upon their memories. Knowledge rather than style, thought rather than memory, and practical mindedness rather than literary skill were the features which he sought to introduce by his educational reforms.

The ancient bases of selection for government positions emphasized personal character, knowledge of the classical literature, government administration, and literary skill.[1] It seems that Wang An Shih had all these in mind, and kept them in much the same order of relative importance. For he was always stressing the importance of personal character in the officials. " The keeping of the laws depends upon the officials. If the officials are of unworthy character, the laws, no matter how good and complete they may be in themselves, will not be kept." [2]   He thought the school system the best that could be devised for discovering the personal character of the official candidates, but until that method was available he thought that close investigation of their record and recommendation by worthy men were the best substitutes. The period of trial was also emphasized by him, a method which in name at least was already in vogue, but which he sought to make more effective by stressing the investigation side of a man's official record.

His actual work of reform on the National College or University was all in line with these broad principles. He extended the accommodation, increased the numbers of students in residence, offering especially greater facilities for students not of the official clan, and by adding to the curriculum such practical subjects as Law, Medicine, and Military knowledge he was seeking to impart that note of utility to education which he was ever stressing as being of first importance.

By limiting the sphere of study each year to one classic, he aimed at thoroughness, and by combining personal character

---

[1] Chu Hsi, Complete Works, vol. lxiv, p. 12.
[2] See Chap. VII, Vol. I, Memorial of a Myriad Characters.

with general learning in the grading of the men he was laying the emphasis in the right place.

One could have wished that he had had a longer period in which to extend his contribution to education. In the times of Chu Hsi the latter stressed almost identically the same points as Wang An Shih. "He deplored the lack of emphasis on personal character in the selection of officials in his day, and stressed the fact that this was the main object of the ancients in establishing their school system. He affirmed, too, that as the government school system had ceased to emphasize character, the educated class had perforce gone to the Buddhists and Taoists for religious and ethical conceptions, and that instead of making personal character the main criterion of a man's capacity for an administrative post, literary ability was regarded as of chief importance." [1] All this might have been written by Wang An Shih himself, and serves to enhance the value of his own theories and contribution.

In the foregoing discussion we have endeavoured to give the reader some account of the motives which inspired Wang An Shih in embarking upon his career of political reform. We have also tried to indicate the aim he had in view in devising his various measures. These again have been outlined in some detail, the nature and value of each have been estimated in some degree, and some insight has been gained into his difficulties and the character of the opposition. We must now attempt to view his policy as a whole and seek to evaluate his political contribution in general.

The fact that the Emperor Shen Tsung maintained Wang An Shih's policy without any important change for the whole of his reign (1068–1085) is not without significance. It must be remembered that Wang An Shih resigned in 1076, so that for a period of nine years, although Wang An Shih was living in retirement, his policy was considered so satisfactory to the Emperor that he thought it unnecessary to introduce any serious modifications. It may, however, be urged that Shen

---

[1] Chu Hsi, Complete Works, vol. lxiv, pp. 15 and 16.

Tsung's interest in the maintenance of Wang An Shih's policy may have been dictated by purely personal considerations, as he had been so intimately associated with his minister in the formulation of it. Further, in support of this it may be said, and justly, that the Emperor was first and foremost concerned with the securing of increased revenue and the creation of a more effective fighting force, and that these were the very things which Wang An Shih's policy was designed to produce. It is therefore only natural that the Emperor should maintain it without change. It may further be urged that mere maintenance of such a policy does not of necessity imply that it was beneficial to the people at large. Shen Tsung's interest in securing increased revenue might easily conflict with the welfare of the people, and the maintenance of a larger and more effective fighting force might be secured at the expense of the people's well-being.

Against such plausible arguments as these we would urge the following considerations.

Firstly, there is the account of Shen Tsung's character, as found in the Dynastic Histories, and which is quoted at the beginning of this chapter. A monarch who was keenly interested in the economic conditions under which the people lived, who was merciful to the poor and aged and generous to those in distress, could scarcely be willing to maintain a policy which "took away all joy in life", even though it happened to be a policy in which he was personally interested, as suggested above.

Secondly, there is no account in the Histories of the time of any serious uprising of the people against the measures introduced by Wang An Shih. As Liang Ch'i Ch'ao says, "If the people had been suffering hardships they would certainly have rebelled. For, under the provisions of the Militia Act, they were well organized and trained, and large numbers of them were provided with the weapons necessary for such a move." [1]

[1] Liang Ch'i Ch'ao, p. 245.

It may be urged that argument from silence proves nothing. But when the biased character of the Dynastic Histories in reference to Wang An Shih and his policy is taken into account, the argument from silence becomes particularly potent. For we may be quite sure that if such a rising of the people had occurred it would most certainly have been included in the records.

There are, however, other evidences of a literary and circumstantial character which can be adduced in support of our contention that Wang An Shih's policy functioned beneficially during the reign of Shen Tsung (which is the only period to which criticism of it can logically apply), and that the country generally was quiet and peaceful.

Wang An Shih wrote five poems in praise of the period known as " Yuan Feng " (元 豐), i.e. the part of Shen Tsung's reign between 1078 and 1085. An attempt at a translation of two of these is given below, viz. :—

" THE EMPEROR'S GIFT OF FELICITY." [1]

" Bare are the hills in the glaring sun,
  Cracked are the fields with the blazing heat,
  As I squat in my hut to the south of the lake,
  My hope is centred in my water-wheel.
  Now the thunder rolls, and the lightnings flash,
  The clouds bank themselves dark in the heavens above,
  The rain crashes down in torrential gloom,
  Flooding the fields and the plain.

" The blasted grains rear their heads again,
  O'ertopping the beasts and their drivers,
  The dead pulse revives with luxuriant beards,
  Our hosepipes may be laid on the rafters,
  Let us eat and drink with our farm-hands.

" Grain has been cheap for three years now,
  This year is one of rich promise.

[1] Poetical Works, vol. i, p. 1.

Our Emperor Yuan Feng is in league with Heaven,
We shall have felicity for ever.
E'en a man in the wilds need not be poor,
So this poor man of the soil,
Sings his Emperor's praise."

A second poem, written later, but with the same title,[1] is as follows :—

"I sing of Yuan Feng,
Every few days we are blessed with rain,
And the crops hide the ground from our view.
The hills are covered with luxuriant green,
The pools with pure rice are filled.
Our hosepipes are dry through lack of use,
The fish are plenteous and fine.
The flavour of reeds is sweeter than milk,
A bushel of wine costs but a hundred cash,
Though 'tis no festal day you can hear the drums,
And the singing and dancing of youth.
Joy abounds everywhere, grief is unknown.
As I sail towards the south in my small willow boat,
I sing or I snooze as I float by Chiang Ning,
For I meet only gladness and laughter."

Such poems suggest a time of peace and prosperity, such as was typified by the times of Yao, when the people were accustomed to sing—

"At sunrise I go to my work,
At sundown I return to my rest,
What power has the Emperor over me ? "

It would seem that at least the times of Shen Tsung's later reign were not such as Ssu Ma Kuang described when he said that the people dare not plant an extra mulberry or buy an extra cow for fear of being taxed out of existence.[2]

That, however, is evidence from Wang An Shih, and if it stood by itself might possibly be discounted.   However, it is

---

[1] Poetical Works, vol. i, pp. 1 and 2.
[2] Liang Ch'i Ch'ao, p. 247, referring to the times of Ying Tsung.

not to be ignored when supplemented by such witness as the following letter from Su Shih (蘇 軾), a former opponent of the reform policy, written to his friend T'eng Ta Tao (滕 達 道):—

"I should like to take the opportunity to talk over with you the way in which we showed our prejudices when the reform measures were under discussion, and how we were led to take up an opposing attitude. Although I feel that possibly at that time we thought we were acting sincerely and reached our position out of a real regard for the welfare of the country, I have now come to see that we were wrong and in the main unreasonable.

"Now that the grace of the Emperor is constantly renewed, and his rule obviously successful, I perceive, looking back, that the attitude I then took up was far from what it should have been. Naturally one does not change one's point of view simply out of personal interest, or in order to enhance one's prestige and influence. I really do feel that unless we desist from our querulous opposition we shall have greater regrets than ever." [1]

The testimony of this letter, that the rule of Shen Tsung was obviously successful, and other indications of a *volte face* on the part of so prominent an opponent of the reform policy as Su Shih, add considerable weight to the evidence already produced that Wang An Shih's measures could not have been acting in the oppressive manner suggested by Chu Hsi.

Other signs that Su Shih had changed his views on the reform policy are not lacking. For instance, it is recorded that during Wang An Shih's retirement at Chiang Ning, Su Shih visited him and that they enjoyed many pleasant rambles together in the surrounding hills.

There is evidence even from the school opposed both to Su Shih and Wang An Shih. Take for instance what Chu Hsi records about Ch'eng Hao's attitude to the Agricultural Loans Measure. He writes, "Although our master Ch'eng Tzu formerly criticized the measure severely, yet he could not

[1] Liang Ch'i Ch'ao, p. 248.

avoid expressing his regrets later that he had been too extreme in his opposition." [1] There are also the words of Ch'eng Hao himself that the unreasonable opposition of his party had driven Wang An Shih to proceed to extremes in his policy.

The fact that we have such evidence from the leaders of two of the great opposing parties to Wang An Shih's policy proves that there must have been many good features in it, sufficient at least to disprove Chu Hsi's contention that he pursued a policy of reckless and rigorous oppression. We do not hold a brief to prove the flawless character of Wang An Shih's administration. What has been said in our detailed discussion of the various measures is sufficient to show that. The new laws had their defects, and did not always or in every case work out in the best interests of the people. There were reasons for that, which we shall now proceed to discuss. But what we are at this point concerned to prove is that during the reign of Shen Tsung there was not the clamorous opposition on the part of the people which Chu Hsi's statement would lead us to believe. If there was clamorous opposition at all, it most probably emanated from the wealthier and more influential sections of the populace, who had many of their cherished privileges taken away by the operation of the new measures.

We have just suggested that the measures had their defects and that in some cases they were administered in such a way as to give just cause for resentment. We might venture to inquire into the reasons for that.

First as to the defective character of the measures themselves. This is attributed by Wang An Shih's critics to his depending too much upon his own knowledge and experience, upon his unwillingness to listen to the advice of others, upon his obstinacy, his unpractical mentality and the like. All of which, either openly or tacitly, assume that if he had subordinated his wilful ideas to the opinions of his so-called " loyal and worthy " contemporaries, he would have produced much better measures and thereby avoided the opposition and enmity which proved so serious an obstacle to the success of his policy later on.

[1] Chu Hsi, Complete Works, vol. lxii, p. 34.

It is evident upon the face of it that for some reason or other Wang An Shih failed to secure the co-operation of those officials at Court whom posterity has regarded, justly in many cases, as able and honourable men. It is also quite reasonable to suppose that if he could somehow have enlisted their sympathetic co-operation, his reforms would have been more fruitful of beneficent and lasting results.

Chu Hsi, representing the opposition, attributes Wang An Shih's failure to secure this co-operation to his impetuosity and extreme self-confidence. He admits, however, that Wang An Shih had the right ideas for his day, and confesses that his critics failed to present sufficiently cogent reasons for their opposition, and that their alternative suggestions were nothing like so good as his proposals. He goes further, and says that he is not surprised that this made Wang An Shih more confident than ever that he had got the right way of doing things, and that it made him more than ever determined to carry out his own ideas. He blames Wang An Shih, however, for not having the patience to expound his ideas more fully. For if he had done so, instead of pressing them upon the Court with such arrogant self-assurance, the results would not have been so disastrous.[1]

He says again, " When the new laws were first propounded, the loyal and worthy officials were sincerely desirous of co-operating, even Ch'eng Hao thinking it right to do so. That was because they perceived that such reforms as were suggested were called for by the nature of the times. However, when they found that they could not altogether approve of his ideas, Ch'eng Hao took it upon himself to remonstrate with Wang An Shih, exhorting him to desist from pursuing a course which was so obviously contrary to the general opinion. It was only after Wang An Shih had spurned the advice of the majority, and had made it quite obvious that he was going to push his own ideas with greater determination than ever, that the great body of worthy officials deserted the Court." [2]

It is interesting to compare with this the opinion of Chang

[1] Chu Hsi, Complete Works, vol. lix, p. 24.
[2] Chu Hsi, Complete Works, vol. lxii, p. 32.

Ju Ming (章 汝 明) of the Ming Dynasty, who wrote an
Introduction to Wang An Shih's works. He says, "Wang An
Shih had the real interest of the State and the welfare of the
people at heart. He had not even the vestige of self-interest.
If only the great officials of his day could, out of sympathy with
his real purpose, have given to his proposals the attention they
deserved, or if only they could have admitted their good points
and set themselves sincerely to remedy their defective features :
If, again, they had only been broadminded enough and
magnanimous enough to inquire about the matters which they
did not fully understand, or if they had been willing to ' give
and take' subduing their prejudices and desire for victory at
any cost : If further they had been ready to co-operate with
him with the sole purpose of seeking the good of their country,
and helped him to find the right men to adminster his measures,
his policy would most assuredly have been of real and lasting
value." [1]

Chang Ju Ming cannot be regarded as unduly prejudiced in
favour of Wang An Shih, for lower down, in this same Introduction, he refers to his lack of patience with the opposition,
to a certain unreadiness to heed criticism, to his mistaken
assumption that the opposition could be overcome by the
exercise of disciplinary and punitive measures, and to his not
being free from prejudices himself.

It seems to an observer, endeavouring to be impartial, that
Wang An Shih's failure to secure the co-operation of the able
and more famous men of his day was due to Wang An Shih's
temperament on the one hand and the disposition of his
opponents on the other ! There is no doubt that he started out
in the hope of co-operating with these talented and worthy
men, but that he found them extremely difficult to get on with.
He had his strong mind, and they had their prejudices. He was
a Radical, and they were inclined to be strongly Conservative.
He had the ear of the Emperor, and this excited their envy and

---

[1] Ts'ai Shang Hsiang, "Shou Chuan" (巷 首), Introduction to Works
of Wang An Shih, by Chang Ju Ming, p. 4.

jealousy. He was perhaps a little too ready to dub them "conventional" and they were too ready to bark back and term him "bigoted". While admitting that there were faults on both sides, one's sympathy goes out to Wang An Shih, for he perceived that the nature of the times called for drastic and speedy action, and that the condition of the country was such that radical and far-reaching reforms were urgently needed. He was obviously sincere in his motives, as even his most doughty opponents are ready to admit; he had the right ideas for the times, as even Chu Hsi confesses. He had the confidence of the Emperor, and considerable influence over him. Both monarch and minister were out for the good of the country, and had constructive proposals to suggest. It was undoubtedly the duty of every right-minded and patriotic official to put up with Wang An Shih's idiosyncrasies and co-operate to the very utmost with him and their common ruler.

"But what were the facts?" continues Chang Ju Ming. "The publication of every new measure was accompanied by vituperous opposition. One day his opponents were denouncing him personally with the utmost vehemence, and the next vociferously decrying the character of the measure itself. The censors availed themselves of the opportunity this afforded to seek the reputation of a "courageous utterance", while the influential officials seized the opportunity to buy a name for "mercy" and sympathy with the people. The subordinate officials in the provinces flattered their patrons at Court by allying themselves with their particular faction. The result was that the Court "parliament" was transformed into a "bear-garden".

During all this fuss and palaver at the capital, no instance of the people making the character of the new measure a pretext for raising the flag of rebellion occurred, nor did the border tribes make them an occasion for unfriendly overtures.

Although everyone knew that the old methods of administration were imperfect, his opponents must of course decry the necessity of making any changes. Though the new measures

met with their unequivocal denunciation, they were not of necessity deserving of it.

But how inconsistent many of his main opponents were ! Ideas which they themselves had mooted earlier on they must perforce attack when Wang An Shih proposed them. Take for instance Su Che and his attitude to the Agricultural Loans Measure ; Ssu Ma Kuang and the Public Services Measure ; Su Shih in connection with the north-western policy, the Public Services Measure, and the Militia Act. Others like Han Ch'i and Ssu Ma Kuang opposed the Agricultural Loans Measure as being detrimental to the people's livelihood, but what alternative had they themselves to suggest for their relief ?

Surely Wang An Shih had some justification for terming such opponents " conventional ". [1]

It seems inevitable in such circumstances that Wang An Shih should have taken things on to his own shoulders, although it is admittedly unfortunate that by so doing he lost the advice and the countenance which the support of these famous men would have given him.

Chu Hsi thinks that it was not the character of the measures so much as Wang An Shih's administration of them which made them deleterious, and that if Ch'eng Hao had headed them up the results would have been quite different.[2] But he also says that Su Shih, if he had been given the scope that Wang An Shih had, would have made a much more disastrous job of things than *he* did.[3] On the whole, one's opinion inclines to the view that considering all the circumstances Wang An Shih made an extremely creditable and valuable contribution.

As has just been suggested, Chu Hsi hints that the real fault lay not so much with the character of the measures as with the way in which they were administered. This brings us to the second suggested reason for failure, namely, the character of the men engaged on the actual prosecution of the reform

---

[1] Ts'ai Shang Hsiang, "Shou Chuan" (巷 首), Introduction to Works of Wang An Shih, by Chang Ju Ming, pp. 1–8.
[2] Chu Hsi, Complete Works, vol. lxii, p. 32.
[3] Chu Hsi, Complete Works, vol. lix, p. 8.

policy. As to Wang An Shih's immediate associates, we have reached the conclusion that in the main they were quite good and able men. There were a few exceptions, as has been pointed out. But as far as the legislative side of things is concerned, little fault can be found with the character and the ability of the men engaged.

But when one considers the rapid and wide-sweeping changes which Wang An Shih introduced and the enormous number of subordinate officers that were required for the execution of them, it would have been surprising if there had been no occasion for complaint about the practical administration of the new laws.

Ts'ai Shang Hsiang has a most apposite criticism in this connection. He says, " Wang An Shih had the right ideas for his day, but failed to discover the right method of carrying them out. He was able to supervise everything himself in a county district, and so made a great success of his political theories there. But when he tried to apply them to the whole country, he was naturally compelled to devolve responsibility on to a great number of others. These ' others ' had not his spirit of conscientious responsibility nor his interest in the well-being of the people. They were covetous and unreliable. In thus failing to secure the right men, confusion and failure resulted." [1]

The reasons for Wang An Shih's failure in this matter have been fully discussed in the chapter on his character, and need not be repeated here. Suffice it to say that such features as were deemed unjust or " oppressive " in the operation of his measures in his own day were all practically due to the character of the local officials administering them. Wang An Shih was fully alive to the danger of not securing the right men, especially when they had to administer such measures as he proposed. One of the great objects of his educational policy was to devise a method whereby the numbers of able and worthy officials might be greatly increased. But for the short time he was in power he was dependent upon such men as were available,

[1] Ts'ai Shang Hsiang, vol. vi, p. 15.

and these, as Ts'ai Shang Hsiang points out, were far from being satisfactory. It was therefore Wang An Shih's misfortune rather than his fault that certain oppressive practices developed in the carrying out of his reform measures.

If in the actual drawing up of his measures he depended upon younger and less experienced men than the " old guard " of loyal and worthy officials represented, and thus failed to produce as perfect a series of reform laws as he might have done, then the " old guard " who deserted him must share the blame for the defects which the measures show. If the character of the local officials prevented the laws from functioning as fairly and beneficially as they might have done, then he may be said to have been unfortunate rather than blameworthy. For in such conditions no one could have done any better, probably not even Ch'eng Hao.

To sum up. It is admitted by friend and foe alike that Wang An Shih had the right ideas for his day, that the times called for such reforms as he proposed, and that he had the welfare of the country and the prosperity of the people generally as his aim. But the need for urgency on the one hand, and the clash of temperament between him and his political opponents, led him to push measures, which though in the main apposite and timely, were not without defects. These defective features arose through the limitations of one-party politics, but for this not only Wang An Shih is to blame. His political foes must share it. The character of the local officials accounts in the main for whatever was " unjust " or " oppressive " in the actual execution of the measures, and it is quite evident that these features were deplored equally by Wang An Shih and his opponents. Throughout his political career Wang An Shih aimed at the relief of the poorer classes and the more equitable sharing of the country's burdens by the classes most able to carry them. It was inevitable in these circumstances that he should meet with the enmity and opposition of the more influential classes, who were naturally more " vocal " than those whose cause he championed. So that in the historical records of the time, we read more of disapproval than approval of his policy. In addition to this general consideration we must not ignore the fact that the Histories were compiled by his political foes, and so still greater injustice is done to him in the records of the period.

All that has been said above applies to the period covered by Shen Tsung's reign. We have deliberately confined our discussion to that period because anything which comes later is complicated by factors extraneous to Wang An Shih's policy as such, and cannot justly be related solely to him and his work. It is, however, necessary to summarize the succeeding history, as it is upon that, in the main, that later critics have based their judgment. For when they talk about the ruinous effects of Wang An Shih's policy, and the confusion which resulted, they have in mind mainly the course of events during the forty years subsequent to his death, and which culminated in the national disaster of 1126, when the Sungs migrated to the south.

To begin with, we must account in some way for the extraordinary fact that immediately Shen Tsung had passed away, and the regime of his mother was instituted, she and Ssu Ma Kuang deliberately abrogated the whole of Wang An Shih's reform measures. Were they justified in so doing? To answer this in the affirmative would be to contradict all that we have said above about the real nature of the new laws. We must therefore inquire whether there were not reasons other than the character of the measures themselves for Ssu Ma Kuang's action.

Ts'ai Shang Hsiang says that "Wang An Shih and Ssu Ma Kuang were as mutually incompatible as water and fire ".[1]

It is evident from the account of the memorable discussion which took place between Wang An Shih and Ssu Ma Kuang shortly after the promotion of both men to the Literary Council, on the subject of the national finances, that their political viewpoints were irreconcilable.[2] Further, as Wang An Shih was so obviously the favourite of the Emperor, and his views were in

---

[1] Ts'ai Shang Hsiang, Tsa Lu (雜 錄), vol. i, p. 13.

[2] " T'ung Chien," Hsi Ning, 1st year, 11th month.

absolute harmony with those of the ruler, it was but natural
that Ssu Ma Kuang should harbour envious feelings, to say
the least. As time went on, and Ssu Ma Kuang found it quite
impossible to gain the upper hand over his political adversary,
they drew more and more apart. In the 9th month of 1069
they had another serious difference of opinion as to Wang An
Shih's employment of Lü Hui Ch'ing, followed by a first-class
debate between the latter and Ssu Ma Kuang about the necessity
for revision of the existing laws and regulations. In this debate
Ssu Ma Kuang had advocated a decidedly conservative policy,
practically amounting to the assumption of the position that
no changes should be made unless circumstances absolutely
left no other alternative. This attitude naturally aroused the
animosity of Wang An Shih, and still further widened the breach
between them.[1]   Then in the second month of 1070 Ssu Ma
Kuang refused the proferred post of Vice-President of the Board
of War, after, according to the Historical account, Wang An Shih
had raised the serious objection that Ssu Ma Kuang was adamant
in his opposition to the views which he and the Emperor held,
and that all their political opponents would rally round him as
their leader if he were given such an important appointment.
Ssu Ma Kuang refused the appointment on the ground that
even though he were to accept such a post his advice would
not be heeded. As a final thrust he further suggested that he
would be adequately recompensed for the loss of this post if
the Emperor would abolish the Financial Reorganization Bureau,
recall the superintendents of the reform measures from their posts
in the provinces, and rescind the Agricultural Loans Measure and
the Public Services Act.[2] Matters were finally brought to a head
in the 9th month of 1070, when Ssu Ma Kuang resigned his
position in the Literary Council, and was appointed Prefect of
Yung Hsing Chun. This was after Su Shih and Lü Kung Chu
had felt constrained to leave the Court, both of whom, on Ssu
Ma Kuang's showing, had been former friends of Wang An
Shih but later had found it impossible to co-operate with him.

[1] " T'ung Chien," Hsi Ning, 2nd year, 9th month.
[2] "T'ung Chien," Hsi Ning, 3rd year, 2nd month.

He therefore feared that to try to hold on any longer at the capital would only result in disaster for himself. So he decided to retire to a provincial post.[1] He had not been long in this appointment before he divorced himself entirely from political affairs, for in the 4th month of 1071 he appealed for, and was granted, a sinecure at Lo Yang, where he continued his famous work on History. His memorial of appeal for resignation bears the impress of great personal chagrin at the favour and confidence which the Emperor had extended to Wang An Shih and at the unjustifiable neglect in which he and other opponents of the reform policy had been allowed to lie.[2] Thus, the breach between the two great men was complete. They had been former friends. Political differences had caused a breach of that friendship, and other considerations entering in, notably the growing influence of Wang An Shih and the decreasing influence of Ssu Ma Kuang, had contrived to kindle a fire of resentment in the heart of the latter which, smouldering through the twelve long years of seclusion, burst into flames on his restoration to power, and only died down again when it had accomplished the complete devastation of his opponent's policy.

There are signs that after the death of Shen Tsung, Ssu Ma Kuang hesitated [3] to return to what was obviously a very critical situation, involving, from his point of view, in the light of his previous relationships to the protagonists of the new measures, action of a drastic character. But having once returned, it is equally evident that he was out deliberately to overthrow the work of the previous regime in its entirety.

How otherwise can we explain his statement that " the laws which Wang An Shih and Lü Hui Ch'ing had propounded were so detrimental to the people's livelihood that it was as important to save the people from them as to save a man from drowning or fire " ? [4]

[1] " T'ung Chien," Hsi Ning, 3rd year, 9th month.
[2] " T'ung Chien," Hsi Ning, 4th year, 4th month.
[3] " T'ung Chien," Yuan Feng, 8th year, 4th month.
[4] " T'ung Chien," Yuan Feng, 8th year, 5th month.

It is true that he is also reported to have said, that " all which was good in Shen Tsung's regime might be preserved for a century ".[1] But his later action speaks louder than his words, for he proceeded to abolish every trace of that regime.

Further, we read in the historical comment on Wang An Shih's death that, in the latter's opinion, " the one who deemed the new measures impracticable from beginning to end was Ssu Ma Kuang." [2]

There is no doubt at all about Ssu Ma Kuang's sincerity in opposing the reform policy on the one hand and his personal regard for Wang An Shih's character [3] on the other. But there is also no doubt that in overthrowing the policy of Wang An Shih he was actuated by ulterior motives. We know that he had no use at all for Lü Hui Ch'ing, who had been one of Wang An Shih's chief colleagues, and that he had suffered tremendous loss of face and influence through Shen Tsung's support of the policy Wang and Lü had advocated. From the general tenour of the history of his relationships to the reformers and their policy, his various expressions of opinion about them and their work, and his obvious haste and " obstinacy " after his return to power, one cannot escape the inference that in overthrowing the previous regime he was venting his personal spleen and satisfying his desire for " redress " to a very considerable extent.

He did not, of course, act solely on his own initiative in this matter. The Regent, Hsuan Jen, had already taken strong action with regard to the reform policy before recalling Ssu Ma Kuang to office,[4] and unquestionably she was as desirous as her new minister of eliminating all traces of the previous regime. For when Su Shih remonstrated with Ssu Ma Kuang for being too rash and drastic, he replied, " I am reforming the son (Shen Tsung) according to the will of his mother (Hsuan

---

[1] " T'ung Chien," Yuan Feng, 8th year, 5th month.
[2] " T'ung Chien," Yuan Yu, 1st year, 4th month.
[3] See Chap. VIII, Vol. II.
[4] " T'ung Chien," Yuan Feng, 8th year, 4th month.

Jen)." [1]   Hsuan Jen had no love for Wang An Shih, and had often urged upon Shen Tsung the desirability of getting rid of him.   So that in her case, as well as in that of Ssu Ma Kuang, personal considerations were not entirely absent in the determination of political policy at this juncture.

Another person of considerable influence at this time was Lü Kung Chu.   Just before his death Ssu Ma Kuang is reported to have said, " The matter of my health I have committed to the care of my physician, my private affairs I have committed to my son, and the concerns of the government I must entrust to Lü Kung Chu." [2]

We know that the latter was connected with Wang An Shih's regime, both during the time he was in office himself and also later after his retirement.   However, he had found himself unable to remain at the capital on account of his opposition to the policy then advocated.   According to the statement of Ssu Ma Kuang, Lü Kung Chu had not only been promoted by Wang An Shih, but had also been cashiered by him, and that this change of attitude on the part of Wang An Shih implied lack of confidence on one side or the other. [3]

Lü Kung Chu is one of those men whose attitude is peculiarly difficult to explain.   It may be because the historians have so cleverly related events connected with him that, as Wang An Shih states in his letter to Chang Tien Ch'eng, it is impossible for anyone living to ascertain the real facts of the case. [4]   But, with a view to getting as near the truth as possible, we will sketch his career as found in the Histories.

He resigned from the post of Chief Censor under Wang An Shih's regime in the 4th month of 1070, after opposing the Agricultural Loans Measure on the ground that the promulgation of it against the opinion of the majority of Court officials was wrong, and also on the ground that the promotors of the

---

[1] Liang Ch'i Ch'ao, p. 275 (太 皇 太 后 以 母 改 子 非 以 子 改 父).

[2] " T'ung Chien," Yuan Yu, 1st year, 2nd month.

[3] " T'ung Chien," Hsi Ning, 3rd year, 9th month.

[4] Works, vol. xviii, p. 8.

measure had unjustly dubbed the opposition " conventional " and their criticisms " worthless ". But the occasion and possibly the real reason for his resignation was that he was asked to appoint Lü Hui Ch'ing to his department, a move which he absolutely refused to make, on the ground that although he had distinct abilities he was of evil character. This, according to the record, incited Wang An Shih's wrath, and he proceeded to falsely accuse him of having made the statement that Han Ch'i was plotting rebellion against the government. For this he was transferred to Ying Chow.[1]

Nothing more is heard of him until after Wang An Shih had definitely resigned in the 10th month of 1076, when the History relates that on Wu Ts'ung assuming the reins of the Grand Council, he wished to make some changes, and proposed the recall of Ssu Ma Kuang, Lü Kung Chu, and eight others, all of whom had been opposed to Wang An Shih's policy.[2] One cannot say definitely whether he returned to the capital at that time or not, but there is a note of his appointment, together with that of Hsieh Hsiang, to an important post in the Military Board in the 6th month of 1078.[3]

In the 9th month of 1080 he was promoted to the Vice-Presidency of the Board of War, and in the 1st month of the following year he was made acting-supervisor of the Board with Han Chen, but in the 4th month of 1082, for some reason not stated, he was either dismissed or took the initiative himself and resigned.[4]

Then, after the death of Che Tsung, and the restoration of Ssu Ma Kuang to power, he was recalled in the 7th month of 1085 to take up an important post in the Shang Shu Sheng. The commentator on this appointment states that he had been at Yang Chow, so we infer that he may have been appointed to that post on his leaving the capital in 1082. The narrative here also includes the following interesting comment, viz. " The

[1] " T'ung Chien," Hsi Ning, 3rd year, 4th month.
[2] " T'ung Chien," Hsi Ning, 9th year, 10th month.
[3] " T'ung Chien," Yuan Feng, 1st year, 6th month.
[4] " T'ung Chien," Yuan Feng, 5th year, 4th month.

Regent asked him to express his mind on things. He said,
' The real idea of Shen Tsung was to make the relief of the
distresses of the people his prime concern, but those who were
advising him then were more concerned with changing the
existing laws and mulcting the people than anything else.
They also got rid of all who were of different opinion from
them. So with the lapse of time the injurious character of their
policy became more and more apparent and the distress of the
people was greatly intensified. If, however, we can secure men
of impartial views and good character to investigate the real
condition of the country and co-operate for its relief, it should
not be difficult to save the situation.' " [1]

The commentator continues, " After he had resumed his
place in the government, he was of one heart and mind with
Ssu Ma Kuang in fulfilling the real purpose of Shen Tsung.
All that he had wished to reform but had not been able actually
to accomplish, and all the reforms he actually made but had not
been able to complete satisfactorily, they carried out *in toto*,
to the great joy of the people." [1]

So that, as in the case of Ssu Ma Kuang and Hsuan Jen, it is
not unreasonable to suppose that Lü Kung Chu, in supporting
so wholeheartedly the abolition policy of Ssu Ma Kuang, was
not altogether free from personal prejudices. It will be noted
that he, like Ssu Ma Kuang, had strong personal objections
against Lü Hui Ch'ing, and that he, like Ssu Ma Kuang, had
been compelled to retire from the Court during the period of
his opponents' greatest influence.

The traditional historians highly praise Lü Kung Chu for
his *volte face* in regard to Wang An Shih's policy.[2] He
became Prime Minister in the 4th month of 1088, but died
in the 2nd month of 1089.

From the above it also appears that Ssu Ma Kuang and Lü
Kung Chu were ready to attribute a considerable portion, if
not the greater portion, of the blame for the injurious character

[1] " T'ung Chien," Yuan Feng, 8th year, 7th month.
[2] Liang Ch'i Ch'ao, p. 290.

of the reform policy, to Lü Hui Ch'ing. In the biographical notice on Lü Hui Ch'ing which is found in the Dynastic Histories, it is said that Ssu Ma Kuang made Lü Hui Ch'ing responsible for the ideas behind the new measures, and that Wang An Shih was merely his instrument.[1]

The latter seems quite unreasonable on the face of it. For of the two Wang An Shih was obviously the chief promoter of the reform policy. If definite evidence were needed, one might quote the letter which he wrote to Lü Hui Ch'ing after his retirement from the Court, in which he states clearly that Lü Hui Ch'ing had "helped" him to carry the measures through when all others had deserted him.[2]

The fact that in the Dynastic Histories Lü Hui Ch'ing is branded as an "evil official" (奸 臣) and that Wang An Shih is included by Chu Hsi in his "Lives of Famous Officials" shows the trend of popular opinion on the relative merits and demerits of these two men. Looking at the matter all round, it would appear that there seemed more justification for blaming Lü Hui Ch'ing on the grounds of personal character than there was for blaming Wang An Shih. But the general impression created by these various attitudes towards one or other of these prominent protagonists of the reform policy is that critics felt compelled to find some "scape-goat" on whom blame might be thrown and so justify Ssu Ma Kuang in pressing for total abolition. So they blamed Wang An Shih rather than Shen Tsung, and Lü Hui Ch'ing rather than Wang An Shih, in order to make their case more credible.

We have gone into some detail in connection with Lü Hui Ch'ing to show that Ssu Ma Kuang and Lü Kung Chu, in eliminating all trace of Wang An Shih's policy, may have been actuated, in part, by their personal antipathy to the one who was most prominently associated with him in the promulgation of the reform measures.

There are, however, still more cogent reasons for assuming that their policy of abrogation was determined not so much

[1] Liang Ch'i Ch'ao, p. 294.
[2] Works, vol. xviii, p. 9.

because they considered Wang An Shih's measures injurious but from ulterior motives. There is for instance a certain inconsistency observable in Ssu Ma Kuang's attitude to those measures. During the promotion of them by Wang An Shih and his associates, Ssu Ma Kuang had presented uncompromising opposition. But in the eighth month of 1086, after he had rescinded them all, he said, in reference to the Agricultural Loans Measure, that " in its main idea it was of benefit to the people, but that compulsory practices in connection with its administration should be given up ".[1]

This indicates a certain measure of repentance in reference to his own action in rescinding this particular measure, and the reason is not very far to seek. For in the third month of this same year Fan Ch'un Jen had appealed for the measure to be revived (it had been rescinded in the second month) on the ground that signs of stringency in the national finances were already apparent.[1]

Evidently it was easy enough to rescind such a measure by the stroke of a pen, but not so easy to supplant it by a measure that would ensure a sufficiency of revenue in the national treasury.

The character of the opposition to total abolition also lends strength to our assumption that the new measures were not of such a worthless character as to merit Ssu Ma Kuang's total abrogation of them.

There was, for instance, the rigid opposition of Fan Ch'un Jen, who had no particular love for Wang An Shih, yet who exhorted Ssu Ma Kuang to deliberate very carefully before he took such extreme action. He urged that only certain " extreme " features of the measures should be eliminated. With regard to the Public Services Act and Ssu Ma Kuang's determination to supplant it by the old Labour Conscription Measure, he urged him to be extremely cautious in doing so, and warned him that any changes which he intended to make should be introduced very gradually, otherwise the sufferings

[1] Liang Ch'i Ch'ao, p. 127.

of the people would be greatly intensified. He further exhorted him to clear his mind of all preconceptions, and not to depend upon his own ideas solely, but to consider other points of view. Ssu Ma Kuang, however, ignored this advice, which caused Fan Ch'un Jen to remark, " This is stopping men's mouths. If I am to flatter you to gain your approval, I might as well have co-operated with Wang An Shih in my early days, and long ago have attained to wealth and position." [1]

Fan Ch'un Jen, as has been shown above, also appealed for the revival of the Agricultural Loans Measure. But he had been one of the most prominent antagonists of both these Measures during the period of their promotion by Wang An Shih.

The same is true of Su Shih, who formerly had said that conscripted labour was essential to the State, but now objected more strenuously than any other individual to the abrogation of the Public Services Measure by Ssu Ma Kuang, urging that not even a sage could improve on the " hiring " system, and that the revival of the " Labour Conscription " idea would add ten-fold to the sufferings of the people.[2]

Li Ch'ing Ch'en (李 清 臣) was another prominent man to raise his voice in protest against the abrogation of these two measures.

It is quite likely that there were other instances of opposition to Ssu Ma Kuang's action which are not recorded in the Histories. For the foundation of the traditional Histories lay in the work of Fan Tsu Yü (who was a follower of Ssu Ma Kuang) and of his son Fan Ch'ung, and it is only reasonable to suppose that they would be unlikely to add to such " damaging " evidence as these instances of opposition afford against the reasonableness of " total abrogation ".

Ch'en Ju Ch'i has an apposite criticism of Ssu Ma Kuang's action, which we will summarize, as follows [3] :—

---

[1] " T'ung Chien," Yuan Yu, 1st year, 3rd month.
[2] " T'ung Chien," Yuan Yu, 1st year, 3rd month, and Liang Ch'i Ch'ao, p. 150.
[3] Ts'ai Shang Hsiang, Tsa Lu (雜 錄), vol. i, p. 12.

" The New Measures were the product of much thought and corporate counsel. Shen Tsung was a man who understood the circumstances of the common people, and had given so much heart-searching thought to the proposals of Wang An Shih that not even the tears of his mother, the fears of his brother, and the importunity of officials great and small were of any avail to turn him from his purpose.

" Although it may be admitted that in the carrying out of the measures, those administering them proceeded to a certain excess ; that some features of them were of doubtful benefit, and that in certain cases the effect produced was contrary to the original intention of the promoters, yet the most important thing (for Ssu Ma Kuang to do) was to follow on the lines already laid down as far as possible, and plan for what revision was necessary, thus freeing the measures from their defective aspects and fulfilling their fine possibilities. In that way they could have prevented them from functioning in any way detrimental to the people's livelihood, and would not have failed to carry out the manifest intention of Shen Tsung. If that had been done, mean men would have been given no opportunity for their nefarious schemes, and the disastrous effects of the ensuing policy of mutual recrimination and revenge would have been avoided.

" But instead of this, he (Ssu Ma Kuang) must go his own way and completely overthrow the preceding regime. The Regent and others who had opposed Wang An Shih fruitlessly before (now seized their opportunity). Others like Fan Ch'un Jen and Su Shih opposed Ssu Ma Kuang fruitlessly now. The moment a flatterer like Ts'ai Ching appeared expressing his joy at the prospect of carrying out Ssu Ma Kuang's intention (promising to supplant the Public Services Measure by the Labour Conscription Measure in five days) it led to the total collapse of the previous regime before the corpse of Shen Tsung had had time to get cold."

Our conclusion on this matter of Ssu Ma Kuang's action in abolishing the whole of Wang An Shih's policy is that he went far beyond what the circumstances called for, and that he was

actuated by personal feeling rather than consideration for his
country's well-being. It is said that Ssu Ma Kuang formed no
faction, but it is certain that his colleagues interpreted his
extreme action at this time as equivalent to that of a political
partisan. He may have been sincere in opposing Wang An
Shih's policy, but there were obviously many good features
in his regime which were well worthy of perpetuation. And
no matter how far he himself may have felt justified in taking
the action he did, the results turned out to be disastrous.
For whether his action was based on personal considerations
or on partisan lines or not, it is certain that he paved
the way for the entrance of the deplorable spirit of faction into
the national politics of the next forty years.

Chu Hsi affords evidence in support of our contention that
Ssu Ma Kuang overstepped the mark in overthrowing the
whole of Wang An Shih's policy. On being asked by one of
his pupils as to what he thought of Ssu Ma Kuang's action, he
replied, " The one thought that obsessed his mind was that
Wang An Shih was wrong, and so he took a one-sided view of
things." [1] He agreed that " The action of the Yuan Yu party
in completely rescinding the Militia Act, led to the ruin of
a successful piece of policy ".[2] And again, " The officials
of the Yuan Yu regime, generally speaking, had their prejudices." [3] He also tacitly confesses that the later restoration
of the territory to the Hsi Hsia which had been taken from them
during Wang An Shih's regime led nowhere.[3] Yet again, " The
proposals of the Yuan Yu officials were the outcome of
a fixed idea that they should correct the faults of the
previous regime, but they were unaware that their actions
betrayed them as conventionalists. For it was essential to the
welfare of the State that the army should be drilled, that reforms
should be instituted when there were obvious faults in the
administration, and that adjustments and changes should be

---

[1] Chu Hsi, Complete Works, vol. lxii, p. 31.
[2] Chu Hsi, Complete Works, vol. lxii, p. 32.
[3] Chu Hsi Complete Works, vol. lxii, p. 33.

made. How can it be said that all the measures of the previous regime were failures ? " [1]

We are not concerned to prove that the downfall of the Northern Sungs in 1126 was due to this action of Ssu Ma Kuang, as some have endeavoured to do. There were other and more cogent reasons for that, as will be explained below. But we do contend that his extreme action so disturbed the minds of political leaders of the succeeding period that the affairs of the nation got neglected, and unworthy men rose to power and influence, with the result that the national defences fell into disrepair, and the Tartars, against whom Wang An Shih had planned with such foresight and effectiveness, conquered the whole of North China with little or no resistance. Had Ssu Ma Kuang shown a more reasonable attitude towards his political enemies, and had he not been so blinded to everything but the vindication of his former opposition so that nothing but complete abrogation of the New Laws would satisfy him, it is difficult to imagine that the party spirit would have waxed so fierce as it did and pursued such a calamitous course.

Ts'ai Shang Hsiang quotes from Wang Ming Ch'ing (王 明 清), a writer of the Sung times, as follows :—

" The Yuan Yu party has been held in the greatest respect by succeeding generations. In the time of Shao Sheng (when Wang An Shih's party was in power) thirty-two of the Yuan Yu officials were blacklisted. Later on, when Ts'ai Ching was in power, no less than 309 of his political foes were proscribed. The source of these actions must, however, be traced to the extreme enmity and hatred of the Yuan Yu party. For Lü Kung Chu, Liang T'ao, and Liu An Shih first proscribed thirty of Wang An Shih's following, including Lü Hui Ch'ing and Chang Ch'un. They also blacklisted ten of Ts'ai Ch'üeh's following, including An T'ao and Tseng Pu. The appeal of Fan Ch'un Jen that only the chief leaders should be proscribed went unheeded. So he proceeded to warn the ringleaders that they would meet with a similar fate later on. Sure enough, this prophecy was fulfilled when Chang

[1] Chu Hsi, Complete Works, vol. lxii, p. 33.

Ch'un set up his tablet incriminating the Yuan Yu officials. All this unseemly conduct on the part of the great officials of the time was the outcome of that spirit of vengeance and recrimination which dominated their minds and, what is more deplorable, eventually culminated in national disaster." [1]

It may be urged that Wang An Shih failed to win the co-operation of a large number of famous officials of his day, and that large numbers of them were constrained to leave the Court and take up subordinate posts in the provinces. Further, that this may be interpreted as action akin to that of Ssu Ma Kuang, and therefore prime blame for the initiation of the faction spirit should be attributed to him. Against that, however, there is ample evidence, both from friend and foe alike, that in all that Wang An Shih did he was actuated solely by patriotic considerations, however faulty his methods may have been. That cannot be said of Ssu Ma Kuang. He introduced the element of vindictiveness into politics which changed the spirit of the national leaders, and so he is relatively more blameworthy for ensuing events than Wang An Shih.

The course of politics during the next forty years makes pitiable reading. First one party and then another came into power, each making the policy of Wang An Shih either its " butt " or its " banner ". But the interests of the nation were gradually subordinated to the interests of the particular party which happened to be uppermost at the time, and political interests got gradually submerged in a flood of personal recrimination, wholesale proscriptions of opponents, banishments, imprisonments, and the like.

The policy of Wang An Shih, although it seemed to be the *casus belli* between the factions, was not really so. For those who later adopted his policy as their warcry did so mainly with the idea of making it a pretext for exacting vengeance on their particular enemies. His policy was never really revived.

But Ts'ai Ching, who was the most influential man during the reign of Hui Tsung (1101–1126), adopted the revival of a

---

[1] Ts'ai Shang Hsiang, " Chuan Shou " (巷 首) (玉 照 新 志 二 則).

semblance of Wang An Shih's policy as a means of satisfying his personal ambition and thus gave a handle to Wang An Shih's critics, who, led by Yang Kuei Shan, began to attribute the cause of the downfall of the Northern Sung Dynasty to Wang An Shih and his policy.

"That however," says Ts'ai Shang Hsiang, "is sheer blasphemy."

This is part of a quotation from an unknown writer, which we will give in full, as follows :—

"During the time that Wang An Shih was in power the whole country greatly prospered, the great victory of the Hsi Ho had led to extension of the national territory by several thousands of li, a successful state of things which had not obtained throughout the hundred odd years of the Sung Dynasty. But after the transfer of the Dynasty to the south, the descendants of the officials of the ' Yuan Yu ' regime, the adherents of the ' Su ' (蘇) and ' Ch'eng ' (程) schools, and those officials who belonged to their parties, yielded themselves up to faction strife with disastrous consequences. Some, thinking it not sufficient to attack Ts'ai Ching, began to attribute the downfall of the Northern Dynasty to Wang An Shih. But that is sheer blasphemy. The downfall of the Northern Sung was actually due to Ts'ai Ching."

The writer then points out that Ts'ai Ching gained no office under Wang An Shih, although his younger brother was married to Wang An Shih's daughter, and that Ssu Ma Kuang was really the first to give him prominence in political life. Yang Kuei Shan, to whom the above charge against Wang An Shih is traceable, was indebted to Ts'ai Ching for past favours, as well as fearful of his influence at the particular time he made this statement, so he thought it preferable to throw the blame on a regime long defunct rather than on that which was extant.[1]

We have already suggested that there were other reasons for the downfall of the Northern Sung Dynasty than either the promulgation of the reform measures in Shen Tsung's

[1] Ts'ai Shang Hsiang, vol. xxiv, p. 7.

day, or their rescindment in the earlier part of Che Tsung's reign. The rise and progress of the spirit of faction and feud which followed on their abrogation certainly was one of the determining factors in the situation, as the real interests of the country went begging whilst the factions glutted themselves with mutual recrimination and vengeance. But as the unknown author of the last quotation suggests, the real cause of the disaster is to be found in the administration of Ts'ai Ching.

Let us take another extract from the writings of Ch'en Ju Ch'i, as found in one of his essays on Wang An Shih. He says :—

"A slavish devotion to the vague and airy teachings of Taoism, lavish expenditure on buildings and other public works, with the people suffering from cruel and burdensome taxation, and indolence and indulgence rampant in high places. These and other features of the national life, injurious to the state and people alike, are alien to the spirit of the Wang An Shih regime, but they are characteristic of the Ts'ai Ching administration.

"Think again of Ts'ai Ching's associates. Men like T'ung Kuan (童貫), Li Yen (李彥), and Liang Shih Ch'eng (梁師成) as Court Chamberlains. Specious and clever opportunists like Ch'ung Mien (冲酌), father and son. Ministers like Wang Fu (王黼), Pai Shih Chung (白時中), Li Pang Yen (李邦彥), and other war-inciting and confusion-creating councillors. Not one of these was associated with the Wang An Shih regime. Ts'ai Ching himself was not employed by Wang An Shih, even though his younger brother was his son-in-law.

"In all this there is no traceable connection with Wang An Shih, and yet it is said that he was the cause of the ensuing disaster.

"The fact that Ts'ai Ching honoured Wang An Shih with special homage in the Confucian temple was simply with a view to deceiving his ruler, of currying special favour for himself, and with the idea of cloaking his own evil purposes." [1]

[1] Ts'ai Shang Hsiang, Tsa Lu (雜錄), vol. i, p. 10.

Reverting now to the opinions of Chu Hsi, we find that he suggests that this national disaster of 1126 can be traced to a number of infamous men who continued Wang An Shih's tyrannical policy. He must have had men like Chang Ch'un, Ts'ai Ch'üeh, and Ts'ai Ching in mind. The policy of vengeance which these three men pursued so relentlessly one must thoroughly deplore. But they were not the prime instigators of such a policy, as has been shown above. And though they made the revival of Wang An Shih's policy their rallying call and battle cry, none of them, excepting perhaps Chang Ch'un, were seriously concerned with the carrying out of Wang An Shih's ideas. The attempted revival of his policy in the period of Che Tsung's independence was but half-hearted, and represented little more than a bare semblance of his regime. Whereas the pretence at revival under Ts'ai Ching was a mere mockery of Wang An Shih. So that it is quite unfair either to say that these men were continuing the labours of Wang An Shih or to attribute their revengeful and cruel tactics to their connection with him. How glaring is the contrast between the way he treated his political antagonists and that in which these men and their opponents treated each other !

But it is easy to see how this slanderous opinion that Wang An Shih was primarily responsible for the calamity of 1126 gained ground and became the permanent tradition. Yang Kuei Shan, who first mooted the idea, was a disciple of the Lo School, and Chu Hsi was his successor. The Lo School was antagonistic to Wang An Shih, and their opinions got incorporated in the Histories.

By way of summing up our views of Wang An Shih as a reformer, we will attempt to rewrite T'o K'o T'o's quotation of Chu Hsi's opinions, endeavouring to be as impartial as possible.

"Wang An Shih was a peer among his fellows both in scholarly attainments and personal character. He realized the urgent need of his country's condition, and devoted himself with an utter disregard to personal consequences to the reform of the moral and social order of his day. The

Emperor Shen Tsung was determined to redeem the national shame of many generations, to replenish the depleted exchequer, and so to strengthen the military resources of the empire that the menace of the northern foe could be thwarted and prosperity and stability restored to the nation. He found in Wang An Shih the one man who possessed the ideas for the fulfilling of this great purpose. He was also possessed of a real spirit of sympathy with his monarch's ideals, and had the resolution to labour for their realization, so he appointed him his High Minister of State.

"His reputation for good work, high character, wide learning, and practical experience of political matters, combined as it was with a fine mentality and noble ideals for his country, was so great that everyone thought he would make some great contribution to the solving of the nation's problems. In fact, so great was their expectancy that they even began to think they might witness a revival of the splendour and prosperity of the Golden Age.

"It certainly was Wang An Shih's purpose to make of Shen Tsung an ideal ruler, and to bring the blessings of peace and prosperity to his people.

"He devoted himself, with rare zeal and courage, to the reform of the national finances and to the strengthening of the military resources of the country. These he considered fundamental to the execution of his purpose. His conviction that he had the right ideas for the times, and a sense, common to both the Emperor and himself, of the urgency of the need for reform, led him to override the opposition of his famous official contemporaries in a manner seemingly arrogant and contemptuous. So their antagonism was aroused, and they began to oppose everything which he suggested in an unreasonable and prejudiced manner. This in its turn reacted on Wang An Shih in such a way that he felt constrained to eliminate their obstruction by transferring large numbers of them to provincial appointments. Others resigned of their own accord. Thus deserted by those whom posterity has deemed loyal and upright, he was compelled to seek for assistance elsewhere, and amongst those whom he introduced to the government service were a few who proved unworthy of his trust.

"The various measures which he and his colleagues devised for the salvation of their country were every one good in intent. But they had their defects, largely through their being the product of the thinking of a few men of like mind and kindred aim. And in the actual application of them to the whole empire they were hampered by having to depend upon a great number of local officials who, either from a desire to win a reputation for zeal and efficiency, or out of lust for personal advantage and gain, administered the measures in such a way that they partially failed of their original objective, and in some respects and amongst certain classes of the people were deemed oppressive.

"The fact that he was attempting a task of radical and empire wide reform, which inevitably meant depriving the wealthy of some of their hoary privileges and much of their ill-gotten gains, naturally aroused their resentment and clamorous opposition.

"At last Wang An Shih, through ill-health, and worn out with his herculean labours for the State, was compelled to resign. This was due to no lack of confidence in him on the part of the Emperor, but to sheer physical and mental inability on the part of his minister to carry any longer the heavy responsibilities of such high office. He was loaded with honours, and continued to be the recipient of his monarch's most earnest solicitude.

"Further, the Emperor for the rest of his reign maintained intact the policy which he had formulated with many signs of success.

"However, after the death of Shen Tsung, the Regent Hsuan Jen, aided by Ssu Ma Kuang and Lü Kung Chu, who were all strongly opposed to the previous regime, completely over-turned Wang An Shih's policy. This extreme action, based as it was on the desire to vindicate their opposition and to vent their personal spleen, paved the way for the entrance of a ruinous spirit of faction and feud into political life.

" Those who succeeded Ssu Ma Kuang began to proscribe
the supporters of Wang An Shih's policy, and to inflict punishment and personal disgrace upon them. But when Wang An
Shih's supporters under the independent rule of Che Tsung
were once more restored to power, vengeance was promptly
and severely exacted of their political foes. Later again, during
the reign of Hui Tsung, when Ts'ai Ching was in power, still
more severe punishment was meted out to those who had
been antagonistic to Wang An Shih's followers.

" This deplorable spirit of vengeance and party strife led
to affairs being seriously neglected, but as Ts'ai Ching had
pretended to revive Wang An Shih's policy, and as he was
mainly instrumental for the downfall of the Northern Sung
Dynasty, critics began to blame Wang An Shih for this national
disaster.

" This opinion, unjust as it was, became the general opinion,
because the historical records which have persisted, and which
have been accepted as ' canonical ', were compiled by writers
who belong to that ' school ' which was antagonistic to Wang
An Shih." [1]

---

[1] T'o K'o T'o probably took this extract, here rewritten, according to my
own ideas, from the commentary in the T'ung Chien, under date recording
Wang An Shih's death in the 1st year of Yuan Yu, 4th month. I have not been
able to trace this extract, or the one which immediately follows it in the T'ung
Chien, in any of Chu Hsi's works. Normally one would expect to find such a
statement in his chapter on Wang An Shih, vol. lix of his Complete Works.

CHAPTER XI

THE LIFE AND ECONOMIC POLICY OF SANG HUNG YANG [1]

(BEING A SYNOPSIS OF THE "LIFE OF SANG HUNG YANG"
AS FOUND IN "THE LIVES OF FAMOUS CHINESE" (中 國
歷 代 名 人 傳 畧) PUBLISHED BY THE ASSOCIATION
PRESS OF CHINA)

SANG HUNG YANG was the son of a Loyang merchant. He was born in 143 B.C. and died in 80 B.C. At the early age of 13 he was appointed a clerk in the government estimating department. In 115 B.C. he devised his "Chün Shu Fa" (均 輸 法) or "Distribution Measure", which comprised the purchase of native products by the government when prices were cheap and transporting them to places where they were required for sale at a fair price. The government sought only to cover transport charges from the operation of this measure.

In the year 110 B.C., in addition to a military appointment, he was promoted to the Presidency of the Board of Revenue, and supplanted K'ung Chin (孔 僅) as Superintendent of the Government Salt and Iron Monopolies.

He at once proceeded to establish Government Bureaus in each district for the purpose of supervising the transport and interchange of commodities, thus eliminating the current practice of competition for this traffic amongst the officials, which had led to increases in prices and losses on transport charges to the government. Thus the government undertook to transport the goods from distant places which hitherto had been transported by the big commerical combines, accepting local products in lieu of taxation. In addition he set up a Central Bureau at the capital which regulated the prices of all commodities and supervised their distribution throughout the country.

[1] The material in Chaps. XI, XII, and XIII is included in this work to give the reader some idea of Wang An Shih's forerunners in the world of Chinese political reform.

The big commercial firms were thus deprived of the opportunity to make enormous profits, and the prices of all commodities throughout the country were regulated by the government to the relief and satisfaction of the people everywhere. The savings effected by the government control of transport and prices were not only sufficient to meet the enormous outlay involved, but led to reduced taxation.

The system of regulating prices was termed " P'ing Chun " (平 準).

He appealed to the Emperor to institute a system whereby subordinate officials could secure their promotion to higher rank by offerings of grain, and also that grain should be exacted in criminal cases in lieu of monetary fines. Every district was also commanded to pay taxes in grain only. As a result of these innovations, in the province of Shantung alone an increase of 6,000,000 piculs of grain was recorded annually in the government revenue. Should grain not be available in any district, silk was to be received. From this source 5,000,000 pieces of silk were received annually. In this way, without the addition of taxation, the government revenue became adequate for all requirements.

As a reward for his successful policy, the Emperor not only promoted Sang Hung Yang in rank, but presented him with two hundred catties of pure gold.

But although his policy was so successful, both in regard to meeting government needs and relieving the general populace, considerable opposition was aroused in official circles on the ground that such financial policy as he formulated was beneath the dignity of scholarly rulers. On an occasion of drought, one Pu Shih (卜 式) demanded that he should be boiled alive, and prophesied that then the rain would come. The Emperor, however, did not take this advice, but banished Pu Shih for his pains.

Han Wu Ti then placed Sang Hung Yang in complete control of the government revenue services, and in 98 B.C. he proceeded to make wine, as well as salt and iron, a government monopoly.

In 87 B.C., just prior to Han Wu Ti's death, along with Ho Kuang (霍 光), Chin Jih Shan (金 日 磾), and Shang Kuan Chieh (上 官 桀), he was commissioned to aid his heir, Han Chao Ti. When the latter came to the throne the next year, Ho Kuang was appointed regent.

In 81 B.C., due to the administration of the government monopolies and the Distribution and Control Measures being in the hands of men like Tu Yen Nien (杜 延 年), although receipts continued to be enormous, a policy of militarism and extravagance resulted in general distress and impoverishment, not only amongst the populace generally, but also in the government exchequer. This led to Ho Kuang calling in the advice of the scholarly class to ascertain the cause of the prevailing distress. This type of scholar, being by training and tradition opposed to such economic policy as Sung Hung Yang had initiated, and seeing an opportunity to curry favour with influential men like Ho and Tu, unanimously appealed for the abrogation of all government monopolies, and the various Distribution and Control Measures, as they involved the government in commercial competition with the people.

Both Ho and Tu approved of this appeal, but Sang Hung Yang made a vigorous defence, asserting that if his policy were abandoned, the economic stability of the empire would be seriously imperilled. But by way of compromise, he suggested, in concert with Ch'e Ch'ien Ch'iu (車 千 秋), that the latest government monopoly, viz. in wine, might be surrendered.

Tu Yen Nien and his confrères, however, in fear lest their efforts should fail, once more incited the scholars. This led to a vigorous attack upon the scholars by Sang Hung Yang. He used very strong language in his indictment, asserting that they were an impracticable, useless, hypocritical, and bigoted crowd. Then Huan K'uan (桓 寬) sought to make the peace by producing a treatise entitled " A Discussion on Monopolies " (鹽 鐵 論), which presented both points of view. The immediate upshot of this was that the scholars lost the day.

However, Ch'e Ch'ien Ch'iu, in his fear of incurring the enmity of Tu and Ho, resigned his position in the Cabinet, leaving Sang Hung Yang alone to meet the onslaught of his political opponents.

In the ninth month of 80 B.C. a plot of rebellion against the government, hatched by Yen Wang Tan (燕 王 旦), Shang Kuan Chieh (上 官 桀), and others, came to the knowledge of Tu Yen Nien. He thereupon accused Sang Hung Yang of being an accomplice. He was therefore incriminated of rebellion and put to death with the others.

Later writers are of the opinion that he was unjustly done to death by Tu Yen Nien, who in his hatred of Sang Hung Yang, also executed his son, Sang Ch'ien (桑 遷).

CHAPTER XII

THE FIVE EQUALIZING MEASURES OF WANG MANG (ACCORDING TO HU SHIH) [1]

THE most interesting feature in the programme of economic reform under the New Dynasty was the so-called " Five Equalizations ". They were chiefly directed to stabilizing the prices of commodities in general use. They may be characterized as a government control of trade in useful goods operated for the benefit of the general public. The surplus profit was to be used in making loans to the farming and working classes.

The organization for this purpose consisted of seven directorates stationed at seven of the commercial centres of the empire, namely, Ch'ang An (長 安), east, Ch'ang An, west, Lo Yang (洛 陽), Han Tan (邯 鄲), Wan (宛), Lin Tzu (臨 淄), and Ch'eng Tu (成 都). Under each directorate there were five Trade Commissioners and one Commissioner on Banking and Credit. Each directorate was to be in charge of the five " Equalizations " which are described in the Han Shu (漢 書), viz. :—

1. *The Determination of the Index Number of Prices.*— " Each directorate shall use the second month of each season for the determination of the equitable price of the commodities under its management. It shall note down the highest, lowest, and the mean price of each commodity in each district. The mean price shall be the equitable price of that particular locality, and shall not be applied to the places where the other directorates are situated."

2. *The Buying of Unsold Goods from the Market.*—" The Office of Equalization shall buy up all such goods as wheat, rice and other foodstuffs, cloth, silk and silk-fabrics—goods which are needed by the people for everyday use but which the merchants have not been able to sell at a particular time. The

---

[1] See footnote, p. 233.

237

cost price shall be paid to the dealers in order to insure them against loss."

3. *The Stabilization of Prices.*—" As soon as the price of any of these useful commodities rises one cash beyond the ' equitable price ' for that particular season, the Equalization Office shall sell out its accumulated stock at the equitable price so that the people may be protected against those who make extravagant profit by cornering the supplies and manipulating the market."

4. *Loans without Interest.*—" Persons who need ready money for funeral, burial, or sacrificial purposes may be given loans by the Commissioner of Credit from the proceeds of trade. Such loans should be without interest, but must be repaid within the specified period of time. Loans for sacrificial purposes shall be repaid within ten days ; those for funerals and burials within three months."

5. *Loans to be used as Working Capital.*—" Poor people who need capital to start productive work may also secure loans from the Commissioner of Credit who shall charge them a moderate rate of interest."

According to Bk. 99*b* of the Han Shu, the ratio was 3 per cent per month, but according to Bk. 24*b* it was " not to exceed an annual interest of 10 per cent ".

Wang Mang issued a decree in A.D. 10 in which he said in part : " I have now inaugurated the loans to the people, the Five Equalizations and the various State controls, all aiming at an equitable distribution of goods among the people, to prevent them from being exploited by the rich and strong."

Seven years later he issued another decree to explain further the purpose of the Six Controls, which now included the Five Equalizations. He said :—

" Salt is the chief seasoning of all food. Wine is the leading element of medicine and the favourite beverage of all gatherings of conviviality. Iron is the basis of all agricultural implements. Mines and forests are the storehouses of national wealth. The object of price stabilization and banking is to protect the people and supply their needs. Money and coinage furnish the necessary medium of exchange. None of these six can be operated by the average citizen, who must depend upon the professional trader for the satisfaction of these needs. Therefore he becomes the victim of economic exploitation, and must accept whatever price the rich and strong are pleased to dictate to him. The sages of the ancient times realized all this evil and resolved to check it by means of government control."

How exceedingly modern these words sound in our ears! These two edicts certainly deserved to be ranked as the earliest conscious statement of the theory of state socialism in the history of the social and political thought of mankind.

But Wang Mang and his assistants were nineteen centuries ahead of their time. In an empire almost as large as the modern China Proper, without any modern facilities of check and control, they were destined to fail in their ambitious schemes of economic and political reform. There were not enough men trained to carry out these complicated undertakings. Those who were employed for this work were largely shrewd merchants and capitalists of Lo Yang and Shantung, who were more interested in raising revenues to please the new Emperor than in caring for the welfare of the people. And above all, these great capitalists, whose names are preserved in the Han Shu, were most keenly interested in making money for themselves at the expense of the people and to the discredit of the government.

The net result of it all was the rise of banditry and insurgency everywhere throughout the empire. And the New Empire fell in A.D. 23. Wang Mang was killed by a merchant named Tu Wn and his body was dismembered by a number of soldiers of the victorious army. And for nineteen centuries his name was a curse. No historian, however liberal, has ever said a word in his defence.

Note.—The above is taken with a few verbal alterations from vol. lix of the *Journal of the North China Branch of the Royal Asiatic Society*, from an article by Hu Shih, entitled " Wang Mang, the Socialist Emperor of nineteen centuries ago ".

CHAPTER XIII

THE CAREER OF LIU YEN (劉 晏)[1]

TAKEN FROM THE TWENTY-FOUR DYNASTIC HISTORIES,
BOOK OF THE OLDEST T'ANG DYNASTY (舊 唐 書),
vol. 123, LIEH CHUAN (列 傳), No. 73

LIU YEN, also known as Liu Shih An (劉 士 安), was a native of Ts'ao Chow Fu (曹 州 府), Shantung province. He was something of a mental prodigy, being given the designation of "Shen T'ung" (神 童), or "Marvellous Child", at the age of 7. In his earlier years he occupied many provincial posts with credit, and gained a great reputation for exceptional ability. He acted as prefect of Hang Chow (杭 州), Lung Chow (隴 州), and Hua Chow (華 州) successively. After that he was appointed to the Censorate, and acted as Secretary to the Ministry of Finance. Later he was appointed to the Intendancy of the Honan Circuit, but owing to rebellion in the area he was unable to assume his duties. He therefore devoted himself to river conservancy work for a period, and was then appointed Intendant of the Capital Circuit.

Promotion followed rapidly. He was made president of the Board of Revenue, and concurrently Chief Censor and Head of the Estimating Department of the Ministry of Finance. After suffering indictment by Ching Yü (敬 羽) he was temporarily transferred to T'ung Chow (通 州), but was soon recalled to the capital to take up his old work.

In A.D. 763 he was appointed Chief of the Civil Service and Grand Councillor, and was given a special commission to supervise all matters pertaining to the national finances, the Salt and Iron Monopolies, and the transport and revenue services. After another temporary setback due to his getting involved in a lawsuit connected with Ch'eng Yuan Chen (程 元 振), which led to his losing his place in the Grand Council, and his being appointed Companion to the heir-apparent, he was once more restored to favour and given control

1 See footnote, p. 233.

of the chief circuits of the empire, like Tung Tu (東 都),
Honan (河 南), Chiang-Huai (江 淮), Shan-Nan (山 南),
etc., with prime responsibility for Transport, Revenue, and
Government Monopolies, much as before.

At this particular period prices of foodstuffs were extremely
high, owing to war and disorder, flour selling at the capital for
as much as 1,000 cash a bushel. The Court and Army supplies
were so scarce that the farmers were ordered to reap their grain
before it was ripe to supply urgent needs. This led Liu Yen
to make a close investigation into the reasons for this stringency,
and he set to work to devise improved transport facilities for
grain from distant places like Chiang Su, Che-chiang, Chiang
Hsi, Hunan, etc., direct to the capital. This meant a good
deal of work on the rivers Huai (淮), Ssu (泗), Pien (汴),
Huang (黄 河), etc. But in the face of many difficulties, such
as lack of men in the devastated areas, the presence of bandits
along the route, and the corruption of the military on the
waterways, he managed to secure the transport of hundreds of
thousands of piculs of grain from distant areas to the capital.

His administration of the Salt Monopoly, which had been
initiated by Ti Wu Ch'i (第 五 琦) in 756, but who was
later displaced by Liu Yen, was evidently extremely efficient.
When he took over, the proceeds from this only amounted to
600,000 " strings " annually. After several years Liu Yen
increased this to 6,000,000, without inflicting undue distress
upon the people. In the year 766, the total revenue from
monopolies and taxation amounted to 12,000,000 " strings " of
which more than half came from the Salt Monopoly.

A rebellion organized by Li Ling Yao in Honan temporarily
deprived the government of considerable revenue from that area,
but Liu Yen kept the government going on his surplus receipts
so that there was no need to resort to additional taxation.

He also instituted a news agency, whereby conditions and
prices in every part of the empire were rapidly transmitted to
the capital, enabling him to take steps to control prices of
foodstuffs and other commodities and prevent profiteering by
the wealthy traders. It is said that in five days the news of

such conditions in the furthest part of the empire reached the capital.   This also enabled him to balance up "plenty and dearth" to the great benefit of the people, and also to the great enrichment of the national exchequer.

He mostly employed young and able men, who made it their object to get things done as speedily as possible, and this roused the whole country to emulate his ideas in this respect.   He encouraged "nepotism" but only up to a certain point.   He gave rank and emoluments to the relations of his associates, but actually employed only the best brains and most energetic and able men of his time.   For twenty years after his death in 780, by far the most able financiers of the time were drawn from the ranks of his associates.

But his methods and fame were bound to bring resentment in their train.   His own system worked so efficiently that the local officials found it impossible to get their tribute goods to the capital before those of his agents.   However, from the period 766–780 little interference occurred with his policy.

But on the accession of Te Tsung (德 宗) in 780, many appeals were made for the rescindment of his economic policy, and when Yang Yen (楊 炎), an old enemy, was promoted to the Grand Council, he accused Liu Yen of having unjustly done Yuan Tsai (元 載) to death and of having suggested to Tai Tsung (代 宗) that he should raise one of his concubines to the position of empress and thereby make her son the heir to the throne.   This led to Liu Yen being cashiered and sent to Chung Chow, where he was executed a little later at the age of 66.   The whole country, however, resented this action, deeming that Liu Yen had done nothing worthy of such a penalty.

His family and associates were, however, all banished to Kuangtung.

In 789 the Emperor Te Tsung repented of his severe action and gave his two sons official recognition, and on the appeal of the elder, bestowed on Liu Yen himself the posthumous rank of magistrate of Cheng Chow (鄭 州 刺 史).

Chapter XIV

THE COINAGE, LIFTING OF EMBARGO ON EXPORT OF COPPER, Etc.

During the Sung Dynasty the coins in use varied in size and in the metals used. As the size varied, it was necessary to fix the value of the larger coins in terms of the smaller, with due regard, of course, to the component metal. As a rule copper coins were classed by themselves, as were those minted chiefly of iron.

Copper was the rarer metal of the two, and of course much lighter in weight and more convenient. The general standard for copper coins in the earlier years of the Sung Dynasty was as follows [1] :—

Five catties of metal in the proportions given below made 1,000 coins, viz. :—

Copper . . .	3 catties (斤)	10 oz. (兩)
Lead	1 „	8 „
Stannum or Tin . .	„	8 „

Iron coins were minted in various weights and sizes. Those turned out from the Kansu mint (prior to the reign of Jen Tsung, 1023–1063) weighed 12 catties 10 oz. per thousand (nearly 17 lb.). Those turned out from two mints in Ssuch'uan were roughly twice the size of the Kansu coins, a thousand weighing 25 catties 8 oz. (32 lb.).

A rough idea of the relative value of the two metals in Jen Tsung's day may be gained from the fact that iron vessels weighing 25 catties could be bought for 2,000 copper coins. The labour on the vessel would have to be allowed for, but as a rough estimate it would appear that copper was worth two or three times as much as iron.

In the year 1045 bronze coins (copper and stannum) were being minted in two places in Shensi, and a brass coin was being

---

[1] Sung Histories, Shih Huo Chih, vol. 133, chap. 2, from which much of the material relating to the coinage is taken.

turned out at I Chow (益 州), also in Shensi. But iron coins were also in circulation and considerable confusion arose.

As a rule the bigger the coin the bigger its value in proportion to the small coins. At one time one big copper coin was worth two small ones, the same holding true of the iron coins. But it is noted that at one period three small copper coins could by smelting be made into one of the big coins which was reckoned as equal to ten small ones. This led to a great deal of illicit minting, it being highly profitable to melt down small coins to make big ones.

In 1048 an attempt was made to fix the value of coins of one metal in terms of the other. In the Hotung Circuit one copper coin was to equal five iron coins (size unknown). In Shensi in the same year coins both of copper and iron were standardized into two classes, big and little, the big coins being fixed at a value equivalent to two small ones in the same metal. In this way the current value of the big coins greatly decreased, and a check was put upon illicit minting.

Coming now to the times of Wang An Shih's regime, we find that in the year 1071 P'i Kung Pi, the Transport Officer of Shensi, sent in the following memorial, viz. :—

" Since it was decreed that the big coins minted in Shensi were to be reckoned as equal in value to two small coins of the same metal, making the current value of the coin and its intrinsic value (i.e. of the composite metals) practically equivalent in each case, illicit smelting has been stopped. As this has proved to be a very satisfactory measure, I appeal that all the available stocks of copper and lead might be used for the minting of the big coins."

"This request," records the History, " was granted, and from this time it was made the universal rule that one big coin was to equal two small ones (presumably in the same metal)."

Although the appeal from P'i Kung Pi (皮 公 弼) was made in 1071, the note of his request being granted and the promulgation of the subsequent decree appears under the date of the 10th month, 1073.[1]

[1] " T'ung Chien," Hsi Ning, 6th year, 10th month.

This is connected in the records with the lifting of the ancient embargo on the export of copper, attributed to Wang An Shih. It is also related in such a way that the reader will get the impression that the standardizing of the currency (one big coin equal to two small ones) [1] was necessitated by the shortage of copper which had come about through this lifting of the embargo. The inference which the writer would have the reader make is that Wang An Shih found it necessary to enhance the current value of the small coins far and away above their intrinsic value.

The Historical account [2] reads as follows :—

" From the time when Wang An Shih came into power and lifted the embargo on the export of copper, evil men began to melt down the coins and make them into vessels and implements, as on the coast and borders they ceased to inspect or take any note of coins going out of the country. This led to the constant diminution of the number of coins in circulation. Chang Fang P'ing (張 方 平) submitted a memorial denouncing the lifting of the embargo."

Extracts which are apropos to the subject under discussion are taken from this memorial as below [3] :—

" During the last few years money has become very scarce, both in government and commercial circles. Trade is suffering seriously and the people are greatly distressed. The situation is so serious that it is spoken of as a ' Money Famine '.

"No one knows where all the coins that have been minted in such enormous quantities the last hundred years or so have gone to. The regulations prohibiting the export of copper and illicit minting are very ancient, and were still extant until the seventh year of Hsi Ning (熙 寧), i.e. 1074, when new regulations were issued lifting the embargo. This has resulted in cartloads of money being taken out of the country and boatloads of the coins sailing from our shores. I hear that

---

[1] " Che Erh Ch'ien " (折 二 錢).
[2] "T'ung Chien," Hsi Ning, 6th year, 10th month.
[3] Sung Histories, Shih Huo Chih, vol. 133, chap. 2, p. 4.

on the borders money passing through for export is simply subject to a tax on each string. In this way the money which is China's natural and most valuable commodity, is being used by the barbarians equally with us.

" Further, since the embargo was lifted the people have been melting down great quantities of the coins, for from ten coins they extract one ounce of pure copper. With this they make vessels and get five times the value of the original coins. Merely to urge the districts to establish more mints and to order all the mints to increase their output is like pouring water into a stream which runs off to the sea."

The History further relates that Chang Fang P'ing asked Wang An Shih what his idea was in rescinding a Measure (the embargo) which had been extant for so long. This excited Wang An Shih's enmity, and from this time the law was promulgated that one coin was to be reckoned as two (really one big coin equal to two small ones) and that this was to be observed throughout the country with the exception of the capital circuit.

But the order about unification of the currency was issued before the lifting of the embargo on export of copper, according to Chang Fang P'ing's own showing, so the former cannot have resulted from the latter.

We conclude, therefore, that the unification Measure was designed to prevent illicit smelting by making the coins, whether large or small, of proportionately intrinsic value, and as such was a definitely good measure.

It was neither due to shortage of copper caused by the large exports of that metal, nor was it a currency inflation measure.

It is difficult from the facts available to estimate the merits or demerits of the lifting of the embargo measure. It is known that very heavy penalties had been exacted under the older regulations for this exporting of copper. Before 1041, when the chief culprit discovered exporting 1,000 copper coins was executed forthwith, the regulations were not quite so stringent. Still they were stringent enough, for if one was caught exporting

2,000 coins the punishment was banishment for one year, and if the amount was 3,000 then the culprit was executed.

We infer that Wang An Shih in lifting the embargo was seeking the economical advantage of the country. We do know that these big coins (one equal to two variety) were ordered to be minted off in large quantities. For instance, in 1074 the two mints in Kuangtung were ordered to produce not more than 500,000,000 of these, the Honan Mint being given similar instructions. These were not the only coins produced, however, for in addition the former mint was ordered to turn out 1,100,000,000 coins of the smaller variety. As there were sixteen mints working under government auspices at this period, some idea of the enormous number of coins being produced at this time can be gained.

The Mint at Sianfu, Shensi, was allowed to increase its normal output by 100,000,000 coins, to be used in connection with the Trade and Barter Measure. The Mint at Hsing Chow (興 州) was permitted to increase its output by 72,000,000 coins, and three other Mints in Shensi were permitted to increase their output by 50,000,000 coins each annually. In 1075 the Hotung Mint was ordered to produce 700,000,000 big coins and 300,000,000 small ones.

These figures indicate two things—one that coins must have been either leaving the country in considerable quantities as Chang Fang P'ing suggests, or that they must have been a continuance of the smelting down process as he also suggests. Possibly both were operative. The question is whether the country suffered financially from these things, as he further suggests.

It is evident that notice was taken of the coins going out, and that taxes were imposed on their export. So that probably the government finances gained rather than lost by this lifting of the embargo. It is equally evident that there could have been no serious shortage of copper in the country at this particular time, otherwise how can one account for the enormous quantities of coins that were being minted ? It is more than probable that illicit smelting went on, for there is an order issued before

1078 strictly prohibiting such practices. The fact that at the same time an order was issued that defective coins in the hands of the officials were to be melted down and reminted might have indicated scarcity or it might have been merely an economical measure to prevent waste. That proves nothing. Some of the mints were closed about this time, too, the History says, "on account of shortage of metal." That might have arisen later.

There is, however, a note applying to the period 1078–1085 that 200,000,000 of these "one equal to two coins" (折二錢) were sent to the west from the No. 2 Mint at Hsü Chow (徐州). That scarcely indicates "a money famine".

The embargo on copper exports was revived in 1086 when the whole of Wang An Shih's policy was reversed. In 1104 all the "one equal to two coins" were called in and reminted, being reissued as "one equal to ten".

In an attempt to evaluate Wang An Shih's lifting of the embargo and its probable effects on the economic situation one notes therefore that export of the metal was subject to regular taxation, that the terrible penalties of former reigns were rescinded, that for a time at least no serious shortage of money or the metal resulted, and that it was not necessary to inflate the currency as the Historian would have us infer. It is quite possible that these large quantities of coins exported were due to the working of the Trade and Barter Measure on the frontiers, the tribes taking money from China in exchange for goods. If so, then we should say it was a decidedly beneficial measure, as the taxing on money going out would be paid by the foreign trader. In this way goods of equivalent value to the money exported would be imported and in addition there would be receipts from the tax on money going out.

If these two measures, thus attributed to Wang An Shih, had been so important and reacted as seriously on the national finances as some critics make out,[1] it would appear reasonable to expect that in the Sung Biography it would have least been

[1] Cf. J. P. Bruce, in *Chu Hsi and His Masters*, p. 12.

mentioned. But it is not, although such minor matters as bidding for market stands and increases in the quantities of salt and tea which the people were compelled to take, find a place. Moreover, in the T'ung Chien the matter is disposed of in the vaguest and most summary fashion. Inquiry into the subject from the Sung Huo Chih reveals the information as given above. Moreover, the matter of the coinage and the lifting of the embargo on export of copper is not mentioned by Wang An Shih's contemporary critics, if we except the memorial of Chang Fang P'ing.

CHAPTER XV

WANG AN SHIH'S FAMILY

WANG AN SHIH had two sons and three daughters, one of whom died as a baby in Chin Hsien (鄞 縣).[1] The sons were named F'ang (雱) and P'ang (旁) respectively. Little is known of the latter, apart from the mention of his name in one poem by his father.[2] The former attained to considerable importance and more will be said about him below. The two daughters [3] married into official families, the elder becoming the wife of Wu An Ch'ih (吳 安 持), the son of the Grand Councillor Wu Ts'ung (吳 充), who succeeded Wang An Shih on his retirement from that office. She was possessed of considerable literary ability, and often engaged in poetical correspondence with her father. The following may be quoted by way of illustration, viz.[4] :—

The daughter wrote—

"Into my lattice blows the mild west wind,
The Autumn air breathes my longing for home,
My distant home in Chiang Nan.
My tears unchecked do flow,
But my feelings I must restrain,
As I gaze on the drooping flowers."

Wang An Shih replied to this, also in poetical form, the last word of each line being either the same as or rhyming with the last word of each line in his daughter's poem. He wrote as follows :—

"There's a bird on the wing in the west,
Who knows your heart's longing for home,
Separation we must all endure,
But soon on a bright Summer's day,
We shall be gathering flowers together."

---

[1] See Vol. I, Chapter III, pp. 19–20.
[2] Liang Ch'i Ch'ao, p. 312.
[3] Liang Ch'i Ch'ao, pp. 317–18.
[4] Liang Ch'i Ch'ao, p. 318.

He wrote many poems to his daughters, all of which breathe a spirit of true fatherly affection.

His second daughter was married to Ts'ai Pien (蔡 卞), the younger brother of Ts'ai Ching (蔡 京).[1] Both gained considerable notoriety for their opposition to the anti-Wang An Shih faction. Ts'ai Pien, however, later incurred the displeasure of his older brother, and lost his high official position at the capital in consequence.[2]

Now we will give some account of his son Fang.[3]

He is reported to have been of exceptional intelligence and ability. Before he had reached the age of 20, the "capping" stage of Chinese manhood, he had many published works to his name, and gained his Doctor's degree (進 士) at the age of 24. Later he was appointed to a post in Ching Te (旌 德) in An Hui province, whence he wrote over a score of State pamphlets, showing a keen interest in current politics. He wrote two larger works, one entitled "The Teachings of Lao Tzu" (老 子 訓 傳) and the other "An Interpretation of the Buddhist Canon" (佛 書 義 解). He was also associated with his father and Lü Hui Ch'ing in the preparation of the series of New Classical Interpretations, the one on the Book of History being his work in the main.

The Sung Histories [4] make Fang responsible for much of his father's policy, as the following quotations will show :—

"When he was 13 years of age, Fang received certain information from a soldier just returned from the T'ao River district. This led him to make the following suggestion (to his father) : 'By taking strong action we can recover this territory. If the Hsi Hsia are allowed to hold it, it will contribute to the strengthening of our enemies, and our border difficulties will be increased.' Later on, when Wang Shao undertook the reclamation of the Hsi Ho (熙 河) territory, Wang An Shih

[1] Liang Ch'i Ch'ao, p. 319.
[2] "T'ung Chien," Ts'ung Ning, 4th year, 1st month.
[3] Liang Ch'i Ch'ao, p. 312.
[4] Dynastic History of Sung, "Pen Chuan," Life of Wang An Shih.

lent him his full support. But that was because it was in line
with the suggestion made to him by his son Fang."

"When Wang An Shih was in office as Grand Councillor
he used young men for the most part to help him in government
affairs. Fang was anxious to gain some post under his father,
with whom he had the following conversation : ' It is true that
a son of a minister may not hold any administrative post, but
he is eligible for an expository position.' "

So Wang An Shih, with a view to bringing his son's name
before the notice of the Emperor, printed his tracts on politics
and his exposition of the Tao Te Ching (道 德 經) and put
them on sale. Thus it came about that reports of Fang's
literary ability reached the ears of the Emperor. Teng Chien
and Tseng Pu, proteges of his father, took the opportunity to
recommend Fang for a post at Court. He was granted an
interview with the Emperor and appointed as Chamberlain
to the Heir-Apparent,[1] and also as expositor in the Ts'ung
Cheng Tien (崇 政 殿).

The Emperor (Shen Tsung) often held private conversation
with him, and he was later commissioned to write commentaries
on the Odes and History Classic. On the completion of this
work he was promoted to the " T'ien Chang Ko " (天 章 閣)
as adviser and expositor, and appointed as tutor to the
Emperor.[2] Later again, he was offered another post in the
" Lung T'u Ko " (龍 圖 閣), but this he refused on the
grounds of ill-health.

The reforms of Wang An Shih were instigated by Fang, for the
latter was always praising Shang Yang as a man of great courage
and ability.[3] The opponents of his father's reform policy

[1] 太 子 中 允.
[2] 侍 講.
[3] Shang Yang (商 鞅), famous statesman and legalist of the State of Ch'in
(秦), who was supreme in the time of Duke Hsiao, 360–336 B.C., whom
he inspired with an insatiable ambition. He showed him that the coveted imperial
throne of the fallen Chow dynasty was not beyond his reach. He introduced
for him certain radical reforms and made a new code of laws whose chief feature
was relentless severity and whose only aim was the attainment of wealth and

ought to have been summarily dealt with, if the following account is true,[1] viz. :—

"Once when Wang An Shih was conversing with Ch'eng Hao, Fang approached, with dishevelled hair and swaggering gait, and carrying a woman's hat in his hand. He inquired of his father in very rude fashion as to what they were talking about. Wang An Shih replied that certain aspects of the New Measures were arousing the opposition of the people and they were talking the matter over. Fang shouted out, 'If you hang the heads of Han Ch'i (韓 琦) and Fu Pi (富 弼) in the market-place, your New Measures may be promulgated all right.' Wang An Shih hastily rejoined, 'You are mistaken, my son.'"

Fang died at the early age of 33, and was given the posthumous title of "Tso Chien I Tai Fu" (左 諫 議 大 夫).

One of the Histories [2] makes Wang An Shih responsible for Fang's death, saying that it was the outcome of his father's reprimand concerning the part which Fang had played in the affair of Chang Jo Chi and Lü Hui Ch'ing, which was the

power for the state. In short, it may be said that it was Shang Yang alone who started the dukedom of Ch'in upon a path of expansion and conquest and laid the foundation for the final triumph of the so-called First Emperor (秦 始 皇 帝), 220-209 B.C. On the death of his master, Duke Hsiao, Shang Yang was compelled to flee for his life, on the advent of the heir-apparent, whom he had seriously offended by punishing and branding his tutor and guardian for failing to keep his young charge within the limits of his duty. He fled to the state of Wei (衛) which he had formerly attacked, and which by sheer treachery he had compelled to cede a large slice of territory in order to ennoble himself as the Prince of Shang (商 君). There the injury he had done to it was still fresh in the memory of the people, and he was driven back again to the country from which he had just fled. It was on this occasion that he was caused to taste the bitterness and severity of his own laws. He was refused shelter in an inn because, as the innkeeper pointed out, he had not, in accordance with his own regulations, provided himself with a passport. A little later he was caught and put to a terrible death. Thus ended the career of a genius, as pitiful as it was meteoric. From *Ancient Chinese Political Theories*, by K. C. Wu, who summarizes his political policy in the phrase : "It had been Shang Yang's whole scheme to make fighting and farming the only source from which fame and profit can be made to light upon the people" (p. 173, op. cit.).

[1] See criticism of Liang Ch'i Ch'ao (below).
[2] Dynastic History of Sung, Pen Chuan, Life of Wang An Shih.

occasion, if not the cause, of Wang An Shih's retirement from the Grand Council. It is narrated that in consequence of Fang's anger at his father's words, an abscess or carbuncle broke out on his back, and this led to his death. But this account is strangely like that of the death of T'ang Chieh,[1] and it appears as though it may have been wilfully applied to Fang's death to blacken still further the character of Wang An Shih.

This account of Fang's character and supposed influence upon his father's policy is severely criticized by Liang Ch'i Ch'ao.[2] The following passages are taken from a work reputed to be by Shao Pai Wen (邵 伯 温),[3] but which some critics affirm to be the work of his son Po (博). They base their judgment on the ground that a man like Shao Pai Wen could not possibly have written such slanderous stuff as is here and there found in it. But we give the accounts relative to Fang for what they are worth, as follows :—

" Fang was a wicked and treacherous fellow, responsible for everything that was oppressive in his father's policy, and who received the slavish and servile obedience of Lü Hui Ch'ing and his associates. When Wang An Shih first established the Financial Reorganization Bureau, he engaged Ch'eng Hao, a very worthy man, to assist him. One day, when they were holding some conversation, at the season of great heat, Fang broke in upon them." (Here the narrative follows on the lines of the incident already recounted above), but adds the following :—

" Ch'eng Hao added, ' Children should not be allowed to interfere when politics are being discussed. Will you please

---

[1] See Vol. I, Chapter XI, p. 125.

[2] Liang Ch'i Ch'ao, pp. 312–13.

[3] Shao Pai Wen (邵 伯 温), whose reputed authorship of the " Wen Chien Lu " (聞 見 錄), in which these extracts referring to Fang are found, is doubted by Liang Ch'i Ch'ao. It is suggested that his son Po (博) wrote this work after his father's death, in the year 1132, when the whole literary world was opposed to Wang An Shih, and when it seems feasible to surmise that Po sought in this way to curry favour. Anyway, it is thought improbable that a man of Shao Pai Wen's character would descend to such base slanders as this work contains (see Liang Ch'i Ch'ao, p. 315).

leave us.' Fang left them in a very unhappy frame of mind.
From this time Wang An Shih and Ch'eng Hao began to
draw apart.

" After the death of Fang, Wang An Shih had a dream in his
residence at Chung Shan, in which he saw the ghost of Fang
wearing the cangue and burdened with chains. This led him
to give up his residence to be used as a monastery in order
that he might make some atonement for the crimes of
his son.

" When Wang An Shih was seriously ill, he ordered his niece
to burn his diary. His niece made only a pretence of so doing,
actually burning some other books instead. Wang An Shih
died soon after this. The reason for his wanting his niece to
burn his diary possibly is to be found in the fact that he saw
other ghosts ! "

The above extracts are taken, as is said above, from the work
of Shao Pai Wen or his son Po, entitled the " Wen Chien Lu "
(聞 見 錄). Although this work is considered to be generally
reliable, Li Fu (李 紱) contends that in these references
to Fang it is quite erroneous. He thinks that such conduct as is
here posited of Fang is inconceivable in the light of his general
character as depicted in other records. Further that the time
when the incident is supposed to have happened (i.e. the
breaking in on the interview with Ch'eng Hao) cannot be right,
as it was impossible for Fang to have been in K'ai Feng Fu then.

Ts'ai Shang Hsiang says that all this about Fang is mere
fabrication, and that the Histories copied it from this particular
work (i.e. the Wen Chien Lu). The fact that Chu Hsi (朱 熹)
also included it in his two works, " The Extraneous Records
of the Ch'eng Family " (程 氏 外 書) and " Biographies
of Famous Officials " (名 臣 言 行 錄), has led to the
persistence of this traditional account of Wang Fang's
character.

As to the manner of Fang's death, it is well known that he
had been in poor health for some time before he died. It is
related in the Histories that Wang An Shih had frequently
asked to resign on the grounds of his son's ill-health. There

is a letter [1] of Wang An Shih, written in 1074, thanking the Emperor for a gift of medicine sent to his son. So it is highly improbable that his death should have occurred in the manner stated. And no matter how true it might have been that Fang was loud and persistent in his praises of Shang Yang, it is absurd to attribute Wang An Shih's reform policy to that.

Liang Ch'i Ch'ao is of opinion that these statements of Li Fu and Ts'ai Shang Hsiang are true. The imputations on Fang's character all date from the times of the Southern Sung Dynasty, when the faction spirit was at its worst.[2]

He is further of opinion that the reason for attributing all that was oppressive in Wang An Shih's policy to his son, is the same as that which led the Historians to lay all the blame for the supposedly bad features of Shen Tsung's reign on Wang An Shih rather than on Shen Tsung himself. They were anxious to find a scapegoat in each case, in the latter case the person of Shen Tsung being regarded as sacrosanct, and in the former the character of Wang An Shih being above reproach.

Wang An Shih's wife, who was styled the Lady of Wu (吳 國 夫 人), had distinct literary gifts. But her ability in this direction was overshadowed by that of his younger sister, styled the Lady of Ch'ang An (長 安 縣 君), who was married to Chang K'uei. She was the author of many beautiful poems, and much beloved by Wang An Shih, who visited her frequently. His eldest daughter was styled the Lady of P'eng Lai (蓬 莢 縣 君).[3]

We will now give some account of the lives of his more famous brothers, An Li and An Kuo. The following are the

---

[1] Works, vol. xv, pp. 21 and 22. See also Works, vol. x, p. 11, where, in his letter appealing that Fang might be allowed to refuse the appointment of librarian to the Lung T'u Ko, Wang An Shih refers to the prolonged illness of his son.

[2] As further evidence of Fang's good character Liang Ch'i Ch'ao cites the silence of Lü Hui and others, on the ground that those who were so ready to vilify the father would certainly have taken advantage of any serious flaws in Fang's character to dilate upon them (see Liang Ch'i Ch'ao, p. 316, also Ts'ai Shang Hsiang, vol. xviii, p. 14).

[3] Liang Ch'i Ch'ao, p. 317.

more important portions of the biographical record of An Li as found in the Sung Histories,[1] viz. :—

"Wang An Li was also known as Ho Fu (和 甫). He was the younger brother of Wang An Shih. His degree of Chin Shih (進 士), or Doctor of literature, was gained while he was quite young, he being recommended for that degree by T'ang Chieh.

"During Shen Tsung's reign, between the years 1068–1077, Han Chiang formulated a project for transferring 40,000 men from the Ho Tung Circuit, for the walling of the town of Lo Wu (囉 兀) in north-west Shansi. Wang An Li opposed this scheme, saying, 'The people's levies have received no military training, yet you are sending them off into the remoter regions of the empire. The enemy will seize the opportunity of this crowd of men going there to make war, and they will be destroyed. Any who should escape slaughter will most certainly perish of starvation. The scheme ought to be abandoned and the people sent back to their homes.' Whereupon Lü Kung Pi (呂 公 弼), who was on the point of committing himself to the project, dropped it."

The Historical note adds that people sent from other districts to carry out this work were many of them slaughtered as they came into contact with the enemy.

For his wisdom and foresight in this and other matters, Lü Kung Pi recommended Wang An Li for preferment. Wang An Shih, however, who was then in supreme power, prevented the Emperor from giving him very high office (probably lest he should incur the suspicion of showing favouritism for his own relatives), and suggested that he would be better employed in literary work. So he was appointed to the Ts'ung Wen Yuan (崇 文 院) as keeper of the books.

The Emperor evidently was inclined to treat An Li with unusual consideration, and permitted him to sit in the Imperial presence. This was criticized, as An Li was only of the eighth grade of official status, and this was too low to entitle him to such a privilege. Later on he was appointed to the Chi Hsien

[1] Pen Chuan, Biography of Wang An Li.

Yuan (集 賢 院), given provincial posts at Jun Chow (潤 州) and Hu Chow (湖 州), and later again was given the important position of assistant governor of K'ai Feng Fu. The Emperor continued to show him special favour, and often detained him for private audiences.

At the time when Su Shih (蘇 軾) was in prison, and his life was in considerable jeopardy, no one else had the courage to come forward and endeavour to save him. But Wang An Li appealed in his behalf, as follows :—

"It is unknown for such a great Emperor as your Majesty to punish men for their exercise of the right of criticism." He dilated further upon the ability of Su Shih, and warned Shen Tsung that if he took drastic action against him he would expose himself to the censure of future generations in that it would demonstrate his inability to recognize and use men of real talents.

As a result of Wang An Li's intervention, the punishment inflicted upon Su Shih was very light compared with the penalties imposed on those who had been impeached along with him, viz. Li Ting (李 定) and Chang Tsao (張 璪).

A little later he was promoted to the Edicts Office with the rank and title of "Chih Chih Kao" (知 制 誥).

He submitted a memorial after the appearance of a comet, affirming that the big officials near the throne were neither loyal nor honest, and that judgments of men's loyalty were utterly confused, also the estimation of their worth. Many of the officials were concerned first and foremost with matters of financial advantage. These were the features of the government which had led to the appearance of the comet. He considered that the prayers which had been offered, and the minor adjustments which had been made in the laws and regulations of the land, were utterly inadequate as a response to this warning from Heaven.

Promotion to the Literary Council (翰 林 院) followed on this, and later he was appointed as Governor of K'ai Feng Fu.

During his term of office there he is reported to have cleared the courts of nearly ten thousand outstanding cases of law. The decisions on these cases were posted up outside the Courts of Justice in the capital in such numbers and with such expedition that the ambassador of the "Liao" (遼), who was visiting the capital at the time, was greatly astonished. The Emperor was also tremendously impressed with his efficiency in this direction, and promoted An Li one degree in official rank.

As the Emperor had lost several sons who might have become his heirs, the Imperial diviner suggested that the cause for these losses lay in the graves which had accumulated in such large numbers in the vicinity of the city. He proposed that an edict should be issued ordering the removal of these graves, and promised that such calamities as had hitherto troubled the Imperial family in the matter of securing an heir would thereby cease. When this project was noised abroad amongst the people it naturally aroused a great outcry of opposition. Wang An Li also opposed the move, warning the Emperor against it by quoting ancient precedents, and the Emperor was persuaded to drop the idea.

Wang An Li also attacked a member of the Royal Household named Ling Fei (令 騑) for ill-treatment of one of his concubines, and resisted his appeal for the return of the money he had paid for her. He also appealed that Ling Fei should be heavily punished for his conduct and attitude on this matter. This appeal was granted, Ling Fei being deprived of his emoluments. An Li also exposed another instance of corruption amongst the members of the Royal Household, and his courage in these directions gained for him the respect and fear of the whole palace.

In the fourth year of Yuan Feng (元 豐), i.e. 1081, Wang An Li was appointed to the position of Yu Chêng (右 丞) of the Shang Shu Sheng (尙 書 省), and later promoted a further step in rank to that of Tso Ch'êng (左 丞). This carried with it the privilege of membership of the Grand Council.

His next achievement of note was to prevent Wang Kuei (王 珪) and Li Hsien (李 憲) from launching a fresh attack upon the Hsi Hsia. They had accumulated 5,000,000 "strings"

for this purpose, but it was all in paper money. Wang An Li
suggested that they could not use the notes as food for the
troops. There was an interval of only two months before the
date fixed for the start of the expedition, the notes would have
to be turned into real coin, and then the grain would have
to be purchased and convoyed to the army in the field. The
time was altogether too short for adequate preparations to be
made. The Emperor postponed the expedition in consequence
of this statement of the case.

Later he was impeached on some count or other by the
Censor Chang Ju Hsien, and he left the capital with the rank
of Grand Literary Councillor of the " Tuan Ming Tien "
(端 明 殿 大 學 士) to take up the post of Governor of
Chiang Ning Fu.

During the reign of Che Tsung, period 1086-1093, his rank
was enhanced to that of " Ts'ung Cheng Tien Hsueh Shih "
(崇 政 殿 學 士), and he held appointments successively
at Yang Chow (楊 州), Ch'ing Chow (青 州), and Ts'ai
Chow (蔡 州). Then he had a short spell in the Censorate,
was again impeached, deprived of his rank of Literary
Councillor, and transferred to Shu Chow (舒 州).

Prior to this he had opposed a proposition of one Hsü Hsi
(徐 禧) that a certain border campaign might be undertaken.
However, on this occasion his advice was not taken, and the
expedition was launched. Defeat resulted at Yung Lo (永 樂).
When the news of this defeat reached the Court, the Emperor
said, " Wang An Li always opposed military expeditions, giving
as his reason the fact that such movements only increased
trouble and involved the promoters in severe punishment.
He was quite right in the stand he took."

During the period 1094-7, under Che Tsung, Wang An Li
was appointed to Yung Hsing Chun (永 興 軍) and later to
T'ai Yuan Fu (太 原 府). He died there at the age of 62.

Wang An Kuo (王 安 國) was the younger brother of
Wang An Li, and was also known as P'ing Fu (平 甫). As
a boy he achieved a reputation for cleverness. Although he
had not been to any school, nor received any regular instruction,

his literary ability was soon discovered to be of an unusual character. Before he reached the age of 10 he composed many poems, essays, inscriptions, etc., which aroused great wonder. Later he became famous as a writer and was very widely read.

He failed several times to gain his doctor's degree (進 士). He was, however, given the classification of Special " Mao Ts'ai " (茂 才) scholar, being placed first on the list for the excellence of his composition. His mother's death then intervened, and he desisted from further attempts to take his doctor's degree on that account. He was greatly devoted to his mother, and spent three years in a small hut erected by her grave, occupying his time reading and composing. It is related that he wrote a number of Buddhist books with ink in which he had mingled his own blood.[1]

In 1068 Han Chiang recommended him for the doctor's degree, which the Emperor conferred upon him. Wang An Shih wrote the Emperor a special letter of thanks for this particular favour shown to his brother.

After this he was given an appointment as teacher in the Lo Yang Academy (洛 陽), being styled Professor of the Western Capital College (西 京 國 子 教 授).

On the completion of his term there, and because of the prestige of his elder brother, Wang An Shih, he was received in a special audience by the Emperor, at which the following conversation is reported to have taken place, viz. :—

To the Emperor's question as to what he thought of Han Wu Ti (漢 武 帝) as a ruler, Wang An Kuo replied, " He has had no equal since the time of the Three Dynasties." The Emperor rejoined, " But he created no new laws and made no reforms of note." " That is true," said Wang An Kuo, " but after he had entered the Royal Palace [2] from his district of Tai (代) he took very little time in reducing the country to good order. Had he not had considerable ability that would have been impossible. Further, he availed himself of the help

---

[1] Works, vol. xxiii, pp. 4 and 5.
[2] The " Wei Yang Kung " (未 央 宮), located near Hsi An Fu.

of Chia I (賈 誼) and brought all the various princes and rulers of states into willing co-operation, and by the kindliness of his rule won the affection of the people throughout the land. So I think he should be considered as an exceptionally able man."

The Emperor asked the further question, "Wang Meng (王 莽) helped his ruler Fu Chien (苻 堅)[1] in such an efficient way that throughout his small kingdom his orders were effectively carried out. How is it that I, who rule so vast a domain, cannot find someone (who could help me to secure like result)?"

Wang An Kuo replied, "Wang Meng advised Fu Chien to institute a most rigorous regime of punishment and death, and this accounts for the fact that the regime which he inaugurated lasted only forty-four years. Doubtless there are some mean and grasping officials who will quote such precedents to mislead you. I hope you will adopt Yao, Shun, and the regime of the Three Dynasties as your models, and then there will be none who will dare to disobey your orders."

The Emperor then asked as to what the outside opinion of Wang An Shih's policy was. Wang An Kuo replied, "There is dissatisfaction with his judgment of men and with his haste to accumulate revenue."

This reply evidently displeased the Emperor, for he maintained silence. No more special favours were conferred upon Wang An Kuo after this. He received only the appointment to the Ts'ung Wen Yuan (崇 文 阮) as redactor. Wang An Shih wrote the Emperor a letter of thanks for this appointment.[2] He was later transferred to the Mi Ko (秘 閣) as librarian, which was a slight improvement on his old post.

The Histories[3] record that Wang An Kuo frequently criticized Wang An Shih's reform policy, that he accused Tseng Pu of misleading his brother, and hated Lü Hui Ch'ing, regarding him as a villain.

---

[1] Fu Chien was the first ruler of the Former Ch'in Dynasty, one of sixteen states in the Western Chin period. The Former Ch'in Dynasty was inaugurated in 351 B.C.

[2] Works, vol. xv, pp. 2 and 3.

[3] Pen Chuan, Life of Wang An Shih.

They also relate that during Wang An Kuo's term at Lo Yang he was inclined to lead rather a loose life. Wang An Shih wrote him a letter reproving him, and warning him against the " licentious music of Cheng ".[1]   To this Wang An Kuo replied, warning his brother against contact with specious men. Evidently Lü Hui Ch'ing took the latter as referring to himself, so after Wang An Shih's resignation from the Grand Council (the first time) he deprived Wang An Kuo of all rank and office for his part in the Cheng Hsieh (鄭 俠) incident and sent him home.   Wang An Shih wept copiously when the news reached him.

Wang An Kuo died at the age of 47, just as his rank was about to be restored to him.   The actual date of his death is not given, but on the tombstone inscription [2] it is related that he did not rise from his bed after the 17th of the 8th month of 1074, and that he was buried near his mother's grave at Chung Shan on the 27th of the 4th month of the year 1080.

At the end of the biographical notice the Historian [3] adds, " Wang An Shih was an enemy of Su Shih, but Wang An Li took steps to save the latter from his accusers.   Wang An Shih was slavishly addicted to Lü Hui Ch'ing, a man whom his brother Wang An Kuo despised.   Critics attach no blame to the brothers of Wang An Shih for their contrary attitude, for they did what was right in the matter.''

[1] Ts'ai Shang Hsiang, vol. xviii, pp. 12 and 13, discovers three different sources for this supposed incident, all differing from one another in details.   In the " Tung Hsien Pi Lu " of Wei Tao Fu it is related as having occurred between Wang An Kuo and Lü Hui Ch'ing in a discussion as to the propriety of Ministers of State composing love songs.   In the " Wen Chien Lu " of Shao Pai Wen it is related as having occurred between Wang An Shih and Wang An Kuo, in connection with the latter's flute playing during a conversation between the former and Lü Hui Ch'ing.   In the " Su Shui Chi Wen " of Ssu Ma Kuang it is related to have occurred in correspondence between Wang An Shih and Wang An Kuo during the latter's term of office at Lo Yang, in which there is no reference to Lü Hui Ch'ing's resentment against Wang An Kuo's innuendo.   In the " Ming Ch'en Yen Hsing Lü " of Chu Hsi the incident occurs as included in the Sung Histories, which probably copied it from that work.   But in this account the incident shows signs of being a collation from two of the former writings, viz. the " Su Shui Chi Wen " and the " Wen Chien Lu ".
[2] Works, vol. xxiii, pp. 4 and 5
[3] Pen Chuan, Life of Wang An Shih.

CHAPTER XVI

THE LITERATURE AND ITS HISTORY

WANG AN SHIH was not only a political reformer; he was a prolific writer of both prose and poetry, and attained to considerable fame as a literary genius. Many who despised his statesmanship lauded his gifts as essayist and poet. Even the historians of the period, who normally are anything but complimentary to Wang An Shih as a politician, praise the essays written in his younger days as fine examples of style and form, while his later work, in the opinion of many critics, entitles him to an honoured place on the scroll of China's most famous writers and poets.

We have seen that he was a voracious reader. Philosophy, Medicine, Religion, Agriculture, History, Fiction, even works on Embroidery, as well as the whole gamut of Classical Works, were given close attention, and made to yield their treasures to his mind, and add interest to his later years.

The following is a list of his works, as far as is known to us, viz. :—

1. Complete works, comprising poems, letters, essays, memorials, government orders, and mandates issued by him during his terms in high office, Inscriptions, Classical Interpretations, Introductions to books, etc., etc. This consists of 24 vols. in the modern edition (王 臨 川 全 集).[1]

2. Complete Poetical Works, comprising 50 vols. in the modern edition (王 荆 文 公 詩).[2]

[1] According to Liang Ch'i Ch'ao the original edition comprised 180 volumes. Later these were reduced to 130, and then 100, and now there are only 24. But the reductions were not due to elimination of material necessarily, but to re-arrangement.

[2] This is noted separately, not because it comprises fresh work from the pen of Wang An Shih, but because it is valuable for the commentary and introductory matter. The modern edition of Wang An Shih's complete works (above) does not contain the introductions found in this edition of poetry only, and the poems comprised in the modern edition have no commentary.

3. The Chow Kuan Hsin I (周 官 新 義) or New Interpretation of the Chow Li (周 禮), 22 vols.[1]

4. Commentary on the "Hung Fan" (洪 範 傳) or "Great Plan" Section of the Book of History. This is contained in his Prose Works,[2] but is worthy of special mention as a work of considerable length.

5. Anthology of the T'ang Poets (選 唐 百 家 詩).[3]

All the above are extant and of unquestioned authorship, with the possible exception of a few poems. The following are also recognized as being wholly his work, but unfortunately have been lost, viz. :—

6. Commentary on Tso's Interpretation of the Annals, 10 vols. (春 秋 左 氏 解).

7. The Main Ideas of the Li Chi (禮 記 要 義), 2 vols.

8. Interpretation of the Hsiao Ching (孝 經 義), 1 vol.

9. Commentary on the Analects, 10 vols. (論 語 解).

10. Commentary on Mencius, 10 vols. (孟 子 解).

11. Commentary on Lao Tzu, 2 vols. (老 子 注).

12. Dictionary of Chinese Characters (字 說), 24 vols.

There are two other works, in the compilation of which his son Fang and also Lü Hui Ch'ing assisted, but which have been lost, viz. :—

13. New Interpretation of the Odes, 30 vols. (詩 經 新 義).

14. New Interpretation of the Book of History (書 經 新 義).

In addition to the above there is another work attributed to Wang An Shih, but generally considered to be of doubtful authenticity, entitled "Interpretation of the Book of Changes"

[1] Now only 16 vols, with two additional on the Artificers' Record. This, however, comprises all that is found in the Ssu K'u Ch'uan Shu.

[2] Prose Works, vol. xvi.

[3] As this is an anthology only, and not original work, it is not included in Liang Ch'i Ch'ao's list of Wang An Shih's works, as given in his Life of Wang An Shih. We mention it here, however, as the work is extant, and because it illustrates his choice of poetry.

(易 義). This is said to have consisted of 14 vols., but is not extant.

When we consider the bitterness of the strife which was aroused by Wang An Shih's political theories and measures, and the odium which attached itself to his name in succeeding generations, it is remarkable that so much of his written work has been allowed to survive. It will be recalled that the blocks of the New Interpretation of the three Classics, i.e. History, Odes, and Chow Li, were destroyed, and that his works were banned in connection with the official examinations.

The earliest edition of his work, of which we have any trace was published by Chan Ta Ho (詹 大 和) in the tenth year of the Southern Sung emperor, Shao Hsing (紹 興), i.e. A.D. 1140. It is to him that we are indebted for a detailed biographical table of Wang An Shih, which has formed the chronological basis for this present study.[1] This edition was based on two prior works known as the Fuchien, or " Min " (閩) edition, and the Chechiang, or " Che " (浙) edition, respectively. All traces of these two prior works have been lost.

Opinions vary as to the number of volumes which originally comprised Wang An Shih's work, some saying that there were 130 vols., and others 180. The general consensus of opinion, however, which is represented by the Dynastic History, in the Arts and Literature Section, styled " I Wen Chih " (藝 文 志), is that there were 100 vols. It is quite reasonable to surmise that Chan Ta Ho in editing his work, re-arranged the contents of the two preceding editions, and compressed them into 100 vols. for convenience.

To the edition of Chan Ta Ho an Introduction was written by Huang Tz'u Shan (黃 次 山) in the year of its publication. He was a native of Chiang Hsi province, hailing from the district of Feng Ch'eng. He gained his Chin Shih degree in the period 1119–1126, and held government office during the early years of Ch'in Tsung's reign (欽 宗) 1126–1162. He was a great friend of Li Kang (李 剛) who, during the last

---

[1] Found in the prolegomena to the Poetical Works. (See n. 2, p. 264.) Translated at the end of Vol. II of this work.

critical days of the Northern Sung dynasty, was a staunch advocate of armed resistance to the Chins. As a matter of fact he lost his position through the stand he took on that occasion.[1]

As this Introduction is the oldest writing extant on the subject of Wang An Shih's Literary Work, we will attempt to translate the whole of it as follows :—

This work was published in the time of Shao Hsing (紹 興), being styled " the new edition of the Lin Ch'uan Chi " (重 刊 臨 川 集). It contains the original compositions of Wang Chieh Fu (王 介 甫), a native of my own prefecture. The work was collated and edited by Chan Ta Ho, a sub-prefectural magistrate and a native of T'ung Lu (桐 廬).

The first emperor of the Sung Dynasty, Sung T'ai Tsu (宋 太 祖), also styled the Accomplished (藝 祖), gained the empire by warlike measures. Since his day the empire has been maintained by his sage-like successors through their holding the civil arm in high esteem. Many scholars and officials from the Chiang Hsi district became famous for their literary and administrative gifts, which they actively applied in a time most favourable for administrators of their calibre.

Wang Yuan Chih (王 元 之) and Yang Ta Nien (楊 大 年) were famous for their poetry and rhyming essays, and they, together with Yen Yuan Hsien (晏 元 獻), were the most skilled in this art. Liu Chung T'u (柳 仲 塗) and Mu Pai Ch'ang (穆 伯 長) were amongst the first to attempt to revive the ancient style of composition, but Ou Yang Hsiu was the one who brought it to the highest pitch of excellence. In this connection Tseng Tzu Ku (曾 子 固) and Huang Lu Chih (黃 魯 直) are also worthy of a place on the roll of honour.

In early years Wang An Shih was a disciple of Ou Yang Hsiu, whom he soon equalled in literary ability. Later on he became the compeer of Yen Yuan Hsien in poetical gifts.

[1] See Chinese Biographical Dictionary (中 國 名 人 大 辭 典) in loco.

He was a very intimate friend of Tseng Tzu Ku. Huang Lu Chih affirmed that his poetry would abide.

The writings of these famous men have all been collected and published during recent years by their fellow provincials. But although the works of Wang An Shih are current in Fuchien and Chechiang, they have so far been neglected by the people of his own province. Chan Ta Ho set himself the task of publishing a complete edition. Having collected his materials for the work, he was hesitant about publishing them. One day he remarked to a guest, " The work of a literary critic demands wide research and is extremely difficult. Unless one should possess the ability of Liu Hsiang or Yang Hsiung, the task had better not be attempted. The material I have collected is confined to the Min and Che editions, which are in confused order and contain many mistakes. My own idea is that by taking a little more time I might be able to rectify all the errors that are found in them. But time flies too rapidly. What would you suggest in such a case ? "

His friend replied, " You are mistaken in delaying publication. Although Kao (皋) and Su (蘇) do not appear in every generation, the composition of music has not on that account ceased. Although Yang and Liu are not found in every generation, that is no reason why books should cease to be issued. Your one object is to preserve the record of the achievements of Wang An Shih. If because of minor imperfections in your work, you commit the greater fault of not publishing your material the result will be that later generations of students who wish to refer his works will be unable to do so. I think myself that now is the most propitious time to publish. Your concern about the defective character of your work is commendable, but you will be seriously at fault if you delay its publication.

" Possibly you humbly imagine that you have no real contribution to make. But if such thinking were to become the norm, even if Yang and Liu were to rise from their graves, they would refrain from doing any literary work."

Chan Ta Ho perceived that his friend's judgment was right,

so he requested me to write this Introduction. Then follows the Subscript, viz. :—

(Written in the 10th year of Shao Hsing, 5th month. By Huang Tz'u Shan (黃 次 山) of Yü Chang (豫 章) styled Chi Ch'en (季 岑).)

The Index to the famous Encyclopædia of Chinese Literature [1] which was published in the times of Ch'ien Lung, 1783, contains a reference to this edition of Wang An Shih's works. It claims that the edition included in that great work was the redaction of Chan Ta Ho, so we may conclude that the extant edition of Wang An Shih's Works is substantially the same as that published in 1140. That was only fifty-four years after Wang An Shih's death.

The Index quotes the opinion of Ts'ai T'ao (蔡 條) of the Sung Dynasty, that included in this edition of Wang An Shih's works there are some poems which are the work of Wang Yuan Chih (王 元 之), Wang Chun Yü (王 君 玉), and Wang P'ing Fu (王 平 甫), the younger brother of Wang An Shih. It also asserts that there are other writings of Wang An Shih which are not included in the Works as now printed. " But," it continues, " in these volumes his best work is found, and his style and method are such as entitle him to everlasting fame."

According to Ts'ai T'ao (above) and Ch'en Shan (陳 善), also of the Southern Sung, the writings of Wang An Shih were collected in the first instance by his friends and disciples, and right from the beginning there arose some discussion about the presence of spurious elements in the work. But, as hinted above, these are of a negligible character,

In the Addendum to Ts'ai Shang Hsiang's Work, written by Yang Hsi Min (楊 希 閔), the date of which is unknown, but which is stated by the Yenching School of Chinese Studies to have been written some tens of years after Ts'ai's work was published, there is included a list of the various editions of

---

[1] i.e. the Ssu K'u Ch'uan Shu, of which the index or synopsis is termed the Ssu K'u Ch'uan Shu T'i Yao (四 庫 全 書 提 要).

Wang An Shih's Works. In this there is no reference to the various editions of Wang An Shih's Poetry only, which receive separate mention in this chapter. But according to this list, the second edition of his Works was published in 1188, by Ch'ien Hsiang Shan (錢象山) accompanied by an Introduction by Lu Hsiang Shan (陸象山).

So far as the investigations of the writer carry him, no trace of this edition is found in any of the Works on the subject. But the famous Memorial Shrine Inscription to Wang An Shih was composed by Lu Hsiang Shan. The renovation of the shrine was undertaken by the official Ch'ien, and as the date of the inscription referred to is given as 1188, one wonders whether this may not have been misinterpreted by Yang Hsi Min as indicating that another publication of Wang An Shih's Works was made then. However, as the official Ch'ien was sufficiently interested in Wang An Shih as to renovate his shrine, and enforce regular obeisance to his memory, and as further he is stated to have been specially interested in promoting literary and educational work in his district, it is not unreasonable to assume that he actually did publish an edition of Wang An Shih's Works, traces which of have been lost. There is, however, no such Introduction as is referred to above contained in the edition of Lu Hsiang Shan's works which has been used by the writer.

The next edition,[1] in order of time, was confined to Wang An Shih's poetry, published in 1214 by one Li Hsi Mei (李西美). He was a pupil of Li Pi (李壁), who was a great admirer of Wang An Shih's poetry, and in his leisure time had written his comments on a considerable number of the separate poems. The Introduction to this edition was written by Wei Liao Kung (魏了翁), a famous scholar and official who was a friend of Fu Kuang (輔廣), the disciple of Chu Hsi (朱熹). Wei Liao Kung has works to his own name amounting to

[1] The edition of 50 vols. of poetry, No. 2 in the list of Works, as given above.

109 vols., which are known as "Ho Shan Ch'uan Chi"
(鶴 山 全 集).[1]

As this Introduction is of great interest and value, we will
attempt a fairly complete translation, as follows :—

"During the period 1102–1119 our Dynasty undertook
the collection of literary works, and carried it out fairly completely and carefully. The works collected and edited comprised
Classics, History, Art, Geography, Letters, Music, Ceremonies,
Mandates, Records, Religions, Medicine, etc.

" Although very few of the writings of officials got into this
Collection, those of Wang Ching Kung of Lin Ch'uan, thanks
to the efforts of Hsueh Chao Ming (薛 肇 明), were included.

"It is quite true that Wang Ching Kung departed from
traditional practices in his method of government and the
appointment of officials, and it may even be said that this was
due to his natural predilection for that sort of thing (i.e. love
of change). But his wonderful literary gifts made him a peer
among his fellows. So that in the times of Yuan Yu (元 祐),
while there were a great many notable officials who opposed
his government policy, there were none who did not recognize
and admire his literary skill.

" The collections got together by Hsueh Chao Ming [2] and
his associates suffered greatly from the great calamity of Ching
K'ang's (靖 康) day, and some sections of Wang An Shih's
works got lost. So that in the commonly accepted edition
we have not the complete works as they came from his hands.
There is probably some confusion in the order, some portions
are missing, and works of other writers may have got included.
However, while all that may be true, the defects are in no wise
serious.

" Wang An Shih had read widely on every subject, including
the Classics, Philosophy, History, commonplace writings, those
written hastily for some special purpose, heresies, religious

[1] Chinese Biographical Dictionary.
[2] Referring to the proposed Imperial Collection of literature attempted in
the period 1111–1118.

treatises of a bygone age, writings of minor officials, and even
novels. There was nothing he had not read, marked, and
inwardly digested. He became fully conversant with all that
he read, so that when he put pen to paper he caused the reader
to read and reread, astonished at the scope of his knowledge. Some applied the epithet of ' walking encyclopædia '
to him.

" Li Pi,[1] a famous writer and minister of the time of Ning
Tsung (1195–1225) who had lived at Lin Ch'uan, and was a
great lover of Wang An Shih's poetry, used to make comments
on such sections as specially appealed to him. This work
he continued for a considerable time, when he ordered one of
his subordinates to put the material in order. At this time Li
Pi's work on the poetry was practically complete, although he
had not shown it to anyone.

" When I (Wei Liao Kung) came to Mei Shan (眉 山) to take
up my official duties, I was shown this work of Li Pi, and at
once perceived that it was of unusual merit and insight. I
received such enlightenment from it myself that I was led
to remark, ' This is no ordinary commentary, for it criticizes
the text in impartial fashion, and is entirely free from the prejudices of the various literary schools. This gives the work
peculiar value, not only in that it tends to give the real meaning
of the text, but also because of its contribution to the ethical
side of literary exposition.'

" Li Pi has helped to demonstrate Wang An Shih's fecundant
style, and to reveal the wonder of his simple and beautiful
writing, which leaves the writer in no doubt as to his meaning.
He was also able to bring to light Wang An Shih's vast stores
of learning, his colossal memory, his suggestive phraseology,
his unusual rhymes. The commentator has done his work so
well, that the reader is enabled to understand each passage
clearly without effort.

" This, however, must be said, that Wang An Shih's learning
shows now and again the defect of his self-confidence. . . ."

---

[1] Also known as Li Shih Lin (李 石 林).

(Written in the 7th year of Chia Ting (嘉 定), i.e. 1214, in the 11th month.)

Another edition of Wang An Shih's poetry was issued in 1302 by Liu Chiang Sun (劉 將 孫), whose father, Liu Hsü Hsi (劉 須 溪), added the " dot and circle " annotations to the poems.[1]

In the Introduction to this edition,[2] Liu Chiang Sun mentions that Li Pi made his commentary on Wang An Shih's poetry in the period 1205–8. He adds that his father, " who was very fond of reading Wang An Shih's poems, was accustomed to make marginal comments on Li Pi's notes. After some time he handed over his work, after eliminating from it all unnecessary details, to some of his pupils and myself. I yielded to the importunity of Wang Shih Chi (王 士 吉), also one of my father's pupils, and consented to issue another edition of Wang An Shih's Poetical Works, complete with Li Pi's commentary, and supplemented by my father's marks and notes."

" Wang An Shih was a great literary genius of the Sung Dynasty. It is unfortunate that his political ideals and activities put him into the bad books of his opponents, and that this odium was extended to his writings. If only he had confined himself to literary pursuits he would have attained to great fame." The subscript reads as follows :—

(" Written in the reign of Ch'eng Tsung (成 宗) period Ta Te (大 德), ' Hsin Ch'ou year,' i.e. 1302.")

In the year 1306 yet another edition of the Poems [2] was issued by one Mu Feng Ch'en (母 逢 長) of Lung Men Hsien (龍 門). This was probably identical with the edition of Liu Chiang Sun (above).

Mu mentions that " Pan Shan " (半 山) was a later designation of Wang An Shih, given because his home was situated

---

[1] Also known as Liu Ch'en Kung (劉 辰 翁).
[2] Found in edition of poetry of 50 vols., mentioned above.

half-way between the city of Nanking and Chung Shan (鍾 山).
He also mentions that Wang An Shih made a collection of
the T'ang Poets,[1] and that he himself is worthy of being styled
" The T'ang poet of the Sung Dynasty ".

　　The next edition was one of both Prose and Poetry,[2] published
in 1308 by one Wei Su (危 素), a famous literary light of Chin
Hsi (金 谿), who held office under the Mongols.　He was
distressed to discover that Wang An Shih's Works were in a
very fragmentary condition, so he collected all he possibly
could, revising where he thought it necessary to do so.　When
his work was finished, it was more complete than the editions
of Lin Ch'uan (臨 川) or of Chin Ling, Ma Sha (麻 沙)[3] or
that of Che Hsi (浙 西).
　　Wu Ch'eng (吳 澄) of Ch'ung Jen (崇 仁) was requested
by him to write an Introduction.　This Wu Ch'eng, although
a very famous scholar, lived more or less of a hermit life in
a mat shed, on account of which he became known as " Ts'ao
Lu Hsien Sheng " (草 廬 先 生).[4]
　　From his Introduction we extract the following interesting
paragraphs, viz. :—

　　" Wang An Shih was a man of lofty character, being absolutely
devoid of self-interest.　He maintained his high principles
throughout his life.
　　" In the times of Cheng Ho (政 和), A.D. 1111–18, when
literary works were being collected by Imperial decree, Wang
An Shih's works were the only writings of the officials to be
included.　But during the commotion caused by the Ching
K'ang disaster and the removal of the capital, the books in

---

[1] Viz. his T'ang Pai Chia Shih Hsuan (唐 百 家 詩 選).
[2] See introduction of Wu Ch'eng, found in Complete Works (under note 1,
p. 264).
[3] Chin Ling refers to modern Nanking.　Ma Sha (麻 沙) is Chien Yang
Hsien (建 陽 縣) Fukien.
[4] Chinese Biographical Dictionary.

the Imperial library got scattered and lost. Private collections existed it is true, but they were mostly incomplete. The works of Ou Yang Hsiu (歐 陽 修) and the two Sus (二 蘇) became much better known than those of Wang An Shih. . . .

" Wang An Shih was a man of exceptional gifts. The literary men of his day, though differing from him on matters of Government policy, sincerely admired his literary genius. Later generations of scholars, however, even those who are accounted worthy by conventional standards, because they hated the very name of the measures which he introduced during his term of high office, allowed his writings to fall into neglect. . . .

" The reason I have consented to write this Introduction is because I believe that the circumstances which led his contemporaries to oppose and reject him, have not yet been fully and impartially investigated. . . .

" My own opinion is, that although his learning was vast, and his ability great, he was not fully conversant with the teachings of Confucius and Mencius. I feel, too, that he falls behind I Yin (伊 尹) or Chow Kung (周 公) in respect of ability. He was not conscious of this as being in any way a defect, and pressed his views rigorously without any idea of changing his purpose. This to my mind was a flaw in his character. . . .

" Still, one must not overlook the fact that the critics of his day were either prejudiced in their views, or nourished private grudges against him, so that they were not only unable to help him to overcome the difficulty of his own obstinate temperament, but actually failed to do him justice. . . .

" The only men who are entitled to the designation of impartial critics are the two Ch'engs (二 程), Chu Hsi (朱 熹) and Lu Chiu Yuan (陸 九 淵)."

The next edition of Wang An Shih's works was published by Ying Yün Yüeh (應 雲 鶯), a native of Hsiang Shan (象 山), in the year 1546, when he was in office as magistrate of Lin

Ch'uan. He prepared a complete new set of blocks for the printing of the edition.[1]

He states as his reason for doing so that the local people did not possess a complete edition. As he had travelled to and fro in the district, he had observed that on stones, trees, etc., were many references to Wang An Shih's writings or extracts therefrom. Formerly he had though of Wang An Shih as a mere stylist, but after having paid a visit to Chin Hsien (鄞 縣) he had discovered that certain of his political ideas as later embodied in the Agricultural Loans Measure, the Militia Act, the Trade and Barter Measure, and the River Conservation work, had all been successfully carried out there.

He considers that the reason for the lack of success attending his reform policy is to be found in his self-confidence and assertiveness. His contemporaries however should share some of the blame as they offered him no help. If this had been forthcoming, it might have enabled him to overcome the defects of his own disposition.

He is of opinion that it is quite unjust to attribute the disaster of Ching K'ang's day to him, although this was often done. That it was so attributed he considers was due to the tendency of the majority to follow the lead of one or two. He concludes with the following paragraph, viz. :—

" I am ignorant as to the site of his grave, so I made the suggestion that we might erect a temple to his memory. This, however, did not materialize. However, the twenty-second direct descendant of his line, Wang Sheng Jui (王 生 瑞), besought my help in the securing of a piece of land which might be reserved for the purposes of sacrificing to the spirit of his famous ancestor. This, after preparing the blocks for the printing of his works, I enabled him to accomplish."

This Introduction by the publisher of the above edition is accompanied by another from the hand of Ch'en Chiu

---

[1] Found in edition of Complete Works, referred to under n. 1, p. 264 (above).

Ch'uan (陳 九 川),[1] styled Wei Chun (惟 濬), a native of Lin Ch'uan. He gained his Chin Shih degree sometime between 1506–1522, and held official appointment at the Ming Court.[2] He wrote his Introduction or Addendum [3] at the request of Ying Yün Yüeh (above) and it was written at the same time as the latter's Introduction, viz. in the 9th month of 1056.

The critical matter in this Introduction is valuable, so a fairly complete translation follows, viz. :—

"Wang An Shih's literary ability was based on Classical learning, and for moral courage and clarity of ideas he was the one man of his day. Yet his native place possesses no complete copy of his works, probably because the literary men of his time thought so little of his policy when he was minister of State.

"Ming Tao (明 道) [4] and Hsiang Shan (象 山) [5] have left us fair and well-informed criticisms of his work in high office. Although his laws and regulations were not all good, his ideas were of the noblest character. Despite that, he incurred such displeasure and aroused such opposition by his policy, that he was termed a traitor. This was due to the fact that the Sage's doctrine had ceased to control the minds of the great and influential, and because real learning had become decadent.

"Amongst those of the Ch'un Ch'iu days who are praised by Confucius, was Kuan Chung (管 仲), the record of whose achievements has persisted to the present day. Had it not been for him, we should long ago have become the slaves of the barbarous north. So goes the common saying among the people. When he became Prime Minister he punished the

[1] Found in edition of Complete Works, referred to under n. 1, p. 264 (above).

[2] Chinese Biographical Dictionary.

[3] Yang Hsi Min (楊 希 閔) states in the addendum to Ts'ai Shang Hsiang's Work, that Chang Ju Ming (章 汝 明) also wrote an introduction to this edition. As free use of this introduction has been made in the chapter on Wang An Shih's policy it is not reproduced here.

[4] i.e. Ch'eng Hao (程 顥).

[5] i.e. Lu Hsiang Shan (陸 象 山).

officers who had thrown the government into confusion. But what is his achievement compared with the way in which Wang An Shih dealt with the situation in his day, when the barbarians threatened to overrun the whole of our country, and when public life was characterized by the moral decadence which had wrought such havoc for over a thousand years ?

" Even the best of men are not free from prejudice, and often lack foresight. They are afraid of innovations, and are prone to follow their own faction. In mid-Sung times the Imperial prestige was very low, and the patriotic spirit of the people very weak. The Liao and the Hsia were the most pressing and persistent of foes. The Chinese nation was like a sick man with sores on both shoulders. For although the generality of the officials realized their weakness and ineptitude both in material resources and national spirit, to them the situation did not seem particularly perilous, and they persisted in the blind hope that everything would turn out all right in the end.

" Wang An Shih alone perceived the perilous nature of the situation. He repeatedly exhorted his rulers, Jen Tsung and Shen Tsung, to take steps at once to avoid the threatened calamity. But he was so hated by all the great officers, that they sought by every means in their power to ruin him, even resorting to geomantic futilities in their attempt to lessen his influence with the emperor.

" In the times of Yuan Yu (元 祐) all the new measures devised by Wang An Shih were rescinded. Later, in the time of Ching K'ang, when disaster overtook the nation, although it was entirely due to the *laissez-faire* policy of those then in power, the latter must perforce throw the blame on Wang An Shih. As a matter of fact he was the only man who had exercised any forethought in the matter. If men like Ming Tao, i.e. Ch'eng Hao, had succeeded Wang An Shih, the results would fully have justified his government policy. But probably because he did not positively oppose Wang An Shih, he was not mentioned as his successor when he resigned from the office of Prime Minister [*sic !*].

" It may be asked why Wang An Shih himself did not suggest Ch'eng Hao for his successor. Possibly because to do so would have been contrary to his general policy of letting his old associates of great reputation go for a time thinking that this was in the interest of the empire ; while, at the same time, hoping that later on, when the new laws were well and satisfactorily established, he might recall them to share in the joy of achievement. Or possibly seeing that Ch'eng Hao had advised him that his methods were impracticable, and that he had refused to heed the advice, he thought that Ch'eng Hao had repented of his action too late to make him an effective associate.

" It may be true that Wang An Shih was not more deeply versed in the Confucian code than any others of his day. But what of his foresight ? The policy of Chung Ting (忠 定), i.e. Li Kang (李 剛), and his achievements were relatively insignificant. But even Li Kang brought upon himself the calumnies of his opponents and involved himself in considerable personal danger. How much more likely were similar results to occur in Wang An Shih's case, who had to take action before the danger had manifested itself ?

" In his time public criticism of an impartial character was unknown. At Court there were no thoroughly reliable historiographers. That later generations should impute the blame for this national disaster to Wang An Shih is absolutely unreasonable.

" Chien An Tzu (介 菴 子) has demonstrated with great detail that not all Wang's measures could be bad. I, too, have gone into the matter in some detail, but here have mentioned only the more important but hitherto unnoticed features. Although it may fairly be said, that Wang An Shih did not conform to the methods of the ancient kings in every detail, yet he is truly entitled to an illustrious name in this respect. Those who read his works as they should be read will discover this for themselves.

" In the Chin Hsien district Wang An Shih was worshipped with divine honours and this respect for his memory persists to this day. During his term of office there Ying Yün Yüeh

heard so much of Wang An Shih's achievements in that district
that he had his writings reblocked."

The next edition was published in the 4th month of 1561
on the initiative of Ho Chi Yang (何 吉 陽), the governor of
Chiang Hsi, who had the blocks prepared at Fuchow. This is
accompanied by an Introduction by Wang Tsung Mu (王 宗 沐),[1]
a native of Lin Hai (臨 海), in Chiang Hsi province. He was
Education Commissioner for Chiang Hsi and Kuang Tung,
and attained to considerable fame as a writer, his works being
styled the " Chi Yang Wen Chi" (吉 陽 文 集).[2] The introduction reads as follows :—

" In setting out to aid one's sovereign to reform the country's
ways one must naturally act in concert with others, although
of course one's own ideas will be incorporated in any schemes
that are propounded. In attempting such a task, difficulties
of an unexpected character are sure to be encountered. Even
a moral philosopher finds it extremely hard to carry out his
principles perfectly, but how much more difficult is it for one
in high government position to carry out his plans completely.

" It was possible for Wang An Shih to carry out his peculiar
ideas in a small and relatively unimportant sphere, such as a
district ' hsien ' represents, but it is an entirely different matter
to contemplate the carrying out of similar plans for the whole
country when in office as High Minister of State. There were
others, already steeped in traditional practices, who had to
be convinced, their ideas revised, and whose personal confidence
had to be secured. It was very difficult for Wang An Shih
to conceal his own self-confident disposition; in fact, it was
inevitable that it should emerge in some form or other. Although
his position compelled him to enter into conflict with others
in an enterprise of this public character, it was inevitable also
that he should try to carry out his own ideas, and this naturally

[1] Found in Complete Works, modern edition, referred to under n. 1, p. 264
(above).
[2] Chinese Biographical Dictionary.

led to differences and rivalries. Self-confidence in such circumstances leads to criticism and opposition, whereas constantly
to urge others to follow one against their will inevitably leads
to rebellion. How truly difficult it is to get help or achieve
success when one's method is faulty !

"Wang Ching Kung, when minister to Shen Tsung, was
greatly concerned about the weakness of the country, and the
defects in national life which were ever growing more serious.
He determined to make a Yao or Shun of his ruler, change the
laws and reform the administration.

"He truly was a peer among his contemporaries, as far as
personal character is concerned. He was widely read and of
exceptionally clear judgment. He was favoured with unusual
intimacy on the part of the emperor. As one reflects on his
purpose, his ability, and his policy, one is bound to admit his
uniqueness as a minister since the time of the Three Dynasties.

"At the same time we notice that whenever a new law was
promulgated, the whole country was thrown into a state of
disturbance and disputation, and that opposition and desertions
among the court officials were of constant occurrence. In
the end Wang An Shih was compelled to resign. Even those
whom he had encouraged and promoted deserted him, attacked
him, and described him as heterodox. Some even ascribed the
disaster of Ching K'ang's day to his policy.

"There have been those of more lowly rank whose self-
confidence has not been reckoned unto them for guilt by
later generations. But Wang An Shih, who was out to make
a Yao and Shu of his sovereign, is dubbed a criminal.

"Undoubtedly he was self-assertive and determined to
carry out his ideas at all costs, although it was quite natural
for him to disparage such unreasonable criticism as characterized
the opposition. But his obstinacy and assumption of superiority
over all others led to the experienced and trusted ministers
deserting him, and this desertion by the able and the good
afforded the opportunity for inferior folk to come in. . . .

"The remark of Ch'eng Hao that ' the affairs of the empire
are not the sole concern of one man ' brings Wang An Shih's

great defect to light.   So that although it is unreasonable to attribute the blame for the disaster of Ching K'ang's day to Wang An Shih, yet viewing the matter in this light, we can see the reason why these statements were made.

" The literary work of Wang An Shih is based on the Classics, and embraces all subjects. His style is direct, penetrating, and pure.   He really forms a school by himself.   I consider his Wan Yen Shu (萬 言 書) the best of his compositions, for as we read it, we see that his attitude is comparable with that taken by I Yin (伊 尹) when T'ang (湯) called him from his agriculture to take charge of the government.

" Later generations, because of their attitude to his political policy, ignored his literary work.   But although it may be reasonable to term his career as a high officer a failure, one should not on that account despise his contribution to literature."

According to Yang Hsi Min (楊 希 閔), who published an Addendum to the Work of Ts'ai Shang Hsiang, another edition of Wang An Shih's Works was published in 1612, by a direct descendant of the reformer, called Wang Feng Hsiang (王 鳳 翔) or Wang Ching Ch'in (王 荆 芩).   This edition was styled the " Kuang Ch'i T'ang Pen " (光 啟 堂 本), and was accompanied by an Introduction from the pen of Li Kuang Tsu (李 光 祚) of Feng Ch'eng (豐 城).   It was published at Chin Ling, i.e. Nanking.

The following is a summary of the subject matter in this Introduction, viz. :—

" The secret of deliverance for the Sung dynasty considering the conditions that existed in those days, lay in changing the old order and not in maintaining it.   In the most flourishing days of the empire the farming classes depended upon some sort of loan system.   No one can deny that Wang An Shih, in devising his Agricultural Loans Measure, had the interests of the farmer at heart, for it was infinitely preferable to offer them government loans at a reasonable rate of interest, than to allow private money-lenders to rob the people by exacting double or even five times those rates.

" Then in regard to his Public Services Measure, as it was impossible for everyone actually to engage in public work, it was better to free all without discrimination from such a duty and tax the people, according to their economical status, so as to provide the means of hiring the necessary labour. There was nothing oppressive in the measure, for according to the provisions of the Act, the people were entitled to exemption in times of stringency.

" His Militia Act was in line with ancient practices, for in those days the people were called upon in times of war to act as the nation's soldiery. In the Han dynasty animals were impressed for public use at such a time. His measure has been adopted by our own Dynasty (Ming).

" His Civil Service examination system has also been revived in recent times, and has led to the securing of a large number of capable men for government work.

" It cannot be claimed that his measures were all equally good, but neither were they all indiscriminately bad. It is absurd to make him responsible for the national calamity of 1126, as his policy was definitely devised to forestall such a disaster. For on its financial and military sides alike, it aimed solely at the peace and stability of the empire.

" He was absolutely oblivious to personal considerations. He acted always on principle, so had no regrets when slandered, and no fear of personal defamation and loss. He would rather stand alone than win the plaudits of his contemporaries by compromising his principles. He had absolute confidence in his theories, being sincerely convinced that if they were carried into effect, prosperity and stability would result.

" It was his great aim to revive the military glory of T'ang and the civil glory of Yao and Shun. But the influential officials of his day, actuated by a spirit of envy and hate, overthrew his policy. Their opposition was of such a character that it was impossible for anyone, no matter how wise and sound his plans might be, to overcome it. But no matter how cleverly his adversaries may try to misrepresent him, it is impossible for them to conceal his fine qualities, whether we think of his literary ability or his political achievements."

The most recent edition of Wang An Shih's poetry was published in 1922, or as the publisher, Chang Yuan Chi (張 元 濟) of Hai Hsien (海 鹽) terms it, the 180th year since the 6th year of Ch'ien Lung (乾 隆), when his ancestor Chang Tsung Sung (張 宗 松) furnished the edition which was included in the " Ssu K'u Ch'uan Shu " (四 庫 全 書).[1]

The account of his labours in this connection and reasons for publishing another edition are given in an Addendum to the modern edition, the gist of which is given below :—

" The poems of Wang Ching Kung were edited and commented upon by Li Yen Hu (李 雁 湖). My ancestor of six generations back secured a copy of the edition published by Ma of Hua Shan (華 山 馬 氏) comprising fifty volumes. In the year 1742 (the 6th year of Ch'ien Lung's reign) he prepared new blocks of the poems. However, owing to the outbreak of the T'ai P'ing rebellion these blocks got lost, and the books which had been printed from them became most difficult to obtain.

" In my youth I had cultivated a liking for this work, and after searching diligently for ten years I found a copy in Peking. I discovered that no edition of his poetical works had been issued since the year 1307, apart from the work of my ancestor included in the Ssu K'u Ch'uan Shu. There were some editions of Wang An Shih's works extant in Japan, but in China they were very scarce. My ancestor had been exhorted by a friend, Yao Shu Hsiang, to seek to preserve the work not by keeping it under lock and key at home, but by printing it and publishing it abroad. I remembered this remark, and became desirous of publishing a modern edition to fulfil my ancestor's purpose.

" In the copy which I had found I discovered that there were two pages missing, the last page of the 30th volume, and also

[1] See below.

the last page of the 50th volume. I tried hard to find these. My friend Yang Hsing Wu, who had been in the Chinese Legation in Japan, possessed a complete type-printed copy of a Korean edition of Wang An Shih's works, including a biographical index. I wrote to him, and he gladly sent me the missing pages together with the Index.

" I was sent to Europe after this, and on my return to China I found everything in confusion and that this work had got lost together with many of my other books.

" Fortunately again, a fellow student of mine, Fu Yuan Shu, told me that on his way through Suchow he had seen a Mongol edition of Wang An Shih's poetry, and he had pleasure in buying this and sending it to me. I found that the two pages which had been missing from my old copy were here complete, and that in addition to a biographical Index the name of another was appended. My friend urged me to print another edition from this, including Liu Hsü Hsi's (劉 須 溪)[1] commentary. This was not in accordance with my original purpose, yet as it tended to preserve the ancient character of the work, I considered it in line with my ancestor's wish. Alas, on looking further into it, I found that some ten pages were missing, so I refrained from printing at that time.

" Then a Japanese friend of mine, Ch'ang Wei Yu Shan, informed me that there was a copy of this work in the Imperial Library in Japan, which he had copied and sent to me. There was still one page missing from this work, but fortunately I discovered this in a dilapidated copy found in the Library at Chiang Nan.

" Li Yen Hu (李 雁 湖), who wrote the original commentary on Wang An Shih's poetry, got Wei Huo Shan[2] (魏 鶴 山)[3] to write an Introduction. My ancestor had been distressed that he had been unable to obtain this for his edition. Later on, however, one Pao of Ch'eng T'ang obtained a copy of this,

---

[1] The same as Liu Ch'en Kung (劉 辰 翁).

[2] i.e. Wei Liao Kung (魏 了 翁).

[3] Liang Ch'i Ch'ao, p. 331, where he also states that the 100 volume edition includes the material contained in the older edition of 180 volumes.

which later editions of the work mostly included. It was, however, only a copy.

"Then I learned that my friend Liu An I of Wu Ch'eng had a dilapidated copy of the Sung edition which included the original text of the Introduction by Wei. He gave me permission to include this in front of my edition, and so I was able to fulfil the wish of my ancestor in that respect.

"In the copy which Yang Hsing Wu had sent me from Japan, there was included the Introductions by Liu Chiang Sun (劉 將 孫) and Mu Feng Ch'en (母 逢 辰). In these Wang An Shih was styled Wen Cheng (文 正) and there were several phrases very hard to understand. This had aroused my suspicions as to the genuineness of these documents. But when I took my edition to pieces for photographic purposes, I discovered right at the beginning, in front of the biographical index, and tightly nipped in the binding thread, two sheets of paper, which I surmised must be the two Introductions referred to, and that the doubtful passages must have been the result of Korean copyists' errors. So I managed to secure both Introductions.

"So after a long lapse of time, by the greatest good fortune and by the co-operation of many friends, I have fulfilled my ancestor's purpose, and secured a complete copy of the Work.

"(Written in the 180th year after the 6th year of Ch'ien Lung, the year in which my ancestor published his edition.)"

The edition of Wang An Shih's complete works, which has been used in the preparation of this book, is that published in 1918 by the Sao Yeh Shan Fang Publishing Co. (掃 葉 山 房). It is stated to be a copy of the Sung Edition of Wang An Shih's Complete Works (仿 宋 本 王 臨 川 集).

Liang Ch'i Ch'ao states that the modern editions of Wang An Shih's Works are the same as the edition of Wei Su (危 素) of Chin Hsi, of the Mongol Dynasty, who assisted T'o T'o in his compilation of the Dynastic Histories of Sung, Liao, and Chin.

Chapter XVII

WANG AN SHIH'S CONTRIBUTION TO PROSE AND POETRY [1]

Wang An Shih's government policy and methods of Classical interpretation aroused general and noisome opposition, but his literary gifts excited universal admiration.

Wu Ts'ao Lu (吳 草 廬), in his introduction to Wang An Shih's Works, says, " During the T'ang Dynasty there were only two men who did anything towards reforming the defects of the writing of the preceding eight dynasties, and who may be said to have attained to the high standards of the earlier Han period. These were Han Yü (韓 愈) and Liu Tzu Hou (Liu Ts'ung Yuan) (柳 宗 元). Han Yü must be regarded as the more famous of these two.

" The literati of the Sung Dynasty held the writers of the T'ang period in the highest esteem. But as a matter of fact men of the Sung period like Ou Yang Hsiu (歐 陽 修), Su Hsün (蘇 洵), Su Shih (蘇 軾), Tseng Kung (曾 鞏), and Wang An Shih may be regarded as compeers of Han Yü and Liu Tzu Hou. These seven, from the standpoint of purely literary merit, are the most famous names on the records of the T'ang and Sung Dynasties.

" Later critics added to these the name of Su Tzu Yu (蘇 子 由), i.e. Su Che, making eight in all. Not that these were the only men of the period entitled to fame for their literary work, but they excelled in their own day, and have not been surpassed since. So they are deserving of a place on the scroll of literary renown.

" In speaking of the literary ability of Wang An Shih, it should be observed that while the merit of the other seven is ascribed chiefly on the grounds of literary ability, and that alone, the work which he has left is distinguished by remarkable intellectual power. Not that the others were not men of great learning, but they lacked Wang An Shih's depth of thought

---

[1] The material in this chapter is mostly taken from Liang Ch'i Ch'ao, chap. 22.

and breadth of reading. They also lacked his wide sweep of the mind, and the directness, combined with grace, of his literary composition.

" These characteristics tend to make Wang An Shih distinctive as a writer.

" I should place Wang An Shih as one of the four relatively greater writers of the period, along with Han Yü, Ou Yang Hsiu, and Su Shih, i.e. Su Tung P'o (蘇 東 坡). If I were asked to carry the comparison further I would say that Su gave more attention to style than logic, while Wang An Shih excels in the much more important feature of cogency of reasoning. A comparison of Wang An Shih's Memorial of a Myriad Words with Su's Memorial to Shen Tsung, reveals their individual characteristics. Wang An Shih learned from Han Yü, and in this he is like Ou Yang Hsiu. Comparing Ou Yang Hsiu and Wang An Shih one might say that the former may be regarded as half-teacher, half-friend.

" In a poem written in Wang An Shih's honour, Ou Yang Hsiu states that he is the only one who could ever hope to compete with Han Yü for the mastery of Letters. In his reply, Wang An Shih says it is inconceivable that he should ever attain to such a pinnacle of literary excellence. He also states his chief object to be the propagation of ethical principles, which would leave neither the time nor the strength to devote to other aspects of literary work.

" My own opinion is that if due regard is paid to learning as well as to purely literary gifts, Wang An Shih may be said even to excel Han Yü, though of course from the standpoint of literary merit alone, the latter is pre-eminent. In this latter respect Wang An Shih may be termed ' a good son of Han Yü '.

" Tseng Kuo Fan (曾 國 藩) says that the main thing to observe in Wang An Shih's writing is the forcefulness of his style. He is like Han Fei Tzu (韓 非 子) in the cogency and perspicacity of his reasoning, while in the forceful pertinacity of his composition he may be likened to Mo Ti (墨 翟). In these respects neither Han Yü nor Ou Yang Hsiu can equal him. . . . "

It is generally acknowledged that Wang An Shih's essays and discussions are worthy of note, but few realize that his best work is to be found among his memorials, obituary notices, and records. His obituary notices alone number over two hundred, and reveal many varieties of style. Some are composed in the progressive, flowing style of composition, others gather in cogency line upon line as the argument advances. In some he leads the mind from a consideration of details to the discussion of great principles. In others again, he compresses great ideas in very compact form. He is master of every form of composition, and has every art and device of fine writing at his command. In this respect he is the only man who can be compared with Han Yü.

Tseng Wen Cheng says, " A free and flowing style is essential to literary art. To attain this, it is important to observe that while the different sections of the essay should be distinguished, it should be done in such a way that the various divisions are not too obvious."

This is the opinion of a great literary critic, and of one who was thoroughly acquainted with Wang An Shih's writings, and is a very fair criticism of his style.

For models of his best style the reader is referred to his " Yen Shih Shu " (言 事 書), his memorial on " A Century of Peace " (國 家 百 年 無 事 劄 子), his " Ts'ai Lun " (材 論), his " Reply to Ssu Ma Kuang's Criticisms " (答 司 馬 諫 議 書), the Introduction to the New Interpretation of the Odes (詩 義 序), the Introduction to the " Chow Kuan Hsin I " (周 官 義 序), the addendum to the Hung Fan Chuan (洪 範 傳 後), and his treatise entitled " After reading Lao Tzu " (讀 老 子).

Should further evidence be sought as to Wang An Shih's literary merit, the following extracts from introductions to various editions of his Works may be quoted, viz. :—

Huang Tz'u Shan writes in 1140 : " In his youth Wang An Shih was a pupil of Ou Yang Hsiu, but soon equalled his master in literary ability."

Wei Liao Kung writes in 1214 : " In the times of Yuan Yu

there were a great many notable people who were directly antagonistic to Wang An Shih's government policy, but there were none who did not recognize and admire his literary merit."

Wu Ch'ung writes in 1308 : " When literary works were being collected by the Government in the time of Cheng Ho (1111–1118) only the works of Wang An Shih were included out of all the writings of contemporary officials."

The above is a summary of the main features of his prose style, and represents an attempt to estimate his place in the galaxy of literary talent which is such a marked feature of the Sung Dynasty. As a writer of poetry also, Wang An Shih is entitled to some renown. He wrote poems in early life, and continued to be prolific in this sphere to the end of his days. The modern edition of his Poetry runs into fifty volumes. The actual number of poems included is over 1,500. This gives some idea of the extent of his poetical work.

As with the criticism of his prose writing, so in regard to his poetry we cannot do better than give the gist of Liang Ch'i Ch'ao's opinions on the subject.

" The usual criticism of Wang An Shih's poetry is that it is not of the same standard as his prose. But he may be regarded as the founder of the Hsi Chiang (西 江 派) School of poetry and also as the originator of a particular style of poesy in the Sung period. So that he holds an extremely important place in the history of Chinese poetical composition.

In this sphere, Tu Fu (杜 甫) has, for over a thousand years, held the field. But much of his later fame is due to Wang An Shih's notice of him. For he not only wrote a very complimentary tribute to Tu Fu, to be subscribed to his picture, but was also the means of recovering over two hundred poems of his, and including them in his already known works. In the Introduction Wang An Shih states that the world is indebted to him for the possession of Tu Fu's complete works. He also states that it was only after acquaintance with Tu Fu's poetry that men learned to write at all. Wang An Shih's admiration for and imitation of Tu Fu's work contributed towards the latter's fame.

During the early days of the Sung Dynasty, the ' Hsi K'un ' (西 崑 體) style of poetry held the field. This had been carried over from the later T'ang times. Wen T'ing Chun (温 庭 筠) and Li Shang Yin (李 商 隱) were the protagonists of this style of writing. It is an inferior form of poetry, and Ou Yang Hsiu and Mei Sheng Yü (梅 聖 俞) tried to improve upon it. During the Sung Dynasty, Yang I (楊 億), Liu Chun (劉 筠), and Ch'ien Wei Yen (錢 惟 演) made parallel rhymes, which were styled Hsi K'un T'i (西 崑 體). These men followed in the footsteps of Wen T'ing Chun and Li Shang Yin.

After Ou Yang Hsiu and Mei Sheng Yü had improved on this style somewhat, a separate School was formed, of whom the most famous exponents were Wang An Shih, Su Tung P'o, and Huang Shan Ku (黄 山 谷). But the one who made the biggest contribution to the improvement of the style was Wang An Shih. He transformed it from its high colouring and sickly conceits to a bold, concise, and direct style of composition.

The most illustrious poets of the Sung Dynasty are Su Tung P'o and Huang Shan Ku, and it is not claimed that Wang An Shih was their compeer. But it is wrong to regard Huang Shan Ku as the founder of the Hsi Chiang School, for that honour belongs to Wang An Shih.

In the ancient style of poetry Wang An Shih imitated Han Yü, and it is almost impossible to say of certain odes whether they are from the pen of Wang An Shih or Han Yü. In other poems he imitated Tu Fu, but he developed his own style which was based on Tu Fu, and which Huang Shan Ku adopted later His style generally is characterized by variety, impressiveness, and richness of suggestion.

But special mention must be made of his twenty poems in a simple moralizing style, all in five-character lines. An example of this is given below :—

我 曾 爲 牛 馬	" Were I a cow or a horse,
見 草 豆 歡 喜	Straw and beans would delight me.
又 曾 爲 女 人	Were I a woman weak,

子　　　The stronger sex would attract me.
我此定使夫己　But were I my own true self,
男是如不物丈　My natural bent I should follow,
見眞長惡為大　For if my desires are unmoored,
喜若合好知堂　Environment will enslave me.
歡我祇若應堂莫　But a really great man,
　　　O'er environment rules supreme."

This is scarcely worthy of the name of poetry. But since Su Tung P'o began to write, it became the common practice to introduce tags of Buddhist philosophy into poetry. This style may be said to have been originated by Wang An Shih.

But his real fame as a poet lies solely in his adaptation of the "Antiphonal Couplet" (排偶之句) style [1] to modern poetry. His seven-character liners follow the later patterns of Tu Fu, which later Huang Shan Ku brought to perfection. It was because of this that the latter gained the reputation (false as shown above) of being the founder of the Hsi Chiang School.

Another feature of Wang An Shih's poetry is his skill in plagiarism. He had a perfectly wonderful aptitude for taking sentences from different poems by other hands and weaving them together, into a new poem. This was his innovation, and was termed the "Chi Chü style" (集句之體). His gift in this direction resulted from his colossal memory, for he could reel off these at random."

The following critiques of Wang An Shih's poetry will be of interest :—

In the Man Sou Shih Hua (漫叟詩話) we read, "Wang An Shih's poetical efforts which are later than the Ting Lin (定林) exceed greatly his earlier attempts for clearness, fluency, and polish, and also in the art of his composition."

Ch'en Shih Tao (陳師道), of the Northern Sung Dynasty, in the Hou Shan Shih Hua (後山詩話) says, "Huang Shan Ku agrees that it was only in his later years that Wang An Shih wrote really fine poetry."

[1] See Lin Yü T'ang, *My Country and my People*, pp. 245–6.

Another quotation from Huang Shan Ku is found in the T'iao Hsi Yü Yin Ch'ung Hua (茗 溪 漁 隱 叢 話) as follows :

"The shorter poems written by Wang An Shih in later life are unequalled for their purity, elegance, and perspicacity. He rose far and away above current styles of writing."

The work from which this quotation is taken was by Hu Yuan Je of the Sung Dynasty.

In the "Shih Lin Shih Hua" (石 林 詩 話), also of the Sung Dynasty, occurs the following: "Great improvement is noticeable in Wang An Shih's poetry, as he grows older. At first his style was direct and obvious, but later much progress is observable in art and depth. His writing became so concise and the language so apt that it could not be improved upon."

In the "Leng Chai Yeh Hua" (冷 齋 夜 話) we read : "Wang An Shih's poetry, together with that of Su Tung P'o and Huang Shan Ku, embraces the best poetry both in ancient and modern style."

Su Tung P'o, referring to a poem sent to him by Wang An Shih, writes, "Since the time of Ch'ü Yuan (of the Chan Kuo times) I have not seen anything so closely to resemble his work."

In the "T'ang Tzu Hsi Yü Lu" (唐 子 西 語 錄) Wang An Shih's five-character liners are commended as being the equal of Tu Fu's work of that type.

As to Wang An Shih's plagiarisms, the "T'ien Chai Hsien Lan" says that they were unique. He could collate lines from different poems and make them fit beautifully both in rhyme and sense."

His best and most renowned works of this character are the eighteen poems styled Hu Chia (胡 笳), the thirteenth and eighteenth of these being real masterpieces of collation.

We have noted that Wang An Shih made a collection of the work of the T'ang Poets. This was made during the period he was in the Board of Finance, at the request of one Sung Tz'u T'ao. In the Introduction to this work, Wang An Shih writes : "If one should wish to know the character of the T'ang poetry, it should suffice to study this Anthology."

CHAPTER XVIII

WANG AN SHIH'S CONTRIBUTION TO CLASSICAL EXPOSITION

IF Wang An Shih's contribution to the subject of Classical Exposition is to be rightly estimated, it is essential that the history of this subject should be outlined. Liang Ch'i Ch'ao has a concise sketch of this in his Work on Wang An Shih, which we cannot do better than translate here.

"For a period of over two thousand years education in China has been related to the Classical literature. The methods of interpretation have naturally changed during this long period of time.

During the times of the Western Han Dynasty (206–23 B.C.) writing on silk and bamboo were rare accomplishments, and as the Classics had mostly been destroyed or lost in the Ch'in Dynasty (255–209 B.C.), the task of restoring the ancient literature was dependent upon the memory of a few men, who dictated what they could recall of the old texts to scribes. As an example we may quote the Book of History, which was rewritten in the Western Han Dynasty by Ch'ao Ts'o (鼂 錯) at the dictation of Fu Sheng (伏 生) of Tsinanfu.

"This scarcity of written texts naturally led to a great deal of oral instruction being given, and also resulted in a great variety both in the subjects and methods of classical exposition. As a matter of fact classical instruction in the accepted sense of the word, scarcely existed. Most of the expositors based their interpretations on Astrology, Geomancy, and the like.

"However, interpretation was not all of that type, for even in those benighted times there were such as Tung Chung Shu (董 仲 舒) who gave us his 'Fan Lu' (繁 露) or Interpretation of the Annals, and Liu Chung Lei (劉 中 壘), who wrote his 'Introduction to the Odes' (新 序 之 說 詩). In their expositions they included not only the traditional views, but added their own individual ideas, and in this respect they may be said to have founded a new school of Interpretation.

" Towards the end of the Eastern Han Dynasty (A.D. 25–220), when the traditional oral method had practically ceased, Chia Kuei (賈 逵), Ma Jung (馬 融), Fu Ch'ien (服 虔), and Cheng Hsuan (鄭 玄) began to analyse the text, splitting it up into chapters and verses, and expounding it clause by clause in the greatest detail. The result was that the main idea of the literature was generally overlooked.

" From this time up to the beginning of the T'ang Dynasty (A.D. 618–905) scholars gave their main attention to essay writing, neglecting the study of the Classics, relatively speaking. However, a few great writers are found amongst the followers of Buddhism, Confucianism in that age being considered as being in need of Buddhistic teachings to supplement it. Such scholars included Hsü Tsun Ming (徐 遵 明) of the Later Wei Dynasty (A.D. 386–543), Liu Cho (劉 焯), and Liu Hsuan (劉 炫) of the Sui Dynasty (A.D. 589–618), Lu Te Ming (陸 德 明), K'ung Ying Ta (孔 穎 達), and Chia Kung Yen (賈 公 彥) of the T'ang Dynasty.

" The work of this School, while more extensive than that of the scholars of the Eastern Han times, was not so important in respect of their contribution to the progress of the subject.

" During the times of the Sung Dynasty (A.D. 960–1278) four Schools of Interpretation may be distinguished. These were the ' Lo ' (洛) School represented by the two Ch'engs (二 程), the ' Lien ' (濂) School represented by Chow Tun I (周 敦 頤), the ' Kuan ' (關) School represented by Chang Tsai (張 載), and the ' Min ' (閩) School represented by Chu Hsi (朱 熹).

" All these concentrated on the attempt to get at the inner meaning of the Classics, and in that respect they represent a new phase in the development of Classical Interpretation. But for the most part they laid emphasis on the ethical, psychological, religious, and philosophical ideas of the literature, neglecting, generally speaking, the practical and political significance of the text. Their theory was that if the philosophical and ethical implications of the Classics were thoroughly apprehended the rest would follow as a matter of course.

" Therefore the Analects, Mencius, Great Learning, and the Doctrine of the Mean were given prior place, other sections of the Classical literature being regarded as of secondary importance. It should, however, be noted that of the Classical literature viewed as a whole only ten to twenty per cent may be said to be related to ethics and philosophy.

" During the Mongol and the Ming Dynasties no appreciable change was made in the method of approach to the Classics, the interpreters following in the steps of their Sung predecessors.

" During the Manchu Dynasty (A.D. 1583–1911), while at first the tendency was to follow along the traditional lines laid down by the Sung and Ming Schools, there arose later a new party whose tendency was to oppose this traditional method, and which aimed at reverting to the more ancient practice of interpretation. Hu Wei (胡 渭), Yen Jo Chü (閻 若 璩), Chiang Yung (江 永), and Hui Shih Ch'i (惠 士 奇) were the chief exponents of this revival, and were supported by Tai Chen (戴 震), Tuan Yü Ts'ai (段 玉 裁), Wang Nien Sun (王 念 孫), and Wang Yin Chih (王 引 之) and his son.

" Beginning with the times of Ch'ien Lung (乾 隆) and Chia Ch'ing (嘉 慶), A.D. 1736–1821, thanks largely to the labours of these men, all the Classics were re-edited and reinterpreted, each section of the text and each explanation being traced to its source, and all baseless or heretical interpretations eliminated. The result was that every character in their editions could be vouched for, and every sentence explained. Viewed from that standpoint, their labours are worthy of commendation. But they were practically only following in the footsteps of the Eastern Han and T'ang Schools, for they largely, if not altogether, confined themselves to a literal exposition of the text.

" We may say, therefore, that for a period of two thousand years or more, the great idea of Classical interpretation, viz., the search for, and exposition of, the meaning behind and beneath the text, has received comparatively little attention. The credit for initiating this method must be given to Tung Tzu Show of the Western Han and Liu Chung Lei of the same period.

" But the one who carried out their ideas more comprehensively and more completely was Wang An Shih of the Northern Sung." [1]

The selections from Wang An Shih's essays given in succeeding chapters of this book are sufficient to justify the contention that he in no way neglected the ethical and philosophical implications of the Classical literature. It has already been noted that he read widely in Buddhist and Taoist literature, and that he was steeped in the Confucian writings. But, as Liang Ch'i Ch'ao suggests, in the above sketch of the history of Classical Exposition, his most notable contribution is in his efforts to bring out the practical value of the Classical texts for matters of government.

It will also be noted from several passages in this work, that in regard to his suggestions for the reform of the examinations for the Civil service, Wang An Shih laid the greatest emphasis on the candidate's knowledge of the possible application of the classics to everyday affairs. It was with that in view, that the New Interpretations of the Classics, for which he was primarily responsible, were produced and issued to the Schools.

These new Interpretations, as has already been noted, consisted of the Book of History, the Odes, and the Chow Kuan. Of these, only the last-mentioned is the sole work of Wang An Shih himself. In the other two, the work was largely undertaken by his son Fang, Lü Hui Ch'ing, and other associates. However, he must have given oversight to their labours on these two Classics, and at least, the finished work must have been in line with his own ideas on the subject.

The Introductions to each of these three works were, however, written by Wang An Shih, and as these give the reader

---

[1] Liang Ch'i Ch'ao, summarized from pp. 320–4.

a general idea of their character and also his object in producing them, we will attempt a translation of them, as below :—

He introduces the Chow Kuan Hsin I (周 官 新 義) [1] thus :—

" The emperor, with a view to reforming the traditional methods of classical interpretation which have obtained for so long, and with the idea of developing true scholarship, called together a group of scholars from amongst his officials, requesting them to attempt to elucidate the real meaning of the books, with the object of distributing them for use in the Schools.

" My part in this work has been to expound the meaning of the Chow Kuan.

" The application of ethico-philosophical principles to matters of government, will ensure an observance of correct distinctions between the worthy and unworthy, and official positions will thereby be properly regulated. Matters of economy will be dealt with in due proportion, and full consideration will be given to the time when things should be done.

" It should be the chief concern of everyone making the laws of the State to see that moral principles are embedded therein, so as to ensure that in the actual execution of the laws, those who are administering them will naturally be fulfilling the moral obligations of their own being.

" For emphasis on these matters, the Chow Kuan stands supreme in history. It stresses the necessity for moral character in the officials administering the laws, and also for the observance of the ethical implications of the laws themselves. The actual laws enunciated in the work are worthy of perpetuation, the government system outlined therein being more perfect than any other which is available in literature.

" This is accounted for by the fact that the rulers of Chow held the laws and ordinances of previous regimes in the highest regard, and continued their efforts in the developing of them until they reached perfection. The result was that the system of governments which they represent became the model for

---

[1] Chow Kuan Hsin I ; Introduction by the author (自 序).

succeeding generations, and needed no additions. But that was not the sole credit of Wen, and Wu, and Chow Kuan (i.e. some of the credit was due to their predecessors, Yao, Shun, and Yü, etc.), just as the temperature of the atmosphere represents the results of accumulated action of generations of natural laws.

" Over a thousand years have elapsed since the Chow Dynasty decayed, and after this prolonged period the very traces of that peaceful age have been eliminated.

" It has, moreover, been very difficult, in fact impossible, to secure a copy of the ancient classic in its original form. So that it is with a full sense of the difficulty of expounding the text, that I have undertaken the task committed unto me, regardless of my own incapacity for such an undertaking. If it is so difficult to expound, it is still harder to estimate the place it should have in matters of government policy, and to restore it to that place.

" However, in sympathy with the sovereign's determination to set up good laws, and in response to the fine example he has given to all his officers, it behoves each minister and official to strive earnestly to co-operate with him in the attempt to usher in a virtuous Age. When I regard my own observations of the present, and what I have learned of the past, I must admit that it is only by disregarding my own lack of what is termed real knowledge of the subject, that I have presumed to think I might get somewhere near the goal set. . . .

" I have, however, arranged the work in 22 volumes, comprising over a hundred thousand words, and now present the result of my labours to the throne, and to the supervisors of examinations, to await official approval before publication and distribution to the schools."

As Wang An Shih contended that most of his so-called innovations in government represented a revival, in spirit at least, of ancient methods and practices, and as these in the main are such as is found in the Chow Kuan, it will be of interest at this point to translate the Addendum to Wang An Shih's New Interpretation of it, which is found at the end of

the modern edition.[1] This is by Wu Ts'ung Yao (伍 崇 曜),
and was compiled in 1853. It reads as follows :—

"The new interpretation of the 'Chow Kuan' (周 官)
comprising sixteen volumes, and the new interpretation of the
'K'ao Kung Chi' (考 工 記) or Artificers' Record, in two
volumes, are the work of Wang An Shih, of the Sung Dynasty.

"The 'Life of Wang An Shih' is included in the Dynastic
History of Sung. These particular works from his pen are
included in the 'Ssu K'u T'i Yao' (四 庫 提 要). The originals
were lost for a long time, but were eventually found and
included in the Yung Lo Ta Tien (永 樂 大 典), from which
work they were later transferred to the 'Ssu K'u Ch'uan Shu'
(四 庫 全 書). One Ch'ien Hsin Hu (錢 心 壺), a censor of
edicts, added thirty additional sections and printed a new
edition at Chung Chow (中 州).

"Everyone is acquainted with the common saying that
Wang An Shih brought disaster upon the House of Sung by
his advocacy of the Chow Kuan (周 官). His contemporaries
rose in opposition to his policy, and later adherents of his
political opponents attributed the real cause of the national
catastrophe to this work.

"As a consequence of this, it became the current theory that
the Chow Kuan could not be the work of the Duke of Chow.
But after an examination of the subject in the Sung Histories,
I find the following facts.

"In the second year of Hsi Ning's reign, i.e. 1069, when
Wang An Shih was vice-Grand Councillor, and it was proposed
to initiate the reform programme, he affirmed that the Dynasty
of Chow organized the 'Ch'uan Fu Chih Kuan' (泉 府 之 官)
or Financial System, with a view to controlling the monopolizers
of wealth, and to relieving the poor and distressed by a more
equitable distribution of that commodity. He also asserted
that in later times only Sang Hung Yang (桑 宏 羊) and Liu
Yen (劉 晏) were roughly acquainted with the idea of this
system, and revived the method with a view to restoring to
the government the supreme authority in matters of finance.

---

[1] Chow Kuan Hsin I Pa (周 官 新 義 跋).

" Han Wei Kung (韓 魏 公), however, asserted that he had wantonly misused the Chow Li (周 禮) so as to give the emperor a false idea of its character.

" Sun Chueh also stated that the ' Kuo Fu Chih Hsi ' (國 服 之 息) was not understood by those who attempted to explain it, so commentators endeavoured to elucidate the expression by referring to the financial method of Wang Mang (王 莽), who in estimating the surplus income (which might accrue from government loans to the people) fixed the maximum rate of interest on these loans at 10 per cent. He reasoned from this that under the government system in vogue during the Chow Dynasty it was inconceivable that they should exact higher rates of interest than Wang Mang. He argued further that if the statement was true that all the government revenue was taken from the ' Ch'uan Fu ' (泉 府) as sole source, how are we to explain the use of the ' Chung Tsai Chiu Fu ' (冢 宰 九 賦) or ' Nine kinds of taxes ' imposed by the Prime Minister ?

" Such questions as these induced scholars to doubt the authenticity of the Chow Kuan.[1]

" After the New Laws had been promulgated for some time, in the eighth year of Hsi Ning, i.e. 1075, the New Interpretations of the Odes, History, and the Chow Li, which Wang An Shih and his associates had been freshly expounding, were formally presented to the throne, and ordered to be used by the

---

[1] Cf. Wylie, *History of Chinese Literature*, p. 5, where he says : " In the eleventh century a minister under the Sung dynasty, named Wang Gan Shih, introduced some changes in the system of levying duties, and rested them on the authority of the Chow Li. The countenance which this unpopular measure seemed to receive from the Chow Li, drew forth much apposition, in the way of counter-exposition, and afterwards led to the declaration, on the part of the literati generally, that the work was unworthy of credit : while one Hu Gan Kuo (胡 安 國) declared that it had been fabricated by Lew Hin, for the purpose of supporting the pretensions of the usurper Wang Mang. These opinions were widely received until the time of Choo He (朱 熹) who investigated anew the claims of the Chow Li, the result of his researches being to confirm the view that the work was composed by Chow Kung, or some sage during the Chow dynasty. Since that time, the question of genuineness may be considered as set at rest, scholars with slight exception giving in their adherence to the views promulgated by Choo Foo Tsze.

educational authorities. The name given to these works was the ' San Ching Hsin I ' (三 經 新 義) or ' New Interpretation of the Three Classics '. The educational officers in charge of the Civil Service examinations made the candidates' knowledge and use of these works the basis of their selection, the traditional commentaries being discarded in favour of these new Interpretations.

" According to Ts'ai T'ao (蔡 條) in the ' T'ieh Wei Shan Ch'ung T'an ' (銕 圍 山 叢 談) the New Interpretation of the Odes and the New Interpretation of the History were the work of Wang An Shih's son (Yuan Tse) and other followers, but the New Interpretation of the Chow Kuan was by Wang An Shih himself. This we presume was because he had special reasons for giving his own time and thought to the production of such a work. The motive behind it was that Wang An Shih, who was of a very obstinate, strong minded, and self-willed disposition, in starting out to make his unrighteous proposals for the financial and military rehabilitation of the empire, attributed his ideas to the ancients, in his desire to deliver the House of Sung from the accumulated weakness of many generations.

" He could not, however, muzzle men's mouths, so he produced this work with the object of forcing all men of all time to accept his particular point of view.

" It is obvious from his prose and poetical writings that he was a man of unusual gifts and extraordinary ability. The ' Sung Pai Lei Ch'ao (宋 稗 類 鈔) says that when he was living in retirement, he was accustomed to sit quietly pondering on the meaning of the Classics, and states further that he worked with such concentration as is rarely seen. He would place about a hundred lotus seeds on his desk, munching at them to help his thoughts. When he had consumed one lot (unless a servant put out more) he would go on biting at his fingers, all unconsciously, until they bled. It is inconceivable that he should not get something out of the classics by such concentration.

" It should also be observed that promulgating new laws

and producing a new interpretation of the Classics are essentially different things, and that the New Interpretations were published later than the time when he was advocating the promulgation of new Measures of reform. It should not therefore follow as a matter of course, that because his new Laws are deemed impracticable, there is nothing worthy of consideration and adoption in his new Interpretations. When this is taken into account there is some reason for the statement of Ch'ien Hsin Mei (錢 辛 楣) in his ' Ch'ien Yen T'ang Wen Chi ' (潛 研 堂 文 集) that ' Wang An Shih made no use of the Chow Li '.

"In the Imperial edition of the Chow Kuan I Shu (周 官 義 疏) selections from the works of Wang An Shih were included, which shows that his comments were deemed worthy of being preserved.

"Wu Tseng Neng (吳 曾 能) in his ' Kai Chai Man Lu ' (改 齋 漫 錄) says that before the times of Jen Tsung (1023–1063) commentaries explaining the textual details were held in high esteem. But Liu Yuan Fu (劉 原 甫) in his ' Commentary on the Seven Classics ' (七 經 小 傳) first departed from the traditional interpretations of the Confucian School. Wang Ching Kung, in his New Interpretations, followed on the lines laid down by Liu Yuan Fu.

"Ch'ao Kung Wu (晁 公 武) in his ' Tu Shu Chih ' (讀 書 志) expresses a similar opinion.

"While it is true that the statements of the historiographers of Yuan Yu's time cannot altogether be relied upon, yet this Commentary on the Seven Classics has been preserved, so why should we allow this work of Wang An Shih to perish?

"Another of Wang An Shih's works on the Interpretation of Characters (字 說) has been reviled as a worthless work for generations. One of his contemporaries, Chang Yu (張 有), in his work the ' Fu Ku Pien ' (復 古 編) criticized its faulty character. The commentary on the ' K'ao Kung Chi ' contains many examples of Wang An Shih's interpretations of the characters. But it is well known that the commentary on the ' K'ao Kung Chi ' was edited by Cheng Tsung Yen (鄭 宗 顏), and so it might be urged that it need not be retained in this work. However, as the original edition included it, I keep it in this form."

A critical study of this particular work by Wang An Shih would demand a separate book, as comparisons with the traditional interpretations of the Chow Kuan would have to be made in detail. A cursory reading of the work, which is all the writer has been able to give to it, shows that Wang An Shih took every opportunity to make the text yield meanings which were in line with his own theories of government, whether rightly or wrongly one is not in a position to judge.

Evidently his interpretations could not all of them have been forced, otherwise why should so many of his opponents seek to throw doubts on the authenticity of Chow Kung's authorship of the Chow Kuan ? This movement suggests that many of Wang An Shih's interpretations were justifiable.

Others of his opponents suggested that he simply emphasized those sections of the Chow Kuan which suited his purpose.[1] That is at least evidence that such sections could be made to carry the meaning he found in them.

Liang Ch'i Ch'ao says the new ideas in Wang An Shih's work are very numerous and beyond the comprehension of later Confucian scholars. He says that it is never read by them, and that large numbers are ignorant of its existence.[2]

In the early days of Che Tsung's reign, Huang Yin (黃隱), the Head of the Imperial College, ordered the burning of the type blocks of the New Interpretations.[3] It is most fortunate, therefore, that this particular work, from Wang An Shih's own hand, has been preserved. Unfortunately, the New

---

[1] e.g. Chu Hsi (朱 熹). Complete Works, vol. lix, p. 25.

[2] Liang Ch'i Ch'ao, p. 328.

[3] I have found no reference to the burning of the blocks in the T'ung Chien, although Liang Ch'i Ch'ao says that this was done during the first year of Yuan Yu. Under the first month of the second year of Yuan Yu, there is a note of the banning of Wang An Shih's New Interpretations and Dictionary, on the grounds that they included many Buddhistic ideas, and that their exclusive use had been detrimental to orthodox teachings. (See Liang Ch'i Ch'ao, p. 197).

Interpretations of the History and the Odes seem lost beyond all hope of recovery.

The Introductions to both of these books are by Wang An Shih, however, and are found in his works. The one on the Book of History reads as follows :—

"In the second year of Hsi Ning, i.e. 1069, I acted as Instructor of the Book of History, but later in the year I received the appointment of vice-Grand Councillor. My son, Fang, succeeded me in the Instructor's post, and later was honoured with the Imperial command to present some literary work. In the 8th year of Hsi Ning, the work which he then presented was accepted for use in the Imperial College, and ordered to be used in the schools.

"The literary remains of the pre-Chow and Chow dynasties were practically all destroyed in the times of Ch'in, and were with the greatest difficulty recovered in the Han dynasty by the dictation of scholars who had memorized the Classics.

"The rulers of those days did not fully appreciate the value of these works, but our present ruler, Shen Tsung, with his great wisdom, perceives that in the Book of History we have a work worthy of fresh investigation, and of value for practical affairs of State. So we, father and son, received the Imperial command to prepare a new exposition of the work for the enlightenment of future generations. Not that our learning is equal to the task, but as no one else has come forward to undertake it, we feel honoured in that we have received the emperor's mandate to proceed with the work." [1]

It would appear from this that Wang An Shih had a share in the preparation of this New Interpretation of the Book of History. We cannot say what that share was, or the extent of his collaboration in the actual composition of the work. He would most probably help out with the ideas to be incorporated in the Commentary, and Fang would work them over for literary presentation. It should be noted how Wang

---

[1] Prose Works, vol. xx, p. 14.

An Shih stresses the emperor's view that this work was of value for the practical affairs of State.

The Introduction to the New Interpretation of the Odes is also from Wang An Shih's pen, and reads as follows :—

" The Odes originally number three hundred and eleven, of which six are lost, only the titles and the meaning of these remaining. The emperor commissioned my son Fang to expound the text, while I and others were requested to give an exposition of the application.

" When the work was completed it was handed to the directors of the Imperial College, and received the Imperial permission to be published to the schools. The emperor also ordered me to write an Introduction to the work, which I do in all humility. I am getting old and feeble, but gladly avail myself of this opportunity." [1]

From this again we gather that Wang An Shih was responsible for elucidating the meaning of this classic in so far as it admitted of practical application.

The burning of the type blocks by Huang Yin must have been primarily responsible for the loss of these two works. There must, however, have been a number of copies in circulation at the end of Hui Tsung's reign, for we read of students of that time who had become accustomed to the use of Wang An Shih's Interpretations demonstrating against the dishonouring of his memory.[2] The removal of the capital in 1126 would help also to account for the fact that none of these books have been preserved. The Imperial Libraries got scattered then, and as Wang An Shih's policy was deemed responsible for the disaster which overtook the northern Sungs in that year, it is extremely unlikely that his works would receive any special care. On the contrary, they might deliberately have been destroyed. The banning of his books from the official examinations would also expedite the process of reduction and loss.

[1] Prose Works, vol. xx, p. 13.
[2] T'ung Chien, Ching K'ang (靖 康), first year.

Happily another of his works is available, in a commentary on the "Hung Fan" or Great Plan section of the Book of History (洪 範 傳),[1] which gives us further insight into his method of Classical interpretation. The appendix to this work reads as follows [2] :—

"The ancient teachers of the Classics sought to impart to the students their own idea of the meaning of the text, so the students received from them something which was well worth the time they gave to the study. Confucius said, 'Do not continue to instruct any student who cannot infer three things from one.' By that he meant that he who is not earnest in his own investigation or sincere in his efforts to think out the meaning and relation of things, is not worthy of the teacher's attention.

"After the death of Confucius, and after the commentators had done their work, teachers of the Classics taught without thought of giving any explanations of their own, and the students were content not to ask questions or to think any deeper than the surface of the text. So for over a thousand years the Classics remained unexplained, and students got nothing from them that was of any real help to their day and generation."

This indicates quite clearly the character of Wang An Shih's method of Classical Interpretation. The meaning of the text was more important than the text itself. Careful thought and earnest study were necessary to extract this meaning from the text, and it was to be the chief aim of the student to search in the text for such meaning as would be of value for practical affairs of every age. He would grant to the student liberty of thought to express his own ideas of the meaning without binding him to the traditional interpretations.

Huang Shan Ku (黃 山 谷), one of the most famous writers and poets of the Sung Dynasty, says that Wang An Shih's learning was of the "eternal" kind, i.e. applicable to every age. He says further that unfortunately his followers absorbed the

[1] Prose Works, vol. xvi, p. 17.
[2] Prose Works, vol. xvii, p. 31.

defects of his methods and went off at tangents in their attempt
to imitate him.   This was because they lacked the capacity to
appreciate his finer points.

Ch'uan Hsieh Shan (全 謝 山), the author of the Literary
Survey of the Sung and Yuan Dynasties (宋 元 學 案), says,
" Wang An Shih's method of classical interpretation follows
that of K'ung An Kuo (孔 安 國) of the Western Han, Cheng
Hsuan (鄭 玄) of the Eastern Han, and K'ung Ying Ta (孔 穎 達)
of the T'ang Dynasty." [1]

He further praises Wang An Shih's method of direct and
penetrating interpretation, but at the same time criticizes his
exposition of the actual text, especially the interpretation of
the individual characters, as often erroneous and forced.[2]

This brings us to a consideration of another of Wang An
Shih's works, called the " Tzu Shuo " (字 說), or Interpretation
of Characters.   The work is now lost, but originally it consisted
of twenty-four volumes, and was prepared at great cost of time
and labour by order of the emperor.   Most of the work on this
was done by Wang An Shih after his retirement from high
office.

The following are extracts from a letter written to the
emperor by Wang An Shih when forwarding the completed
work for his approval, viz.[3] :—

" The written characters have long been in use.   Former
rulers established schools that students might be taught them,
officials were appointed for the extension of their use, and
scholars to explain their meaning.   The utmost care should be
exercised to prevent a lax or wrong interpretation of them.
For on that depends the possibility of uniform thinking and
practice.   When the standards of public life are low, the meaning
of characters remains obscure, for when officials fail in their

[1] Liang Ch'i Ch'ao, pp. 328–9.
[2] Liang Ch'i Ch'ao, p. 329.
[3] Prose Works, vol. xv, p. 4.

duty, the study of characters gets neglected. Attention to the study and extension of the knowledge of written characters is the universal concomitant of a great Age. . . .

" Although the written characters are the creation of men, they really have their origin in the natural world. There were lines on the body of the phœnix, and on the map which emerged from the river there were certain diagrams. These were not the creation of men. Men, however, copied these things, giving a visible form to such ideas as higher and lower, inner and outer, beginning and end, before and after, middle and side, left and right. Again, such ideas as horizontal and perpendicular, crooked and straight, pairs and multiples, connections and breaks, opposites, contraries, interchanges, etc., all were expressed in visible form.

" Sounds were also distinguished as free and restrained, by the breath expelled or drawn in, as held in, or let go, as concentrated or dispersed, as weak or strong, as clear or confused, etc.

" We learn by seeing, and by hearing we are induced to think. In that way we arrive at the natural ideas of things. When that is ensured, although the sages may live wide apart from one another, even though their pronunciations should be different, and their manner of writing be not the same, their ideas will be found to be the same when the sounds and signs representing them have been converted from one language into another.

" Progress in the art of writing and in the study of the written characters usually depends upon the progress of moral standards among the people. Where the latter obtains, though times and affairs may change, though the actual letters and sounds may be altered, no permanent change in ideas will be possible. When knowledge is unavailing, and thought fails us, the written characters may be used as proof, and without them learning is impossible. Only the wisest of men can investigate this subject thoroughly.

" Your Majesty, in sympathy with the wonderful art of the Great Heaven, which art is represented by forms and figures, has given thought to the ancient delineations, and is anxious that the work of enlightening the people should go on. If this type of learning is allowed to fall into neglect, and no one is appointed to keep it going, it necessarily means that there is indifference to the intelligence and education of the people. It will mean that fine points will remain hidden from our ken, and hidden things remain unexplored. In which case it cannot be expected that affairs will be brought into line with your sagelike will, for it will be truly difficult to make public expression of your purpose thoroughly and accurately through the medium of letters (without due study being given to the subject).

" For some years I have been at leisure. Although I received your honoured command in person, I have been a long time completing the work owing to illness and grief. Some parts of the work I have already submitted. But in great trepidation lest I might die before completing the work, I decided to forget my illness and grief, and took up the task again with a new energy. I have taken every opportunity of discussing doubtful points with every one who was likely to help, in the hope that in a small way I might make some contribution to the fulfilling of your great purpose.

" The work is now completed in 24 volumes, and I have the great honour of presenting it. . . ."

It is regrettable that this work which cost Wang An Shih so much labour in research, and which aroused so much opposition on the part of conventional scholars, should have been lost. It is therefore impossible to compare it with great Works on the written character like the Shuo Wen (説 文) of Hsü Shen (許 慎) or the Work of K'ang Hsi, the great scholar-emperor of the Manchu Dynasty.

We have, however, examples of his analysis of the characters in certain of his essays, notably in that on the Book of Changes, and in the New Interpretation of the Chow Kuan, illustrations of which are given in the notes.[1]

For footnote see p. 311.

¹大 神 者 昊 天 也 夏 日 昊 天 則 帝 與 萬 物 相 見
之 時 故 王 所 祀 者 昊 天 而 已 五 帝 則 五 精 之 君
昊 天 之 佐 也 凡 在 天 者 皆 神 也 故 昊 天 爲 大 神
凡 在 地 者 皆 示 也 故 大 地 爲 大 示 神 之 字 從 示
從 申 則 以 有 所 示 無 所 屈 故 也 示 之 字 從 二 從
小 則 以 有 所 示 故 也 效 法 之 爲 坤 言 有 所 示 也
有 所 示 則 二 而 小 矣 故 天 從 一 從 大 示 從 二 從
小 從 二 從 小 爲 示 而 從 一 從 大 不 爲 神 者 神 無
體 也 則 不 可 以 言 大 神 無 數 也 則 不 可 以 言 一
有 所 示 則 二 而 小 而 神 亦 從 示 者 神 妙 萬 物 而
爲 言 固 爲 其 能 大 能 小 不 能 有 所 示 非 所 以 爲
神 惟 其 無 所 屈 是 以 異 于 示 也, translated as follows:—

The "great god" is termed the "vast heaven". It is the glory of the summer season that gives rise to the expression "vast heaven", for that is the time when the interaction of God (帝) and Nature are most clearly observed. This is the reason why the ruler worships "vast heaven" and that alone. The five gods (五帝) are the spiritual rulers of the five regions, who co-operated with "vast heaven". All that are in heaven are termed "gods" (神) and so "vast heaven" is termed the "great god" (大神).

All that are related to the Earth are termed "shih" (示) or "manifestations". So the great Earth is termed the Great Manifestation.

The character "shen" (神) is composed of the two elements 示 and 申. The reason for this is that the gods have something to give forth; they never "withhold" (i.e. they manifest their nature without restraint). The character "shih" (示) is comprised of the characters 二 "two" and 小 "small". This is because it too has something to "manifest". But that which is of the nature of imitation is termed "k'un" (坤) (another term for earth), by which is meant that what is manifested in the case of the earth is relative (二) or "secondary" and of lesser import (小).

The character for "heaven" (天) is comprised of the characters "i" (一), which denotes "priority", and "ta" (大), which denotes "greatness". The character 示 as remarked above, is comprised of 二 "secondary" and 小 "small". The latter is termed "shih" or manifestor, but the great priority (天) is not termed "god" (神). The reason for this is that "gods" (神) have no visible form, so that the expression "great" (大) cannot be

Wang An Shih wrote several treatises on the Book of Changes,[1] one of which consists of a definition of the whole of the sixty-four hexagrams.[2] He makes use of the diagrams sometimes in the exposition of Classical passages. But generally speaking Wang An Shih was not prone to giving mystical explanations of things. He thought little of the practice of astrology so prominent in Court circles in his day, and incurred no little odium on account of his contemptuous attitude to so-called heavenly warnings. His mind was essentially practical, which leads one to think that he would be unlikely to give the time and thought necessary to the production of any great commentary on that Classic which is the most difficult of all Chinese books to explain.

Yin Ho Ching (尹 和 靖) says that the authorship of the work styled "I I" (易 義), a very concise commentary on the book of Changes which leaves out difficult passages, while generally attributed to Wang An Shih, is not sufficiently

applied to them. Again, " gods " have no numerical significance and so it is impossible to use the expression —— of them.

That which has something to manifest is termed secondary and small. The " god " (神) character also comprises the character 示 " to manifest ". That is because the " gods " are mysteriously manifest in " nature " (萬 物). By this is meant that " gods " can be " great " and can also be " small " (i.e. they have the capacity for massive and minute manifestations). That which cannot manifest itself cannot be termed a " god " (神). But " gods " withhold nothing, and in this they differ from the earth spirit (示). Chou Kuan Hsin I, vol. i, p. 30.

Translator's Note.—The above will serve as an instance of Wang An Shih's interpretation of characters, in which he definitely differs from the " Shuo Wen " interpretations. It also serves to suggest that Wang An Shih was feeling his way towards a really spiritual conception of " God " as being behind and above, while yet within the visible and material universe. Without form and without number suggests a truly spiritual conception, but one could have wished that he had been clearer in relating " Shen ", which seems to be a generic term for " spiritual intelligences or entites ", to 帝 " Ti ", which he uses as the " great Ruler of Heaven ".

[1] See Prose Works, vol. xvi, e.g. his 易 泛 論, 卦 名 解, 易 象 論 解, and 九 卦 論.

[2] The Kua Ming Chieh (卦 名 解). Prose Works, vol. xvi, pp. 8 and 9.

authenticated.[1] This work is probably identical with the
" I Chieh " (易 解), which is quoted in the Sung Histories
as being of Wang An Shih's authorship.

Considerable controversy has been aroused in literary
circles on the subject of Wang An Shih's opinion of the Annals
or " Ch'un Ch'iu " (春 秋). This, being the only Classic
which is regarded as the actual work of Confucius, was naturally
held in high esteem by conventional Confucianists, and any
seeming despising of the work, such as is laid at the door of
Wang An Shih, just as naturally aroused indignant and clamorous
opposition.

The statement which Wang An Shih is reputed to have
made on this subject, and which was responsible for the outcry,
is as follows :—

" The Annals is but a series of short and scrappy records of
the Court." [2]

That statement evidently *was* made by Wang An Shih,
but when taken in connection with its context, it would appear
that it is anything but a despising of the book.

Li Mu T'ang (李 穆 堂) has preserved the context for us
in his account of the following incident, viz. :—

" I have often heard people say that Wang An Shih criticized
the Annals as being a mere collection of short and scrappy
Court records, and that this statement was included in the
Lin Ju Hsien Shu (臨 汝 閒 書). This remark, however, had
no reference to the character of the Classic itself, but to an
attempt to interpret it. Two of Wang An Shih's best pupils,
Lu Tien (陸 佃) of Shan Yin, and Kung Yuan (龔 原) of
Sui Ch'ang, were working together on a commentary of the
Annals. Lu Tien was to produce an Appendix and Kung the
Commentary. Whenever they came to a knotty section they

[1] Dynastic History of Sung, vol. 202, I Wen Chih (藝 文 志), Section
155, p. 2.
[2] Dynastic History, Life of Wang An Shih.

were accustomed to report to Wang An Shih, and had so often used the remark 'there is something missing from the text here', that Wang An Shih replied, 'If there are as many lacunæ as that in the text of the Annals, it must be merely a series of short and scrappy court records.'"

So that this remark, taken in its context, was far from being a cynical criticism of the work, but was rather a jocular poke at these interpreters of it. [1]

Sun Chueh (孫 覺), a contemporary of Wang An Shih, who, it should be said, also submitted a memorial criticizing Wang An Shih's interpretation of the " Ch'uan Fu " (泉 府) as found in the Chow Kuan, produced a commentary on the Annals. In the appendix to this particular work, Chou Lin Chih (周 麟 之) of the Sung dynasty says [2] :—

" Wang An Shih was also desirous of publishing a commentary on the Annals. But Sun Chueh's commentary having been published first, he was so chagrined that his own work did not come up to it that he began to decry the Classic itself, saying that it was of no value, being a 'mere collection of short and scrappy court records'. He therefore refused to permit its use in connection with the government examination system."

Li Mu T'ang thinks it extremely improbable that Wang An Shih ever saw this commentary of Sun Chueh, as it was compiled late in the life of Sun. He died in the period 1094–7 at the age of 63. But Wang An Shih had died ten years previously. Li Mu T'ang therefore concludes that this statement must be a fabrication on the part of Chou Lin Chih.[3]

As to the reason why Wang An Shih did not include this Classic in the curriculum for the government examinations, the first part of the following quotation from the introduction to Sun Chueh's work (above) is apropos, viz.[4] :—

---

[1] Liang Ch'i Ch'ao, p. 331.
[2] Liang Ch'i Ch'ao, p. 330.
[3] Liang Ch'i Ch'ao, pp. 330–1.
[4] The Introduction is by Yung Kuei Shan (楊 龜 山), a great opponent, of Wang An Shih; see Liang Ch'i Ch'ao, p. 331.

" During the Hsi Ning period (1068–1077) the Confucian Classics were highly esteemed. But because of the mutual discrepancies which existed in the three commentaries on the Annals, and because it was relatively more difficult to interpret than the other classical works, it was not included in the regular curricula of the schools. This did not mean that it was regarded as valueless, but as the students naturally devoted themselves to the prescribed books for the examinations, they neglected to study this particular work."

This, says Liang Ch'i Ch'ao, is fairly convincing evidence as to the reason for the non-inclusion of the Annals in the government examination curriculum at that time, coming as it does from one who normally was opposed to Wang An Shih's methods of literary interpretation.

Further evidence on this point is furnished by Wang An Shih himself, for in his reply to Han Ch'iu Jen (韓 求 仁), who had written for his opinion on the Six Classics, he says [1] :—

" The Annals is the hardest classic to expound, as the three commentaries on it are untrustworthy."

It was then rather an appreciation of the difficulty of expounding the Annals rather than a cynical despising of the work, which characterized Wang An Shih's attitude to this particular classic. One could almost forgive Wang An Shih if he had really said that it was " a series of short and scrappy court records " and had really meant it. However, some day perhaps a scholar will arise who will justify the labours of Confucius on this particular work.

Included in Wang An Shih's works is one of ten volumes entitled " Commentary on Tso's Interpretation of the Annals " This is probably the one referred to by Chou Lin Chih. Unfortunately there is not so much as even an Introduction extant which might have given us a clue to the character of the work. The fact that he chose the commentary of Tso [2]

---

[1] Prose Works, vol. xviii, p. 3, at the end of the letter.

[2] And yet in his essay on Human Nature (性 說) he says that the work of Tso Ch'iu Ming is unreliable, at least in one particular. (See Essay, p. 324.)

indicates, however, that he evidently considered it superior to those of Kung Yang and Ku Liang.

His attitude to the Analects, Mencius, the Rites, etc., can to some extent be gauged by the essays which follow. His works on these classics have all been lost, but the samples of his exposition of them which are available give us some idea of his method of approach to the literature, and also of his method of interpretation. He is quite free in his criticisms both of the meaning of the text and also of the character of the personages referred to. In these he is often most unconventional, " heterodox " one might say, if by that we are to understand " divergence from conventional opinion ". In that respect he affords a notable example of his own canon of criticism, viz. " that a man should be allowed to give his own interpretation ".

It has been noted in another section of this work that the classics were the basis of education in those days, so that Wang An Shih's contribution to classical interpretation was in a very real sense part of his contribution to the general educational problem of his times. His originality in the realm of literary pursuits, coupled with the fact that he had the authority to impose his own ideas of the Classics upon the students of his time, no doubt increased the enmity and intensified the opposition of the more conventional literati to his economic policy. Mr. C. W. Allan in his sketch of Wang An Shih's Life [1] wonders how far the opposition of the literary classes was due to the fact that he attempted to introduce reforms in their special realm, and he is inclined to the opinion that these had more to do with his downfall than his economical policy.

Certainly his method of classical interpretation had a good deal to do with the character and extent of the opposition, for it was that which to a large extent accounted for the faction strife of the period. However, the reasons for Wang An Shih's downfall are complex, and while later critics do include his

---

[1] *Makers of Cathay*, p. 110.

heterodoxy in classical interpretation among the reasons for their opposition, it is not by any means the only one.

Of course, Wang An Shih based his economical policy on his interpretation of the classics, particularly on the Chow Kuan, and, as we have sought to show, that raised a great storm of criticism and opposition amongst the official classes. So that viewing the matter all round, we must certainly place his critical attitude to conventional methods of literary interpretation amongst the reasons for the opposition to his general policy.

Liang Ch'i Ch'ao [1] summarizes Wang An Shih's contribution to the educational problems of his day as follows :—

" Viewed from the subjective aspect his method aimed at bringing the student to regard the will of Heaven as the norm (知 命) and to seek to act always in accordance with what was seen to be right (厲 節). In its more objective aspect it sought to make the student relate his studies to the practical problems of his own time and circumstances. One's studies affected one's principles of conduct, both personal and public, and were intended to be a preparation for participation in political life."

So that Wang An Shih regarded education as related to the whole of life. It should therefore occasion no surprise that he went to the classical literature of his country, which was regarded as the chief subject of study in those days, with a view to extracting from it all that he considered it should yield of enlightenment for the development of personal character, the determination of one's social relationships and duties, and for the discovery of the method of government, which was regarded as the *summum bonum* of all educational pursuits.

His countrymen should be grateful to him for emphasizing in such striking manner the right of the individual to think independently and to express one's thoughts freely. They should also be grateful for his emphasis on the practical aspects of education and on personal character in connection with it. Some of these matters are receiving more attention in China

---

[1] Liang Ch'i Ch'ao, p. 320.

since the days of the Republic, and it is largely due to such measure of freedom of thought and expression as has characterized the new age that truer impressions of Wang An Shih and his policy are gaining ground. To him, more than to any other name in China's literary history, must be accorded the honour of giving prominence to these fundamental principles.

ESSAYS

ON ORIGINAL NATURE (原 性)

(Wang An Shih's Works, vol. xvii, pp. 11, 12.)

SEEING that Mencius, Hsün Tzu, Yang Hsiung, and Han Yü are all famous for learning and character, and that the characteristic quality of human nature is a question which is fundamental to everything in this life, it would seem reasonable to expect that these great and good minds would have had no doubts about such a vitally important subject. How is it then that they differ in their definitions of the original nature of man?

My reply to such a question is that I myself am satisfied with the explanation of Confucius, viz. " The Great Extreme (太 極) is the source of the five elements. But the five elements are not the Great Extreme. The Nature (性) stands to the five constant virtues (五 常) in the same relationship as the Great Extreme to the five elements (五 行)." So that the five virtues cannot be said to be the nature. In this respect I disagree with Han Yü. For the latter said [1] that these five virtues are the nature, and yet he also affirmed that the nature is evil. But is it possible to regard these five virtues which constitute the nature as evil?

Mencius said that the nature of man is good. Hsün Tzu affirmed that the nature of man is evil.[2] To revert to the illustration of the Great Extreme again. It was only after it had given birth to the five elements that the possibility of beneficent and injurious activity could be posited. But in regard to the Great Extreme itself, it is not possible to posit either beneficial or injurious activity. The nature gives birth to the disposition, and it is only after the disposition begins to function that good and evil become manifest. But we cannot speak of

[1] Han Yü (韓 子), "Yuan Hsing P'ien" (原 性 篇).
[2] Hsün Tzu (荀 子), "Hsing O P'ien" (性 惡 篇).

the nature itself as being either good or evil. In this respect
I disagree both with Mencius and Yang Hsiung.

Mencius held that all men have a feeling of sympathy (惻隱
之 心), and he deduces from that that every man is loving
(仁) by nature.[1] If nature is as he defines it, then hatred, malice,
rage, and injustice should not be found in man's nature. For
otherwise how could man's nature be said to be good ? Is it
true, however, that such evil attributes are not found in men ?

The reason that Mencius regarded the feeling of sympathy
as innate was because it essentially belongs to the inner life.
But hatred, malice, rage, and injustice, as well as this feeling
of sympathy, all proceed from within, in response to external
stimulation, so where is the difference between them ?

Hsün Tzu said,[2] "He who does a good deed does so
factitiously (偽)." If his view of human nature is correct,
one would have to posit the absence of any feeling of sympathy
in the nature (the presence of which is basic to the position of
Mencius). For then and then only could the good be termed
"factitious". Is it true, however, that this feeling of sympathy
is entirely absent from man's nature ?

Hsün Tzu says again,[3] "A potter uses clay to make the
basic material for pottery, but the material so made is not of
the same nature as the clay." The potter, however, does not
use wood to make this material, as only clay possesses the
nature which makes the manufacture of that material possible.
Where then does the "factitious" idea come in ?

These four philosophers make no mention of the disposition
(情); all their talk is about "conduct" (習), which is not the
same thing as the nature (性). Although the view of Yang
Tzu [4] seems to be fairly correct, yet even he regards the nature
as being inseparably connected with actual "conduct".

---

[1] Mencius, Bk. II, pt. 1, ch. vi, par. 4.

[2] "Hsing O P'ien" (性 惡 篇).

[3] "Hsing O P'ien" (性 惡 篇). But Wang An Shih takes the argument
back a step here.

[4] i.e. Yang Hsiung, who held that human nature comprised both good and
evil capacities. (See Essay, p. 327.)

Among the ancient teachers there are none who do not refer to pleasure, anger, love, hate, desire as belonging to the disposition.

But it is only when one's disposition of pleasure, anger, love, hate, and desire are directed towards a good end that they may be defined as virtuous or right, and when they are directed to ends that are not good, that they may be termed evil and wrong. It follows from this that the disposition must be functioning before good and evil can be distinguished. Therefore " good " and " evil " are terms which are used to denote the character of the " emotions " when they have really manifested themselves as such.

My statement agrees with that of Confucius, viz. " Men by nature are very much alike, but in practice they become different." Is there then any consistent explanation of his other expression, " The superior and intelligent cannot be changed into the inferior and stupid, and vice versa " ? My own opinion is that in making these distinctions between men, he was thinking only of their intellectual faculties, whereas I am arguing about human nature and moral distinctions.

I believe that an evil man, if he desires to do good, and proceeds to do so, may become good, but that an inherently stupid man intellectually cannot even by great effort become wise.

Fu Hsi made the diagrams of the Book of Changes, but amongst the sages of later generations, only those of the highest grade of intelligence and perspicacity could rise to the ideas which Fu Hsi meant to convey. Confucius wrote the Annals, but even Tzu Yu (子 游) and Tzu Hsia (子 夏) could not add a word (to what he wrote). If therefore the wisdom of Fu Hsi could not be matched except by the men of highest intelligence and perspicacity, and if such great minds as Tzu Yu and Tzu Hsia could not equal the wisdom of Confucius, even though they exerted themselves to the utmost, how can it be expected that those of inferior and stupid mind should equal them ? That they could not be changed to that extent is perfectly clear.

Possibly some will say that each of the four philosophers

(mentioned above) has his contribution to make to the discussion of " human nature ". As to that I cannot say. But I do know that the sages sought to make terms denote what they were intended to denote.

DISCUSSION OF HUMAN NATURE (性 說)
(Works, vol. xvii, p. 12.)

Confucius said,[1] " Men by nature are very much alike, but in actual conduct become different." I agree with Confucius in this, but disagree with Han Yü's opinion of human nature.[2]

What then did Confucius mean by his statements,[3] that " Only to men of ' superior ' capacity may higher things be communicated, for to men of ' inferior ' capacity higher things cannot be communicated," and that " It is impossible for a man of ' higher ' intelligence to be transformed into a ' base and stupid ' fellow, and vice versa " ?

I think he meant that the man of " higher " or " superior " intelligence was one who had become accustomed to good habits, and by the expression " base and stupid " he meant one who had become innured to evil habits. He who was partly accustomed to good habits and partly innured to evil habits he would term a " mediocre man ". So that when he used the terms " superior ", " mediocre ", and " inferior " of men, it was the final product or fixed character that was denoted (卒).

So a man before he had done anything evil might reasonably be termed " superior ". But if in the end he should go on to do evil, he might be termed " mediocre ". Likewise a man before he had done anything good, might reasonably be termed " inferior ". But if in the end he went on to do good, he also might be termed " mediocre ". It is only to the man's character as finally fixed that the statement of his not being capable of change either from superior to inferior or from inferior to superior applies.

[1] Analects, book xvii, chap. ii.
[2] Han Yü, ".Yuan Hsing P'ien " (原 性 篇), translated by Legge. *Prolegomena to Mencius*, p. 89.
[3] Cf. Analects, book xx, chap. xix, and bk. xvii, chap. iii.

The theory that a man is born (either good or bad), and is incapable of change, which is the theory of Han Yü, is not worthy of consideration.

Han Yü says, " Human nature is of three grades (superior, mediocre, and inferior) and has five constituent elements, viz., an innate sense of the humane, of justice, of the fitness of things, of right and wrong, and of good faith." Which of these can be considered not to be good ? He says further, " The ' superior ' man makes one of these five constituent elements his ruling principle, and acts in accordance with the other four. The ' inferior ' man violates one of these five, and acts contrary to the other four."[1]

On this view of human nature he only is to be termed " superior " who never fails to act in accordance with these five constituent elemental principles of his nature, while he who is termed " inferior " is he who fails to conform to any one of them.

This certainly, on the one hand, implies the innate goodness of the nature (性) and on the other relates the evil to actual conduct.

What then is to be said about the great historical examples which have been so constantly quoted [1] in illustration of the (innate goodness or badness of human nature) such as Yao and his evil son Chu, Shun and his evil son Chun, the evil Ku Sou and his good son Shun, the evil Kun and his good son Yü : what about Hou Chi, Yueh Chiao (越 椒), and Shu Yü (叔 魚)? or are these latter instances to be regarded as lacking historical foundation ? My reply would be that Chu and Chun became evil because of their evil conduct, and that Shun and Yü, though sons of evil fathers, became good because they formed good habits.

The poem which relates the incident of Hou Chi [2] recounts something which must be termed " abnormal ", whereas my discussion relates only to what is " normal ". The poem refers to a son only, and to a son who had no father. Can

[1] " Yuan Hsing P'ien " (原 性 篇), as above.
[2] Odes, pt. iii, bk. ii, ode 1.

a man who had no father be discussed in the same category
as the " normal " ? When we refer to the " nature " we mean
the normal nature. Otherwise a madman rushing into a river
or dashing into a fire would be said to be acting in accordance
with his nature.

The instances quoted of Yueh Chiao [1] and Shu Yü [2] are
found only in the writings of Tso Ch'iu Ming, and certainly
cannot be regarded as reliable history.

Confucius erred in regard to Tsai Wo [3] (宰 我) because of
his specious utterance, and erred in the case of Tzu Yü [4] (子 羽)
because he judged him by his appearance. Although these
were already fully grown men, with whom Confucius was in
constant companionship, he made erroneous judgments about
them, in one case through speech and in the other through
appearance. Yet as soon as Yueh Chiao and Shu Yü were born,

---

[1] Yueh Chiao (越 椒) was the son of a minister of Ch'u. When his uncle
Tzu Wan saw the child, he said, " You must put him to death. He has the
appearance of a bear or a tiger, and the voice of a wolf. If you do not kill
him, he will cause the extinction of our Jo Ao family." His father Tzu Liang
rejected the idea however. Later on Yueh Chiao became chief minister, killed
the Minister of Works, Wei Chia, and attacked the king. In the ensuing battle,
however, the army of Ch'u under Yueh Chiao was completely defeated and
the king exterminated the clan of Jo Ao. (See Tso Chuan, under fourth year
of Duke Hsuan, Legge, pp. 295–6.) Cf. also Tso Chuan, Legge, p. 254, par. 12.

[2] Shu Yü (叔 魚). " When Shu Yü was born, his mother, perceiving
something unusual in his appearance, remarked, ' He has the eyes of a tiger
and the mouth of a pig, the shoulders of a goose and the belly of a cow. The
deepest ravine may be filled up, but the covetous nature of this child will never
be satisfied. He will die eventually through greed.' " (Taken from the Kuo Yü
(國 語) or " Narratives of the States " (vol. 14, Narratives of Chin (普 語),
i.e. section viii, p. 3).)

There is an account of his death in the Tso Chuan under the fourteenth year
of Chao Kung, as follows : " A land dispute which had been in abeyance for
some time, was eventually entrusted to Shu Yü to settle. One of the claimants,
Yung Tzu, though evidently in the wrong, presented Shu Yü with a daughter
as a gift, whereupon Shu Yü decided that the other claimant, Hsing Hou, who
really had the law on his side, was in the wrong. This so enraged Hsing Hou
that he then and there killed Shu Yü and Yung Tzu in the court." So the
prophecy of Shu Yü's mother that her son would die of covetousness was fulfilled.
See Legge's Classics, " Ch'un Ch'iu," p. 656.

[3] Tsai Wo was a very glib talker but of unsatisfactory character.

[4] Tzu Yü was of an unattractive countenance but of stalwart character.

women predicted their future character either from voice or appearance. Are women then to be regarded as superior to Confucius?

HUMAN NATURE AND DISPOSITION (性 情)

(Works, vol. xvii, p. 4.)

The "nature" (性) and the "disposition" (情) are really (two aspects of) one and the same thing. But there are some who affirm that the "nature" is good, and the "disposition" evil. This is due to their failure to comprehend the real signification of the two terms, and to their ignorance of the real character of the nature of man.

The term "hsing" (性) or "nature" is properly applied to the feelings of pleasure, anger, grief, joy, love, hate, and desire before they have manifested themselves, and while they are still retained in the heart. But when these feelings become manifest and are expressed in actual conduct, then the term "ch'ing" (情) may be appropriately used.

The "nature" is the source of the "disposition" and the "disposition" is the "medium of expression" of the nature. So I affirm that the "nature" and the "disposition" are really one.

Those who affirm that the "nature" is good, do so because they have read the books of Mencius without comprehending his real meaning. Those who affirm that the "disposition" is evil, do so on the ground of their observation that the seven "instincts" lead men into evil, but fail to perceive that these seven "instincts" originate from the "nature" (性).

All men are born with these seven "instincts", which are excited into activity by external stimulation. If these "instincts" are stimulated in accordance with what is right and reasonable, they lead men to act in accordance with the dictates of the highest moral character, so that they become "sages" (聖) and "worthies" (賢). If, however, they are stimulated in

326   WANG AN SHIH

accordance with what is wrong or irrational, they become
degraded and " mean " (小 人).

So that those who say that the " disposition " is evil, do so
because they have merely observed that the " disposition "
when manifested is entangled by external phenomena, and gets
drawn into evil. It is on this ground also that they are led to
say that the " disposition " violates the " nature ".

But have they not also observed that sometimes the
" disposition " is influenced by external stimuli in such a way
that good conduct results ?

For the good man (君 子) cultivates the good part of his
" nature " (性) and his " disposition " (情) also becomes good,
while the " mean man " (小 人) cultivates the evil part of his
nature and his disposition also becomes evil.

Hence the " good man " is good because of his " disposition "
and the " mean man " evil on the same ground. The error of
the exponents of the ideas referred to above lies in the fact that
in their reference to a " good man " they are thinking only of
his " nature " (性), while in their references to a " mean man "
they are thinking only of his " disposition " (情).

Now by " disposition " (情) they mean the seven " instincts "
of pleasure, anger, grief, joy, love, hate, and desire. Shun
was a " sage ". He was joyous when Hsiang (his brother)
was joyous.[1] But would Shun have been a sage if he had not
been joyous when he ought to have been ? Wen Wang was
a sage. He demonstrated his anger. But would he have been
a sage if he had not shown anger when he ought to have done
so ? [2]

If these two illustrations are understood, then the application
to the other cases follows.

If the " disposition " is divorced (from its connection with

[1] Cf. Mencius, bk. v, pt. i, chap. ii, pars. 3 and 4. Legge's second edition,
revised, pp. 346–8. Evidently we are to interpret the incident of Hsiang's
" blush " as evidence of repentance of his purpose to make away with Shun.
Shun rejoiced in a truly filial way with his brother, whom he conceived as being
honestly glad that he had been prevented from carrying his evil purpose into
effect.
[2] Cf. Odes, part iii, bk. i, Ode vii, verse 5. Legge, vol. iv, part ii, p. 453.

the " nature ") then, even though the nature be good, how could it demonstrate that by itself? Then truly it would be as some to-day affirm, that only he who has no " disposition " is good. In which case for a man to be like wood and stone would be considered estimable.

So I conclude that the nature and disposition are mutually necessary the one to the other, in the same way as the bow and arrow are mutually necessary. So that in speaking of good and evil we may use the simile of the arrow hitting or missing the mark.

Is there then such a thing as an evil nature? I would reply in the words of Mencius, that " he who nourishes the higher part of his nature is great, while he who nourishes the lower part of his nature is mean "

Or, in the words of Yang Tzu,[1] that " the nature is a mixture of good and evil ".

So that from these we may perceive that the nature may be regarded as having evil possibilities.

THE POSSIBILITY OF REPENTANCE (原 過)

(Works, vol. xvii, pp. 15, 16.)

Nature in the heavenly sphere is not without faults, as witness irregularities in the seasons, eclipses, etc. Nature in the earthly sphere also has its faults, earthquakes, floods, desiccation, and the like. But yet Heaven and Earth continue to cover and support all things, being in no wise hindered by their defects from so doing. That is because they possess the capacity of reverting to the normal.

Is it reasonable to expect that man, who stands between Heaven and Earth, should be without faults? Why then is it possible for some to become sages and worthies? Because man also possesses the capacity to return to the normal. So

[1] i.e. Yang Hsiung (楊 雄).

T'ai Chia's change after contemplation of the " Mean " (庸),
Confucius' remark that one should not be afraid of reforming
one's faults, and Yang Hsiung's appreciation of the power of
man to revert to the good, are all based on this fundamental
principle.

If a friend of mine regrets a fault, and truly repents of it,
he demonstrates that his former way of life was not the right
one. But some say, " that is merely making a difference between
his former and later ways of life, and his nature is in no wise
affected thereby. He has merely assumed a veneer of goodness
so as to deceive others."

But is that statement reasonable ?

Heaven has endowed all spiritual entities with the five
constant virtues, and men therefore have them in their completeness. But merely to have them, and give them no thought,
results in the loss of them. And if thought only is given to
them, and they are not actually practised, then they may be
said to have deliberately discarded them.

But if on a certain day a man recalling some former evil
deed should not only apply his mind earnestly to it, but carry
out his good intention (to atone for it), it is just the same as if
he had recovered what had been lost, and had restored to its
rightful place what he had previously disregarded.

I therefore assert, that those who say that such a change
in no way concerns a man's nature, lead people to violate the
conception of the " nature " (by robbing it of one of its glorious
capacities).

Take an illustration of a man who has been robbed of some
of his money. After a lapse of time he recovers the money.
But people say, " This is not his money, for it was taken from
him by a thief." Is that statement reasonable ? Certainly not.
Then, if it is unreasonable to say that wealth once lost and
later regained, is not the owner's rightful possession, can it
be reasonable to say that virtue, which belongs by right to
man's original nature, once lost, and later restored, is not the
achievement of his original nature ?

Discussion on the Views of Yang Hsiung and Mencius (楊 孟) on "The Nature of Man" (性) and "The Decree" (命)

(Works, vol. xvi, pp. 13, 14.)

The cause for a good man's becoming good and for an evil man's becoming evil is to be found in his "nature" (性). The fact that a good man is honoured with good position and length of days, and that an evil man experiences poverty, difficulties, and death, is due to such being "decreed" (命).

To this general thesis objections may be raised. Some would say, "The nature of man is good. How can you say that 'an evil man's becoming evil is due to his "nature"'?" Those who argue in that way show that they are acquainted with Mencius's actual statements about the nature of man, but also display their ignorance of what he really meant by it. Others might say, "By the expression 'decreed' is meant those occurrences which are not the direct outcome of what men do or do not do. How can you say that 'the fact that an evil man experiences poverty, difficulties, and death, is due to such being "decreed"'?" Those who argue in that way show that they are acquainted with what Yang Tzu wrote about "the decree", but also display their ignorance of what he really meant by it.

Mencius said, "The nature of man is good," while Yang Tzu said, "The nature of man is a composite of both good and evil." Mencius said of the "decree" that "everything is decreed", while Yang Tzu said, "Those occurrences which are not the direct outcome of what men do or do not do are 'decreed'."

These two philosophers really hold similar ideas on these subjects, for their statements amount to the same thing. We must bear in mind the statement of Confucius, that "a statement may bear more than one possible interpretation, but it ought to be interpreted in the way in which the speaker intended it should be interpreted". Mencius in his discussion of the nature of man was referring to "nature" in its ideal aspect, i.e. human nature as it ought to be, whereas Yang Tzu in his definition of the " nature " of man, includes, not only the ideal aspect, but also the non-ideal aspect of it. Again, Yang Tzu in his remarks about the " decree " refers only to the " orthodox " interpretation of that term, while Mencius in his definition includes not only that, but also the " non-orthodox " aspect of it.[1]

Amongst the things which are " decreed " in man's case is his possession of an innate sense of shame at doing evil. Here is a man, however, who is ashamed of his failure to do good, or to establish a fair name. If he exerts himself to do good with a view to satisfying this demand of his nature, what is there to prevent him from becoming a good man ? This is an instance of a man fulfilling the ideal possibilities of his nature, and is in accordance with what Mencius meant by the " nature of man ".

Take another instance. Here is a man who is ashamed that he has not gained enough profit, or not as much as he might have got. If he devotes himself to gain more profit in order to satisfy this particular demand of his nature, what is there to prevent him from becoming an evil man ? This is an illustration of a man fulfilling the baser possibilities of his nature, and agrees with Yang Tzu's definition of the term " nature of man ".

To continue. Here is a man of naturally inferior ability, who actually attains to only an inferior position, or who, having committed some serious crime, suffers the death penalty.   These are instances of occurrences which are the result of the man's own conduct, and which would be regarded as a " non-orthodox " operation of " the decree ".   But such things as

---

[1] The " cheng ming " (正 命) may be interpreted as that which happens to a man, which is beyond his power to effect or avoid, i.e. something which is not the issue of his own conduct. The orthodox interpretation of (ming) " 命 " would be of that type, and so I have used the term " orthodox " for this aspect of the subject.   That which is the opposite of this, termed " Ming chih pu cheng " 命 之 不 正 也 in the essay, and for which I have used the expression " unorthodox ", seems to mean that which happens to a man as the logical outcome of his own doing or neglect. (See next essay.)

these would be included in Mencius's definition of the term
" decreed " (命).

Take another instance of a man who by nature is equipped
with great ability, but who actually attains only to an inferior
position, or who is of such good character that one would
expect him to live a long life, but who actually dies an early
death. These are illustrations of something happening to a
man which cannot be interpreted as a direct outcome of his
own conduct. These are instances of the operation of " the
decree " in its orthodox aspect, and are in agreement with what
Yang Tzu meant by the term " decreed " (命).

(Carrying the argument a stage further) in regard to the
case of the dissatisfied profiteer, Yang Tzu would certainly
not attribute the outcome of his conduct to the man's " nature "
(性) but would blame the man himself for failing to realize
the good possibilities of his nature. And in regard to the
case of the man of naturally inferior ability who attained to
but an inferior position, Mencius would certainly not attribute
the result to " what is decreed " (命) but would blame the
man himself for failing to realize the good possibilities of
" what was decreed in his case ".

Mencius said,[1] " For the mouth to desire sweet tastes, the
eye to desire beautiful colours, the ear to desire pleasant sounds,
the nose to desire fragrant odours, and the four limbs to desire
peace and rest, these things are ' natural '. But there is the
' appointment of heaven ' (命) in connection with them.[2] The
superior man does not *say* of his pursuit of them, ' It is my
nature ' (性)."

The exercise of love between father and son, the observance
of righteousness between sovereign and minister, the rules of
ceremony between host and guest, the display of knowledge
in recognizing the worthy, and the fulfilling of the heavenly
course by the sage. These are the " appointment of heaven "
(命), but there is an adaptation of our " nature " (性) for them.

---

[1] Mencius, bk. vii, part. ii, chap. xxiv, vv. 1 and 2. Legge, pp. 489–490.
[2] i.e. desires must be regulated in accordance with the will of Heaven.

The superior man does not *say* in reference to them, " It is the appointment of heaven " (命).[1]

What difference then is there between the ideas of Mencius and Yang Tzu in this connection ? For scholars who hold that Mencius is right, regard Yang Tzu as having wrong ideas, while those who hold that Yang Tzu is right consider Mencius to have erroneous opinions. But that is because such scholars, although they are acquainted with what these philosophers have written on the subject, have failed to understand what they really meant. So that when they presume on their knowledge of the philosophy of " the nature of man " and " the decree " they are just displaying their ignorance.

A FURTHER DISCUSSION ON THE " NATURE AND THE DECREE " (對 辨)

(Works, vol. xvii, pp. 12, 13.)

Some people have raised difficulties about my treatment of the discussion of Yang Tzu and Meng Tzu on the subject of " the nature " and " the decree " (性 命), in which I endeavoured to point out the errors of current thought on the topic. It is said that my discussion of " the nature " is quite right, but that in regard to " the decree " (命) I am not sufficiently convincing.[2]

My questioner says, " Here is a man who as far as his abilities are concerned ought to be in a very subordinate position, but actually occupies a very exalted position in the State, who again, as far as his personal conduct is concerned, ought to have met with great misfortune, but has actually attained to the highest felicity. Or take the exact counterpart of these incidents. Such instances are utterly obversive of men's conception of

---

[1] i.e. each man by nature is so constituted that he ought to strive after these ideal relationships, no matter how difficult they seem to be of attainment in his own circumstances.

[2] See Essay on Yang Meng (楊 孟), pp. 329–332.

what ought to be, and are also considered as beyond the power of men to bring about. So the scholars say that such events are wrought by Heaven, and are said to be ' decreed ' because what is decreed has its source in Heaven.

" When Shun was on the throne he promoted to high office the nine famous worthies and executed the four notoriously infamous officials. When Ch'eng Wang was on the throne he highly honoured his two elder uncles and executed his two younger uncles. It would seem that the promotion of the nine was due to their being both able and good, and that the four infamous ones were executed because of their worthless character. The same ideas apply to the actions of Ch'eng Wang. Such results as these were brought about by men's own initiative and therefore in the ' orthodox ' sense, not ' decreed '.

" But suppose that Shun had been an unenlightened ruler and that he had promoted the four infamous ones and executed the nine (good ones), and that Ch'eng Wang likewise had given high honour to his younger uncles and had executed the two older ones. Such actions may be termed as ' beyond the power of men to bring about ', or such as are ' decreed by heaven '.

" But how can effects which are brought about by men themselves be interpreted as ' decreed ' ? "

I should reply, " My opinion is that the reason why the worthy are promoted and honoured and the worthless degraded and punished is also ' decreed '."

Confucius, who embraced in his own person the virtuous character of the nine officers and the two elder uncles, was himself involved in the difficulties attendant upon an age of disorder, and barely escaped with his life on several occasions. He laboured in journeyings to the courts of the princes, seeking for a sphere in which he might employ his gifts. But in the end he died out of office. (That would be commonly interpreted as a true case of what is " decreed ".)

Nevertheless we must also say that in the case of the nine officers and the two elder uncles, despite the fact that they themselves were worthy, that their promotion and honour were decreed.

The wickedness of Tao Chih (盗 跖)[1] greatly exceeded that of the four infamous ones and the two younger uncles, and yet he died a natural death at a good old age. (Such is an instance of what is commonly meant by " decreed ".) But we are bound to say that the four infamous ones, and the two younger uncles, even though they were of vicious character, suffered punishment because it was thus decreed.

So (in regard to such logical issues of conduct) the sages do not speak of " the decree " (命), but in their instruction of men confine themselves to what was within the power of men to perform.

Why confine the operation of what is decreed to matters of rank or position, or misfortune and felicity? Even the very characters of men, as being either worthy or worthless, are also decreed.

Some, however, might say, " Rank and position, felicity or misfortune are the result of extraneous circumstances, but you think that lofty rank gained by the worthy and inferior positions falling to the unworthy are all decreed. That I understand.

" But how can you term ' decreed ' that which you assert is in the power of men to bring about, such as the reason why the worthy are worthy and the worthless are worthless? "

My reply would be that this desire to be worthy and fear of becoming worthless are component elements in the great purpose of the really good man and that all the ancients who were fond of learning held similar ideas to this.

Mencius said, " the exercise of love between father and son, the observance of righteousness between sovereign and minister, the rules of ceremony between guest and host, the display of knowledge in recognizing the talented, and the fulfilling the heavenly course by the sage, these are the appointment of heaven. But there is an adaptation of our nature for them.

---

[1] Tao Chih, a sort of Robin Hood of Chinese History.

The superior man does not *say* in reference to them, ' They are the appointment of Heaven.' " [1]

From this it may be said that the reason why a man of worthy capacity actually becomes worthy, although the superior man, i.e. conventional scholar, *may not term it* " decreed " (不 謂 命),[2] is nevertheless " decreed " in Mencius's meaning of the term. In the case of the worthless man, and the reason why he is such, need we posit anything different?

Discussion on the Canons of Human Relationships
(禮 論)
(Works, vol. xvi, pp. 27, 28.)

How deplorable was Hsün Ch'ing's (荀 卿) ignorance of the true nature of the Canons of human relationship, in that he says, " The sages transformed the original nature of man, making it factitious " (僞).[3] That statement proves that he was obviously ignorant of the real nature of the Canons (禮).

True knowledge of the Canons lies in giving chief regard to the purpose for which they were formulated. But Hsün Ch'ing thinks mostly of the regulations and distinctions which are connected with the Canons, and commends that aspect of them.

But when he says that " they transformed the original nature of man, making it factitious " he cannot be said to understand the real purport of the Canons.

The Canons of human relationships have their origin in Heaven, but receive their fulfilment from men. If there is knowledge only of what is bestowed by Heaven (i.e. of one's

[1] Mencius, pt. ii of book vii, chap. xxiv.
[2] The emphasis in each case is particularly on either the " nature " or the " decree ". Where the rightful emphasis is on the " nature " the superior man does not refer to the " decree " and *vice versa*, though as appears from the text both elements are present in each case.
[3] Cf. Hsün Tzu, " Hsing O P'ien " (性 惡 篇), or Essay on the Evil Nature of Man, vol. xvii, of his Works.

natural endowments) while one is ignorant of man's duty in connection therewith, then one may be said to remain "uncivilized" (野). If one is cognisant only of man's part in the business, and remains ignorant of one's natural endowment, one may be said to have become "factitious" (偽).

It was just because the sages loathed all that is implied by the term "uncivilized" and deplored what is suggested by the term "factitious" that they devised the canons.

Hsün Ch'ing by his expression, "the sages transformed the original nature of man, making it factitious," shows that he is not conversant with the faulty character of what is naturally bestowed. There are, however, those who with a show of reason say, "He who observes the canons must of necessity act contrary to his indolent and self-willed ideas, and act in a manner which is opposed to his real cravings and desires. For there are none who really do not desire to take things easy, and yet they must engage in bitter toil for their superiors ; there are none who do not really desire to get things for themselves and yet they are bound to give way to their elders. It is only by their external demeanour, unnatural and forced, that their respect is shown, in which case how can it be said that the people take a real delight in observing these canons ? They observe them rather because they dread the punishment that would follow on their superiors' and elders' objection to their non-observance of the canons."

But Hsün Tzu, in thinking that the sages devised these canons to control men by fear of incurring the penalties of disobedience to the regulations, shows that he has not given sufficient thought to the subject.

The making of implements from the tree and the training of a horse for the shafts are not only the outcome of natural capacity. The wood has to be cut out with the axe, marked out with ink and line, and shaped by the compass and square. The pieces have to be connected by joints, and glue and varnish have to be applied before the implement can be said to be ready for use. In the case of the horse, the restraint of the bridle and bit have to be imposed, the whip has to be brought into play to frighten the beast, speed and pacing have to be regulated so as to make it serve the will of man, and make it suitable for riding or pulling. From this it would appear that everything is dependent upon external coercion and compulsion.

But the sages' teaching implies that the original tree is essential to the making of the implement, and that you must first have the horse before you can train it to serve you. That these results are possible is because nature makes available the material for men's use.

A man at birth is endowed with respect for his father and love for his mother. The sages devised certain regulations in accordance with these natural desires. So that while these regulations seem to imply a measure of compulsion or coercion, they are at the same time in true accordance with a man's natural desires.

If the sages had not devised the canons of human relationships, then the probability is that men would have come to despise their fathers and hate their mothers. Which may be said to be equivalent to losing that with which they were naturally endowed. If it is to be termed " factitious " to fulfil the (obligations of one's) nature, can it be termed " true to nature " to lose what originally belongs to one's nature ?

So that Hsün Tzu in taking up his attitude to this question betrays lack of thought.

A monkey is similar in physical form to a man. But if you sought to make it observe the distinctions that should subsist between the noble and lowly, and train it to bow and observe the other amenities of polite society, it would hasten away into the deep recesses of forests and hills. It is quite impossible to make it the equivalent of man in these respects, even though you should do all in your power to intimidate it or train it.

But if it is true that something which is absent from the original nature can be produced factitiously by the influence of education, then it should be possible to make the monkey observe the canons of propriety.

So I repeat, that the canons of human relationships have their origin in nature but are fulfilled by the efforts of man.

I remain to be convinced that you can, by human effort, produce what is not originally inherent in man's nature.

On the Superiority of Confucius to Yao and Shun
(夫 子 賢 於 堯 舜)
(Works, vol. xvii, pp. 1, 2.)

Tsai O (宰 我) remarked that in his opinion Confucius far and away superseded Yao and Shun from the standpoint of real worth (賢).[1] The conventional commentator is sure to explain such a remark as this by saying that this is merely the private opinion of a personal disciple of the sage, and is not to be understood as the general and impartial opinion.

But Mencius also said, " There never has been one to equal the master, since man was created." [2] Is that also the private opinion of a disciple, and not the general and impartial opinion ? Those who do hold such an opinion have, I consider, not given sufficient thought to the subject.

When it is said that the terms " sheng " (聖) and " hsien " (賢) have different connotations, there must be some real reason for making the difference. And students should inform themselves as to the reason why they are thus differentiated. The " sage " (聖) is one whose principles of life and actual achievements of character are so wonderful that it is impossible for any of a later age to improve upon them. For if their achievements in these directions can be surpassed, then they cease by virtue of that fact to be " sages "

My opinion, however, is that the statements of Tsai O and Mencius, which have been quoted above, were made with particular reference to the age in which Confucius lived. (See below.)

In ancient times the right way of life was first expounded by Fu Hsi (伏 羲) and carried to completion by Yao and Shun. Then Yü T'ang, Wen, and Wu continued their labours, and extended the scope of their principles. All these occupied

---

[1] Mencius, bk. ii, pt. i, ch. ii, v. 26. Legge.
[2] Mencius, bk. ii, pt. i, ch. ii, v. 23.

the imperial throne, and so laboured that gradually clearness and completeness of the ideal method of government was attained.

There were, too, those in official positions who may be said to have carried on their good work, like I Yin (伊 尹), Po I (伯 夷), Liu Hsia Hui (劉 下 惠), and Confucius.

Fu Hsi originated the idea of the correct way of life and government, but his method was not completed until the times of Yao and Shun. But although Yao and Shun could fulfil Fu Hsi's ideas and help to perfect his method, yet from the standpoint of perfect inclusiveness they did not reach the achievements of Confucius.

What then is the reason why sages with such glorious equipment, with knowledge adequate to the preparation of a method of government for the whole empire, should have to wait for Confucius to make their ideas quite complete?

Because the mind of the sage is not set on seeking for an opportunity to do anything for the State, but waits for the opportune time to arrive, and then in accordance with the needs of the time devises his method. In the times of Confucius the state of the empire was such as called for a complete method, and so Confucius was enabled to devise such.

This is an illustration of the statement which we find in the Book of Changes, viz. " To adapt oneself to the opportunity afforded by changed conditions, and to conduct the government of the people as energetically as possible ".

So we conclude, that the possibility of attaining to the complete and perfect method in the time of Confucius, is not the sole credit of Confucius. For all who are termed " sages " had helped to prepare the way by their efforts. Mencius says,[1] " Confucius was one who concentrated the achievements of the great in his own person." By that he meant that he gathered together all the achievements of all the great men in the past, and brought to a great perfection the method that will be the model for all generations. It is in this respect alone that he may be said to be superior to Yao and Shun.

[1] Mencius, bk. v, pt. ii, ch. i, v. 6.

On Great Men (大 人 論)

(Works, vol. xvi, p. 31.)

Mencius said,[1] " The great man is he whose solid achievements are gloriously displayed, and the sage (聖) is a great
man (大) who exercises a transforming influence. The spirit-
man (神) is a sage who exceeds our comprehension (i.e. no
other term is adequate to describe him)." (But see below.)

These three terms, i.e. " great-man," " sage," and " spirit-
man ", are all designations of the " sage ". The reason why
these different designations are used is simply because by them
different aspects of the character of the sage are denoted. The
term " spirit-man " is used to indicate his principles (道);
the term " sage " is used to indicate his personal character (德);
while the term " great-man " is used to indicate his actual
achievements (事 業).

The sages of ancient time are all entitled to the designation
of spirit-man, on the ground of their principles. The reason
they were only termed " sages " was because their principles
were hidden away beyond men's sight. When, however, these
principles become embodied in the human personality the term
" virtuous " is applied to them. So that although they were
entitled to the designation of spirit-men on the ground of their
principles, they did not actually receive that title, but were
given the title (sage) which their personal character (德)
justified.

The characteristics of the spirit-man in their highest form
cannot be made manifest except by those attributes which the
sage possesses, and even though sage-like attributes should be
possessed they cannot assume tangible form unless they are
embodied in the achievements characteristic of the great-man.

So I repeat that these three designations are all proper titles
of the sage, and that the reason why these different designations
are used is that by them different aspects of the sage's character
are denoted. . . .

[1] Mencius, bk. vii, pt. ii, chap. xxv, vv. 6, 7, and 8.   Legge, p. 490.

Confucius said,[1] "(Principles) are manifested in a man's benevolence, and function (mysteriously) in everything he does. So (the spirit-man) influences everything (beneficially) without experiencing the anxiety of one who is but a 'sage'. He is one who has attained to the highest pinnacle of personal character and through whose activity the greatest possible achievements are wrought." This statement refers to the achievements of the spirit-man. Although his achievements are the greatest possible (to man) they are undiscernible by others, until he makes them manifest by his benevolent nature, and by actual effort produces something of tangible benefit to his fellows.

These are the aims which actuate the sage as he engages in his self-purifying tasks, and cultivates his spirit in secret. But it is only when his benevolent character is displayed in inexhaustible beneficial activity for his fellows, and when he gives tangible evidence by his indefatigable efforts at permanent improvement of the social order, that he is termed " sage ".

So I conclude that the achievements of the spirit-man should be manifest in the spheres of illustrious personal character and great practical achievements, for it is only on the grounds of personal character that he may be termed a " sage " and only on the grounds of practical achievements that he may be termed " great-man ".

But among my contemporaries there are those who merely hold to their own conceptions of " principle " (道) and in their ignorance of the interpretation which is given above of (the characteristics of the " spirit-man ") think that " personal character " and practical achievements (德 業) are something inferior, and inadequate to express what is denoted by " principle " (道) restricting the application of such to the spirit-man (神). So they discard virtuous endeavour as a goal and refrain from making practical applications of it. But if all who termed themselves " superior-men " (君 子) acted in this way, how could anything at all be accomplished?

[1] Book of Changes, " Shang Chuan," chap. v (周 易 繫 辭 上 傳).

So we have the words of Confucius, describing the " spirit-
man " as one who had attained to the highest possibility of
virtuous effort, with the idea of showing that on no account
was such effort to be discarded. For seeing that the spirit-
man's attributes are applied to virtuous effort and practical
achievements, it becomes possible to conceive of the supreme
goal of the same.[1]

Hence it is said, " Unless the ' spirit-man '[2] is a ' sage ' his
spirit-man characteristics will not be manifest, and unless the
' sage ' be a ' great-man ' his sagely qualities will not assume
a tangible form."

Thus perfection is attained, and the goal of the ancients
illustrated.

On Seeking to Apply One's Principles to Affairs of State (行 述)

(Works, vol. xvii, p. 6.)

Those of old, who thought that in wearying themselves
out in seeking for the opportunity to apply their principles
to matters of government, they were following the example
of Confucius, were quite mistaken.

Confucius first accepted appointment in the State of Lu (魯),
but when that state became disorderly he left it and proceeded
to Ch'i (齊). When again he perceived that association with
the rulers of that state was detrimental to his principles, he went

---

[1] It would seem that Wang An Shih in this essay is opposing his own conception of the highest manhood to current opinions of a different character.
To him, the great man is one who makes great contributions to his age in the
way of practical reform. To others " greatness " was confined to the other-
worldliness of the Taoists, which had no place for the practical reformer.

[2] I have borrowed the expression " spirit-man " for 神 from Legge. But
perhaps some other term like " ideal-man ", one whose life is ruled by spiritual,
rather than materialistic, ideals, is nearer the mark. In the Doctrine of the
Mean, we have the expression 至 誠 如 神 " of the utmost sincerity
like the Spirits " to guide us. A man of the utmost sincerity would represent
ideal manhood. (See Legge's Mencius, pp. 490–1.)

back to Lu.[1] When, however, the ruler of Lu accepted a present of dancing girls and musicians, and suspended the Court proceedings for three days holiday and jollification, he felt it incumbent upon him to leave again. Being then in some doubt as to where he ought to proceed next, he said, "Duke Ling of Wei (衛 靈 公) is a thoroughly unprincipled man in himself, but he still retains a sense of the proper way in which to treat worthy ministers." So he set out for Wei. When he discovered that it was impossible to co-operate with Duke Ling, he left at once without having any definite place in mind where he ought to go, and visited in succession the states of Ts'ao (曹), Sung (宋), Cheng (鄭), Ch'en (陳), Ts'ai (蔡), Wei (衛), and Ch'u (楚). In each state his attitude was determined by the same motives as led him to leave Wei and proceed to Ts'ao. Then, feeling the pressure of age upon him, he returned to Lu, where he ended his days.

Such was the way of Confucius. Where in all this can he be said to have "sought" for the opportunity to apply his principles to government? It is clear that the principle governing these matters is that rulers and princes who do not of themselves take the initiative in seeking the help of worthy ministers are not capable of using them. If Confucius was ignorant of that principle, how could he be Confucius? Let us recall his remark, "Sell it! Sell it! (No indeed!) I would 'wait' for one to offer the price."[2]

To weary oneself out in seeking for an opportunity to apply one's principles to affairs is equivalent to "selling" one's principles.

The ideas of Confucius in this connection are exemplified in the words of Tzu Lu (子 路), viz. "The superior man takes up office with a view to doing what he conceives to be right. He knows beforehand when there is no prospect of his principles being put into effect". That reveals the thought of Confucius on this matter.

Are we then to conclude that Confucius had no desire to

[1] Cf. Analects, bk. xvii, chap. iii. Legge's second ed., p. 332.
[2] Cf. Analects, bk. ix, chap. xii. Legge's second ed., p. 221.

co-operate with the officials of his day? We remember that he said, " When my principles are about to prevail, it is so ordained, and when they cannot prevail, that too is so ordained."

In effect, therefore, he said, " Seeing that it is ordained that my principles cannot prevail, of what avail is it to co-operate with the rulers ? " [1]

ON THE ATTAINMENT OF UNITY (致 一 論)

(Works, vol. xvi, pp. 31, 32.)

All things have their ultimate principle of being. He who is quite conversant with the ultimate principle of things is a sage. The way to become conversant with this ultimate principle of things is to attain unto the unity (behind them all). If this is attained to, then all created things can be understood without further thought. . . . As the Book of Changes has it, " Such a man is entitled to the designation of " spirit-man " (神). The " spirit-man " has attained to the supreme height of moral excellence. One who has so attained has reached the stage when without thought or effort, and by a deep and mysterious inactivity, (he brings things to pass).

It is, of course, true that the affairs of government call for thought and activity, and so it is essential that the reason for that should be known. The sages, therefore, held practical ability in highest esteem. But the effect of this practical ability is seen first in one's sense of quiet conviction, so that everything is seen to have vital relationship to my own personality. If I can take advantage of everything to bring about this sense of quiet and settled conviction, then I shall be useful wherever

---

[1] Cf. Analects, bk. xiv, chap. xxxviii, p. 2. Legge's second ed., p. 289. Wang An Shih evidently applies this quotation in his own way, so as to make the principles of Confucius apply to the particular argument of this essay. Confucius did desire to co-operate with the statesmen of his time, but knew that the ruler must himself desire his services if success was to be achieved on the understanding always that Confucius's principles would be observed. The absence of any such ruler in his day prevented him from making the contribution he would like to have made.

I go and whatsoever I do. In which case, my virtuous character is sure to win respect.

So we read in the Book of Changes, " To be so conversant with righteousness as to become a spirit-man and to express one's achievements in a practical fashion, to avail myself of my own quiet personal conviction to secure respect for my character, is the correct order of moral progress."

Confucius, having set forth the various stages of moral progress, and fearing lest his students should not have understood his meaning, illustrated it from the diagrams. To be in difficulties when one ought not to be, to hold on to a position which one ought not to hold on to, to be unashamed of unkind deeds, to have no fear of acting unrighteously, to regard a small deed of kindness as of no use, and a trifling crime as in no way deleterious, all these are reasons for the non-attainment of this quiet personal conviction, and respect for one's character.

The best way to gain respect for one's character and to attain to that quiet personal conviction is to hide your talents in your heart, and wait for the right time to take action. If one can but observe these two principles of conduct, he will illustrate the right method of attaining conviction and gaining respect, for in every case these proceed from the observation of these two principles.

A man who has attained to this standard will be of the greatest service to his day and generation. . . .

Tzu Kung (子 貢)

(Works, vol. xvi, pp. 12, 13.)

I question the accuracy of the traditional records concerning Tzu Kung, for if they are correct, I fail to see how he could be termed a Confucianist. For a Confucianist in government service is necessarily concerned about the same matters as his ruler, and when he is taking his support from the people, he is necessarily distressed about the same things as distress the people. If he finds no master to use his services, then he devotes himself to the cultivation of his personal character, and is concerned about nothing else.

In the times of Yao the people were greatly distressed by the floods. This greatly concerned Yao. So Yü (禹) during his nine years of toil passed by his own door three times without inquiring after the welfare of his child.[1] In the times of Hui (回) the distress of the people exceeded that of the times of the floods, and the concern of the ruler of his day exceeded that of Yao, and yet Hui, who had a character equally worthy with that of Yü, was content to live in his humble alley without as much as giving a thought to the distress of the people or the concern of his ruler.[2]

But are not these two, i.e. Hui and Yü, really observing the same principles of action ? And are not we to seek the reason for their different attitude in the different character of their respective times ? If in the times of Yü, Yen Hui had acted as he did in his own day, he would have been an egoist like Yang Chu (楊 朱). And if he had acted in his own day like Yü did in his he would have been another Mo Ti.

So the definition of the conduct and attitude of the Confucianist (as outlined above) is not concerned with the distress of the people or the concern of the ruler as such, but solely with the question of one's duty in the particular circumstances obtaining at the time. For if the relieving of the ruler's anxiety or the elimination of the distress of the people demands the violation of one's sense of right, then of course the true Confucianist in such a case would do nothing.

In the History we read,[3] " Ch'i was about to attack Lu. When Confucius heard of this, he said, ' Lu is the State of our ancestral tombs, what are you, my disciples, going to do in this time of peril ? Why do you not proceed to its deliverance ? ' "

Tzu Kung (子 貢) thereupon set off, and urged Ch'i to attack Wu (吳), and at the same time urged Wu to save Lu. He further embroiled the states of Yüeh (越) and Chin (晉).

---

[1] Cf. Mencius, bk. iii, pt. i, chap. iv.
[2] Analects, book vi, chap. ix.
[3] i.e. of Ssu Ma Ch'ien.

So (by the counsel of Tzu Kung) these five states engaged in mutual strife, with the object of preserving Lu. He was utterly regardless of the interests of the other states as to whether they should prosper or not, or whether they should be thrown into confusion or not. Looking at his advice and conduct, he appears in no wise different from I, Ch'in, Chen, and Tai (儀 秦 軫 代).[1]

But what about the words of Confucius,[2] " That which you would not desire others to do to you, do not ye that unto them " ? The people of Ch'i and the people of Wu had equal reverence for the country of their ancestors' tombs. They were equally desirous of maintaining their territory intact. What justification was there for throwing them into confusion ?

This is the first reason why I affirm that the historian's account of Tzu Lu must be false.

Moreover, by further investigation into the history of the period, we discover that both Confucius and Tzu Kung were without any official position at that time, and were in receipt of no government emoluments, so that such matters as the ruler's concern and the people's distress were outside the sphere of their duty. (If they had taken action such as the record states) they would have acted contrary to the principles of Yen Hui. That is the second reason for my doubting the authenticity of the historian's account.

The fact that a certain state contains one's ancestral tombs is naturally a matter of deep concern to the superior man, but he would not simply because of this devise wicked schemes

---

[1] I (儀) is Chang I (張 儀), minister of Ch'in Hui Wang (秦 惠 王) who in the Chan Kuo times advocated an alliance of six states on an east and west line, so as to bring back the rebellious states to the allegiance. His policy was opposed by Su Ch'in, named Chin (秦) in the text, whose own ideas were, however, rejected by Ch'in Hui Wang. So the latter travelled to the Yen and Chao states advocating an alliance of six kingdoms on a north and south line, viz., Yen, Chao, Han, Wei, Ch'i, and Ch'u, which eventually materialized. The policy of Su Ch'in is known as Chung (縱) and that of Chang I as Heng (橫), the expression Chung Heng chih chia (縱 橫 之 家) being later used of any statesman who sought to unite sections of the kingdom in any alliance.

[2] Analects, book xv, chap. xxiii.

(to save the situation). Assuming that in cases of concern and distress only the right thing should be done, how could one possibly with the object of preserving one's own State proffer such selfish and evil advice, as would lead to the ruin of another?

This is the third reason why I consider the record to be a fabrication.

Although one cannot say that the conduct of Tzu Kung was absolutely in accord with one's conception of right, he was quite a worthy disciple of Confucius, and it is inconceivable that he should have descended to such base conduct as is attributed to him in the records. It is still less credible that Confucius should have encouraged him to act as he is reported to have done.

Ssu Ma Ch'ien (司 馬 遷) says, " Students in their remarks about the seventy disciples, exceed the facts in their praises, or do less than justice to the facts in their detractions." Although Tzu Kung was fond of argument, could he be so bad as to deserve such serious calumny? I think it is just an instance of a detractor warping the facts.

The Highest Form of Love (荀 卿)

(with reference to Hsün Ch'ing)

(Works, vol. xvii, p. 8.)

Hsün Ch'ing quotes Confucius as saying, " Yu (由), tell me what a wise man is like, and what a good man is like?" Tzu Lu (子 路) replied, " A wise man causes others to know him, a good man causes others to love him." Confucius said, " You may be termed a scholar " (士). He then put the same question to Tz'u (賜), i.e. Tzu Kung (子 貢), who replied, " A wise man knows others, a good man loves others." Confucius said, " You may be termed a scholarly good-man " (士 君 子). He put the same question a third time to Hui (回), i.e. Yen Yuan (顏 淵), who replied, " A wise man knows himself, a good man loves himself." Confucius said,

"You may be termed a truly enlightened good-man" (明
君 子).

I doubt very much whether these are really the words of
Confucius ; in fact I am sure they are not.

For it is a universal principle that only he who can see what
is near at hand can see what is more remote, and only he who
can help in a small way can be of assistance in greater things.
On this basis, it was the ancient teaching that a man should
get to know himself first and then he might be able to know
others, and that a man should first love himself and then he
might seek to love others. That too is a natural principle,
on which not even a sage can alter.

Take an easy example. Here is a man who cannot see T'ai
Shan (太 山) at the distance of a foot. That such a one cannot
see a hair at a distance of a hundred paces, even the most stupid
can perceive. It is then quite clear that a man who cannot see
a nearer object certainly cannot see one more remote.

But Hsün Ch'ing's idea is that one who knows himself is
superior to one who knows others, which is equivalent to
saying that a man who can see T'ai Shan at a foot's distance
is superior in vision to a man who can see a hair at a distance
of a hundred paces.

Take another illustration. Here is a man who has scarcely
enough food to fill his own belly, or clothes sufficient to cover
his own nakedness. The most stupid person knows that it is
folly to expect such a man to do any great thing for his fellow
villagers. For it is clear that a man who is incapable of doing
the lesser thing will not be of much help in accomplishing the
greater.

But according to Hsün Ch'ing, he who loves himself is
superior to him who loves others. Which is equivalent to
saying that the man who has just food enough to fill his own
belly and clothes enough to cover his own nakedness is superior
to him upon whom the whole village depends (for their
livelihood).

This shows how shallow was Hsün Ch'ing's reasoning.

My own opinion is that to know oneself is but the first step which enables a man to go on to know others, and to love oneself is but the first step which enables a man to go on to love others. Further, it is only when one has fulfilled in their entirety the requirements of wisdom and love, that one can cause others to know and love oneself.

For a man who can cause others to know and love him will certainly know others and love others, and he who can know and love others will certainly know and love himself.

But the words of Hsün Ch'ing imply just the opposite of all this. So I am confident that the quotation which he attributes to Confucius cannot have been spoken by him, but must be a fabrication of Hsün Ch'ing himself.

When Yang Chu said, " Self-love is the acme of altruism," he meant that he who can love himself is then able to love others, and not that he who does not love others can love himself.

But, alas, there were among the ancients some who could love others, but were unable to love themselves. But that is not what I mean by " love of others ". It is rather the doctrine of Mo Ti (墨 翟). In the same way those who say that it is possible to know others, and yet not be able to know oneself, cannot mean the same thing as I do by " knowing others ".

LOVE AND WISDOM (仁 智)

(Works, vol. xvii, p. 5.)

Love (仁) is inferior to sagehood (聖), and wisdom (智) is inferior to love. There never has been a loving man who was not wise, nor a wise man who was not loving. Then what difference is there between love and wisdom? The difference lies in the manner in which they attain to that loving disposition.

If I am loving by nature, then even though I act without thought, and speak without conscious deliberation, and yet in one's conduct of affairs there is nothing that is not in accordance with the principle of love, the characteristic nature of the loving man is thereby revealed.

If, however, I am not loving by nature, but understand how one should conduct oneself as a loving man, if I act only after thought and speak with conscious deliberation, and yet in my conduct of affairs there is nothing that is contrary to the principle of love, the characteristic nature of the wise man is manifest thereby.

These two types differ in the way in which they attain to love, but in their actual loving conduct they are the same.

Confucius said, "The loving man is quiescent,[1] the wise man active." On what grounds did he make that statement? Take an illustration. Here are two merchants. One has already attained to great wealth; the other, though not yet wealthy, knows how to become so. In the case of the first, although he should lose all his boats and carts and even give up business, he would still be comparatively well-off. But the other man in such a case must still carry on his business. So the difference between the loving and the wise man lies in one being quiescent and the other active.

If a man's love is adequate to the requirements of heaven, extends in its graciousness to all created things, and overflows even to the border tribes,[2] and even then is not exhausted, what more does one need to seek for? This is the reason why the loving man can be quiescent.

But if all I possess is to know the desire to make my love

[1] There would seem to be contradiction between this passage on "quiescence" (cf. Analects, bk. vi, chap. xxi) and that found in the Doctrine of the Mean, chap. xxvi, section 1, where we read, "To entire sincerity there belongs ceaselessness" (至 誠 不 息). Confucius did not advocate the entire absence of activity. What he was keen on advocating was the opposite of that type of activity which works consciously and deliberately with the end in view. "Activity" for its own sake is the mark of perfection, both in the sphere of human character and in nature. The truly "loving" man loves because it is his nature to love, and not because he aims at it as the ideal end of life. So he is ceaselessly loving, but not for a conscious and deliberate end. It is not "doing by doing nothing" such as the Taoists advocate, but doing "for" nothing. Cf. Fung, *A Comparative Study of Life's Ideals*, pp. 175-7.
[2] Cf. Doctrine of the Mean, chap. xxxi, sect. 4, where this "extension" to the barbarous tribes is related to the reputation of the sage. "Here in making this extension of influence relate to 'love' Wang An Shih is approaching nearer to the ideal of 'internationalism' and Christianity."

adequate to the requirements of heaven, and how to make it extend to all created things, and even to overflow to the border tribes, and yet at times feel that my resources are getting exhausted, then of course it follows that I must still go on seeking. That indicates the reason why the wise man must be active.

Hence also it is said,[1] " The loving man loves the mountains, the wise man loves the flowing streams." The mountains are still and reposeful, and yet how useful they are to men. The streams flow on unceasingly and they too are of use to men. Mountains and streams differ in respect of their being still and active, and yet in their usefulness they are the same.

It is also said,[1] " The loving man lives long, the wise man joyously." But is not the loving man joyful, and does not the wise man live long? I would reply, " The wise man does live long, but not so long as the loving man. The loving man is joyful, but his joy is not adequate to the complete expression of love. For he who can adequately fulfil the law of love is a sage (聖 人)."

But the reason why we do not term such " loving " but regard them as " sages " is because of their transforming influence (化). For those who fulfil the law of love are capable of exerting transforming influences. But he who fails to exercise this transforming influence cannot, as I see it, fulfil the law of love.

Yen Hui (顏 回) was not equal to Confucius. Confucius said of him, " he is capable of not violating the law of love for only three months." Therefore who that is not like Confucius can perfectly fulfil the law of love?

COURAGE AND GENEROSITY (勇 惠)
" RIGHT " THE UNIVERSAL STANDARD OF ACTION
(Wang An Shih's Works, vol. xvii, pp. 4, 5.)

Conventional critics say that a generous man gives lightly, and a courageous man dies lightly. They say further that the

[1] Analects, bk. vi, chap. xxi.

sages approve the man who distributes his possessions without a thought, and him who avoids no danger, and that to act thus is the way of the superior man.

I contend, however, that such is not the correct view of the matter, and assert that the generous man gives after much thought, and the courageous man dies for grave reasons alone. I would contend further that the sages actually disapprove the man who gives lightly or lightly surrenders his life, and that actions of this latter type are the marks of the mean man (小 人).

'So I say that the superior man is characterized by two things. He thinks carefully before committing himself to any course of action, and in actual practice makes " right " (義) his universal standard of conduct. For by careful thought he ensures that any decision which he makes will conform to what is " right ", and by making " right " his standard he is sure that all he does will be in line with what he ought to do in the circumstances. In a word, all he does, he does after due consideration as to what is involved in his conduct.

We read in the Book of Changes : " Felicity or misfortune, regret and shame all arise from a man's conduct. Men are divided into worthy and worthless on the basis of their conduct, so one dare not be in any way casual about such a vitally important matter. So that the superior man, in matters of personal conduct, refrains from activity if he possibly can."

So in cases where it is feasible not to give or not to die, and so to act would be right,[1] should a man feel it incumbent upon him to give either possessions or life, although the generality of men might say that to act in that way in such circumstances is extremely difficult, the superior man will not necessarily approve such conduct. In another case, where it is possible to give or to die, should neither possessions nor life be surrendered, the multitude would deem such conduct easy.

---

[1] To make this quite clear, a clause ought to be added " and yet it might also be right to give or to die ". The case is one in which one's right course is doubtful. So with the next clause, one ought to complete the sense by adding " and yet also permissible not to give or not to die ".

And yet the superior man would not deem his conduct wrong.

Approval of a course of action because it is difficult, and disapproval of conduct on the ground of its being easy, are attitudes of the small minded. To ignore the whole question of ease or difficulty, and to make " right " the sole standard of conduct, is the attitude of the superior man.

We read in the commentary on the Book of Changes (易 經): " The universal rule of conduct is to do what is right. To make any other consideration than this the guiding principle of one's conduct is to class oneself among the mean-minded. It in no way affects the matter that a man, in adopting a certain course of action (contrary to this universal rule), does something which even a sage could not do."

Chi Lu (季 路) is deemed a man of real worth, and yet Confucius said of him, " Yu is a stauncher devotee of valour than I, but in that respect he is not to be taken as a model." [1] It was the great principle of Confucius to approve only that which was " right ", and by this statement that Tzu Lu [2] was a stauncher devotee of valour than he himself, he meant to convey the idea that he had gone beyond what was right. It was therefore quite correct for Confucius to say that conduct which overstepped the bounds of what was right was not to be imitated.

If in this matter of courage, Confucius disapproved the going beyond what was right, we may infer that it is also wrong to go beyond what is right in the matter of " giving ".

Mencius says,[3] " If when it is doubtful whether one ought to give or not, one proceeds to give, that is to do violence to the principle of generosity, and if when it is doubtful whether

---

[1] Cf. Analects, book v, chap. vi. The translation of " ts'ai " (材) gives Legge considerable difficulty. It may be presumptuous to suggest that one's own translation as given above renders better sense, but it seems justifiable. It should be noted also that Tzu Lu in the end lost his life through rashness. Confucius prophesied that he would not die a natural death. Analects, book xi, chap. xii.

[2] Chi Lu and Tzu Lu are one and the same.

[3] Mencius, book iv, pt. ii, chap. xxiii.

one ought to surrender one's life or not, one proceeds to make that surrender, that is to violate the principle of courage."

We see, therefore, that the superior man regulates all his conduct solely by what is considered indubitably right. If he has any doubts about a proposed course of action, then he remains quiescent.

We read also in the Analects: " See much, and put aside the points of which you stand in doubt, while you exercise caution in carrying out the rest, and you will have few occasions for repentance." [1] The meaning of this is that the superior man exercises the greatest care always to keep within the bounds of what is right.

I know, of course, that current critics affirm that in the transmission of the text of Mencius certain errors have crept in, and that the quotation (about generosity and courage) ought to read, " . . . If you do *not* give, you violate the principle of kindness, and . . . if you do *not* surrender your life, you violate the principle of courage."

But that is simply because they have given no real thought to the matter.

THE " MEAN " (中 述)

(Works, vol. xvii, p. 6.)

The superior man makes light demands of others, but draws the distinction between right and wrong quite clearly.

Confucius in blaming Tsai Yü (宰 予) said, " Of what use is it to reprove him ? " [2] And in criticizing Jan Yu (冉 有), he said, " Beat the drum, lads, and attack him." [3]

It would seem, from the way in which Confucius spoke of these two disciples, that they ought to have been dismissed from his fellowship.

---

[1] Analects, book ii, chap. xviii, sect. 2. There is a slight variation from the usual text.

[2] See Analects, book v, chap. ix.

[3] See Analects, book xi, chap. xvi, sect. 2, where Confucius says definitely that Jan Yu was no disciple of his.

However, we find in classifying the disciples according to their qualities, that those whom Confucius specially approved, were a mere handful. Yet he approved of Tsai Yü for his persuasive eloquence, and Jan Yu for his administrative gifts. He did not refuse to acknowledge their good qualities because they chanced to have bad ones as well.

Can it be said then that Confucius showed partiality? No, he made light demands of others. Kuan Chung (管 仲) was one whose achievements made him generally famous. But Confucius thought little of him.[1] Of the three thousand disciples of Confucius, Yen Hui (顏 回) alone was praised by the Master for his devotion to learning.[2] Others, such as Min Sun (閔 損), Yuan Hsien (原 憲), and Tseng Tzu (曾 子), were not so designated. When you add to this the fact that Tsai Yü and Jan Yu were criticized as above, it may reasonably be asked whether Confucius was not given to over-emphasizing men's good points. But not so, he was merely making quite clear the distinction between right and wrong.

In making light demands of others, he praised generously their laudable qualities, and in being punctilious about the distinction between right and wrong he made clear the doctrine of the sages.

For if such men as Tsai Yü and Jan Yu could not be regarded as good disciples, then the vast majority would find it extremely difficult to escape blame. Who indeed could be accepted as being good enough (for his standard)?

On the other hand, if Kuan Chung had not been blamed, then all who follow administration as their calling might rest content with such achievements as he attained to, and make no effort to improve upon them. If all of the seventy disciples had been praised for their devotion to learning, then those who love learning would be content with the standard which they had reached, in which case how could the principles of the sages be clearly expounded?

But by approving men's good qualities as he did, Confucius

[1] See Analects, book iii, chap. xxii, section 1.
[2] See Analects, book vi, chap. ii.

shows that while one should make heavy demands of oneself, one should also encourage others to persevere. By exemplifying this principle as he does, he shows clearly the line both I and my fellows ought to take.

Therefore, to make light demands of others, without concealing their faults, and at the same time to be scrupulously careful in one's criticisms of others, is the way to encourage them towards perfection.[1] The teachings of the sages are simply founded on the idea of the "mean". The main idea of the Annals is in no wise different from this.

On Ceremonies and Music (禮 樂 論)
(Works, vol. xvi, pp. 28–30.)

The will (心) is that which is by divine appointment conferred (as the guide of) the passion-nature of man (氣).

It is by the exercise of the utmost sincerity that looking leads to seeing, listening leads to hearing, thinking leads to perception, and action leads to achievement.

But it certainly belongs to the nature of man and the independent character of his spirit (神) to apprehend without listening, to be intelligent without looking, to perceive without thought, and to attain without action. These may also result from exerting one's will power to the utmost, and exhausting the possibilities of the exercise of the utmost sincerity. So the reason why sincerity may be regarded as "unfathomable" is due to man's "nature".

The "worthy man" (賢) is as sincere as possible with the object of realizing the full possibilities of his nature (立 性), while the sage (聖) exerts his natural capacity to the utmost with the object of being absolutely sincere.

The "spirit" (神) is begotten of the "nature" (性): the "nature" is begotten of "sincerity" (誠): "sincerity"

[1] The general principle advocated by Wang An Shih is enunciated in Analects, book xv, chap. xiv : " He who requires much from himself and little from others, will keep far from incurring resentment."

is begotten of the " will " (心) : the " will " is begotten of the " emotions " (氣), and the " emotions " are begotten of the " physical form " (形). The " physical form " is the foundation of all life. So the nurture of life depends on the preservation of the physical form : the fulfilling of the purpose of the physical form depends upon the education of the " emotional faculty " : the nurture of the emotional life depends upon a " fixed will " (寧 心), and a " fixed will " depends upon absolute sincerity. The culture of sincerity depends again upon exhausting the possibilities of one's nature.

For failure in the latter renders one incapable of nurturing one's life. But he who exhausts the possibilities of his nature is absolutely sincere : he who is abolutely sincere is of a fixed will : he who is of a fixed will educates his emotions, and he who educates his emotions preserves his physical form : he who preserves his physical form nurtures his life.

Failure in the latter renders a man incapable of exhausting the possibilities of his nature.

Life and the nature are mutually dependent; the will (志) and the emotions are related as inward and outward aspects of the one thing.

If the life is not pure, the real character of the nature will remain unrevealed ; if the nature is not pure, then the real character of life will remain hidden, just as the will, when a unity, excites the emotions into activity, and when the emotions are a unity they excite the will into activity.

The ancient rulers, cognisant of the truth of these things, represented in tangible form the nature of man by creating the " rites " (禮), and with a view to harmonizing the nature of man, created music (樂).

The rites are the universal moderator as music is the universal harmonizer. So the ancient rulers utilized the rites and music to nurture the spirit of man, and to control his emotional nature, thereby restoring his original correct nature.

As this was their objective, the greatest ceremonies are extremely simple, and lacking in display, while the finest music is extremely easy and quiet. Simplicity and ease were the fundamental ideas of the ancient rulers in their creation of the rites and music.

The sages esteem lightly that which the ordinary man is greatly concerned about, and the sages grieve over that in which men take pleasure. It is not that the sage and the ordinary man have contrary dispositions, but the sage seeks for an inner satisfaction, while the ordinary man seeks for satisfaction in external things. He who seeks for this inner satisfaction takes a delight in the fulfilling of his natural capacity (for good), while he who seeks for this external satisfaction delights in the fulfilling of his desires.

The desires rise readily, and the possibilities of the nature are hard indeed to explore, and this is the reason why the nature and the disposition are mutually opposed.

Clothes and food are necessary to the nurture of the body and emotional nature of man, rites and music are necessary to the nurture of one's original nature. Rites bring a man back to his primal condition, while music brings him back to his original ideas.

In rites and music as I conceive of them, I find that the sages render the highest homage to the life of man. But the common saying runs, " the nurture of life is not the concern of the superior man." This betrays general ignorance of the ideas which inspired the former rulers to create the rites and music. For one nurtures one's life in order to be benevolent, and preserves one's emotional life in order to be righteous: one eschews evil passions, and represses base desires, in order to realize to the full the capacity of one's human nature; one educates the spirit to the utmost of one's intelligence in order to reach the sagely pinnacle.

Among the sayings of the sages there are none of greater importance than the reply of Confucius to Yen Yuan,[1] viz., " Look not at what is contrary to propriety: listen not to what is contrary to propriety: speak not what is contrary to propriety: make no movement which is contrary to propriety," then one will not be far from the way of benevolence.

[1] Analects, book xii, chap. ii.

The ear does not need to be educated by men to become perceptive, nor does the eye need to be educated by men to become capable of seeing, neither does the mouth need the help of men to enable it to utter words, nor the physical frame of man to begin to move.   To retain these powers is extremely simple, and the help that one needs to maintain them is very near at hand.   Every one who has a " will " and physical form possesses these faculties.

Why then did Yen Yuan find any difficulty about the matter ?   For the simple reason that he had asked about the greatest problem of human ethics.   For the expression " look not at what is contrary to propriety " does not mean that I am to blindfold myself, and avoid the world of sight, for the phenomenal world as such is incapable of confusing my sight. Likewise the expression " listen not to what is contrary to propriety " does not mean that one is to muffle one's ears, avoiding the world of sound, for the phenomenal world as such is incapable of affecting my perceptiveness.   The expression " speak not what is contrary to propriety " does not mean that one is to muzzle oneself, and utter no words at all, for the phenomenal world as such cannot change my speech. Likewise the expression " make no movement which is contrary to propriety " does not mean that all physical activity is to cease, for the phenomenal world as such is incapable of affecting my passion-nature.

For the phenomenal world does not consist solely of visible or material activities; the source from which these spring is of the minutest character.   For before one has heard anything the power of hearing is there : before one has seen anything the capacity of seeing is there : before one has uttered a word the power of speech is present : and before one has moved a muscle the power of movement is there.   Among the disciples of Confucius, only Yen Yuan can be said to have appreciated the import of this.

Therefore if a man considers that the ear is indispensable to the apprehension of sounds, but at the same time is ignorant of the way in which it is capable of so doing, the full possibilities of hearing will not be realized. If a man regards the eye as essential to vision, and yet is ignorant of how it becomes capable of it, the full possibilities of vision will not be realized. The apprehension of sounds and the capacity of vision are faculties pertaining to the physical organs of hearing and seeing, but the source of hearing and seeing is not in the physical organ. It is on this ground that the statement is made that " He who has to wait for the sound of bells and drums before he can experience the feeling of joy is not deeply versed in music, and that he who has to wait for the appearance of gems and silks before the feeling of respect is induced, is not deeply versed in ceremonies ".

All that is essential to complete the requirements of music is a cane drumstick and an earthenware drum. All that is essential to complete the requirements of ceremonies is some roasted millet, a few pieces of pork, and a hollow in the ground from which to drink with one's hands. So the sages in their desire to make quite clear the essential idea of music and cere-monies, were quite unconcerned about the adornment of their furs, or the decoration of their equipages, making the actual observance of the ceremony the real thing.

Those who assert that ceremonies are vitally related to a man's disposition have not penetrated to the core of the meaning of them. Tseng Tzu said to Meng Ching Tzu,[1] " There are three things which the superior man regards as of the highest importance in connection with conduct, viz., that in his deport-ment he should avoid either cruelty or arrogance : that he maintain a correct demeanour so as to approach to sincerity : and that in his speech he descend to no baseness or impropriety. As to the appurtenences of sacrifice there are the proper officers for them."

From this statement of Tseng Tzu it might be asserted by some that even he did not understand the real principle of the matter. But assuming that he did so, then we may say that the principles of conduct are related solely to such matters as deportment, demeanour, and speech, and have no reference

[1] Analects, bk. viii, chap. iv, par. 3.

to anything extraneous to these. It may also be affirmed that when the ancients merely flashed an eye, and the right principles of conduct were observed : when they conveyed their ideas without the medium of words, or roused men to moral enthusiasm without the offering of rewards, or induced dread without warning them of punishments, that they did so on the basis of the same supposition. On the same ground it might be asserted by critics that such portions of the way of the ancient rulers as were transmitted by words, and exemplified by actions, such as, for instance, their laws and regulations, and the formalities of government, would not be the medium which sage-like minds would use.

We read in the Book of Changes [1] : "Spiritual intelligence is something innate in the man. It is a mysterious faculty. To elicit trust without speech, is a faculty pertaining to a man's character." The curbing of one's passions and the control of one's desires, lead to the attainment of this spiritual intelligence. The education of the spirit to the limit of intelligence will lead to natural attainments in the world of affairs. It is this which accounts for the rarity of real super-men. He whose heart is under proper control and fully enlightened, whose character is pure and intelligent, has command of all things under heaven. Though the superior man observes but a few simple rules, the influence of such is very far-reaching. He takes from what is near at hand, but the effect is widespread.

Another quotation from the Changes reads [2] : "Speak only after your mind is made up. Act only after full consideration. For when perfected, determination and thought work a transformation " of such a character that the resultant will be the greatest that is possible either to heaven or to man.

Many sections of the Book of History refer to the principles governing the actions and relationships of heaven and men. In this respect the " Hung Fan " is of the greatest importance. In the " Hung Fan " again, which has many references to the subject, the most important are those relating to

[1] Changes, Hsi Ts'e, vol. ii, chap. xii, at end.
[2] Changes, Hsi Ts'e, vol. i, chap. viii.

demeanour, speech, sight, hearing, and thought. Great indeed are those principles which are discovered solely by the sage, and the words which are the vehicle of their innermost thoughts. The resources of their spirit and their peace of mind enable them to penetrate the deepest spiritual mysteries.

The three things which the superior man will not do are (1) to fail to regulate his countenance in the presence of others, (2) to make a faulty utterance, (3) to take a false step. Not to fail in regard to the first of these indicates perfection of demeanour. Not to err in regard to the second shows that he has attained to perfect understanding of the requirements of speech or silence. Not to fail in the third respect shows that he is perfectly conversant with the implications of action or inaction. The way of the superior man is such that in its furthest reaches it cannot be contained by heaven and earth, but in its minutest aspects it is finer than the tip of a hair. In its might, there is nothing under heaven that can resist it, and in its utter simplicity it is incomprehensible.

Amongst the words of the sages which have been handed down to us we find the following : " The great ceremonies are as chaste as heaven and earth, and great music is as harmonious as heaven and earth."

If " nature " is the topic of discussion, then the great ceremonies are its moderating influence, and great music acts as its harmonizer. Moderation and harmony are as penetrating as spiritual intelligence. . . . The influence of the sage affects all created things.

Mencius said,[1] " I am skilful in nourishing my vast, flowing, passion-nature. . . . It fills up all between heaven and earth."

Yang Tzu said, " Demeanour, speech, sight, hearing, and thought are part of the nature, they are as vast as heaven and as deep as earth."

Alas ! that the real significance of ceremonies and music should have been lost for so long, and that those who discourse of the nurture of life and the cultivation of the nature, should all have recourse to Buddhism and Taoism. Should, however,

[1] Mencius, bk. ii, pt. i, chap. ii, par. 11.

the theories of these cults be afforded a free course, ceremonies and music will become purely conventional.

The rulers of Liang and Chin lost their states through encouraging their people to go in for elaborate ceremonies and musical festivals, hoping by such conventional activities to institute successful government. But the reason that ordinary people are ignorant in this respect is because they fail to appreciate the real significance of ceremonies and music. These are mysterious and difficult to apprehend, whereas the teachings of Lao Tzu are very shallow, and not hard to understand.

The Confucian doctrine has as its object the development of one's personal character, while at the same time encouraging a man to apply his principles to practical affairs, not demanding of him that he withdraw from society. But the Buddhist teachings require that a man should wed himself to poverty, dwelling miserably on the hills or in the woods. That according to their ideas is the one way to nourish one's moral life. This enables us to make a comparison on the grounds of practicability and relative ease, between the tenets of Taoism, Buddhism, and Confucianism.

In the matter of rewards and punishments, they offer much the same teaching as the ancients, but the stimulus and restraint which their teachings induce is not the same. With regard to inculcating sympathetic feelings they teach much the same doctrine, but their idea of love is not the same. They are alike in their discourses on wisdom but differ in their ideas of knowledge. Although their utterances seem to be alike, they are not equally potent, or trustworthy as a guide. The principles which they enunciate seem to be akin, but the motive behind them and their object differ.

Principles cannot be exemplified apart from human relationships. . . .

Nowadays Confucian scholars are zealous enough for the doctrine of the sage, but they have the idea that the quicker they sell their principles, the quicker will be their progress. If they get a good price they will serve their master, but if not, they cast off their Confucian robes and engage in business. . . .

There are very few indeed, who having gained their desire for high office, continue to practise the teachings of the sage without wavering. . . .

Confucius said [1] of Yen Hui that "he did not transfer his anger, neither did he commit the same fault twice". He said [2] of him further, "that he had seen him advance but had never seen him stop." My contemporaries give their minds to other things than Yen Hui studied, for by "not transferring his anger" he implied that he always sought for the wrong in himself, and "by not committing the same fault twice" he meant that he desisted from an evil course as soon as he perceived it to be evil. What the ordinary man means by "retreat" Yen Hui terms "progress" and what he terms "injurious" they call "beneficial". In the Changes [3] we read, "Sun (損), the diagram representing 'Injury', means success after preliminary difficulties." This may be appropriately applied to Yen Hui.

The ear is injured by sound, and the eye by the allurement of beauty, the mouth by speech, and the person by activity. That indicates the preliminary difficulty. But by persevering, the ear hears everything, the eye sees everything, speech is always believed, and one's activity always receives support. Is not that ultimate success?

The superior man, during the term of his novitiate, is like a rustic or a child, but when his ideal is attained heaven and earth are not big enough for him, all created things are not sufficient for his investigation and effort, the spirits and demons cannot conceal their ways from him, all the heresies of the philosophers of all schools cannot disturb him. The height of heaven, the nature of the sun, moon, and stars, nature in its expanding and contracting influences, all alike he is able to calculate. The expanse of earth, with its mountains, streams,

[1] Analects, bk. vi, chap. ii.
[2] Analects, bk. ix, chap. xx.
[3] Changes, appendix iii, chap. vii, par. 51.

all created things, and all the regular products of man, he can discourse upon, use, and control. The calendar, astronomical and geological laws, the reason of everything that is created, have all been invented and expounded by the most sincere and wisest sages of the past.

Later generations have received from them their completed work methods, but how can they be expected to know the origin of it all. The commentary on the " Changes " [1] says, " All great achievements, in all their variety, are the work of sages." Which may be applied appropriately to what has been said above.

Hence the ancients, in their discussion of ethical principles, put heaven and earth in the forefront, then personal character, then the " nature ", then the " spirit ". It is the spirit which makes heaven so high, the earth so vast, and which makes the sages the " mate " of heaven and earth. Of all the able charioteers only Tsao Fu (造 父) is renowned, not because his chariot and animals were different from those used by others, but because he had the real spirit of the charioteer. The same with Yi (羿) and archery. There is no difference between modern men and the ancients, as far as their nature is concerned, but the use they make of their " natural endowment " is different. Tsao Fu used his for charioteering, Yi for archery, and Tao Chih (盜 蹠) used it for banditry !

Knowledge of Men (知 人)
(Works, vol. xvii, p. 18.)

When a covetous man becomes honest, a lustful man pure, and a plausible man straight, he does not remain so permanently, for he has made the change because it is advantageous for him to do so.

When Wang Mang [2] (王 莽) was offered a Marquisate, he

---

[1] Cf. Changes, appendix iii, chap. ii, par. 11.

[2] Wang Mang, known as " the usurper " in the fifth month of the first year of Han Ch'eng Huang Ti (漢 成 帝) dynastic period known as " Yung Shih " (永 始), i.e. 16 B.C., was offered the appointment of Hsin Tu Hou

returned the seal, refusing the appointment. But he arrogated to himself the title of emperor, and having received the imperial seal he was content. Such an instance affords an illustration of a covetous man availing himself of " non-avaricious " conduct to further his covetous purposes.

King Kuang of Chin ¹ (晉 王 廣), with the object of gaining the heirship to the throne, hid away his flutes and lyres in secret recesses in the palace. But later on (after he had assumed the reins of government) he brought the State to ruin by the music and licentious practices which he fostered. He affords an instance of a licentious man assuming a veneer of purity to further his own evil purposes.

Cheng Chu ² (鄭 注), in making his proposals for the stabilizing and progress of the government, by his earnest manner and noble demeanour so impressed the ruler and the people, that they were brought into agreement with his ideas, and adopted his proposals to bring peace. But in the end by his wicked conduct he brought ruin upon the State. He affords an illustration of a plausible man assuming a veneer of straightforwardness to further his own evil designs.

Ability to recognize the real character of a man, is the mark of a really wise man, and the difficulty which faces the ruler of the kingdom in this respect is the same now as of old.

(新 都 侯). There is, however, no note as to his having refused the appointment. In the time of Han P'ing Huang Ti (漢 平 帝), A.D. 6, Wang Mang was regent, and poisoned the emperor. He then set up an infant king, styled Ju Tzu Ying (孺 子 嬰), and in the fifth month of A.D. 6 styled himself the " chia Huang Ti " (假 皇 帝) or " acting emperor ". In A.D. 8 or " Ch'u Shih " first year, he usurped the throne, and received the imperial seal.

¹ Chin Kuang Wang (晉 廣 王) was the second son of Sui Wen Ti (隋 文 帝). He killed his father and assumed the throne with the title of Sui Yang Ti (隋 楊 帝). His elder brother should by right have succeeded to the throne, but as he was of a bad character, his father showed his displeasure with his conduct. Kuang noted this, and although by nature he also was of a dissolute disposition, he deliberately feigned chastity and economical ways. By concealing his licentiousness from his father, he deceived the latter into appointing him his heir.

² Cheng Chu belongs to the T'ang dynasty.

DEVOLUTION OF RESPONSIBILITY (委 任)

(Works, vol. xvii, pp. 17, 18.)

The chief difficulty facing a ruler is connected with the devolution of responsibility, while the chief concern of an appointee to public office is to fulfil the duties of his office without incurring blame. It is reasonable that of a man to whom great responsibilities are entrusted great loyalty should be expected. But it is unreasonable to expect great loyalty of a man to whom only small responsibilities are entrusted. As I lack knowledge of other sources, I will try to illustrate my meaning from the Han times.

Han Kao Tsu's policy in this matter was to appoint to office only those whom he could trust, i.e. those whom he considered capable of discharging the duties of any particular post. Otherwise he would just refuse to appoint him. He recognized, too, that every man had his peculiar qualifications for certain work, but not necessarily for work of another type, so he appointed him for the good qualifications which he possessed and ignored his shortcomings in other directions. Further, he recognized that loyalty and deception are relative terms, so he trusted a man to be loyal and did not suspect him of disloyalty, saying in effect, "I employ a man because he is loyal to me, if he is deceiving others, what does that matter?"

On this basis he employed the lawyer Hsiao Ho in the district of Kuan Chung, and ceased to be concerned about the state of things in the area. He appointed Ch'en P'ing, who was a fugitive in banishment, to disburse a sum of over 40,000 taels, and made no inquiry about the accounts. He entrusted Han Hsin, who was a crafty fellow, with an army of a million, and had no doubts about his loyalty.

These three are not generally regarded as loyal officers, but because Kao Tsu made them feel that they possessed his utmost confidence, he made it impossible for a third person to come between them and exercise any divisive influence, so they each one carried out their commissions successfully.

In later generations, those rulers who followed out Han Kao

Tsu's policy rarely failed in this matter, whereas those who did not copy his example, failed disastrously. . . .

The ordinary man has ability for one kind of work and not for another. He is loyal to one person but not to another. It is the right course to entrust a man with heavy responsibilities if it is seen that he has the capacity for the same. If he is considered loyal, it is right to trust him, for trust begets trust. The entrusting of heavy responsibilities to a man makes him respond with energy and loyalty so that he becomes equal to the discharge of them. When mutual confidence exists between ruler and officer, gratitude will be generated in the heart of the latter, and he will do his utmost conscientiously to display his gratitude. Hence arises the saying, "Have no doubts about anyone or anything, and confidence and trust will be begotten."

Su Ch'in [1] (蘇 秦) was not trusted by Ch'in Hui Wang (秦 惠 王), but he became the trusted minister of the Prince of Yen (燕 君). This resulted in Su Ch'in's being able to form many valuable alliances for his master, and his policy became successful because the Duke of Yen treated him with confidence and respect.

If a ruler treats a man like a dog or a pig, he will behave like a dog or a pig. But if he treats him like an honourable officer of State, then his behaviour will be of that character. So it is said that whether an ordinary man is capable or not, loyal or not, depends entirely on the way his ruler treats him.

On Taking up Office (進 說)

(A Warning to two Friends)

(Works, vol. xvii, pp. 15, 16.)

In ancient times unemployed scholars never sought for positions from their superiors, as it was the constant concern of those in high office not to lose the help of an able man. The promotion of men to official service in the past was made on

---

[1] Cf. Essay on Tzu Kung, note 1, p. 347.

the basis of character, or ability, or gift of exposition, or technical skill.

Nowadays, however, that is not the case. For from the highest grade of scholarship to the lowest, the stages of promotion or degradation are strictly regulated by law. It would be quite possible for those whom the ancients regarded as capable and virtuous to be without position now, and that those whom the ancients regarded as capable expositors might find themselves unable to fulfil modern requirements. For if a man does not proceed according to the graded regulations, even though he should be a truly exceptional man, he will find no one to recommend him for office. And even though he be recommended, unless he should conform in every detail to the literary regulations, he would have no chance of selection at the examinations.

However, for one to strive to get official position in such ways as these, is what I regard as demeaning oneself. Mencius said, "No one who demeans himself can correct others." But as a matter of fact, there are no scholars nowadays who do not demean themselves in this way. For there is only this one way to self-advancement. It cannot be, however, that they all are lacking in that self-respect and dignity which characterized the ancients.

In olden times the system obtained of plotting out the land and entrusting it to the people to cultivate. All scholars who had not as yet been given official appointments were the recipients of a plot of land and a house, and so were enabled to live happily and contentedly with their wives and parents. There were also various grades of schools functioning, ranging from the home-school to the college in the capital. There were village schools, district schools, provincial colleges, and the National University. In these it was possible to stay for a while. Shorter or longer courses were open to the student, and in them students and teachers could delight themselves with the musical praises of Yao and Shun. They could exercise, improve, and embellish any gifts that they possessed, until they became so steeped in learning and mind cultivation, became possessed of such high gifts of character and ability, that they could confidently say, "It is impossible that those in high office shall not find use for me." Those in high office simply could not but find them employment.

Now, however, the plotting system no longer obtains. There is no National University, no provincial colleges, no district high schools, no schools in the villages or in the homes. Scholars with no official appointment have not a sufficiency of the means of life to maintain their wives and parents, and they are deprived of any opportunity of improving their character or completing their ability. Their superiors have ceased to recommend them. How can it be otherwise but that scholars should *seek* to advance *themselves* to official position?

If the scholars of the present day are regarded as inferior to those of ancient times, the difference is not in the men but in their circumstances. For different circumstances account for differences in conduct, even in the cases of those whom we term sages and worthies. The fact that Mencius refused to serve in official families, and that Confucius served the family of Chi in an official capacity, was due to the different circumstances obtaining in their particular times.

I have already suggested that nowadays the promotion or rejection of a scholar depends, not upon character or ability, but upon his keeping to the prescribed regulations. There is, however, still another factor to be taken into account. The prejudices of the supervisor of examinations are not always in agreement with the requirements of the regulations governing the examinations. So it often happens that the promotion or rejection of candidates depends upon their ability to conform to the particular prejudices or partialities of the examiner, as well as upon their keeping to the regulations. Again, these supervisors are frequently changed, and so one can never be sure of the particular prejudices or partialities of the examiner who happens to be in charge at the time. There is therefore no certain standard whereby one might gauge the prospects of any candidate.

It may be regarded as not seriously faulty to base the selection of men upon their particular point of view on affairs, but first to make that the criterion of selection, and afterwards to withhold from such a man the opportunity to carry out his views, is surely a serious blemish. When you add to that the further disability of having to consult the prejudices of the examiners, and also not knowing what those prejudices may be through constant changes in the personnel of that office, the situation is extremely serious. In fact the ancient principles in regard to this matter are no longer discernible in the educational world.

In such circumstances I should suggest that unless a man is compelled through force of circumstances to take up office, he will naturally refrain from doing so. For any who are not thus compelled, and yet seek for office, are usually men of no principle.

Yet Yang Shu Ming and his brother have gained positions at the capital by virtue of their father being in a government post. They were not such as I have referred to above, i.e. their circumstances were not such as would compel them to seek office anyhow. They had sufficient means to support their families. But they have taken the " chin shih " examination by doing despite to their principles, and have secured positions by demeaning themselves to the examiners. And yet one does not see that they are satisfied. These two regard themselves as conscientious men, and consider themselves friends of mine. In my fear lest they should remain unaware of the peril of their situation, I have composed this essay by way of warning.

THE TRUE EDUCATIONAL METHOD (原 教)
(Works, vol. xvii, pp. 14, 15.)

The skilled educator goes to work in such an unobtrusive way that the people are led to conform to the ideas of their superiors without knowing how they have been induced to do so. The unskilled educator proceeds in just the opposite way. Under his method the people perceive how they are being instructed, and so fail to respond in the way that their superiors expect them to.

The method of the skilled educator is to see to it that he himself becomes righteous and loyal,[1] the result being that each ruler and minister in the empire becomes righteous and loyal. He himself becomes filial and loving, with the result that all fathers and sons everywhere become filial and loving too. He exercises a gracious kindness towards his own brothers, and the result is seen in the practice of gracious kindness between brothers everywhere. As a husband he behaves courteously to his wife, and courtesy becomes the rule between husbands and wives everywhere. The ultimate result of this is that all rulers behave as rulers should, all ministers behave as ministers should, every father, son, brother, and husband, every wife likewise, all behave as they should behave the one to the other. This is the outcome of instruction by personal example, and leads the people to inquire what they are dependent upon for their moral improvement (i.e. they have become good without being aware that any particular instruction has been given them).

This is what is meant by the expression, that " the people are led to conform to the ideas of their superiors without knowing how they have been induced to do so ".

The unskilled educator pays no attention to such matters, but busies himself devising stringent regulations and numerous prohibitions, issues numberless mandates and warnings, piles up his statutes in the government offices, posts them in all public places, ordering all the people to obey them. They say, " The minister must act as a minister should, the ruler as a ruler, the son as a son, the father as a father ; brothers must not fail to behave as brothers should, nor must husband and wife fail to treat one another as husband and wife should." They further affirm that those who obey these orders will be rewarded, while those who disobey them will be punished.

---

[1] It is the force of personal example, especially by those who occupy superior and influential positions, that is enunciated in this essay. Cf. Analects, book xii, chap. xix. Legge, pp. 258–9.

Those village leaders and family elders who are somewhat slack read out these injunctions occasionally, while those who are more particular expound them daily. Yet with all this care and detail, there are many who through disobedience involve themselves in punishment. Some are called to face the wall in shame, others to endure the hardship of imprisonment, while the more serious offenders suffer execution or banishment. Despite all this the people do not desist from wrongdoing.

This is what is meant by the statement that " the people perceive how they are being instructed, and so fail to respond in the way that their superiors expect them to ".

The skilled educator gets the inner approval of the people without their being conscious of instruction by eye or ear, i.e. he leads them along the line of their own natural inclination. The unskilled educator uses the obvious method of instruction through eye and ear, striving to get the inner approval of the people by methods of compulsion.

The leading of the people along the lines of their own natural inclinations acts like the call of the hills and woods to the beasts and birds, or the call of the streams and the lakes to fish. What need is there of rules and regulations in their case ? The compulsory and external method is like the caging up of birds and beasts, or the enclosing of fish in an artificial pool. The moment that control is withdrawn, they throw off all restraint.

The reason why the ancient times were so fine is due to nothing else but the following of the first principle enunciated above, and the failure of modern times to reach to the ancient standards is attributable to nothing but the following of the second principle.

Should someone ask, " Then are laws and regulations, warnings and orders useless in the education of the people ? " I would reply, " These are external representations of ideas, whereas that to which I refer is something fundamental in itself. To supplant what is fundamental by what is merely an external representation of it, is, to my mind, quite wrong."

On the Error of Reverting to the Ancient Ways (太 古)

(Works, vol. xvii, p. 14.)

The ancients were only slightly superior to the birds and beasts.[1] The sages in their loathing of this state of things, made their laws and regulations, to emphasize and develop further the distinctions that should subsist between man and the brute creation.

Later on, however, extravagance in the matter of attire and palatial dwellings, and the love of sensuous delights, obsessed the minds of the people to such an extent that the rightful relationships between ruler and minister, father and son, older and younger brothers, husband and wife all failed to be maintained. The principles of benevolence and righteousness failed to nurture the nature of men: ceremonies and music failed to control their passions: laws and ordinances failed to keep them from crime, so that it seemed as though they were recklessly reverting to their kinship with the birds and beasts.

The sages had ceased to arise, the people were so ignorant that they knew of no method whereby they might educate their fellows on to higher planes of life, so they could think only of leading them back to the ancient ways.

But if the way of the ancients had been practicable for ever, what need would there have been for the sages to make their laws and regulations in connection therewith? The fact that it was felt necessary so to do, demonstrates clearly that the ancient way was impracticable (or unsatisfactory).

But now for people to seek to lead their fellows back to that, is like having cast off the ways of the birds and beasts and

[1] Cf. Mencius, bk. iv, pt. ii, ch. xix, par. 1, where Mencius writes, " That whereby man differs from the lower animals is but small. The mass of people cast it away, while superior men preserve it." (Legge's translation.) The difference would seem to be that of moral consciousness, the " tao hsin " (道 心) of the Book of History, part ii, bk. ii, chap. ii, par. 15. But the " tao hsin " itself is regarded there as " minute ". Really the difference between the animals and man may be considered vast, as the implications of the possession of this moral consciousness are exceedingly great. However, Wang An Shih is thinking of the ancient days before this moral consciousness was highly developed, when the differences themselves were not so marked.

then reverting to the same. What help is there in such a method towards the improvement of the social order (or the advance of civilization)?

My own opinion is that responsible officials, in their efforts to deal with a disorderly situation, should advocate some positive method of improvement, and that they are either stupid or misled when they advocate a reversion to the ancient ways.

On Revenge (復 讎 解)

(Works, vol. xvii, pp. 19, 20.)

The question as to the rights or wrongs of "revenge" (i.e. the question of whether he who kills the murderer of his father or elder brother is justified in so doing) should not arise if the empire is properly governed.

With an enlightened ruler on the throne, and loyal officials employed throughout the land, cases of killing without just cause would naturally be very rare indeed. If such a case did perchance occur, the son or younger brother of the victim would have recourse to the local officials. If the officials did not heed his appeal and administer the law justly, he could then carry his complaint to his superior, and so on right to the emperor, who would certainly devise proper measures of punishment, not only for the murderer, but also for the officials who had failed to give proper attention to the case.

However, in a time of prevailing disorder, there would be no officials whom one could inform, and so we find it recorded in the Book of History that "none of the guilty could be dealt with constitutionally, so the people arose and exacted private vengeance". So that the idea of exacting private vengeance arose from the fact that there was no opportunity of laying complaints before properly constituted officials, and because those who were guilty of murder could not be dealt with according to properly constituted laws.

In such times as we have just outlined, and in view of all the circumstances, it would be permissible, according to the

Confucian ideals, for a son or a younger brother to take steps
to exact vengeance on the murderer of his father or elder brother.
It is this which accounts for the fact that we have the duty of
exacting vengeance outlined in the Annals and the Rites (禮 記),
for the reference in each case is to a time of disorder. In the
Annals we read that it was wrong for a son to exact vengeance in
the case of a father suffering death deservedly, for it would be
immoral for one to do violence to public justice simply out
of personal motives. The Annals, however, permit the son's
exacting vengeance in the case of the father's suffering death
from any other cause than violation of the laws, because one's
indubitable sense of filial indebtedness should take precedence
over a doubtful sense of duty.

The statement which is found in the Chow Kuan (周 官),[1]
viz. " That all who kill another man in the execution of vengeance
shall be considered guiltless if they shall have informed the
officials in writing," is to my mind not the true law of Chow
Kung. For, as I have said above, it was only because the
times were disorderly, and because of the impossibility of officials
taking properly constituted legal action, that the system of
private vengeance arose. But in the times of Chow Kung,
when there were such officials, if they did not take proper
action in regard to murder, and permitted the son or younger
brother to devise measures for vengeance on their own initiative,
it seems to me they would be unworthy of the name of officials,
or of their appointments and emoluments. But as a matter
of fact, in those ancient times, cases of murder were investigated
most closely, and there was the greatest apprehension lest justice
should not be done. Hence arose the saying, " Rather err on
the side of leniency in administering the laws, than slay an
innocent man."

But in regard to the expression " That he who kills another
man in the course of executing vengeance shall be considered
guiltless if he shall have informed the officials in writing ".
Does it follow that he who is described as the avenger is thereby

---

[1] See Chow Kuan Hsin I (周 官 新 義), vol. xv, p. 8.

WANG AN SHIH

permitted to take vengeance (on the ground that he was justified in doing so) ? If so, then not only should it have been feasible to have made proper complaint, but the culprit ought to have been dealt with (by the officials). Why then should such a man not have been executed by the officials, instead of allowing the case to be left to the vengeance of a private individual ?

These considerations lead me to infer that this could not have been the law laid down by the Duke of Chow.

Should the question be raised whether in a disorderly time, if private vengeance should be prohibited, it would be right to commit suicide by way of exacting vengeance, or whether no vengeance should be exacted (in this form) so as to preserve the maintenance of sacrifices to the deceased, I would reply, " That if vengeance is permitted, and vengeance is not exacted, it is unfilial. But to exact vengeance at the expense of maintaining the sacrificial succession, is also unfilial. In the latter case, it is better to keep the feeling of vengeance in one's heart to the end of one's day. That vengeance cannot be exacted in such circumstances is the will of heaven (天), but it is still possible for oneself not to forget the feeling of vengeance. To deny oneself in reverence for the will of heaven, while at the same time not forgetting one's father or elder brother, is surely right."

FORTUNE TELLING (推 命 對)

(Works, vol. xvii, p. 20.)

In Wu Li there lived a well-known scholar who was reputed to be skilled in forecasting one's future, who could tell you whether you would attain to high official rank, or would remain a commoner, and whether happiness or misfortune awaited you.

A friend urged me to inquire of him, but I excused myself. A day or two later, he once more urged the matter upon my attention. So I replied, " As to whether I attain to high position or not, that matter is in the ' lap of the gods ', but whether I become virtuous or depraved is entirely within my own power."

So I do not need any other person to tell me about what I know
to be in my own power. And as a matter of fact, I am not
altogether unenlightened as to what Heaven can do for me.
If I am of worthy character, and have qualifications equal to
the demands of high office, then the biggest of official salaries
is mine by right. If in spite of that, I am compelled to pass
my days in poverty and live among the common herd, it must
be due to the fact that my time has not yet come. Should,
however, my character be of the worthless kind, and my qualifications such as do not fit me for high office, then I should have
no regrets if my food is of the simplest. If perchance in spite
of that, I should attain by sheer good fortune to high rank
and become wealthy, it would be quite unjust and morally
wrong. As I am well enough informed about the truth and
cogency of these statements, of what use is it to appeal to a
fortune teller ?

I would urge further, that such matters as suffering and
felicity are alien to the thinking of a superior man. He is of
necessity bound to abide in love and walk in the paths of
righteousness. It is quite foreign to his conceptions that felicity
may be gained by acting contrary to loving and virtuous principles. When through following hard after right and love
he suffers misfortune, even then he does not lightly give up
his principles.

Let us recall that Wen Wang suffered imprisonment in Yu Li
(羑 里), and that Confucius received a fright in K'uang (匡).
Such sagely men as these could not avoid trouble and misfortune,
because they were solely concerned to maintain their principles.

Should the question be raised, that if rank and the lack of
it are the ordinances of heaven, then also any case of the
unworthy gaining high rank, or the worthy failing to get such,
must also be thus decreed by heaven, I would reply that far
from their being so decreed, they are cases of men not con-
forming to the way of heaven.

It is the purpose of heaven in creating men that the worthy
should control the unworthy. It is therefore right that the
worthy should occupy high position, and that the unworthy

should not hold such offices. That I repeat is the ordination of heaven. But it is possible for man to conform to that way or to depart from it. If the way of men agrees with the ideas of heaven, then the worthy will be in office and the unworthy not. If, however, there is conflict between the way of men and the ideas of heaven, then the unworthy will be in office and the worthy out. Of course, there will be times when the ways of men and the ideas of heaven get confused and there is neither complete agreement or disagreement between them, in which event uncertainty in the issue will arise, and you may have the worthy either in or out of office, and the unworthy likewise.

In the times of Yao and Shun, worthy men like Chi, Hsieh, and Kao Yao were in office, and unworthy fellows like Huan Tou, San Miao, Kun, and Kung Kung were out of office. That affords an illustration of the ways of men agreeing with the ideas of heaven. But in the time of Chow and Chieh, the rascal Fei Lien was promoted to high office, and worthy men like Wei Tzu, Chi Tzu, and Pi Kan were rejected. That is an instance in which the ways of men and the ideas of heaven are in conflict.

Since the times of Han and Wei, the promotion of worthy or unworthy men, and the rejection of the same, have been in a state of confusion and uncertainty, because the ways of men and the ideas of heaven have been partly in agreement and partly in conflict.

The ordinances of heaven are single, but the time in which a man lives does not always permit of his career being in line with the same.

Therefore the superior man cultivates his character as he waits for the will of heaven to be fulfilled in his own person, and maintains his principles, so that when the appropriate time comes he will be ready for it. To such a one, rank or the lack of it, misfortune or felicity, alike are no impediment.

If anyone fails to exert himself to maintain the principles of love and right, and relies upon the ability of the fortune-teller to prognosticate his future correctly, all his energy will be dissipated on these trifling and worthless matters, and in the end he will be enslaved by such false and superstitious notions.

On Yang Chu and Mo Ti (楊 墨)

(Works, vol. xvii, p. 9.)

The doctrines of Yang and Mo may be said to attain to the teachings of Confucius in one point, but to fall short of them in a hundred others. Anyway, the doctrines of Confucius embrace the teachings of Yang and Mo, and are applicable to all times and circumstances.[1]

The teachings of Mo Ti are summarized in the sentence, that "if by rubbing his body smooth he could benefit his fellows he would do so". The teachings of Yang Chu are likewise summarized in the sentence, "He would not pluck so much as a hair out of his head for the benefit of his fellows."

Take the illustration of the great Yü, and his attitude to his fellows. In a period of nine years (during his labours on the floods) he passed the door of his home three times, and even though he heard the crying of his child, refrained from entering or saying a word to him. He surely is deserving of the merit of "living for his fellows".

Think again of Yen Hui (顏 回) and his attitude to himself, how he used the meanest vessels and consumed the coarsest

---

[1] Such I take to be the significance of the clause 無可無不可者. For according to the teachings of Confucius, the ruling principle of conduct was to be sought in the nature of the times and circumstances obtaining. Cf. Mencius, bk. v, pt. ii, ch. i, v. 5. Legge's Classics, second edition revised, p. 372, where Legge in translating the phrase 孔子聖之時者也 coins the adjective "timeous" to give expression to the idea that Confucius did at every "time" what the circumstances of it required. According to this tenet it would be possible for a man, in taking a certain line of conduct, to be right at one time and wrong at another. For example, in the instances quoted of Yü and Yen Hui, it would have been wrong for Yü to act as Yen Hui did, and wrong also for Yen Hui to act as Yü had done. The defective character of Yang Chu and Mo Tzu's teachings is seen (thinks Wang An Shih) in relation to this very thing. The former adopted "self-interest" as his universal principle, as the latter adopted "altruistic-love" as his. Both failed to have regard to circumstances, or to adapt their principles to the nature of the times. This "rigidity" was their failing.

food, living a lonely life in the lowliest of humble lanes, utterly disregarding the disorderly state of the country. He surely is worthy of the epithet of " living for oneself ".[1]

Why is it then that in respect of living for others and living for oneself Mo Ti and Yang Chu are said to offend against the teachings of the sages ? Because as has been said above, while their teachings agree with those of the sages in one respect, they are at variance with them in a hundred others. So that those who follow Yang Chu's doctrines are regarded as unrighteous, and those who follow Mo Ti's doctrines are deemed non-benevolent (不 仁).

Only the followers of Confucius neglect no single aspect of righteousness and benevolence and in practice fail in nothing that may be considered as essentially related thereto.

In their failure in respect of righteousness and benevolence, and in the failure to view the world (of ethical relationships) as a whole, Yang and Mo are alike. But in respect of the reason why their teachings are considered an offence to Confucianism, the matter is worthy of discussion.

The main tenet of Yang Chu's teachings is " self-interest ". But " self-interest " is but the first principle of the Confucian doctrine. The *summum bonum* of Mo Ti's teachings is " altruism ". But " altruism " in the Confucian system is only of secondary importance (末).

The " candidate " of the Confucian school puts himself and his interests first, and only when he has surplus (thought and energy) should he, in accordance with the circumstances obtaining at the time, devote himself to the concerns of his fellows. For then, it is incumbent upon him to do so. So it may be said that the learning of the Confucian disciple, while at first it is not directly related to " living for others ", in the end enables him to do so. When he begins his studies, should his moral reserves be insufficient for the control of himself, he would be using his energies mistakenly in attempting to live for others. If he misuses his energies in this way, although his object may be to live for others, he will be unable to do so.

<hr />

[1] Cf. Mencius, bk. iv, pt. ii, ch. xxix.

Looking at the matter in this way, Yang Chu's doctrine, although it is inadequate from the standpoint of "living for others", is certainly fully enlightened on the subject of "living for oneself".

But as regards the object of Mo Tzu, although he aimed at living for others, I am convinced that he could not attain to it. Alas, alas! that Yang Chu who knew the importance of living for himself, fell short of the way of the great Yü, so that he is deemed to be imperfectly enlightened, and that Mo Ti broke down the distinctions (which should subsist) between men and things, and near and remote relationships, and at the same time accepted the concerns of the whole world as his responsibility. It is this which transformed his desire to benefit others into a universal calamity. Was that not too extreme a doctrine?

The conclusion of the whole matter is that Yang Chu's teaching is relatively nearer to the doctrine of Confucius, and that of Mo Ti relatively remote from orthodoxy. They are both different from Confucianism, but distinctions should be made between them in regard to the reason why they offend the Confucianists.

On Lao Tzu (老 子)

(Works, vol. xvii, pp. 9, 10.)

" Tao " (道) has primary and secondary aspects. In its primary aspect it is the cause of all existing things, whereas in its secondary aspect it brings all things to completion. In its primary aspect it may be said to belong to the "natural sphere", for it produces all things without the aid of man. In its secondary aspect, when it assumes form and substance, it needs the aid of man to complete it.

It is in connection with its primary aspect as defined above that one may speak of a sage as using neither speech nor energy. But in its secondary aspect as defined above, the sage cannot dispense with either speech or energy.

This accounts for the fact that in ancient times, when the throne was occupied by sages, who felt responsible for all affairs, they realized it was incumbent upon them to devise ceremonies, music, laws, and regulations, in order that all things might be made complete.

It can be said, therefore, that the sages devoted themselves solely to the work of bringing things to their realizable perfection, and that they did not discourse upon the cause of all things. For the creative cause wields its effortless sway in the natural sphere where the efforts of man are unavailing.

Lao Tzu, however, would disagree with this point of view. For he considered that the material universe was unworthy of discussion or human effort, so he rejected all discourse upon ceremonies, music, laws, and regulations, and talked only of " tao " (道). That, however, is due to his shallow thinking on the ultimate nature of things, and to his excessive concentration on matters too high for the human intellect.

For if " tao " is entirely natural, what need is there for anyone to do anything? But it assumes form and substance (as has been explained above), and in that aspect of it it is essential that the speech and energy of man should be employed.

In his writings Lao Tzu says, " The thirty spokes of a cart wheel are related to one hub. But before they have their use in relation to the cart they already have their use (in principle)." But labour such as is involved in cutting and shaping, cannot be employed on something which has no material existence. But the " wu " (無), or immaterial principle, belongs to the " natural " sphere, and cannot be worked on.

The cart-builder knows how to make spokes and hubs, but is unconcerned with the immaterial principle of things. But it is only when the cart is complete with spokes and hub that it is of any real use. If the cart-builder only knew about the utility of the immaterial principle, and refrained from making spokes and hubs, then his cart-building method would be extremely irrational.

There are some who while cognizant of the fact that immaterial principles are essential to the utility of a cart, are unable to explain how these may contribute to the same, as there are others who know that immaterial principles are essential to the government of a State but cannot explain wherein their utility consists. The fact that immaterial principles are of use to the cart is due to the presence of spokes and hub in the cart structure, and the fact that immaterial principles are of use to the government of the state is due to the existence of ceremonies, music, laws, and regulations in connection with the same. A person who imagines that he can dispense with spokes and hubs in the making of a cart, or with ceremonies, music, etc., in the government of a state, is something of a greenhorn.

On Chuang Tzu (莊 周 上) I

(Works, vol. xvii, pp. 10, 11.)

There are various opinions extant upon the teachings of Chuang Tzu. Earnest devotees of Confucianism assert that his writings are deliberately opposed to Confucius, as he believed that his heresies represented the truth. They affirm that his books should be burnt, and his disciples boycotted, as the question of the correctness or otherwise of his teachings is not worthy of discussion.

Such are the opinions of the earnest Confucianist.

On the other hand, those who are partial to Chuang Tzu affirm that his strong point lies in the fact that according to his faith material things are of no concern. They also deny that he was ignorant of the main tenets of Confucianism, viz. practical sympathy and sense of duty (仁 義), asserting that he regarded these as comparatively of minor significance in that they are altogether inadequate to represent the goal of man's moral effort. They deny also that he was ignorant of ceremonies and music (禮 樂), asserting that he regarded these as of comparatively little worth in that they are incapable in themselves of transforming the characters and lives of the people.

Lao Tzu said, " It is only when a man fails to attain to ' tao ' (道), i.e. the ideal of life, that he is termed virtuous (德) : it is

only when he fails to attain to virtue that he is termed
'sympathetic' (仁): it is only when he fails to attain to
'sympathy' that he is termed 'dutiful' (義): and it is
only when he fails to attain to a sense of duty that he is termed
'considerate' (禮)." [1]

This statement shows that he was by no means unacquainted
with the main tenets of Confucianism (仁 義 禮 樂), but also
shows that he regarded them as being of secondary importance
to " tao " or " the supreme principle of life ".

While the opinion of the devotees of Confucianism may be
considered laudable, I must say they have come to it without
really trying to arrive at Chuang Tzu's real meaning, while
that of those who are partial to Chuang Tzu shows that they
are acquainted with what he wrote, but that they too have
failed to perceive his real intent.

The beneficent influence of the ancient rulers had exhausted
itself by the times of Chuang Tzu. Public life had become
thoroughly artificial and depraved, honesty and simplicity
being marked by their absence. Even the scholarly and official
classes had lost all real sense of proportion, despising the virtue
of self-respect and devoting themselves to self-interest. They
utterly failed to comprehend the inner significance of " con-
siderateness " and " sense of duty ", rejecting them as of no
account, and devoted themselves solely to the securing of
personal advantage and the avoidance of personal loss. This
they did with such shamelessness, that they would not regret
the loss of life itself in their lust for gain. Gradually they got
so immersed in this struggle for material prosperity that it
became practically hopeless to redeem the situation.

Chuang Tzu perceived the ruinous effect of all this, and
thought out his doctrine as a remedy for the universal disease,
hoping thereby to reform public thought and practices, and
bring back the people to a truer conception of life. But in his
over-anxiety to bring about a better state of things, he overstepped the mark. For in regarding the Confucian ethic

---

[1] Tao Te Ching (道 德 經), chap. xxxviii.

ESSAYS

387

(仁 義 禮 樂) as inadequate for his purpose, and by making
out that right and wrong were the same, that one's neighbour
and oneself were of equal importance, that advantage and
disadvantage were in no wise different one from the other,
and by seeking for an inner sense of satisfaction as the supreme
good, his efforts at reform were defective. For supposing that
his ideas were adopted, one would fear, and I think that he
himself would fear, that if later generations accepted his theories
at face value the really pure doctrine of heaven and earth, and
the great model of the ancients which was based on that, would
be lost to their view.

So Chuang Tzu repented, and in his later tracts explained
himself as follows: "The Odes morally instruct the will:
the History is useful for everyday life: the Rites are a guide
to conduct: Music inclines to harmony: the Changes instruct
one in the operation of the great natural forces: and the Annals
enlighten one as to one's duty." [1]

In the light of all this we cannot say that Chuang Tzu was
unacquainted with the sages.

He says again, " Just as in the case of the eye, the ear, the
nose, and the mouth, each has its peculiar function, and none
is able to take the place of the other, so the various schools of
philosophy have each their own peculiar contribution to make
to their age." [1]   He used this illustration in reference to the
doctrine of the sages, so that he must have thought of completeness in connection with their doctrines and not in connection with his own teachings or those of any other school.
Moreover, Chuang Tzu himself classes his teachings with those
of Sung Yen (宋 鈃), Shen Tao (愼 到), Mo Ti (墨 翟), and
Lao Tzu (老 聃), describing them all as teachers who emphasized
one aspect of truth and not the whole, and with the object of
showing that while their teachings were of practical and
particular value they did not necessarily represent the complete
and universal doctrine.

So it is impossible to deny that Chuang Tzu had the idea of

[1] Chuang Tzu, T'ien Hsia P'ien (天 下 篇). Works, chap. xxxiii.

reforming his age and maintaining the position of the sages' teaching.

The chaste purity of Po I, and the compromising policy of Liu Hsia Hui, both had their contribution to make to the reform of their particular age.[1] Chuang Tzu in his effort may be said to be their compeer.[2] But in his actual statements he must be regarded as heretical, comparatively speaking. For he must be said to have proceeded to excess in his reform policy. In correcting a crooked stick the object is to make it straight, but if the correcting process is carried too far, it becomes crooked again. Chuang Tzu himself said, " Mo Ti was all right in his purpose, but in carrying it out he erred." [3] As we endeavour to estimate the nature of Chuang Tzu's ideal, and investigate his method of carrying it into effect, one finds no difference between him and Mo Ti.

So that readers of Chuang Tzu's works, who approve of his idea in writing his books, but disapprove of the ideas expressed therein, may be said to be intelligent readers of his writings. For that is the way in which Chuang Tzu himself would wish later readers to read him.

But modern students of Chuang Tzu use him to do despite to Confucius, saying, " Great are the teachings of Chuang Tzu, so deep that Confucianists cannot comprehend them."

That such, in their ignorance of his real meaning, should regard as valuable anything that is different from the sages' teaching is truly pitiable.

On Chuang Tzu (莊 周 下) 2

(Works, vol. xvii, p. 11.)

Scholars revile Chuang Tzu for his opposition to the teachings of Yao, Shun, and Confucius. But in my reading of his works,

[1] Mencius, bk. v, pt. ii, chap. i, pars. 1–5. Also cf. bk. ii, pt. i, chap. ix, pars. 1 and 2.
[2] i.e. Chuang Tzu was like Po I and Liu Hsia Hui in that he adopted an attitude to current thought and practice which was designed to correct the evil of his particular age.
[3] Chuang Tzu, T'ien Hsia P'ien (天 下 篇), as above.

I find that there is much that is of a deep parabolic nature. Mencius said, " Those who explain the odes may not insist on one term so as to do violence to a sentence, nor on a sentence so as to do violence to the general scope. They must try with their thoughts to meet that scope, and then we shall apprehend it." [1] Those who defame Chuang Tzu do so because they have read his works without penetrating to the meaning.

Chuang Tzu said,[2] " The ruler should control the empire without effort. But the people must strive to be of service to the empire."

Moreover, he himself lived in a disorderly age, and experienced many difficulties, so that he remained in obscurity and afforded no opportunity to men to estimate his practical ability. But who can say that none of his ideas could be used in practical affairs of state or in the family ? The character of the age in which he lived, and the character of the rulers who were then in power, led to their not availing themselves of his help.

When he refused the call of the ruler of Ch'u by quoting the illustration of the sacrifical animal for the Imperial court,[3] he showed in that brave and perilous statement his warning to the men who were desirous of taking up office in a disorderly age. For we cannot think that a man of Chuang Tzu's ability could act stupidly in the matter of taking or refusing office, or that he would shrink from sacrificing his own interests (if principle demanded it).

He was rather one of those who Confucius referred to as [4] " living in retirement, but expressing his mind freely upon everything ".

But as the theories he advocated were contrary to the orthodox teaching, it was natural that he should be regarded as an offence to the followers of Confucius.

Such attainments as were possible to the mediocre man, were carefully expounded and meticulously illustrated by the

---

[1] Mencius, bk. v, pt. i, chap. iv, par. 2. Following Legge's translation.
[2] Chuang Tzu, T'ien Hsia P'ien. Tract 33 of Works.
[3] Chuang Tzu, Works, Tract 32. " Lieh Yü K'ou " (列 禦 寇).
[4] Analects, bk. xviii, chap. viii, par. 4.

sages. If their exposition failed to be sufficiently clear or if in carrying out their instructions they failed to exercise sufficient care, then the public life suffered proportionately.

But that which is beyond the capacity of the mediocre man is held by the sage in the innermost recesses of his heart, and he describes it in vague fashion. Should he attempt to go into too much detail in this connection, the people would be led astray. If tremendous labour is requisite to get the people to understand one's meaning, and if argument of the greatest detail is necessary to persuade them to carry out the teaching, it shows that they are not capable of receiving instruction in higher things.

How sad that Chuang Tzu, who was so able at propounding truths, remained unenlightened on this point (i.e. he had erred in his attempt to expound deep truths to those who were incapable of receiving them).

APPENDICES

CHRONOLOGICAL TABLE OF THE SUNG DYNASTY

A.D. 960–1278

NORTHERN SUNG

Emperor		Accession	Title of Reign		Date adopted
T'ai Tsu	(太祖)	960	Chien Lung	(建 隆)	960
			Ch'ien Te	(乾 德)	963
			K'ai Pao	(開 寶)	968
			T'ai P'ing	(太 平)	976
T'ai Tsung	(太 宗)	976	Hsing Kuo	(興 國)	976
			Yung Hsi	(雍 熙)	984
			Tuan Kung	(端 拱)	988
			Shun Hua	(淳 化)	990
			Chih Tao	(至 道)	995
Chen Tsung	(眞 宗)	998	Hsien P'ing	(咸 平)	998
			Ching Te	(景 德)	1004
			Ta Chung	(大 中)	1008
			Hsiang Fu	(祥 符)	1008
			T'ien Hsi	(天 禧)	1017
Jen Tsung	(仁 宗)	1023			
Ying Tsung	(英 宗)	1064			
Shen Tsung	(神 宗)	1068			
Che Tsung	(哲 宗)	1086			
Hui Tsung	(徽 宗)	1101			
Ch'in Tsung	(欽 宗)	1126			

4 7 0 2 7okstop

Emperor		Accession	Title of Reign		Date adopted
Kao Tsung	(高 宗)	1127	Chien Yen	(建 炎)	1127
			Shao Hsing	(紹 興)	1131
Hsiao Tsung	(孝 宗)	1163	Lung Hsing	(隆 興)	1163
			Ch'ien Tao	(乾 道)	1165
			Shun Hsi	(淳 熙)	1174
			Shao Hsi	(紹 熙)	1190
Kuang Tsung	(光 宗)	1190			
Ning Tsung	(寧 宗)	1195			
Li Tsung	(理 宗)	1225			
Tu Tsung	(度 宗)	1265			
Kung Ti	(恭 帝)	1275			
Tuan Tsung	(端 宗)	1276			
Ti Ping	(帝 昺)	1278			

FROM THE DATE OF WANG AN SHIH'S BIRTH TO THE REMOVAL OF CAPITAL
TO SOUTH

Emperor	Title of Period	Year	Date	Emperor	Title of Period	Year	Date
Chen	T'ien	5th	1021			3rd	1043
Tsung	Hsi					4th	1044
(眞 宗)	(天禧)					5th	1045
	Ch'ien	1st	1022			6th	1046
	Hsing					7th	1047
	(乾 興)					8th	1048
Jen Tsung	T'ien	1st	1023		Huang Yu	1st	1049
(仁 宗)	Sheng	2nd	1024		(皇 祐)	2nd	1050
	(天 聖)	3rd	1025			3rd	1051
		4th	1026			4th	1052
		5th	1027			5th	1053
		6th	1028				
		7th	1029		Chih Ho	1st	1054
		8th	1030		(至 和)	2nd	1055
		9th	1031				
					Chia Yu	1st	1056
	Ming Tao	1st	1032		(嘉 祐)	2nd	1057
	(明 道)	2nd	1033			3rd	1058
						4th	1059
	Ching Yu	1st	1034			5th	1060
	(景 祐)	2nd	1035			6th	1061
		3rd	1036			7th	1062
		4th	1037			8th	1063
	Pao Yuan	1st	1038	Ying	Chih	1st	1064
	(寶 元)	2nd	1039	Tsung	P'ing	2nd	1065
				(英 宗)	(治 平)	3rd	1066
	K'ang	1st	1040			4th	1067
	Ting						
	(康 定)			Shen	Hsi Ning	1st	1068
				Tsung	(熙 寧)	2nd	1069
	Ch'ing Li	1st	1041	(神 宗)		3rd	1070
	(慶 曆)	2nd	1042			4th	1071

Emperor	Title of Period	Year	Date	Emperor	Title of Period	Year	Date
		5th	1072		Ching Kuo	1st	1101
		6th	1073		(靖 國)		
		7th	1074				
		8th	1075		Ts'ung	1st	1102
		9th	1076		Ning	2nd	1103
		10th	1077		(崇 寧)	3rd	1104
						4th	1105
	Yuan	1st	1078			5th	1106
	Feng	2nd	1079				
	(元 豐)	3rd	1080		Ta Kuan	1st	1107
		4th	1081		(大 觀)	2nd	1108
		5th	1082			3rd	1109
		6th	1083			4th	1110
		7th	1084				
		8th	1085		Cheng Ho	1st	1111
					(政 和)	2nd	1112
Che	Yuan Yu	1st	1086			3rd	1113
Tsung	(元 祐)	2nd	1087			4th	1114
(哲 宗)		3rd	1088			5th	1115
		4th	1089			6th	1116
		5th	1090			7th	1117
		6th	1091		Ch'ung	1st	1118
		7th	1092		Ho		
		8th	1093		(重 和)		
	Shao	1st	1094		Hsuan	1st	1119
	Sheng	2nd	1095		Ho	2nd	1120
	(紹 聖)	3rd	1096		(宣 和)	3rd	1121
		4th	1097			4th	1122
						5th	1123
	Yuan Fu	1st	1098			6th	1124
	(元 符)	2nd	1099			7th	1125
		3rd	1100				
					Ching	1st	1126
Hui	Chien	1st	1101		K'ang		
Tsung	Chung				(靖 康)		
(徽 宗)	(建 中)					2nd	1127

394

OUTLINE OF THE REFORM POLICY

Date.	Event.
1069, 2nd month.	Wang An Shih appointed vice-Grand Councillor.
1069, 2nd month.	Financial Reorganization Bureau established, with Wang An Shih, Ch'en Sheng Chih, Lü Hui Ch'ing and Tseng Pu in charge.
1069, 4th month.	Commission of eight appointed to make tour of inspection of economic conditions throughout the country. This commission included Ch'eng Hao.
1069, 6th month.	Wang An Shih impeached by Lü Hui.
1069, 7th month.	"Economical Transport and Distribution Measure" promulgated.
1069, 9th month.	"Agricultural Loans Measure" promulgated.
1069, 11th month.	Han Chiang succeeds Ch'en Sheng Chih in the Financial Reorganization Bureau.
1069, 11th month.	Appointment of forty-one officials to supervise the operation of the New Laws in all districts.
1070, 1st month.	Ssu Ma Kuang appeals for abolition of the Financial Reorganization Bureau, and for the abrogation of the Agricultural Loans Measure.
1070, 2nd month.	Ssu Ma Kuang refuses preferred appointment of vice-President of the Board of War.
1070, 3rd month.	Reforms in the Official Examination System instituted.
1070, 4th month.	Chao Pien (vice-Grand Councillor) resigns as a protest against the numerous retirements of important officials for their opposition to the Reform Policy. Han Chiang appointed in his place.

Date.	*Event.*
1070, 5th month.	Financial Reorganization Bureau affiliated with the Board of Finance, and Lü Hui Ch'ing appointed as Head of the Revenue Office, under which the Financial Reorganization Bureau would be placed.
1070, 5th month.	Authority for the appointment of military officials transferred to the Civil Affairs Legislative Assembly.
1070, 7th month.	Su Shih criticizes the Reform Policy and is transferred to Hang Chow.
1070, 8th month.	Lü Hui Ch'ing resigns on account of mother's death.
	Ssu Ma Kuang transferred to Yung Hsing Chun.
1070, 10th month.	Ch'en Sheng Chih resigns on account of mother's death.
1070, 12th month.	Redistribution of Regular Army in different centres.
1070, 12th month.	" Militia Act " promulgated.
	Wang An Shih promoted to Grand Councillor.
	" Public Services Act " promulgated.
1071, 1st month.	Stocks of Kuang Hui Granary converted into capital fund for the operation of the Agricultural Loans Measure.
1071, 2nd month.	Revised regulations for the " Chin Shih " or D.Litt. examination promulgated.
	Wang An Shih in sole power in the Grand Council.
	Special Inspectorate set up to report on officials hindering the Reform Policy.
	Deepening of the Pien River started.
1071, 4th month.	Ssu Ma Kuang granted a Sinecure at Lo Yang.
1071, 5th month.	Corea sends tribute to the Chinese Court.
1071, 6th month.	Ou Yang Hsiu stops distribution of Agricultural Loans in Ch'ing Chow Fu, and eventually resigns all offices.

Date.	*Event.*
1071, 8th month.	Wang Fang, son of Wang An Shih, appointed as Teacher in the Imperial family.
1071, 10th month.	National University divided into three Departments.
1072, 1st month.	Bureau set up for the intimidation and control of recalcitrant officials.
1072, 3rd month.	" Trade and Barter " Measure promulgated.
1072, 5th month.	" Militia Mounts Measure " promulgated.
1072, 5th month.	Wang An Shih threatens to resign but is persuaded to continue in office.
	? Wang An Shih presents his memorial of " Five Matters ".
1072, 8th month.	T'ang Chung attacks Wang An Shih in Imperial presence.
1072, 8th month.	" Equitable Land Tax Measure " promulgated.
1072, 10th month.	Hsi Ho territory made a Circuit of the Empire.
1073, 3rd month.	" Bureau for editing new interpretation of the Classics " established, with Wang An Shih, Wang Fang, and Lü Hui Ch'ing in charge.
1073, 6th month.	Organization of Arsenal Board at Wang Fang's suggestion.
1073, 9th month.	Celebration of Wang Shao's victory in the north-west.
	" Trade Tax Measure " promulgated.
1073, 10th month.	Scheme for straightening Yellow River started.
	Unification of Copper currency (noted).
1074, 3rd month.	" Liao " or Iron Tartars send an embassy to discuss the northern boundary.
1074, 4th month.	Drought and incident of Cheng Hsieh.
	Temporary suspension of the various new Measures, followed by rain.
	Restoration of all new Measures with the exception of the " Trade Tax Measure ".
	Wang An Shih resigns from Grand Council and is appointed as governor of Chiang Ning Fu.

Date.	*Event.*
	Han Chiang appointed Grand Councillor and Lü Hui Ch'iang vice-Grand Councillor. Reform Policy maintained in general by the influence of these two.
1075, 2nd month.	Wang An Shih returns to his post as Grand Councillor. Second embassy from the Iron Tartars anent the northern boundary.
1075, 4th month.	Ch'en Sheng Chih transferred from Board of War to Yang Chow.
1075, 6th month.	New Interpretation of the Odes, History, and Chow Kuan, presented to the throne, and ordered to be used by the Educational Authorities.
1075, 7th month.	The demands of the Iron Tartars *re* northern boundary conceded.
1075, 8th month.	Han Chiang resigns on grounds of illness.
1075, 10th month.	Lü Hui Ch'ing transferred to Ch'en Chow. Appearance of comet causes consternation at Court, followed by numerous appeals that the New Laws should be rescinded. Wang An Shih threatens to resign but is once more induced to stay on.
1075, 11th month.	Annamese invade China.
1075, 12th month.	Revision of Salt Regulations.
1076, 2nd month.	Punitive expedition against Annam ordered.
1076, 7th month.	Wang Fang attacks Lü Hui Ch'ing, who impeaches Wang An Shih.
1076, 8th month.	Edict issued forbidding sale of temple property.
1076, 10th month.	Wang An Shih resigns office at the capital, and returns to Chiang Ning Fu as Commissioner for civil and military affairs.
1085, 3rd month,	From this time to the death of Shen Tsung in the Reform Policy was maintained in its entirety, a period of over eight years.

Date.   *Event.*

Shen Tsung's mother, Hsuan Jen, assumes the regency, as Che Tsung, the new emperor, was only ten years of age on his accession.

1085, 3rd month.   Special Inspectorate abolished.

"Trade Tax Measure" rescinded.

River Conservancy Bureau abolished.

1085, 4th month.   ? Ssu Ma Kuang restored to power.

1085, 7th month.   "Militia Act" rescinded.

1085, 11th month.   "Equitable Land Tax Measure" rescinded.

"Militia Mounts Measure" rescinded.

1085, 12th month.   "Trade and Barter Measure" rescinded.

1086, 2nd month.   "Agricultural Loans Measure" rescinded.

1086, 3rd month.   "Public Services Act" rescinded.

Bureau of Appeal established in the interests of officials who had suffered under previous regime.

1086, 4th month.   Hsi Ho Finance Bureau abolished.

Death of Wang An Shih.

Mandate issued for revision of Educational System.

1086, 6th month.   Banishment of Teng Chien and Li Ting.

1086, 7th month.   Ssu Ch'uan Tea Monopoly abolished.

1086, 9th month.   Death of Ssu Ma Kuang.

1087, 1st month.   The New Interpretations of the Classics, and Wang An Shih's Dictionary, put under the Imperial ban.

1088, 5th month.   Ts'ai Ch'üeh banished.

From this time on the faction spirit becomes the most serious factor in government circles, the Loyang and Ssu Ch'uan parties being in constant conflict for power, with the party claiming loyalty to Wang An Shih's policy awaiting their opportunity to return.

1093, 9th month.   Death of the Regent Dowager Hsuan Jen.

Che Tsung assumes the reins of government.

Date.	Event.
1093, 12th month.	Chang Ch'ün and Lü Hui Ch'ing (Wang An Shih's party) restored to power.
1094, 2nd month.	Li Ch'ing Chen and Teng Jun Pu, also of Wang An Shih's party, appointed to the Grand Council.
1094, 3rd month.	Tseng Pu, also of Wang An Shih's party, recalled.
1094, 4th month.	Chang Shang Ying, also of Wang An Shih's party, recalled.
	Return to Court of Ts'ai Ching " The Wobbler ".
	Dynastic Title fixed as " Shao Sheng ", or Revival of Shen Tsung's policy.
	Edict issued ordering the rewriting of the History of Shen Tsung's reign. Ts'ai Pien, son-in-law of Wang An Shih, commissioned for this work.
1094, 4th month. } Intercalary. }	" Ch'ang P'ing Granary Laws " revived as a semblance of the Agricultural Loans Measure.
1094, 5th month.	Candidates for the Official examinations ordered to specialize in the meaning of the Classics.
1094, 6th month.	Ban lifted on Wang An Shih's Dictionary.
1094, 7th month.	Proscription of officials of Hsuan Jen's regime.
1094, 8th month.	" Trade Tax Measure " revived.
1094, 12th month.	New History of Shen Tsung's reign, styled the Vermilion Record " by Ts'ai Pien, presented.
	Banishment of editors of previous record.
1095, 2nd month.	" Militia Act " revived.
1096, 7th month.	Fan Tsu Yü and Liu An Shih banished.
1097, 1st month.	Ssu Ma Kuang and associates, some living, some dead, degraded in rank and titles.
1097, 1st month.	Banishment of Lü Ta Fang, Liu Chih, Su Che, and Fan Ch'un Jen.
1097, 5th month.	Ch'eng I banished.
1097, 11th month.	" Trade and Barter Measure " revived.

Date.	Event.
1098.	Dynastic title changed to "Yuan Fu" on discovery of ancient seal.
1098, 3rd month.	Wen Yen Po's son imprisoned.
	Descendants of Liu Chih and Liang T'ao banished, the latter having died in banishment.
	" Sins of the fathers visited upon the children."
	Chang Ch'un and Ts'ai Pien attempt to deprive the late Regent-dowager Hsuan Jen, of her royal titles.
1098, 4th month.	Split between Chang Ch'un and Tseng Pu.
1099, 3rd month.	Treaty of Alliance betwene the Tanguts (Hsi Hsia) and the Iron Tartars (Liao).
1099.	Special Inspectorate revived. 830 people punished.
1100, 1st month.	Death of Che Tsung, without heir.
	Tuan Wang, younger brother of Che Tsung, and son of Shen Tsung succeeds him, adopting the Imperial title of Hui Tsung.
1100, 11th month.	Dynastic title adopted as " Chien Chung " or " Establishment of Neutrality ", indicative of purpose to eliminate the extreme faction spirit.
	Banished and defamed officials of previous regime restored to their homes and ranks.
	Chang Ch'un banished : Ts'ai Ching degraded An Ch'un cashiered.
	Ch'eng I restored.
1101, 11th month.	Ts'ai Ching restored.
	Dynastic title changed at the instigation of Tseng Pu to " Ts'ung Ning " or " Reverence for the regime of Shen Tsung and Wang An Shih ".
1102, 5th month.	Ssu Ma Kuang and forty-three of his associates once more defamed. Over fifty officials of opposing regimes proscribed.

Date.	*Event.*
	Ts'ai Ching attains to supreme power after split with Tseng Pu, who is degraded.
1102, 8th month.	" Public Services Act " revived in different form.
1102, 9th month.	" Traitor's Tablet " set up, inscribed with names of 120 officials opposed to Reform Policy.
1103.	Revival of Tea Monopoly.
1103, 4th month.	Portraits of Ssu Ma Kuang and nine associates removed from the Ching Ling Tien.
	Salt Ticket Regulations revived.
	" Traitor's Tablet " ordered to be set up in each county.
1104, 4th month.	Officials ordered to report on the progress of Reform measures.
1104, 6th month.	Wang An Shih's tablet placed in Confucian temple.
	Stone tablet erected in the Ming T'ang at the capital, inscribed with the names of 309 " traitors ".
1104, 7th month.	" Equitable Land Tax Measure " revived.
1105.	Ts'ai Ching and Ts'ai Pien part company, the latter being degraded.
1105, 5th month.	" Ban " lifted on descendants and relatives of the " traitors ". Banished officials allowed to return and reside in the provinces, but not in the capital.
1106, 1st month.	Appearance of another comet.
	Emperor orders the " Traitors' Tablet " to be destroyed.
	Lifting of the ban on all " traitors ", and all banished officials restored to favour.
	Suspension of the " Equitable Land Tax Measure ".
1106, 2nd month.	Ts'ai Ching degraded.
1107, 1st month.	Ts'ai Ching restored.

Date.	*Event.*
1110.	Ts'ai Ching once more degraded.
1112.	Ts'ai Ching once more restored.
	" Equitable Land Tax Measure " revived.
1113.	Wang An Shih given posthumous title of " Wang " or " Shu Wang " (Prince of Shu).
1120.	Ts'ai Ching again degraded.
1121.	" Equitable Land Tax Measure " rescinded.
1123.	Ts'ai Ching again restored.
1124, 12th month.	Ts'ai Ching in supreme power.
1125, 12th month.	The Golden Tartars (" Chin ") advance into Chinese territory.
1126, 2nd month.	The Golden Tartars appear before the walls of K'ai Feng Fu, and return with Imperial family as hostages.
	Dictionary of Wang An Shih banned.
1126, 5th month.	Wang An Shih's tablet removed from Confucian temple.
1126, 7th month.	Ts'ai Ching banished to Chan Chow and dies on the way.
1127, 4th month.	Complete rout of the Sungs by the Golden Tartars.
1127, 5th month.	The Sung capital transferred to the south.

BIOGRAPHICAL TABLE OF WANG AN SHIH

(According to Chan Ta Ho)

Year.	*Event.*
1021.	Born.
1036.	Accompanies his father from Shao Chow to the capital.
1039.	Father dies.
1042.	Gains " Chin Shih " degree.
	Appointed to Yang Chow as Under-Secretary to Military Yamen.
1046.	Appointed to Chin Hsien as District Màgistrate.
1051.	Appointed to Shu Chow as prefect, after refusing to sit for the " kuan chih " examination.
1053.	Refuses position in Imperial Censorate, for which he had been recommended by Ou Yang Hsiu, on the grounds of his grandmother's advanced age.
	Grandmother dies.
1054.	Appointed to concurrent posts of Redactor of the Chi Hsien Library and Assistant Superintendent of the Imperial Stud.
1056.	Appointed magistrate of one of the " hsien " in the capital Circuit.
1057–8.	Appointed to Ch'ang Chow as prefect.
1060.	Appointed Chief Justice of the Chiang-Tung Circuit (提 點 江 東 刑 獄).
1060–1.	Takes up appointment in Accounts Department of Board of Finance.
	Appointed Librarian of the Chi Hsien Library.
1062.	Keeper of the Emperor's Diary (同 修 起 居 注).
	Writer of Edicts (知 制 誥).
	Secretary of the Board of Works (工 部 郎 中).
	Inspector of Justice at the capital (糾 察 在 京 刑 獄).
	Head of Imperial Bodyguard (personal) (管 幹 三 班 院).

Year.	Event.
1063.	Death of the Emperor Jen Tsung, succeeded by Ying Tsung.
	Death of Wang An Shih's mother in the 8th month.
	Wang An Shih in mourning for three years.
1066.	Refuses appointment at the capital, but appeals for an appointment at Chiang Ning Fu.
1067.	Death of the Emperor Ying Tsung, and accession of Shen Tsung.
	Appointed Governor of Chiang Ning Fu, in the 3rd intercalary month.
	Appointed Literary Councillor in the 9th month.
1068.	Accepts the appointment of Literary Councillor, proceeding to the capital in the 4th month of this year.
	Appointed Expositor of the Literary Council.
1069.	2nd month. Appointed Vice-Grand Councillor of State (參 知 政 事) with status of Adviser to the Legislative Assembly (右 諫 議 大 夫).
1070.	Threatens to resign on account of opposition in the 2nd month, but resumes his post on being reassured of the Emperor's favour, 12th month. Appointed Grand Councillor of State (同 中 書 門 下 平 章 事) and Grand Councillor of the Board of History (史 館 大 學 士).
1071.	3rd month. In sole power in the Grand Council.
1072.	5th month. Once more threatens to resign, but is persuaded to continue in his office.
1074.	4th month. Resigns from position of Grand Councillor and is transferred to Chiang Ning Fu as Governor.
1075.	2nd month. Recalled from Chiang Ning Fu to resume position as Grand Councillor of State (平 章 事) and Grand Councillor of the Chao Wen Kuan (昭 文 官 大 學 士).
	Promoted to Left Imperial Bodyguard (左 僕 射) and Presidency of the Men Hsia Sheng (門 下 侍 郎) on completion of his New Interpretation of the Classics.
	Death of his son Fang.

Year.	Event.
1076.	10th month. Retires from position of Grand Councillor and is appointed Imperial Commissioner for Chiang Ning Fu (以 使 相 鎮 金 陵). Resigns executive responsibilities for the Governorship of Chiang Ning Fu, and after being commissioned as Right Imperial Bodyguard (右 僕 射) resigns all executive responsibilities and is appointed Warden of the Hui Ling Kuan (會 靈 觀 使), a sinecure, carrying with it certain emoluments by way of pension.
1077.	Granted honorary title of " K'ai Fu I T'ung San Ssu " (開 府 儀 同 三 司) and invested as Duke of Shu (舒 國 公), which later was altered to Duke of Ching (荊 國 公). Also given title of " T'e Chin " (特 進).
1078.	Appointed Warden of the Chi Hsi Kuan (集 禧 觀 使) with honorary rank of Grand Scholar of the Kuan Wen Tien (觀 文 殿 大 學 士).
1082.	Dictionary completed and presented (字 說 成 進). Some time prior to this he had been given additional rank of " Shang Chu Kuo " (上 柱 國), which was now prefixed to his old title of " Ching Kuo Kung " (荊 國 公).
1083.	Winter. Ill.
1084.	Spring. Offers his residence for use as a temple, and his lands for support of a monastery. Rents a house in Chiang Ning Fu.
1085.	Death of the Emperor Shen Tsung in the 3rd month, succeeded by Che Tsung. Offered appointment as Minister of Works, but refused on grounds of ill-health.
1086.	4th month. Dies. Posthumous title of " T'ai Fu " (太 傅) or " Grand Tutor " conferred upon him.

NOTES ON BIOGRAPHICAL TABLE OF CHAN TA HO

The table as compiled above follows with minor alterations the Biographical Table of Chan Ta Ho (詹 大 和) found in the prolegomena to the Poetical Works of Wang An Shih. Chan Ta Ho was a native of T'ung Lu, who published a complete edition of Wang An Shih's works in the 10th year of Shao Hsing (紹 興), i.e. A.D. 1140. His dates have been compared with those given by Liang Ch'i Ch'ao in Chapter IV of his Life of Wang An Shih (王 荆 公 傳) and also with the actual dates given in the " T'ung Chien " for the period of Wang An Shih's Court appointments. Minor divergences between Liang Ch'i Ch'ao and Chan Ta Ho may be accounted for by the fact that one relates the dates when appointments were offered, and the other the time when these appointments were actually accepted, amounting in certain instances to a difference of seven months. As Liang Ch'i Ch'ao is following Ts'ai Shang Hsiang, who has the reputation of having given the greater part of his life to preparing the Life of Wang An Shih, we translate both these tables on separate sheets for purposes of comparison.

NOTE.—The divergence of a year which sometimes occurs in the different Tables may be accounted for by the fact that the period title of a reign was often changed in the middle of a year. It is possible that one writer may be using the older designation of the year and another the newer.

BIOGRAPHICAL TABLE

(As given by Ts'ai Shang Hsiang)

Year.	Event.
1021.	Wang An Shih born. (According to one authority, Wu Jung Kuang (吳 榮 光), on the 12th of the 11th month.)
1030.	Father appointed to Shao Chow.
1033.	Returns with father from Shao Chow to Lin Ch'uan.
1036.	Accompanies father to the capital.
1037.	Father appointed to Chiang Ning as assistant-prefect.
1039.	Father dies on the 13th of the 2nd month, aged 46 at Chiang Ning.
1042.	Gains degree of Chin Shih, in the 3rd month. Appointed to Yang Chow as secretary.
1043.	Returns home on leave.
1045.	Tseng Kung recommends Wang An Shih to Ou Yang Hsiu.
1046.	Visits the capital (probably on completion of his term at Yang Chow).
1047.	Appointed as magistrate of Chin Hsien.
1048.	Gains leave of absence to bury his father.
1049.	Still at Chin Hsien.
1050.	Returns to Lin Ch'uan. (There is an inscription by his hand in the district dated the 25th of the 5th month of this year.)
1051.	Commanded to take the " kuan chih " examination, but appeals for delay. Death of eldest foster-brother, Ch'ang Fu. Appointed to Shu Chow as prefect (local inscription, 16th of 9th month).
1052.	Still at Shu Chow.
1053.	Still at Shu Chow. Death of grandmother Hsieh (謝).

408

Year.	*Event.*
1054.	Offered appointment as Redactor of the Chi Hsien Library (first refusal dated the 22nd of the 3rd month).
1056.	In office in the Imperial Stud.
1057.	Magistrate of Ch'ang Chow. Appointment altered to that of Chief-Justice of the Chiang-Tung Circuit.
1058.	Submits the memorial of a myriad characters.
1059.	Still holds the Chiang-Tung appointment as Chief-Justice.
1060.	Appointed to the Ministry of Finance in the 5th month.
1061.	Secretary to the Edicts Board in the 6th month. Submits the memorial on current affairs (時 政 疏). His brother Wang An Li gains his Chin Shih degree in the 3rd month.
1062.	Still secretary to the Edicts Board.
1063.	Death of mother in the 8th month at the capital.
1064.	In mourning for his mother at Chiang Ning.
1065.	On the completion of two years' mourning called to take up appointment at the court of Ying Tsung, but refuses. (Date of proferred commission 27th of 7th month.)
1066.	Still at Chiang Ning without appointment.
1067.	Death of Ying Tsung in the 1st month, and accession of Shen Tsung. Wang Fang (son) gains his Chin Shih degree in the 2nd month, and is appointed to Ching Te Chun. Wang An Shih appointed Governor of Chiang Ning in the 3rd intercalary month. Appointed Literary Councillor in the 9th month.
1068.	Admitted to Imperial Audiences by special decree in the 4th month. Submits memorial on A Century of Peace (百 年 無 事 劄 子). Brother Wang An Kuo gains Chin Shih degree in the 7th month.
1069.	Appointed Vice-Grand-Councillor in the 2nd month.

Year.	*Event.*
1069.	Appointed with Ch'en Sheng Chih to draw up the regulations for finanical reorganization (also in the 2nd month).
	Submits the memorial of warning (進 戒 疏), 5th month.
	Lü Hui submits memorial of indictment, 6th month.
1070.	Still Vice-Grand Councillor.
	Threatens to resign in the 3rd month, but continues in office.
	Appointed Grand Councillor, together with Han Chiang in the 12th month.
	Appointed Imperial Historiographer.
1071.	Still Grand Councillor.
	Brother An Kuo promoted to hierarchy (kuan chih) (館 職).
	Wang Fang appointed Tutor to Hier-apparent and Imperial Expositor.
1072.	Still Grand Councillor.
	Submits the memorial on Five Matters (五 事 劄 子).
1073.	Still Grand Councillor.
	Bureau for New Classical Interpretation set up with Wang An Shih in charge, assisted by his son Fang and Lü Hui Ch'ing (3rd month).
	Receives gift of jewelled belt from Emperor on celebration of Hsi Ho victory (10th month).
1074.	Still Grand Councillor.
	Resigns in the 4th month and appointed as Governor of Chiang Ning.
	Death of brother Wang An Kuo on the 17th of 8th month.
1075.	Recalled to old office of Grand Councillor in the 2nd month.
	Promoted to Left Bodyguard and Presidency of Men Hsia Sheng in the 6th month.
	Reappointed Imperial Historiographer in the 9th month.
	Lü Hui Ch'ing transferred to Ch'en Chow in the 10th month.
	Punitive Expedition against the Annamese launched in the 12th month.

Year.	*Event.*
1076.	Death of son Fang in the 7th month.
	Resigns office at the capital and is appointed as Governor of Chiang Ning, in the 10th month.
1077.	Appointed Warden of the Chi Hsi Kuan in the 6th month.
1078.	Still Warden as above. Appointed Duke of the State of Shu (舒 國 公), with rank of Left Bodyguard of the Shang Shu Sheng.
1080.	Granted honorary title of " K'ai Fu I T'ung San Ssu ".
	Invested as Duke of Ching State (荆 國 公) in 9th month.
	Dictionary completed and presented.
1082.	Wang An Li appointed to Grand Council as Shang Shu Yu Ch'eng, in the 4th month.
1083.	Wang An Li promoted a further step, as Shang Shu Tso Ch'eng, in the 8th month.
	Ts'ai Pien, son-in-law, appointed Expositor of Chow Li.
1084.	Wang An Li transferred.
	Wang An Shih offers residence for temple purposes, and land for use of monastery.
1085.	Death of Shen Tsung in 3rd month. Succeeded by Che Tsung, under regency of Hsuan Jen, mother of Shen Tsung.
	Honorary appointment of Minister of Works.
1086.	Dies in 4th month.
	Posthumous title of Grand Tutor conferred.

BIOGRAPHICAL TABLE

(As given by Liang Ch'i Ch'ao)

Date.	Age.	Event.
1021.		Born.
1036.	16	Accompanies father to the capital.[1]
1039.	19	Father dies.
1041.	21	Gains " Chin Shih " degree.
1042.		Appointed to Huai-Nan (淮 南), i.e. to Yang Chow (楊 州).
1047.	27	Appointed to Chin Hsien as District Magistrate.[2]
1051.		Finishes a four-year appointment at Chin Hsien.
1052.		Appointed to Shu Chow as prefect.[3]
1054.	34	Offered appointment of Redactor of Chi Hsien Library [4] (集 賢 校 理).
1056.	36	In Imperial Stud as Assistant Superintendent (群 牧 司 判 官).[5]
1057.		Appointed to Ch'ang Chow as prefect, but this appointment altered to that of Chief-Justice of the Chiang-Tung Circuit the same year.[6]
1058.		Returns to capital to report, and sends in his memorial of a myriad words (萬 言 書).
1059.		Chief-Justice of Chiang-Tung Circuit (in office).
1060.		Appointed to Accounts Department of Board of Finance.[7]
1061.	41	Writer of Edicts, an office which he retained for three years.[8]
1064.	44	In residence at Chiang Ning Fu, mourning for his mother.
1067.		1st month, death of Ying Tsung and accession of Shen Tsung.
		3rd month. Appointed Governor of Chiang Ning Fu.

Year.		Event.
1067.		9th month. Appointed Literary Councillor.
1068.	48	4th month. As Literary Councillor given special privilege of attending Imperial audiences.
1069.		2nd month. Appointed Vice-Grand Councillor.
1071.		Appointed Grand Councillor of State.[9]
1074.		6th month. Resigns office at capital and appointed Governor of Chiang Ning Fu.[10]
1075.		2nd month. Returns to capital and resumes post of Grand Councillor.
		6th month. Promoted to Left Imperial Bodyguard.
1076.	57	10th month. Resigns and returns to Chiang Ning Fu as Imperial Commissioner.[11]
1078.	58	Given honorary title of " K'ai Fu I T'ung San Ssu ", invested as Duke of Shu, and appointed Warden of the Chi Hsi Kuan.
1080.		Appointed Duke of Ching (荆 國 公).
1085.		3rd month. Death of Shen Tsung and accession of Che Tsung, with the Empress-dowager Hsuan Jen in regency.
		Appointed Minister of Works.
1086.	66	4th month. Wang An Shih dies.
		Posthumous title of " T'ai Fu " (太 傅) conferred upon him.
1094–7.		Posthumous title of " Wen " (文) conferred upon him.

NOTES ON BIOGRAPHICAL TABLE AS GIVEN BY LIANG CH'I CH'AO

[1] Liang here gives the age of Wang An Shih as 16, but gives no date. The question arises as to whether Liang is using the Chinese or Western mode of calculating ages. The Chinese method is to count a child 1 year old at birth. In instances where Liang gives the date as well as the age, e.g. 1054, his appointment to the Redactorship of the Chi Hsien Yuan is given when he was 34, it is evident that he is using the Chinese method. Wang An Shih was born in 1021, so according to Western reckoning he would be 34 years of age in the year 1055. In general then we assume that Liang is following the Chinese method, so where he gives the age only and not the Chinese date we have fixed the date at one year earlier than the foreign method of calculating would give.

[2] Chan Ta Ho gives the date of 1046 for this appointment but, as we have remarked in the note on the Biographical Table as compiled by him, this may be

accounted for by the fact that Chan Ta Ho gives the date when the appointment was made public, while Liang may be giving the date when the appointment was actually taken up. It is quite possible that the mandate conferring the appointment was issued late in 1046, but that Wang An Shih proceeded to Yang Chow and actually took up his duties early in 1047.

³ Here again there is a discrepancy of one year between Chan Ta Ho and Liang Ch'i Ch'ao, probably accounted for by the same reason as that given in the preceding note.

⁴ Liang says that Wang An Shih refused this appointment. Certainly he did so at first. But according to Chan Ta Ho the appointment to the Imperial Stud which was made at this time was styled a concurrent (兼) appointment, which may be interpreted to mean that the Redactorship to the Library was also accepted.

⁵ Liang uses the expression "wei" (為) in connection with this appointment, so it may be that there is no discrepancy here between him and Chan Ta Ho. The latter says this appointment was made in 1054. He may have held it for two years, and Liang simply states the fact that he was in this appointment at that particular time.

⁶ Liang makes the appointment at Ch'ang Chow a very short one, and the appointment as Chief-Justice of Chiang-Tung a long one.

⁷ Chan Ta Ho makes this appointment date in 1061, but in the "T'ung Chien" under Chia Yu 5th year 5th month (1060) this appointment is said to have been offered then. Liang uses the same expression "chao" (召), which may be interpreted to mean "called to the post". It may be that he waited until the following year before actually taking it up.

⁸ The "T'ung Chien" dates this appointment as in the 6th month of the 6th year of Chia Yu (嘉 祐), i.e. 1061. Chan Ta Ho makes it to take effect in 1062.

⁹ The "T'ung Chien" gives the date of this appointment as the 12th month of 1070. Chan Ta Ho gives the 10th month of that year.

¹⁰ "T'ung Chien" gives the 4th month of this year for his resignation.

¹¹ If Wang An Shih proceeded to this appointment in 1076 his age would then be 56 only, according to Chinese reckoning. Perhaps Liang reckons that he actually took up office the following year, when he would be 57 years old, as stated.

INDEX

Agricultural Loans, I, 142–176, 263, 267, 272, 278, 281, 372, 382, 384; II, 12 36, 42, 43, 51, 134, 166, 171, 174, 198, 205, 222, 276, 283
Aid Money, II, 38, 42, 171
Allan, C. W., I, 8; II, 183, 316
An Ch'un, I, 209; II, 17, 18
Ancient Ways, Return to, I, 49, 50, 51, 52, 54, 55, 56, 57, 58, 60, 66; II, 30
An I, II, 87
Annals, The, I, 340, 341; II, 55, 265, 313, 314, 315, 321, 357, 377
Annamese Expedition, I, 274, 304, 319, 321; II, 51, 191, 195, 196, 197, 198
An Shou, II, 94
An T'ao, I, 372; II, 2, 12, 13, 65
Anthology of T'ang Poetry, II, 265, 274, 293
An Tu, II, 16
Appeal, Bureau of, I, 384
Army Distribution, I, 251, 254; II, 190
Army Reduction, II, 187
Army Regular, I, 113, 185, 186, 187, 194, 215, 251, 252, 254; II, 20, 76, 77, 187
Arsenal Board, I, 251, 258, 276, 278
Artificers' Record (K'ao Kung Chi), II, 300, 303
Assassins, Record of, II, 145

Baldwin, Mr. Stanley, II, 181
Banishment of Officials, II, 13, 14, 15, 16, 18, 26, 41
Black Ink Record, II, 66, 67
Bruce, Dr. J. P., I, 8
Buddhism, II, 54, 56, 201, 251, 292, 295, 363, 364

Censorate, I, 172; II, 33, 40, 41, 95, 101
Ceremonies, National, II, 78
Chan Ta Ho, I, 15, 26, 34, 97, 108; II, 92, 266, 267, 268

Chang Chi, I, 41
Chang Chien, II, 41, 129
Chang Chueh, I, 76
Chang Chun, I, 123, 208, 239, 271, 273, 277, 315, 316, 317, 356, 372, 381, 383; II, 7, 8, 10, 13, 14, 16, 17, 18, 21
Changes, Classic of, I, 63; II, 310, 312, 313, 321, 339, 344, 345, 353, 354, 362, 365, 366
Chang Fang P'ing (An T'ao), I, 158; II, 110, 115, 128, 152, 153, 155, 157, 246, 247
Chang Jo Chi, I, 360; II, 48, 51, 253
Chang Ju Ming, II, 208, 209
Chang K'uei, I, 7; II, 256
Chang P'i Kuang, I, 129, 130; II, 106, 107
Chang Shang Ying, I, 273; II, 10, 13, 23
Chang T'ang, II, 152
Chang T'ien Ch'eng, II, 61, 62, 217
Chang Tsai, I, 157, 276; II, 21, 295
Chang Tsao, I, 273, 372, 383; II, 2, 94
Chang Yu, II, 303
Chang Yuan Chi, II, 284
Ch'ang An Min, II, 13
Ch'ang I Fu, II, 99
Ch'ang Pien, II, 68
Chao Hsieh, II, 125
Chao I, II, 59
Chao K'uang Yin, II, 73
Chao Pien, I, 138, 160, 165; II, 129
Chao Ting, I, 135; II, 54
Chao Tzu Chi, I, 224
Chao Yen Jo, II, 13, 66
Ch'ao Kung Wu, II, 303
Ch'ao Ts'o, II, 294
Ch'e Ch'ien Ch'iu, II, 235, 236
Chen Tsung, Emperor, I, 215; II, 74, 83
Ch'en Chien, II, 41
Ch'en Chih Chai, II, 151
Ch'en Chiu Ch'uan, I, 23; II, 277

415

418INDEX